LIBERALIZING THE
EUROPEAN MEDIA

LIBERALIZING THE EUROPEAN MEDIA

Politics, Regulation, and the Public Sphere

SHALINI VENTURELLI

CLARENDON PRESS · OXFORD
1998

Oxford University Press, Great Clarendon Street, Oxford OX2 6DP

Oxford New York

Athens Auckland Bangkok Bogota Bombay Buenos Aires
Calcutta Cape Town Dar es Salaam Delhi Florence Hong Kong Istanbul
Karachi Kuala Lumpur Madras Madrid Melbourne Mexico City
Nairobi Paris Singapore Taipei Tokyo Toronto Warsaw

and associated companies in
Berlin Ibadan

Oxford is a registered trade mark of Oxford University Press

Published in the United States
by Oxford University Press Inc., New York

British Library Cataloguing in Publication Data
Data available

Library of Congress Cataloging in Publication Data

Venturelli, Shalini.
Liberalizing the European media : politics, regulation, and the
public sphere / Shalini Venturelli.
Includes bibliographical references and index.
1. Mass media policy—Europe.   2. Communication policy—Europe.
I. Title
P95.82.E85V46   1998   302.2'094—dc21   97-47468
ISBN 0-19-823379-5

JK

1 3 5 7 9 10 8 6 4 2

Typeset by Regent Typesetting, London
Printed in Great Britain
on acid-free paper by
Biddles Ltd, Guildford and King's Lynn

TO
Philip AND *Ophelia*

Contents

Introduction

THE IDEA of the 'information society' has become a generally accepted way of referring to the image of society inscribed in the autonomous processes of technological innovation. The process is thought to possess a force all of its own which sweeps along individuals and societies into an ambiguous future of transformed work, wealth creation, and cultural practice constituted by complex, intelligent multimedia networks. As popular discourse, it may be dismissed as a phenomenon of technical romanticism such as may periodically punctuate the imagination of the modernist age. But it would be a mistake to treat the notion of 'information society' entirely as a mythic form of contemporary cultural experience since it may now have passed beyond the banalities of technological and engineering determinism, to occupy a place at the highest level of political and economic priority in the industrial, economic, and social projects of national policies, transnational directives, multilateral agreements, and international law.

A universally networked broadband, interactive, multimedia information society could be the richest source of creative, diverse, empowering, and democratizing communication ever to connect humanity. It may perhaps evolve into the world's first true 'mass medium' by allowing anyone with a few simple tools to communicate ideas to thousands of persons at once. It inspires a notion of tolerance and promotes the possibility of mutual understanding in the idea of connecting people of all origins around the world. It could serve as a tool of community organizing and citizen involvement.

Yet all of the technological innovation on its own may not guarantee a universal network constituted by the unimpeded flow, exchange, and production of knowledge and information, because the realization of this form of an information society in reality depends less on technological choices than on the political decisions—that is, the economic, social, and cultural decisions of societies and states. On the one hand, it is argued, we cannot return to the comfort of the status quo before the microchip. On the other hand, in the absence of a political will to shape the technological revolution towards the progressive ends envisioned, we may end up with a transformed public space characterized by fracture and segregation, incapable of supporting the structures of civil society and the democratization of participation and interests in the determination of common concerns.

It is suggested, therefore, that what may be at stake in the information society debate is not merely economic growth and international competitiveness, but the fate of a political form of society we call democracy. The exploitation of print communication arose in a form that invited the enlargement of knowledge, participation, and public debate beyond the monopoly of information held by clerical and aristocratic elites, ultimately bringing about the democratization of feudal society. It was not the technology itself but the socio-legal and political basis of its exploitation to widen the public realm to participation in the production of political and cultural expression, which brought about social transformation.

The information revolution of the late twentieth century is also supported by a socio-legal basis we may call liberal internationalism which requires liberalization of the information sector in societies worldwide. The advanced industrialized economies recognize that the expansion of the global economy is dependent upon development of global information intelligent networks and services in the exploration of new markets. This dynamic can no longer be guaranteed by individual states but must be supported by an increasing emphasis on supranational regulation. While the benefits of information liberalization are promoted by organizations such as the World Trade Organization and the World Bank, there are many important issues which are not being addressed at the supranational and transnational levels.

One of the greatest advantages of information liberalization claimed by economists is increased competition which they anticipate will benefit the global economy in every part of the world. High-tech firms would bring prosperity to affluent corporate and individual users even in lower-income nations such as India and China; computer software and assembly is evolving into an economic force in special economic zones of lesser developed nations; and international business demands for telecoms infrastructure in order to locate in different regions of the world would bring employment and prosperity to underdeveloped economies. Some economists have argued that competitive forces in the communications market can supply the developmental needs of all economies more efficiently than state-managed development strategies because greater competition works on the basis of greater standardization of information networks and services; free entry into the communication market enabled by standardization, interconnection, and absence of restraints on tariffs and movement of capital resources; and by the creation of incentives in the spread of information technology and services from the promise of higher rates of return to investors. This benefit is expected to pass down to the rest of society through job creation and higher wages.

To achieve the benefits of information liberalization, a supranational governance structure embedded in transnational regulation and trade agreements is required. By supranational governance is meant an international system of supranational institutions,[1] which articulate, at minimum, principles and standards of regulation for states. The effect of this system is to transform most states into law-takers rather than law-makers. So, for example, the General Agreement on Tariffs and Trade (GATT) contains principles and standards of regulation in areas as diverse as food standards, services, and intellectual property. Countries that are signatories need to make significant changes to their national regulatory and legal systems. The dominant feature of the supranational governance structure, especially in the information sector, is that it is primarily concerned with the principles, standards, and articulation of transnational policy that are binding on participant countries, which means that the supranational order is both based on, and expresses itself in terms of, the rule of law. This is especially so in the case of the European Union (EU) which, as a legal entity, can employ the treaties of the Community as a constitution in the production and interpretation of information policy and law that is binding on a union of member states. It is important to emphasize this in order to argue the significance of the implications and complexities inherent in the radical restructuring of the public sphere in democratic states, undertaken in the production of law for the information society. What appears as economic or trade policy for the information market has in reality profound implications for the political and cultural constitution of free societies.

Under the supranational governance structure, environmental policies may be invalidated as trade barriers; so may anti-concentration competition policies to ensure information diversity, cultural policy to provide pluralism in cultural expression, and even constitutional guarantees of political rights, communication rights, and human rights as expressed in information policy and social policy can be contested on the grounds that they act to constrain international trade through a set of interventionist, non-commercial public interest requirements imposed on the communications industries, whether in infrastructure or content. Similarly, policies that lead democratic societies to determine a need for direct or indirect 'subsidies' because of issues that concern the common welfare or the general interest, ranging from universal service to programming requirements for educational or cultural content, may be rendered illegitimate under the supranational governance structure for

---

[1] Examples include the European Union (EU), World Trade Organization (WTO), World Intellectual Property Organization (WIPO), World Bank, International Monetary Fund (IMF), Organization for Economic Cooperation and Development (OECD), and the International Telecommunications Union (ITU).

the information society. The cumulative delegitimization of national policies in all areas of information policy and law would redefine the ability of democratic societies to decide the meaning of the public interest for their citizens in those areas most closely tied to the survival of democracy itself, namely, the structure, form, content, and accessibility of the information environment.

Thomas Jefferson, for example, would find his theory of the republic in violation of information liberalization policies since there would be an immediate international challenge mounted to his rather interventionist idea of guaranteeing education and access to knowledge and information as public goods set aside from trade and proprietary governance because he claimed these are essential to the functioning of democracy and to the practice of political freedom. Such a constitutional defence of the role of the state in guaranteeing information access and diversity because of the inherent relationship between information conditions and democratic conditions, may not be supported under the emerging information-society supranational framework which, instead, is being designed to treat most state intervention in the information sector as 'discriminatory' to international information industries. In fact, the 'non-discriminatory' principle of supranational regulation is rapidly emerging as the pre-eminent form of international law, taking precedence over most other levels in the hierarchy of legal systems and regulatory traditions, from the transnational to the municipal level.

This study examines a few of the central components of the political and socio-legal basis of liberalization of media and the design of an information society in Europe. The question of an information society is approached from the perspective of the restructuring of the public sphere which serves as the conceptual and empirical grounds for examination of the evolving political order in the European Union. In this respect, the study departs from the understanding of an information society solely as an economic, industrial, technological, even social-policy question, and treats its construction as first and foremost a political question.

With respect to a rationale for the relevance of a political and democratic approach to an area generally held to be of technological and economic concern, this study will argue that problems and conditions of the information age have recentred a set of moral and political arguments which have been at the heart of modernity's core enterprise and yet continue to remain unresolved: namely, the proposal that information and knowledge are central to the progressive emancipation of all social groups and hence the conditions of public space for deliberation, participation, and political practice are irrevocably tied to the quality of human life and to the universalization of political freedom.

In order to address the information society in political terms, it is necessary first to explore the normative basis of information policy, establishing its validity and relevance to the evolution of democracy in modernity. It would also be necessary to clarify the conflict among the principal paradigms of public space which inform the underlying assumptions and justifications in the state's identification of particular options for the regulation of the public realm. Moreover, it would not be sufficient to specify this array of paradigms without an exposition of their implicit limitations and whether an alternative approach may be better suggested in the context of the functioning of democracy and the structures of civil society. This responsibility is addressed in the attempt to develop a participatory paradigm of public space more appropriate to the claims and promises of the information revolution, and which improves upon the liberalization model. Concepts and issues developed in the exploration of public space are then employed in the analysis of key sectors of the design of an information society in the European Union.

While addressing the information policies of the EU, the study will evaluate initiatives for liberalization of telecommunications, including the approach to universal service and public service for the information infrastructure. Thereafter, the analysis shifts to policies concerning content or expression which economists treat as the primary source of wealth creation in the information economy. The study will explore the question of who would own and control content in the public sphere of an information society as prescribed in emerging policies and laws for intellectual property, including the issue of which social groups are likely to benefit, and the implications for the forms of expression that would be favoured under current initiatives. The second question determining the structure of content in the multimedia broadband-network environment would involve the legitimacy of content regulation on grounds of public interest or cultural policy. The study identifies the struggle over content regulation in the audiovisual sector as significant to the larger framework for regulation of expression in cyberspace and for the role of the state in the information age. An inquiry of this nature would necessarily require that models of content regulation in Europe be examined for their mutual tensions, contradictions, and convergences in the determination of the relationship of society and state to forms of cultural expression that prevail and dominate in the public realm, and to forms of expression that do not or cannot arise under the emerging policy environment.

The third question concerning content in the information society is perhaps the most important: namely, information rights. The analysis will confront the development of information rights in the EU as emerging from a complex set of sources in the socio-legal construction of the Community, including ownership regulation, the treaties, the jurisprudence of the European Court, human-rights traditions and principles, the regulatory interpretation of these principles in information policy, and the problem of implementing constitutional guarantees. Finally, the study will address the emergence of a competitive order of information liberalization that may ultimately define whether the initiatives for the information society would have real meaning in any given discretionary application of competition rules. This competitive order, it is argued, shows distinct signs of an evolving logic which reveals its political aims and underlying use of the state to achieve those ends. During the course of the theoretical exploration and policy analysis, the study will identify patterns and systematic tendencies which can assist in clarifying the political order of the information society emerging from these crucial policy initiatives, in an effort to understand the transformation of the public sphere and the conditions of democracy these policies would bring about.

Some conflicting aspects and ambiguities in the political conceptions of information liberalization that are addressed in this study include: the paradox of competition policy and realist basis of information liberalization as developed from liberal political foundations; the dilemma of universal service and public service in Europe as developed from public interest political foundations; nationalism or cultural essentialism in European information regulation as developed from expressivist political foundations; and the place of political rights of participation in the information age arising from tensions between public interest constitutional law and private contractual law.

While examining specific forms of information policy and the social conceptions which define them, this book will attempt to argue from a socio-legal basis drawn, in part, from Hegel's (1952*a*) concept of the central role law plays in the social order. By relating Hegel's political theory to information policy through a deliberative paradigm, this study provides a way of examining the legitimacy of policies for the information society against requirements of democratic will-formation, principles of public reason, and political rights of expression and information. To this end, the first three chapters are devoted to the development and exposition of a participatory theory of public space which is then followed through in subsequent stages of policy analysis.

The investigation will raise a set of fundamental social issues which democratic societies must necessarily confront, namely: whether and in what form the structure of the broadband multimedia network will create possibilities for extending the information revolution to all citizens in a democratic society; and, as seen in the case of the European

Union, whether convergence of EU information policies with those emerging at the global level in multilateral agreements and treaties to advance the fundamental restructuring of public space in free societies, assumes a mode of the democratic social order that is indeed more participatory as claimed by most parties to the policy debate. This understanding is absent from prevailing analyses of the information infrastructure (Ciborra, 1992; Ungerer and Costello, 1990; Lanvin, 1989; Antonelli, 1985) which are dominated more often by debates over economic and technical issues in the diffusion of technical systems, and by efficiency and performance assessments or aggregate statistical indicators, than by the recognition that there is something fundamental at stake in the evolution of the intelligent network involving the further development of democratic political community, the practice of political self-determination, and the values and possibilities of participatory citizenship.

This study attempts to refocus and enlarge the policy debate by proposing that the structure of the information system, and not merely procedural voting rights, is one of the original problems of democratic freedom. It is relevant therefore to compare the status of the fundamental rights of man to information and knowledge as the normative foundation of public policy in its relation with the rights of contract and competition in the constitution of the information society. The problem of a normative foundation, therefore, begins the task of this inquiry.

Research Undertaken

The following research activities were undertaken for this study: Documentary search was undertaken for data investigation in the EU, with visits to the European Commission and European Parliament in Brussels and in Strasbourg, and to government ministries and agencies in some member states such as Germany, France, and the UK. On-site archival and institutional investigation was necessary to compile the background documentation for key policy and legal instruments and to interview policy sources. Approximately one hundred interviews were conducted with law-makers, policy-makers, communication-industry representatives, regulators, and citizen-action groups throughout the European Union for the purpose of examining central issues in the policy debate.

I

The Normative Grounds of Information Policy

THE ANALYSIS here will identify the normative grounds of public policy with respect to the information sector in a way which carries the problem beyond the conceptual limits of utilitarian liberalism and its qualified rationale for the meaning of information in democratic societies as a market or as identical to the free circulation of contractual and proprietary structures. The notion of a substantive normative foundation for communication policy has in large part been denied both in policy-making and in scholarship over the course of this century, during which period public-space policy traditions have been established by the principles of capitalist market competition, proprietary rights and freedoms, totalitarian domination by the state, strategic interests in the project of state-building, or by cultural–nationalist collective interest (discussed in the next chapter).

This chapter will therefore introduce a theoretical–historical argument that a substantive moral basis for guaranteeing public space in the common interest exists at the core of liberalism's political project for self-determination and participatory inclusion. It is further argued that this foundation must be revived and reconstructed in light of the continually valid concerns regarding the collapse of this promise as criticized by Marx and by Weber, and an attempted reconstruction by Habermas who identifies the conditions of the public realm as the measure of the reality of freedom, although Habermas's theory is still unable to engage with the question of policy and political practice as is discussed more fully in this and subsequent chapters. Finally, recovering this foundation has become imperative in view of the contemporary policy debate over the information society and the significance of the debate's outcome for social and cultural development and for the future of democratic community.

The notion of the 'promise' of modernity as a promise of communication will be addressed through the thought of Kant who provides the best defence (Taylor, 1993, 1985, 1979; Cohen, 1989; Rawls, 1971; MacIntyre, 1966) of the ethical basis of the modernist historical movement and of one its most influential outcomes, the liberal democratic polity. The difficulties which this moral defence presents for the disjuncture between the historical reality of modernity and the core of its covenant with democratic transformation is then explored in the critique of modernity articulated by Marx and by Weber. As critics of modernity's social forms, they reassert the value of this promise in terms of its relation to degenerative tendencies in the modern social order manifested in diverse formations of domination and distortion which obstruct realization of the true conditions of public freedom. In a general sense, their perspectives construct the causes of domination, and the perpetuation of oligarchic social relations to stem from modernity's economic form of monopoly, and from its particular mode of integration into the normative and structural foundations of the liberal democratic system as increasingly organized on a world scale.

Antinomies and inconsistencies between concepts of public communication centred on the political promise of modernity as defended by Kant, and those implicated within the reality of modernity's social forms, as assessed by Marx and Weber, will then be elaborated as one of the central problems in the construction of public-space and information policy. This problem has lately been underscored by Habermas, and thus his response to the social critique of Marx and Weber is then elaborated in so far as it touches on reconstructing the rational grounds of freedom as participation. Assessment of Habermas's effort to redeem reason is undertaken while keeping in mind certain unresolved difficulties in his approach to the problem of modernity which, as argued later, derive from limitations in his dialogical concept of the public sphere.

Finally, this chapter concludes by redefining this problem of divorce between the promise and reality of modernity, demonstrated in the communication-policy debate in the European Union, as a significant issue in the continuing historical development of modernity's political undertaking of constructing self-determining communities.

INFORMATION RIGHTS AND LEGITIMACY

Because individual rights, freedom, free speech, and the free market comprise a specific normative system, the essential grounds of modern liberal democracy can be said to be primarily normative. As Rawls (1971) argues in his treatise on the moral foundations of liberalism, the most significant articulation and justification of these values is furnished, not in the utilitarian rationale of Locke, but in the non-instrumental defence of Immanuel Kant. The first full expression of the modern view of freedom, emancipation, and a just social order, according to MacIntyre (1966), is discovered not so much in the civil-society thesis of Hobbes (1991) as is sometimes maintained (Gray, 1989; Oakeshott, 1975), but in Kant's defence of liberal democratic values, the 'supreme representation of the Enlightenment' (MacIntyre, 1966: 190). This argument arises from:

his [Kant's] belief in the power of courageous reasoning and in the effectiveness of the reform of institutions [when all states are republics there will be no more war]; supreme because in what he thought, he either solved the recurrent problems of the Enlightenment or reformulated them . . . for emerging liberal individualist society in a way that makes the individual morally sovereign. And it leaves the individual free to pursue whatever it is that he does . . . His wish is to exhibit the moral individual as being a standpoint and a criterion superior to and outside any actual social order. (MacIntyre, 1966: 190–8)

The central value in modernity's enterprise, namely the cause of freedom, is defined within a Kantian moral framework whereby 'Man is a free being only in the sense that he is meant to find his paradigm purposes within himself, and not out of the order in which he is set' (Taylor, 1985: 319). Hence, in the political realm, human freedom is assured prior to legitimate order and is part of the natural condition of man's reason—the 'state of nature'; political structures come later.

The unhooking of the notion of freedom from all social context, in contrast to the ancient view of the preconditions of political society (Aristotle, 1981), renders it non-contingent, absolute, and inalienable, thereby transforming the hope of emancipation effectively into a promise. The promise of universal human rights, directly drawn from the Kantian moral framework, also distinguishes itself from Hobbes's (1991: 38–9 and 90–1) freedom as purely naturalistic self-love which is similarly detached from social context. This is because the Kantian doctrine of freedom as reason is uncompromisingly part of the moral order, therefore normatively inscribed in the historical ascendancy of liberal democracy, whereas Hobbesian freedom has nothing to do with moral law for it is simply part of the state of nature as perpetual desire and supposedly justifies the imposition of political power.

The inquiry here turns to this promise of freedom expressed as an aspiration to total liberation, which defines the modernist enterprise. In an effort to elaborate the essential characteristics of the hope of self-determination which has cast liberal democracy as morally superior to competing political doctrines in our time, the discussion will attempt to examine the place of communication within the modernist conceptual scheme. In so doing, it may be possible to elucidate the problem and place of information policy within the constitution of liberalism's freedom, the moral legitimacy of the democratic state, and its relation to the value and status of the individual.

According to Kant (1990: 52), individuals are morally sovereign, therefore ends in themselves, because they are endowed with reason, as opposed to passion, or desire, or competitive self-interest. Persons do not have a market value but possess intrinsic worth, that is, dignity, from the a priori capacity to give themselves their own laws (ibid. 38). Thus for Kant, the condition of membership and the communal end, is rationality where 'each man is left free to make use of his reason in matters of conscience' (ibid. 88). While this elevation of the individual to unqualified eminence in the natural hierarchy forms the body of Kant's moral framework for liberalism's rights-based theory of freedom (see discussion of this aspect in Chapter 2), it becomes substantively extended, perhaps even transformed, by his political philosophy. In the political domain, Kant insists on a set of conditions accounting for the reality of the practice of freedom as reason, and it is at this level, the one that also concerns the discussion here, that freedom involves certain fundamental prerequisites of communication and a set of public policies guaranteeing its necessary structure in order for political legitimacy to prevail.

Requirements of social reality in the actualization of freedom—whether religious freedom, freedom of expression, freedom to participate or be included—for Kant, is not private autonomy as one might infer from his metaphysics (ibid. 38–9), but public autonomy. Kant's (1990: 38) abstract 'categorical imperative' with its emphasis on freedom of the will, subjective consciousness, and a transcendental ego which grasps and synthesizes the world through private categories of reason,[1] is a view of freedom largely independent of the empirical world and thus remains a matter of ongoing theoretical debate (Wolff, 1973). But in terms of social validity, it is argued, what Kant means by freedom is public freedom. In 'What is Enlightenment?' (1990), he writes that the promise of self-determination is essentially contingent on using one's reason in public:

It is the freedom to make public use of one's reason at every point . . . . The public use of one's reason must always be free, and it alone can bring about enlightenment among men [in so far as each] . . . regards himself at the same time as a member of the whole community or of a society of world citizens . . . (ibid. 84–5)

Thus only the public practice of reason constitutes freedom for Kant and he goes so far as to assert that social and political arrangements as well as public policies which create obstructions to knowledge,

---

[1] For a full elaboration of Kant's moral philosophy based on private reason, see his *Foundations of the Metaphysics of Morals* (Kant, 1990). A critical assessment is provided by C. Taylor (1985), *Philosophical Papers*, ii, 319–37.

information, and progressive public participation amount to a violation of the moral–political rights of mankind (ibid. 87). Any

contract made to shut off all further enlightenment [knowledge] from the human race, is absolutely null and void even if confirmed by the supreme power [sovereign head of state], by parliaments, and by . . . treaties. An age cannot bind itself and ordain to put the succeeding one into such a condition that it cannot extend its knowledge . . . and progress in general enlightenment. (ibid. 87)

The origin of liberalism's political and moral basis, as articulated in this view, does not cast the question of liberty to be autonomous from contingency as Kant would have us believe in his metaphysics, where freedom stands above contingent factors. Rather, the practical problem of freedom is one of public communications: the preconditions of access to knowledge, to public space, to ever-extending forms of participatory experience.

As Velkley (1989) observes, without the meaning of freedom as public reason, liberal values work only in individual relations, not in social-political relations nor in resolving the question of public policy in democratic states. Kant's (1991b) approach to civil society and the state[2] argues that citizenship requires of the individual autonomous rational judgement, but this is only possible in a particular kind of political order and within particular kinds of public arrangements without which freedom remains a mere ideal, an aspiration, or worse, an ideology. Consistent with liberalism's framework, Kant is not interested in inequalities and social justice; however, he is deeply interested in the conditions which guarantee the public practice of freedom. Thus citizenship is not neutral with respect to the social order, as may be suggested from Kant's metaphysics alone.

The roots of freedom in the moral system of the modernist movement contain, therefore, a necessary concept of communication expressed as the 'principle of publicity'—that is, the principle of independent thought, normally addressed in liberal political theory under the heading of 'freedom of expression'. Beyond the negative concept of liberty which the conventional free-speech right invokes, the 'principle of publicity' bears an ethical force in Kantian liberalism, for its rule requires widespread inclusion of citizens in public debate as well as their rights to be informed, without which the state forfeits its legitimacy. It thus represents a first principle of a democratic order:

The citizen must . . . be entitled to make public his opinion on whatever of the ruler's measures [law or policy] seem to him to constitute an injustice against

---

[2] See Kant's essay, 'On the Relationship of Theory to Practice in Political Right', in H. Reiss (ed.) and H. B. Nisbet (trans.), *Kant: Political Writings*, 73–87 (Kant, 1991b).

the commonwealth . . . for in all matters concerning universal human duties, each individual requires to be convinced by reason that the coercion [social contract] which prevails is lawful, otherwise he would be in contradiction with himself. (Kant, 1991*b*: 84–5)

In his essay on 'Perpetual Peace' (1991*b*: 93–130), Kant describes the principle of publicity as a 'transcendental [i.e. universal] concept of public right' (ibid. 126). By this he means, Williams (1983) explains, that any political issue or state policy which cannot be adequately and fully debated in public cannot also be made compatible with the idea of justice. The fundamental legitimacy of liberal democracy in the Kantian defence rests on the level of transparency and degree of non-distortion in the structures of public space for sustaining knowledge and debate, which permits lines of common interest to emerge under conditions of political pluralism. The state's legitimacy is linked to the principle of publicity since, from a normative standpoint, the government only holds authority over people if it represents the general will of the community: 'Whatever a people cannot impose upon itself cannot be imposed upon it by the law-maker either', and what a people would impose upon itself can only be determined according to the idea of publicity. Therefore, a guardian of the general interest—public/political authorities—has no reason to fear 'independent and public thought' (Kant, 1991*b*: 85).

The basic case made in modernity's philosophy of freedom of expression is that it is more likely to render the claim of democratic government valid where it allows the public, as against private, practice of freedom for most citizens. The principle of publicity reconciles the requirements of general interest or public interest with the requirements of political legitimacy, a reconciliation exacted by Rousseau's (1973: 135) first fundamental rule of democratic government, that it 'follow in everything the general will'. The general interest through publicity in this framework is essential to the recovery of self-determination and can never be democratic if arrived at through paternalism or authoritarianism or, as in contemporary instances, through unaccountable structures of proprietary governance over the public realm. However, these are the alternatives which automatically arise in the absence of the regulation of the information system for widespread inclusion and undistorted opportunities for participation.

When we join Kant's idea of publicity with contemporary notions of democracy, we arrive at a deliberative theory of democratic legitimacy. Rather than pure consent based on the necessity of state power to contain social anarchy, in the way Hobbes (1991: 138) justifies the existence of the civil state (see Chapter 2), this moral defence of liberal democracy stresses the deliberative processes leading to consent and to the reasons which underpin consent. The central idea is that citizens should be 'convinced by reason' and deliberation in the public realm—not by appeals to desire and entertainment or by false debate, distortion, and inadequacy of information—that the institutions and norms of their political community are in the general interest. Conversely, the social order of a political community, including its institutions, policies, and norms, is not in the public interest when citizens cannot be convinced by reason in the public realm, or else when they encounter barriers to widespread inclusion within information structures for deliberating on matters of common concern and government policy.

Thus the test that reconciles politics with democratic legitimacy is the test of the modes of public space. Politics is coercion (Kant, 1990: 85) and democracy is the moral basis of association. These can only be reconciled by fundamental rights, the foremost being publicity, the information right of knowledge and public participation. Publicity says you are free when you are living under laws you would give yourself. Publicity is therefore a liberal theory of citizenship and asks that citizens evaluate the justice of their policies and laws decided by the creation of consensus through structures of deliberation. Public space, therefore, is the context where the moral legitimacy of democracy is established, for it is only in the participatory structures of public communications that the basis of general interest can emerge. It is not enough to come up with policies and laws, just or otherwise, through the procedures of representative government, voting rights, or benevolent oligarchy. Citizens must be convinced by reason in the exercise of public debate that public policies are just.

As with Mill (1974: 71), this is an argument for freedom of conscience and of speech. Yet Mill defends this first principle of democratic relations on the utilitarian grounds that freedom of expression is functional to peaceful coexistence and to individual self-interest: 'I regard utility as the ultimate appeal on all ethical questions' (ibid. 70). Kant's notion of publicity, on the other hand, is founded on the grounds of the fundamental dignity, the moral sovereignty of individual citizens. Only governments who are not acting in the public interest fear open and encompassing structures of public space and conditions of widely available, undistorted, substantive knowledge: 'All actions affecting the rights of other human beings are wrong if their maxim is not compatible with their being made public' (Kant, 1991b: 126).[3]

The promise of modernity as judged by its powerful ideal of universal self-determination is inherently integrated into the promise of specific modes of the public realm without which self-determination can never be actualized. The obstructions to freedom are not because of a flaw

---

[3] From Kant's (1991b) essay 'Perpetual Peace', 93–130.

inherent in our make-up as human beings (the natural-vices argument), but because of flaws in the make-up of the social order, particularly with respect to the structures and forms of communication. This is the sense in which the moral foundation of liberalism can be said to hold forth a hope for emancipation in the political context of 'publicity'—the responsibility of the democratic state in guaranteeing the conditions of information. Thus the policies of the public realm are inseparable from the primary postulates of the liberal democratic social order.

The right to publicity—or right of public freedom of speech, knowledge, information, and participation—is a moral and political right, not a mere ideological construction or a right constrained to the domain of private conscience. Therefore, the 'right of publicity', unlike the utilitarian right of freedom of expression, has important social consequences. Properly defended, Kant's ideal of the right to participation in public space demands the existence of a set of structures, guaranteed by the policies of the democratic state, in which there are progressively enlarging possibilities for the public exchange of ideas. It is through this public realm maintained in the public interest that citizens and social groups can press for social improvements in the direction of the fulfilment of the promise of emancipation for all.

The Kantian defence serves both as the positive proposition as well as the grounds of social criticism of modernity's development. It has thus worked as a ferment, Taylor (1985) notes, to stimulate critical assessment of modernity's social forms, eventually emerging in revolutionary theories of liberation. In the argument presented here, the standard of freedom as public reason through participation establishes the normative grounds of social criticism for the institutional formations of the modern world, including the fundamental responsibility of democratic governments and the value and place of the citizen. These grounds help to mediate the criticism of Marx and Weber who evaluate the contrast between the promise and the reality of modernity's social order. This polarity, explored below, is relevant to the next stage in elaborating the central problem of this chapter.

COMMUNICATION AND THE REALITY OF MODERNITY

The shift to post-eighteenth-century social thought is a shift in defining the agency of modernization: namely, from the ideal of political agency for individual citizens through participation in knowledge, to the reality of global agency by particular forms of economic forces permeating all modes of life—social, cultural, and political—within enlarging oligarchic systems, some claiming the status of 'democracies'. Modernity's economic form, monopoly capitalism, not accounted for in the normative standard of its political form, progressively appropriates the state in a set of interrelations that is rationalized by an ideology of emancipation, though based on the reality of dependency. In the context of this transformation of the social order of modernity and the salience of the social criticism of Marx and Weber for understanding the general forms of transformation, the dialectic between freedom's hope and actuality becomes directly relevant to the constitution of the public realm and the policies which sustain it.

The collapse of the possibilities for a concept of freedom contingent on the public sphere parallels the social ascendancy of civil society as a private sphere, revered as the primeval site of individual being. Thus entailed in the reorganization of modernity's social forms is a transformation in the value and status of the individual and a reordering of the relation of the democratic state to that value. The social criticism drawn upon here pertains to the degeneration of democratization suggesting a normative test of public freedom in contrast with liberalism's test of private rights.

Marx recognizes the ideal of modern individualism as its own telos when he writes that 'Present-day society is the realised principle of individualism; the individual existence is the final goal; activity, work, content, etc., are mere means'[4] (Marx and Engels, 1975: 81). Modernity's social form has cast up the individual as solitary and abstract rather than an agent of participation in self-determination, for the latter would inherently conflict with the maintenance of a social order whose essence is domination. Modernity's doctrine of individualism is in reality one in which 'individuals appear to be independent . . . appear to collide with one another freely and to exchange with one another in this freedom' (Marx, 1974: 100), with no reference to the particularities of concrete circumstance. It is to this doctrine that Marx assimilates the significance of equality and freedom in the Rights of Man (French Declaration, 1789) which he regards as an ideology rationalizing the conditions of subordination and inequality that prevail in the guise of citizenship.

Marx's critique suggests that the grounds of practice of individual freedom in modernity are essentially contradictory, even irreconcilable with its moral contract, since this freedom derives not from participatory rights of knowledge and agency in the public realm but from the structures of dependency inherent in forms of productive social relations. For Marx, this renders modern freedom 'merely imaginary', and individual independence 'merely an illusion' (Marx, 1974: 100).

---

[4] From 'Contribution to the Critique of Hegel's Philosophy of Right', see Marx and Engels, 1975.

Fromm (1992) argues that Marx does not dismiss human rights altogether for that would be inconsistent with the hope implicit in his criticism for recovering modernity's promise of development and emancipation for mankind (Fromm, 1992: 42). Marx's point is simply that given the social reality of the modern age, freedom and other rights of the individual remain largely chimerical because, in Sayer's words, 'they do not extend to that arena which he considered the foundation of being, the production of life' (Sayer, 1991: 65–6).

In this argument, the 'abstract individual' who is claimed by modern democracies to enjoy political and civil rights is just that: a representation, a subject whose existence remains merely an ideal. However, this subject serves powerfully as a universal reference point for distracting from the conditions of power and structural inequality essential to the maintenance of the existing social order. Elaborating Marx's critique of modern individualism, Sayer observes that 'Modernity constitutes individuals as subjects not through but in opposition to the real sociality which concretely defines and differentiates them' (ibid. 72). Thus the conception of emancipation through participatory self-determination remains an assurance unrealized.

If the constitution of freedom is in contradiction to its ideal, the constitution of the modern state is in substance as much a form in which social power is secured through domination as the pre-capitalist mode of rule from which the political project of modernity struggled to articulate the grounds of liberty. The continuity of power is made possible from the joint domination of class and public power through the democratic state: 'Civil society as such only develops with the bourgeoisie; the social organization evolving directly out of production and commerce, which in all ages forms the basis of the State and of the rest of the idealistic superstructure . . .' (Marx, 1978a: 163). The notion of liberty is institutionalized by securing the conditions under which the dominant social class can operate privately as individuals in civil society. This market freedom is less intrusive than the visible sites of power in pre-modern societies and rests upon the organization of social power in the shape of the democratic political state ostensibly independent of relations based on the ownership of capital.

Thus the free society dreamed of by liberalism is in reality an oligarchy where the maintenance of personal power depends on having to maintain that the power holds good for everybody, and where the ruling class must 'represent its interests as the common interest of all the members of society' (ibid. 174). The notion of the public realm as a realm of progressive inclusion which serves to give rise to consensus regarding the common interest by deliberative, participatory means, becomes irrelevant, perhaps even a serious hindrance to the determination of the public good by the private self-interest of capital. The state thus 'is the form in which the individuals of a ruling class assert their common interests' (ibid. 187) through the political illusion that these interests are the result of the general will. Public power must logically assume impersonal forms such as the rule of law, and representative democracy must function as a strict expression of this exigency. This mode of civil society requires abstractly equal individuals independent of any contingent factors or preconditions, such as rights of knowledge and access to public space, which the moral liberalism of Kant conceives for authentic self-determination.

Fundamental to the modern representative democracies is a separation of 'public' and 'private' whereby the public domain is defined by private categories allowing the growing displacement of issues from the public sphere where they must be addressed collectively, into the private sphere where they are transformed into matters of personal preference. The systematic moral confusion of the public interest and the private interest has a substantive bearing on the value and status of the citizen, the role of public policy, and the place of communication within the modern social order.

Since the citizen is not a normative category, but a 'sheer, blank individuality, a subjectivity without social content' (Marx and Engels, 1975: 77), the state is effectively able to extract legitimacy from the plausibility of its claim to represent the private interests of individual competing entitities. Marx's point here is that, given the social conditions of modernity, in fundamental ways the democratic state is hardly the guarantor of the conditions of participatory citizenship. Rather, it is an ideological project, 'a collective misrepresentation whose real content remains the inequities of capitalism' (Sayer, 1991: 83). The political citizenship articulated in modernity's democratic struggle, and the moral, civil, and human rights which go with it, have never extended to all members of civil society.

Exclusion from the public realm, from access to knowledge, information, and deliberative relations, are exclusions which are fundamental to the construction of the 'freedom of the market' and of private self-interest as the basis of public policy and of membership. The absence of limitations, 'barriers', regulations, and obstructions to competition in international trade, and the commercialization of all spheres of modern life demand an assumption regarding citizenship and the public interest whereby the democratic state is expected to service the domain of private proprietary rights.

It is argued here that Kant's social understanding (Goldmann, 1971) of the preconditions of political practice imbues the moral foundation of liberalism with a standard by which to measure its actualization.

Marx, however, points out that this sense of progress in the modernist movement is flawed because the social circumstances of modernity's economic formation prevent individuals, citizens, or social groups from attaining the promised goal. Marx does not, however, deny the need to strive for the ideal in the sphere of political self-determination—contingent on knowledge and public participation—but even more, in the sphere of material self-determination—contingent on the authentic autonomy of the individual's labour (Marx, 1978*b*: 70). Both, of course, are necessarily related (Fromm, 1992). In democratic societies we strive under the ideals of modernism for information and access to the public realm, as well as for autonomy in our labour, but this is denied us by the exploitative nature of integration between capital and the state. As Goldmann (1971) argues, Marx and Kant are at one in thinking progress is possible and can be accelerated by the notion of intervention, or the public practice of reason, that is, political practice. Yet Marx's criticism implies that the promise of modernity has given individuals a goal it is scarcely possible to realize in the context of the circumstances of modernity.

Even Marcuse (1972: 80), who in general adheres to Marxist disapproval of Kant's liberal philosophy because it does not intend to criticize modern capitalist society in a revolutionary way, recognizes the substantive ideal inherent in the 'principle of publicity' which requires that members of political society be allowed to make public use of their reason in all matters which concern them, that is, in all matters of public policy and law by which they could be governed.

Marx's critique suggests that the political reality of the governed is illusory, whereas Weber's (1946: 224–6)[5] critique supports this thesis in the argument that 'democratization', in the sense intended in liberalism's ideal, does not necessarily mean an increasingly active share of the governed in the authority of the social structure. Weber recognized the major historical relevance of the theory of natural rights which he affirms as the necessity to 'account for the ultimate meaning of one's own conduct' (ibid. 151–2) in his essay, 'Science as a Vocation'. But he believed that under modern conditions the theory had progressively lost its significance and was being replaced by positivistic, formal–legal norms (ibid. 216; 1930: 25), requiring that fundamental rights be interpreted anew in relation to the concrete social relations of late-capitalist industrial societies. Thus the idea of self-determination seemed to Weber to have become largely meaningless under the conditions of advanced industrial societies (ibid. 71). The structure of domination that had become inherent in the democratic system for Weber could be distinguished from that of Marx in the emphasis placed on the

---

[5] See Weber's (1946) essay on 'Bureaucracy', 196–244.

irrevocable progress of rationalization essential to the abstract com-
modification processes of late capitalism.

Weber's precise analysis of the historical reality of capitalist economic
and social organization, following to a large extent Marx's classical
analysis (Mommsen, 1989), offers little, if any, emancipatory hope,
both in terms of modernity's processes and in terms of its ultimate
consequences. Modernity as the process of progressive rationalization
signified for Weber (1947: 123, 184–6) an increase in formal rationality
in all spheres of life, somewhat similar, in a manner of speaking, to the
way in which Marx inferred the gradual assimilation of all social
experience to exchange-value relations. The public practice of reason as
a practice of self-determination affirmed in the moral foundation of
liberalism is observed by Weber to have been paradoxically transformed
in late modernity into a powerful source of domination:

One of the fundamental elements of the spirit of modern capitalism, and
not only of that but of all modern culture: rational conduct . . . building the
tremendous cosmos of the modern economic order. This order is now bound to
the technical and economic conditions of machine production which today
determine the lives of all the individuals who are born into this mechanism, not
only those directly concerned with economic acquisition, with irresistible force.
(Weber, 1930: 180–1)

The transformation of reason into rationality or *Zweckrationalität*
(Weber, 1947: 115) for Weber implies purposive rationality, or the
choice of the most efficient means for realizing final goals. 'Rationalization' as domination is therefore tied up with the increase of economic or
administrative efficiency. It points to the imposition of a coherent and
systematic order upon the indeterminateness of common existence that
ought to have been governed instead by the principles of authentic individual liberties. The tendency to formalization and universalization of
law and bureaucracy (Weber, 1946: 196–244) in rapidly developing
monopolistic-capital structures results in an increase in coherence,
systematic order, calculability, control, and systematic planning, thereby rendering liberalism's hope for citizens' rights obsolete. Weber
concludes that the 'the most urgent task [of rationalization is] the
destruction of spontaneous, impulsive enjoyment, and the most important means is to bring order into the conduct of life' (1930: 118–19).

In *The Protestant Ethic and the Spirit of Capitalism* (1930), Weber
provides a powerful formulation of the actual tendencies of modernity.
If left to run its course undisturbed, late capitalism would bring a
new age of serfdom not unlike the one of late antiquity. Capitalist
industrial society, organized according to the principle of purposive
or instrumental rationality, could lead into a dehumanization of the

world of work and displacement of the individual from economic participation and political participation (ibid. 54–5). The advanced capitalist system is exhibiting increasingly mechanical, ultimately inescapable powers over mankind such as have never before been seen in history (ibid. 181–2), enforcing in the process forms of the regulation of life which are no longer in accordance with liberalism's ideal of emancipation. Thus it is only to the private sphere of preference, desire, appetite, and personal value that the individual can retreat (Weber, 1946: 151–3).[6]

Yet implicit in Weber's theory is a notion of freedom which must derive from rationalization's antinomial social conditions, that is, from those which give rise to possibilities of participation free from distortions of illusion and self-deception. Thus rationalization also implies its opposite: the experience of authentic modes of participation and an optimum degree of individual self-determination for all. His use of the term 'disenchantment' parallels Marx's 'alienation' in reference to the realization of these circumstances in modern liberal democracies: 'The fate of our times', Weber writes, 'is characterized by rationalization and intellectualization and, above all, by the "disenchantment of the world"' (ibid. 155).

One might say that Weber privileges the role of public reason in modern life and develops his critique of modernity based on the circumstances of its deformity which points to an increasing imprisonment of modern experience in dehumanized systems of a new historical kind (Weber, 1930: 181–3). The tendencies of increasing formalization, instrumentalization, and bureaucratization according to an internal systemic logic, steer towards a state of society in which liberalism's ideal of participatory rights becomes more and more of an anachronism, and in which the possibility of information structures which could support the formation of consensus based on political practice has disintegrated into communication structures supporting self-interested pluralism and privatized value choices (Weber, 1946: 151–2).

There is a profoundly pessimistic—though not determinate—philosophy of history implicit in Weber's theory of modern rationalization. The increasing rationalization of humanity by an internal logic triggers historical processes which tend, as elaborated in *The Protestant Ethic*, to depersonalize social relationships, to atomize substantive-rational communication, and to subject human life to the impersonal logic of rationalized, anonymous administrative systems (Weber, 1946: 230–1). In short, Weber's account of historical processes characterizes modernity as the rendering of human life into mechanized, free, and meaningless modes of order and experience; in other words, into an

---

[6] See Weber's (1946) essay 'Science as a Vocation', 129–56.

'iron cage' of rationality, rather than into the possibility of liberty through public reason:

No one knows who will live in this cage in the future, or whether at the end of this tremendous development entirely new prophets will arise, or there will be a great rebirth of old ideas and ideals, or, if neither, mechanized petrifaction, embellished with a sort of convulsive self-importance. For of the last stage of this cultural development, it might well be truly said: 'Specialists without spirit, sensualists without heart; this nullity imagines that it has attained a level of civilization never before achieved'. (Weber, 1930: 182)

The decision whether to submit to the iron rule of formal rationality or not is simply no longer in the hands of citizens and social groups to whom reason was supposed to be applicable, nor in the hands of workers, or individual entrepreneurs. It is simply enforced by market competition, a basic regulative principle of the world capitalist order. Thus the innate tendency of the workings of this principle is to shackle members of political society in a system of unbroken dependence (Weber, 1977: 138), even further accentuating Marx's thesis of substantive irrationality in the modern economic order.

Weber's argument that the hope and expectation of liberalism had turned into a bitter and ironic illusion, therefore, is structured on the premise of the normative grounds of the social practices of reason whereby its forms and modes are necessarily linked to human liberty. He poses this problem in the opposition and irreconcilability of substantive rationality with purposive-instrumental rationality (Weber, 1946: 129–56), the former fundamentally essential to individual self-determination, the latter to continuity of modernity's social order. The hope of recovering substantive reason in the public life of liberal democracies is becoming progressively less and less leaving no possibility whatever of revolutionary transformation of the social order under the 'iron cage' of capitalism.

This sobering thesis has been lately disputed by Habermas (1984) who challenges Weber's fatalism that all hope of emancipation in the structures of substantive reason has been lost to modernity. Habermas recentres the principle of communication into the emancipatory project of modernity by means of a theory of communicative action which redefines the problem of reason and rationalization. While the historical processes of social modernity are by necessity oriented to the 'iron cage' and to the nullity of human life, he argues that instrumental rationality has its legitimate place, but only in the 'systems world'. In Habermas's view, the boundary of instrumental rationality in the service of the systems world is only 'overstepped when systemic imperatives force their way into domains of cultural reproduction, social integration, and socialization' (Habermas, 1987: 374)—in other words into the core zones of the 'lifeworld' of self-determination where a non-repressive form of rationalization ought to prevail. The redemption of Weber's iron cage of rationalization into differentiated forms appropriate and legitimate to distinctive realms of human life thus allows Habermas to return to the spirit of Kant's emancipatory model:

It [Habermas's reconstruction of modernity's hope] is critical both of contemporary social sciences and of the social reality they are supposed to grasp. It is critical of the reality of developed societies inasmuch as they do not make full use of the learning potential culturally available to them, but deliver themselves over to an uncontrolled growth of complexity. . . . This increasing system complexity encroaches upon nonrenewable supplies [in the cultural and natural environment]. . . . Not only does it outflank traditional forms of life, it attacks the communicative infrastructure of largely rationalized lifeworlds. But [critical] theory is also critical of social-scientific approaches that are incapable of deciphering the paradoxes of societal rationalization because they make complex social systems their object only from one or another abstract point of view, without accounting for the historical constitution of their object domain. (Habermas, 1987: 375)

To address the fundamental problem of redeeming the hope of reason and to differentiate rationalization in various historical contexts, Habermas's theory of communicative action moves to restore the principle of public reason in modern liberalism by isolating, identifying, and clarifying the normative conditions required for the practice of social and political communication. The process is accomplished by grounding a theory of rationality in intersubjective relations, or discourse, that no longer entraps us, he argues (ibid. 62), in the monological perspective of the philosophy of the subject whose consequence is the reification of the atomized individual. Communicative action is intrinsically dialogical, a distinctive type of social action oriented to mutual understanding, as opposed to other types of social action oriented to 'success' or the efficient achievement of ends as constitutive of means–ends rationality (ibid. 46).

Ideally, the only force that should prevail in the information infrastructure of society is the force or condition of uncoerced argumentation. While everyday life is certainly characterized by disputes and breakdowns in communication and mutual understanding, Habermas's major point is that a form of rationalization is in fact necessary to this 'lifeworld' of intersubjective relations in order that the human struggle to overcome presumably irreconcilable differences may provide the rational foundations for the emergence of common interests. The mode of public reason he proposes is the notion of universal 'validity claims' (ibid. 69) set in the general structures of public communications and in the intersubjective structures of social reproduction. His overall vision for a form of rationalization proper to everyday cultural life is as follows:

In practical discourse we thematize one of the validity claims that underlie speech as its *validity basis* [original emphasis]. In action oriented to reaching understanding, validity claims are 'always already' implicitly raised. . . . In these validity claims, communication theory can locate a gentle, but obstinate, a never silent although seldom redeemed claim to reason, a claim that must be recognized de facto whenever and wherever there is to be consensual action. (Habermas, 1979: 97)

The pragmatics of everyday reason are stressed further in his assertion that 'again and again this claim [to reason] is silenced, and yet in fantasies and deeds it develops a stubbornly transcending power, because it is renewed with each act of unconstrained understanding, with each moment of living together in solidarity, of successful individuation, and of saving emancipation' (Habermas, 1982: 221).

One of the conceptual strategies Habermas employs for legitimizing rationalization and for rescuing the idea of reason in the process, is to categorically distinguish the rationalization of communicative action from that of purposive-rational action.

Purposive-rational actions can be regarded under two different aspects—the empirical efficiency of technical means and the consistency of choice between suitable means . . . . The rationality of means requires technically utilizable, empirical knowledge. The rationality of decisions requires the explication and inner consistency of value systems and decision maxims as well as the correct derivation of acts of choice. (Habermas, 1979: 117)

The rationalization of communicative action is thus radically and categorically different from *Zweckrationalität*, the form of rationalization process Weber took to be basic to modernization:

Rationalization here means extirpating those relations of force that are inconspicuously set in the very structures of communication and that prevent conscious settlement of conflicts, and consensual regulation of conflicts, by means of intrapsychic as well as interpersonal communicative barriers. Rationalization means overcoming such systematically distorted communication in which the action-supporting consensus concerning the reciprocally raised validity claims . . . [can be measured] against the intersubjectivity of understanding achieved without force. (Habermas, 1979: 119–20)

Thus the significance of Habermas's theory of communicative action is closely linked to, one might even say determined by, the way he addresses Weber's notion of rationalization by differentiating it into two distinct types. Qualifying the notion of rationalization allows him (a) to demonstrate that a theory of communicative action and an adequate theory of modernity to explain the dynamics of historical processes are not two independent endeavours—they are conceptually and inextricably related; and (b) to develop an approach to social analysis that can discriminate the different forms of rationalization processes. Habermas's support of the notion of selective differentiation in rationalization is to recover the possibilities for empirical analysis in the Marxian tradition which has from the very first stressed the fusion of both philosophical and scientific-empirical dimensions of analysis. In an important sense, his approach to this recovery almost requires an inversion of Weber's thought.

In the theory of communicative action, Habermas (1984) supports this basic thesis by showing how both classical social theorists (Marx, Weber, Durkheim, Mead, and Parsons) as well as critical theorists (Lukács, Horkheimer, and Adorno) have all either neglected the significance of rationalization or been blinded from aspects of a comprehensive theory of modernity grounded in a full understanding of the dynamics of public reason and rationalization processes in modernity's social forms. By developing his concept of rationalization's selective differentiation Habermas is then able to propose two mutually exclusive but jointly exhaustive categories to explain modern life, namely, 'systems world' and 'lifeworld'.

Habermas's diagnosis of the historical problem of collapsed substantive reason in the public-communication practices of liberal democracies leads him to formulate what Wellmer calls 'the paradox of rationalization':

The paradox of rationalization is that a rationalization of the lifeworld is the precondition and the starting point for a process of systemic rationalization and differentiation, which then becomes more and more autonomous vis-à-vis the normative constraints embodied in the lifeworld, until in the end the systematic imperatives begin to instrumentalize the lifeworld and threaten to destroy it. (Wellmer, 1985: 56)

The argument that rationalization is a precondition to the normative development of the lifeworld implies there would be no possibilities for conceptualizing the existence of a lifeworld in modernity without a prior conceptualization of a legitimate role for rationalization in the systems world. The lifeworld is only threatened when forms of rationalization valid for the systems world begin systematically to instrumentalize the form of normative public reason valid and necessary to lifeworld processes (Habermas, 1987: 186). Strictly speaking, for Habermas, there is no logical, conceptual, or historical necessity that systemic rationalization imperatives must destroy the lifeworld. While he recognizes that early critical theorists highlighted the real threats modern industrialized societies pose to the communicative integrity of the lifeworld, he veers away from the void to which this must lead and proposes in its place a selective process of differentiated rationalization. In this conceptual transformation of a Marxist–Weberian social criticism, purposive-instrumental rationalization must inevitably prevail in its quite valid domains of state and economy. It only becomes problematic and deserves negation when it encroaches upon and deforms the public sphere, the lifeworld of the citizen's participatory prospects. Habermas suggests this deformation is at present occurring at an alarming rate. As Wellmer puts it:

Against Weber and Horkheimer/Adorno . . . Habermas objects that this paradox of rationalization does not express an internal logic (or dialectic) of modern rationalization processes; it is, strictly speaking, not a paradox of rationalization . . . we have to substitute for Weber's restricted conception of rationality. From an action theory in Weber's sense, there would neither be a paradox of rationalization nor a dialectic of enlightenment for Habermas; rather it would be more adequate to speak of a selective process of rationalization, where the selective character of this process may be explained by the peculiar restrictions put upon communicative rationalization by the boundary conditions and the dynamics of a capitalist process of production. (Wellmer, 1985: 56)

The thesis of the selectivity of rationalization suggests that despair and disenchantment are not inevitable. All lines of Habermas's emancipatory reflections on modernity lead to, and are intended to clarify and support, this thesis. It is only when we grasp the different forms of action and reason, he stresses, that the colonization of the public sphere can be explained by analysing the causes and dynamics of systemic differentiation of reason:

the emergence of modern . . . societies required the institutional embodiment and motivational anchoring of postconventional moral and legal representations; but capitalist modernization follows a pattern such that cognitive-instrumental rationality surges beyond the bounds of the economy and state into other, communicatively structured areas of life and achieves dominance there at the expense of moral-political and aesthetic-practical rationality which produces disturbances in the symbolic reproduction of the lifeworld. (Habermas, 1987: 304–5)

Among the controversial aspects of this argument, according to Jay (1985), is the suggestion that we can accept this differentiation and still seek new ways to integrate participation into our everyday lives, and that we can still seek to restore a proper balance between the legitimate demands of social systems and the public reason of the lifeworld. The prospect of furthering the communicative rationalization of our every-day lifeworld is still, for Habermas, a real historical possibility. The aspirations of modernity are transformed into rational grounds for hope by dealing with the conceptual problem of Weber's disenchantment, inverting it, and redirecting its tendencies. The explanatory power of a theory of communicative action will endure, Habermas claims, because communicative rationality in our everyday social practices has a 'stubbornly transcending power . . . renewed with each act of uncon-strained understanding, with each moment of living together in soli-darity, of successful individuation, and of saving emancipation' (Haber-mas, 1982: 227).

Wellmer argues that Habermas's conceptual strategy for redeeming the potential of reason points to the importance of adequate 'objectification' of communicative rationality in new social and political institutions; that is, ' by institutions which, on the one hand, would represent the normative anchoring of the system in the lifeworld, and on the other, would protect the communicative structures of the lifeworld themselves, and secure a rational and democratic control of the system by the lifeworld' (Wellmer, 1985: 58). According to this view, the insti-tutionalization of rationality in modes appropriate to its social context provides a new meaning for Weber's notion of the discontents of modernity. These discontents, in Habermas's thought, are not rooted in rationalization as such, but in the failure to develop and institutionalize different dimensions of public reason in a balanced way.

Thus, owing to the absence of institutions that could protect the private and public spheres from the reifying dynamics of the economic and administrative systems (the systems world), participatory relations drawn from the public practice of reason have been increasingly pushed to the margin. Owing to lack of feedback relations between a differentiated modern culture and impoverished conditions of public space, the lifeworld has become increasingly desolate. In Habermas's view, the expoitation of the public-communication infrastructure of society on the grounds of instrumental rationality poses a growing threat to the very legitimacy and moral basis of liberal democracy (Habermas, 1987: 361), for it instrumentalizes everyday cultural life which requires widespread inclusion in communicative participation in order to function in the democratization of social life.

The more deeply non-commercial relations in civil society are penetrated by systemic imperatives, the greater the danger of demo-cracy's effective collapse, both in ideal and historical terms. The struggle towards a balanced institutionalization of different modes of reason demands a de-colonization of the public sphere, but not in the sense of insulating it altogether from processes of reason. There is a type of reason proper to the public sphere of the lifeworld which Habermas explicitly defends, namely, an expansion of the areas in which action is coordinated by way of deliberative-communicatively achieved agreement and therefore of chances for consensus over the terms of associational life between citizens and social groups (ibid. 119).

POLITICAL FOUNDATIONS OF INFORMATION POLICY

Discussion here of the conceptual basis of modernity's democratic project has attempted to argue that the core of its struggle for freedom has been inextricably linked to the progressive democratization of the public realm. Liberal ideals of personal autonomy and individual self-development originate both explicitly and implicitly in a root principle of 'publicity' embedded in the moral basis of liberal thought, defended by Kant whose moral framework for universal human rights legitimizes modern democracies (Baynes, 1992; Dworkin, 1978). While the utilitarian origins of liberalism derived from Locke, Hobbes, and Mill have left us with an incoherent concept of the human self and society from an anti-political equation of civil society with the private sphere, the moral origins of liberalism instead provide a substantive equation of civil society, individual rights, or the notion of freedom, with the public sphere. No doubt, moral liberalism is fraught with ambiguity and, in historical terms, has not been as successful in articulating the inter-relation between self-determination and participatory public space. Yet the principles of public reason it expounds stand in direct contradiction to utilitarian liberalism's claim that no necessary interrelation exists other than through the market-oriented economic system.

This latter reasoning has served as grounds for information policy throughout the modern period, experiencing a deepening justification since the 1980s (Ungerer and Costello, 1988; Fowler and Brenner, 1982) and serving as the conceptual-normative basis for a worldwide movement of information liberalization ever since the end of the Cold War (Mansell, 1993; Porter, 1989). Because the public interest is the private interest, it is argued, the role of the state must be to further proprietary rights and private governance of public communications, mediate conflicting proprietary claims, and further competitive practices in the design of policies for the public communication networks of liberal democracies (Fowler and Brenner, 1982; Bork, 1978).

Contrary to misleading liberal conceptions of policy as guarantees solely of the private interests of individual entities against public interference in their commercial freedoms, the discussion here has attempted to show that communication policy in free societies possesses in fact a substantive normative foundation emerging from the very core of modernity's political project for individual self-determination and for the progressive expansion of knowledge and participation to all social groups. The social criticism offered by Marx and Weber demonstrates that the political project of information and participatory rights is far from complete and that attempts to deny or suppress the substantive grounds of this ideal or its realization reflect the governance of civil society by private interests claiming validity as the public interest.

This trend, intensified in recent decades, has derailed the emancipatory movement and constitutes historical modernity's primary pathology. More recently, as shown in the preceding discussion, Habermas (1989) has attempted to reconnect liberalism's principles of individual rights with the political precondition of normative requirements in the structure of public space. Though there may be some conceptual problems (see discussion in Chapters 2 and 3; Benhabib, 1992; Fraser, 1992) in the theoretical procedures by which he attempts this reconstruction, yet the broader issue Habermas raises for the recovery of the public realm if modernity's ideals are not to collapse altogether is the essential point considered relevant to this study and to its examination of the historical problem of contemporary information policy.

The argument in this chapter has attempted to establish the normative, substantive grounds—as opposed to either unitary, neutral, procedural, or competitive grounds—of communication policy, and its place at the heart of modernity's promise of freedom as citizenship rights in knowledge and participation. These normative grounds suggest a way of questioning the policy design of information society on the basis of the normative criteria of publicity and the issues of historical reality raised in the preceding discussion.

In June 1994, the European Council of Ministers adopted a report (Commission of the European Communities, 1994a, henceforth referred to as the Bangemann Report) recommending a complete transformation of the social and economic structure of public space in the European Union (EU). Growing out of the Delors White Paper (Commission of the European Communities, 1993a), which embodies the notion of a revised social contract in European public policy for the next century, the Bangemann Report asked member governments to endorse a fundamental overhaul of public policies and laws in the information sector.

The report represents a synthesis, perhaps an apotheosis, of a particular historical direction in policy for reconceptualization of both the public realm and the projected role of the state which has been evolving and gathering momentum in Europe since the late 1980s.[7] Following a series of initiatives in a wide range of information sectors— from broadcasting and telecommunications to audiovisual production, copyright, and ownership regulation—the Commission has offered a more consolidated vision for a 'European information space' in the interests of citizens and consumers that would constitute 'a new industrial revolution . . . based on information, itself the expression of human knowledge . . . and ensure the cohesion of the new society' (Commission of the European Communities, 1994*a*: 7–8). The proposals also effectively concretize the direction of existing policies recently laid in place, institutionalizing them within an overarching framework that sets the boundaries of legitimate debate over the meaning of the information revolution. The Bangemann Report followed within less than a year of US National Information Infrastructure proposals (US Congress, 1994*b*; US Government, 1993) for bringing about a nationwide broadband multimedia network. As reflected in the Bangemann Report, US policy reasoning also employs the rationale of revolutionary innovation in information technology to argue for radical restructuring, in the public interest, of policies governing public space in most information sectors.

The policy design of the information society articulated in these proposals is indicative of a century of contradictory and confused debate (Porter, 1989; Rowland, 1986) over the fundamental social-political value of the information system in a democratic society and the responsibility of government in ensuring the public realm as a democratic good. Further, the policy framework emerging for the information superhighway in the EU—as also in the USA—signifies the transition of the communication-regulation debate to a new level. This trend may culminate in the institutionalization of a particular approach to information policy which suggests the historical end of the place of the principle of publicity in the normative legitimacy of liberal democracies. As such, it would effectively bring to a close modernity's long struggle for citizenship as participatory inclusion, remove the promise of knowledge and emancipation from liberalism's ideal of the meaning of progress, and substitute in its place the aspiration of proprietary interests and contract law as the solitary rationale and normative grounds of the democratic polity.

While this is clearly foreseen in Marxian–Weberian analysis as the preceding discussion shows, the precise mode by which the principle of publicity as the moral basis of liberalism moves from the condition of

---

[7] The origin of this policy trend can be traced to publication of the European Commission's Green Paper on telecommunication services (Commission of the European Communities, 1987; see ch. 4).

ideology Marx describes to political disestablishment in contemporary policies of the public realm, invites investigation. Examination is needed of the policy basis by which democratic legitimacy is amended from the promise of participation to the promise of technological progress for sustaining competition and consumption.

In the contemporary prevailing vision of legitimacy which new information-society policy initiatives show, the central principle of modern civil society is composed of two premises: first, the unqualified autonomy of proprietary interests from minimal standards of obligation in the common interest, and secondly, a conception of democratic legitimacy in which the primary end of government and public policy is to serve as unqualified instrument of participants in the marketplace. The first premise is offered as a required precondition for technological innovation without which, it is argued, the information age would elude us indefinitely (Ellul, 1990) while the second further minimizes the accountability of the governance structure of economic rivalry thereby forcing both the state and citizens to retreat from civil society, leaving its space of social action almost entirely to market players (Schumpeter, 1991; Hayek, 1982, 1976; Gray, 1989).

A crucial element in this theory of economy and the state (Barro, 1994) is the predominant role played by technological innovation, particularly communication technology, in creating economic growth. Above and beyond any other socio-economic factor, including conditions of investment or lower tax rates on capital accumulation, technological progress is required to fuel economic expansion. This progress is slowed by all government policies, even the most marginal, except for economic policies furthering liberalization. The reasoning claims that proprietary rewards of monopoly power and higher prices above the competitive level must be permissible as the prize for innovation of the products of improved technology in a commercial sense, or else innovators will have no incentive to carry out costly and often unsuccessful research.

Accordingly, it is argued, technological change and growth are contingent on the transformation of the state into an economic instrument for protecting compensation structures, maintaining free markets by keeping market regulation to a minimum, even taking a more favourable view of monopoly in technological sectors such as communications; and finally, eliminating all expenditures for public service such as universal service since these are thought to distort the market by shifting resources to non-productive human capital.

While this approach to liberal social organization has been constitutive of the historical reality of modernity all along as Marx and Weber have shown, nevertheless liberal democracies in this century have

evolved within a relatively broader understanding of the need for institutions to mediate between the private and public spheres, between civil
society and the state, between private property and common welfare,
and between the demands of political participation, communication, or
citizenship, on the one hand, and those of a market-oriented social
order, on the other (Dahlgren and Sparks, 1991). It is this mediating,
nuanced, often contradictory approach that accounts for traditions of
the public interest (Bauby and Boual, 1994) that have developed in
advanced industrialized democracies over the course of this century (see
further discussion on the public service tradition in Chapters 5 and 6).
The result has been a dichotomous policy framework for establishing a
balance of private and public rights in communication regulation which,
while paradoxical and ideological in many respects, has nevertheless
incorporated a set of political struggles over democratizing principles in
public policy, foremost among them being the principle of publicity or
participatory rights (Curran, 1991; Garnham, 1990).

But the technological form of an information society now offered in
information-society proposals of the European Union (Commission
of the European Communities, 1995*a*, 1994*a*), closely following
tendencies gathering momentum in the USA (US Congress, 1996*a*; US
Government, 1995*a*, 1993) is an explicit rejection of evolved traditions
of public-interest information policy in the modern age which, until
recently, preserved a minimal concept of publicity and participatory
rights in the regulation of the public spheres of liberal states. Even
though the function of these traditions may have been none other than
to invoke democratic legitimacy and to marginalize alternative political
conceptualizations of a public realm, yet the explicit rejection of the
moral foundations of liberalism which emphasize progressive democratization through the principle of publicity, and its substitution with a
technological model of economic growth that allows little, if any, place
for democratic objectives in public policy, provides a strong basis for
inquiry.

It is argued that the goal of an analysis of information policy, therefore, should be to re-examine the normative basis of information policy
and to examine those workings, contradictions, and modifications
manifest in the policy design for the information ssociety.

CONCLUSION

The central concern of this chapter has been to underscore the historical
need for assessing information-society public policies in terms of their
potential for addressing the unrealized promise of freedom of public

participatory rights that lies at the heart of the democratic social contract. As the discussion of Kant's political arguments demonstrates, the modern principle of democratic legitimacy rests on the principle of rights as public freedom, and contemporary communication-policy debates echo this discourse in the claim that the information revolution can make possible a new form of public freedom appropriate for a plurality of decentralized, interactive contexts. This chapter suggests a way of asking in what form a coherent conception of a modern and potentially democratic civil society which requires political space for citizens is accounted for in the policy design of the information age.

It is suggested that Kant's principle of publicity serves as the standard for distinguishing between legitimate and illegitimate normative grounds of communication policy, and for defining the validity of state action. For democracy to be valid, the principle asserts, there must exist fully public communicative processes unconstrained by unequal and distorted social and economic forces. The public space of the multimedia age must also be public in terms of participatory access to progressively more citizens and social groups and in terms of real potential for knowledge and not merely for entertainment and commercial expression.

It was observed that Habermas (1990, 1987) reasserts the principle of publicity as a principle of legitimacy based on the way in which it resolves the apparent rift between policy and morality by revealing the political ethic underlying the organization of the public realm. Thus, one of the arguments of this chapter is that Kant's principle of publicity, along with its reformulation by Habermas (1990, 1987, 1984), is a political ethic of legitimacy and fundamental participatory rights. In brief, this principle provides the standard with which to test the legitimacy of the structure of public space since, as held here, it provides the substantive normative grounds of communication regulation.

It is also made clear from the discussion of Marxian–Weberian social criticism that modernity has not developed the principle of publicity as participatory rights in a sufficiently democratic direction. In terms of political philosophy, the historical movement of privatization and deregulation in communication policy unconvincingly maintains that the difference between the private proprietary interests of the information industries and the public participatory interests of citizens can be decided according to the criteria of which dimensions concern only owners and investors of capital—such as copyright law and regulation of capital ownership—and which concern only consumers—such as universal access to infrastructure and information services, access to production and distribution of expression, affordability of information-technology products, and application of competition rules to communication-service providers. But this direction in information policy overlooks that the claim of liberalism from the beginning was to link all politically consequential decision-making to the legally guaranteed deliberative will-formation of the citizenry (Habermas, 1979), not merely to the role of communication-technology innovation in sustaining proprietary growth and product consumption.

As the discussion in this chapter has stressed, the structure of democratic society would need to be accountable to a valid consensus formed in the political public sphere, that is to say, the structure should be accountable to the principle of publicity. But as many have pointed out, including Habermas, Marx, and Weber, the claims of liberalism have hardly been adequately realized. While the principles of formal democracy, universal voting rights, majority rules, freedom of the press, assembly, and opinion are guarantees of liberty, the institutionalization of these rights manifested within particular structures of public space is increasingly biased in the direction of proprietary social interests. Assessment of emerging information-society policies makes apparent that, rather than revolutionizing the information, knowledge, and participatory potential of public space and reversing the anti-democratic tendencies of modern democracies as identified by Marx and Weber, the proposed policy designs for the broadband network would seem to reinforce the purely counterfactual character of the normative principle of democratic legitimacy.

The origin of flawed approaches to the design of information policy is explored next in the exposition of limitations in the principal paradigms of public space from which these policies are drawn.

2

Paradigms of Public Space

Introduction

Among the most significant aspects of the European problem of
common existence is the reconstruction of democracy around policies
favouring the notion of transnational public space, or transnational
communication (Commission of the European Communities, 1990*a*,
1990*b*, 1989, 1987). The significance, of course, is implicit in the
central value placed upon free speech, free press, and open information
within the historical legitimation of liberal democracy from higher
normative standards of freedom, justice, and civil society (Kant, 1991*b*;
Mill, 1974; Habermas, 1989; Rawls, 1993). But the centrality of open
communication to democracy also arises from the link between the
mode of public space and the potential for political liberty, on the one
hand, and between the ideals of modern emancipation and its realities in
the arrangements of political space, on the other.

It will be argued here that the assumptions underlying the forms of
information policy—as examined in subsequent chapters—can be
regarded as the constitutive theory of associational life and democratic
relations defining a given social order. In the structural reorganization
of European information space under information liberalization—
including telecommunications, content ownership, audiovisual and
cultural production, and free expression guarantees—which began in
the 1980s and which has accelerated since (Servaes, 1992; Sepstrup,
1991; Negrine and Papathanassopoulos, 1991), questions have been
raised (Garnham, 1990; Curran, 1991; Porter, 1993*a*) regarding the
political and social conditions of information brought about by these
changes. Indeed, recent transformations of the communication environment—both audiovisual and telecommunication—render problematic
the philosophical grounds of the concept of open communications
emerging in the globalization of the information infrastructure. The
concept generally claims an enlargement, via new communication
technologies, of the liberatory capacity for opinion, action, and thought
among individuals worldwide (Pool, 1990; McLuhan, 1964). It invokes,
therefore, the notion of a transnational public sphere (Jameson, 1991;
Tomlinson, 1991; Sakamoto, 1991) of plural constitution developing as
a natural consequence of convergence in systems of information pro-

duction and distribution among diverse societies, as well as convergence in communication technologies for access and delivery of information services.

In an attempt to reassess the political foundations of modes of thinking about public space, this chapter will examine the conceptual and normative grounds of validity in theories of public space underlying assumptions and claims in contemporary transnational policies for the information society. The notion of the 'transnational' denotes a set of social, political, and economic processes which:

- transcend the political and economic orbits of state actors and delimit their legal and regulatory power (Mowlana, 1994);
- produce a structure of multinational arrangements emerging from globalized market relations which are managed by an alliance of commercial and state proprietary interests with more influence on the lives of individuals and societies worldwide than the national governments they have either elected or been forced to endure (Tomlinson, 1991);
- comprise a cross-border system of communication and cultural forms which render the boundaries of indigenous and exogenous cultural production obscure (Jameson, 1991); and
- provoke the need for a response to life dominated by remote information and cultural oligarchies through the proprietary-oriented instruments of the information society.

Transnational-communication policies in these historical circumstances are those fundamentally implicated in multinational arrangements to enlarge the sphere of negative freedom and the social basis of participation by the consumption and proprietary relations that characterize the competitive order of liberal internationalism. This international order has ascended to great heights in the post-Cold War period, energetically sweeping aside barriers to capital flow, convergence, and consolidation and inducing growing inequalities and concentration in the governance of societies. The competitive order of liberal internationalism has also become the principal regulative mechanism for managing political and social development by the terms of proprietary interests (Wallerstein, 1989; Gilpin, 1987). The emerging competitive order may arise from transnational integration as in the European Union (EU), multilateral trade agreements as in the World Trade Organization (WTO), intergovernmental institutional frameworks for the production of law as in European-level institutions within the Community, or by the internationalization of legal and social models exported from nations such as the USA which exert a formative influence on the regulatory framework of the transnational system.

The modes of transnational communication policy for the information society draw upon national–regional precedents and traditions. They can be said to represent contemporary framework options facing any construction of a transnational public sphere, particularly with respect to the claim within intergovernmental policy deliberations in the European Union that a calculative expansion of cross-border information networks and content distribution implies a progression in the qualities of freedom of speech, consumer choice, and political liberties for individuals and communities. Theories of the press and of media responsibility in modern democracies have been extensively treated. Curran (1991), for example, sheds important light on the divergent interests of these approaches and their social consequences for media systems.

The discussion in this chapter delves several stages beneath press theory to question fundamental conceptions of the good society and notions of freedom for individuals and communities that form the background and define the paradigms of public space and the information policies to which they lead. The political thought of public space embedded in particular frameworks of information policy govern the implementation and interpretation of concepts of political community and categories of rights (Habermas, 1989). To evaluate the principal forms in which a transnational public sphere may be imagined, structured, and institutionalized within socio-legal and intergovernmental arrangements, it becomes necessary to examine the intellectual grounds of theories of public space which establish the meaning and possibilities of common identity in a given political order.

PUBLIC SPACE AS THEORY OF ASSOCIATION

In a wider sense, it is argued here that information policies ought to be regarded as theories of public space, and therefore as political theories of associative relations. For instance, press laws protecting freedom of expression as an intrinsic value can be seen as founded upon a certain concept of the good society: that is, a society in which justice, freedom, and human dignity would be impossible if public language were expunged of honest debate and the critique of existing social conditions, or where knowledge of political, cultural, and social life was unavailable to citizens. Under proposals for the information society, however, public institutions and information industries in the advanced industrialized democracies take pains to differentiate questions of factual truth in information-technology innovation and global market competition, from those of the normative rightness of regulatory arrangements. That is to say, the momentum of information liberalization in public policy—involving information infrastructure, content, and services—has been moving in the somewhat implausible direction of separating the 'is' from the 'ought'. While this technological determinism inherent in the discourse of the information society may claim a more enlightened rationality in policy matters, its reasoning becomes questionable if we consider that resulting laws and policies could not possibly gain social legitimacy, or even coherence, if they did not presuppose a concept of the 'good'. One may conclude then that arguments in defence of the neutrality of policies for the liberalization of the information sector can only be regarded as rationalizations seeking to evade a decision about the form of their political, and therefore ethical, theory.

Such evasions no doubt are routine in the legal and policy histories of liberal democracies. But it may be argued that in no other sphere are the consequences of unacknowledged motivation and the confusion to which it gives rise greater than in the information policies and socio-legal norms that define the public realm of civil society. This is because the actualization of political freedom is fundamentally tied to the potential, the conditions, the structures and organization of public space where common interests are proposed, enacted, deliberated, struggled over, and determined. One of the purposes of this chapter, therefore, is to question the validity of the idea of a context-free technological imperative in legislation, policy, and jurisprudence governing rationalizations of the information society. The perspective here recognizes that a substantive change in moral outlook in the advanced industrialized democracies since the 1970s regarding the meaning of a free society and the status of its citizens has been required in order to accept that no 'ought' in information policy can be derived from any 'is'. Instead, it is held that the emerging initiatives for the information society can be explicitly connected to certain moral positions which these policies presuppose but generally do not acknowledge. Weber (1946: 94–5, 216–21, 299) points to the systematic rationalization of socio-legal and administrative structures of the modern social order, suggesting, as in the case of communication regulation, the imposition of policies and laws in the name of technology, efficiency, and market exigencies. Weber's basic insight into the encompassing reaches of instrumental reason and technical rationalization within all spheres of jurisprudence, economy, and society is useful for probing into the basis of policies regulating the public realm. These policies (for example, US Congress, 1996a, 1994a; and Commission of the European Communities, 1995a, 1994a, 1994b, 1994e, 1994f) are increasingly constructed by premises of the 'technical reasoning' Weber identified, by which policy options can be explained as natural consequences of the laws of technological innovation rather than the outcome of the will of the members of a polity or the participatory requirements of a functioning public sphere.

With respect to the materialist perspective (Schiller, 1996) on the social reality of the information society, while one may rightly posit a correlation between capitalism and liberal democracy, the argument here is that the conditions of emancipation, namely, freedom, rights, equality, and justice, are in fact the measure of democracy and must be regarded as the products rather than the conditions of the political process. The exposition of modes of public space will suggest that private rights—whether as property rights, subjective interests, or the right to creative labour free of domination—do not have any pre-political historical reality. Political community and the terms of associational life precede the claim to these rights and determine the socio-legal basis of economy and society (Barber, 1984; Aristotle, 1981, 1962; Arendt, 1975; Hegel, 1952a). Theories of freedom which envision pre-political, a priori natural states for human freedom (Locke, 1960, Kant, 1990, Hobbes, 1991) may constitute ambiguous, even harmful fantasies (Taylor, 1993) whose social consequences have been the systematic dismantling of the ethical foundations of possibilities for effective political self-determination in late modernity.

To address these problems in the conceptualization of information policies and their implicit vision of political community, I shall elaborate four paradigms of public space which are inscribed in the socio-legal basis of the information society and define its central tensions, structures, and incongruities. Each paradigm derives from distinct though related modes of apprehending individualism and privatism, even though the fourth may appear to project itself as a unitary or collectivist approach to conceiving the public world. The purpose of elaborating these paradigms for this study is to provide the background for the interpretation of the policy design of the information society in the regulation of telecommunications, universal service, intellectual property, audiovisual and cultural production, competition policy, and information rights which are then analysed and assessed in subsequent chapters. The discussion will focus on questions which arise from private versus public conceptualizations of the public sphere, or private as opposed to public reasoning in defining the terms of associational life. The relevance of assessing the assumptions of public space implicit in the design of the information society is that these principal paradigms orient the project of economy and society which are the objectives of the design. The problem is not merely that of constructing the information society by some specific terms of political theory, but of defining particular historical forms in which democracy's promise of political emancipation through access to the public realm for all citizens and social groups is embodied in the information policies which define that realm.

The chapter suggests, finally, the need for further reflection on modernity's accelerating departure from the ideals of political liberty that have been the core of the modernist political enterprise, not simply as an alternative to other principles of associated life (Dewey, 1963) but as the idea of political community itself. Criticism of the distance between the ideal and political realities of modernity has been definitively articulated by Rousseau, Marx, and Weber. For the most part, however, the critique of modern life has tended to neglect the relation between the theory and structure of public space and socio-political development. While some may argue this has informed the Habermas (1989) theory of the public sphere and communication, the discussion will show the political inadequacies of his theoretical project owing to its grounding in Kantian procedural liberalism, while other historical and conceptual problems in his argument of the public sphere have been taken up elsewhere (see Curran, 1991, for example).

Other avenues to the analysis of modernity under the rubric of postmodernism attempt to force a shift from a normative account of human life towards a self-defined free play of human interpretation as a world force. This collapse into subjectivism, as Nussbaum (1992) defines it, is taken up more fully under the second and third modes of public space, illustrating the political and conceptual outcomes of the legitimation of the subject as cultural practice. Postmodernist rejection of the political project of modernity as exemplified in Rorty's (1989, 1983) and Lyotard's (1984) arguments for the eclipse of universalism cannot be disconnected from intellectual Romanticism which began in the middle of the eighteenth century and has provided an eclectic though persistent critique of logical positivism and critical progressivism. Consistent with its historical roots, this Nietzschian revival as some have called postmodernist thought (see Lowenthal's extended reflections in Jay (1987), *The Autobiographical Reflections of Leo Lowenthal*) is not independent of modernity but exists only within and in relation to the structures of modern social experience whose instrumental rationality it attacks from an expressivist, radically subjectivist orientation. And like its conceptual predecessors, the political consequences of postmodernist perspectives reify the status quo through retreat to celebrations of the private, thus reinforcing conservative threats to progressive democratic politics. Evoking the meaning of the modern political project is therefore consciously employed in this essay to distinguish the emancipatory struggle for the democratic revolution that began in the eighteenth century and is still far from complete, from Romanticist postmodernism (see also

Mouffe, 1988; Laclau, 1988; and Keane, 1991, 1988) and its quest for the authentic, passionate, radically indeterminate empty signifier imagined as 'the subject'.

Instead of retreating to a postmodernist analysis, this chapter will argue the historical need for a reconstruction of the philosophical grounds of information rights by returning to the central condition (Tocqueville, 1990; Montesquieu, 1989; Barber, 1984; Aristotle, 1981; Arendt, 1975) which makes freedom politically contingent: the foundations of public space.

PUBLIC SPACE AS INSTRUMENT OF PRIVATE CHOICE

The tradition we allude to as democracy is a far from coherent axiom. Though applied most often as a law-like explanatory thesis, it comprises in fact disparate conceptual systems defining the meaning of freedom. Macpherson (1973) notes that political modernity has at least two traditions, liberal and democratic, which are not necessarily related. But in order to sort out the complex motivations, terms, and implications of communication policy, it is necessary to distinguish democracy even further by more specific sets of assumptions regarding public space and political liberty.

Committing the resources of society to developing maximization of choice in information products and services is commonly recognized today as the meaning of freedom and the primary goal of information policy. This answer to the good society has become so powerful a model in the post-socialist age that sometimes, Barber (1984: 3) observes, 'the very future of democracy seems to depend entirely on its fortunes'. There is historical need, therefore, seriously to address the political premises of human nature and associational conditions which may be genuinely progressive, in the sense of transformational force, but not intrinsically democratic. The discussion here shall be limited to the inherent dependence of contemporary public policy for market-centred democratic values upon a particular assumption of public space and civil society within the work of Locke and Hobbes.

In elaborating the utilitarian paradigm of public space, the term civil society is not employed in the sense of society versus the state but rather signifies the entire complexity of the democratic social order whose system, in the Hegelian meaning of civil society (see Hegel, 1952*a*; taken up by Gramsci, 1971; and more lately by Cohen and Arato, 1992), both incorporates and differentiates the spheres of state, economy, and non-market, non-commercial social networks. While such complexity may be irrelevant to the internal assumptions of utilitarianism, the notion of civil society as political society points to the totality of social life and thus invokes the meaning of the democratic social contract. It is the grounds of political reasoning with respect to this contract which concern this analysis, for the paradigms of public space that underlie judgements in policy discourse may define not simply a notion of society and the state, but which version of civil society is to prevail in the materialization of information policy. Barring an understanding of the premises of the social contract for civil society advanced in the projects for the information age assessed later in this book, it becomes difficult if not impossible to grasp how the functioning of infrastructure and content systems of the technological revolution, broadband, and multimedia systems are described and evaluated in statutes and policies which propose to transform the actualization of public freedom, the structure of the public realm, and the place of the citizen in the social construction of a liberalized society and economy.

The paradigm which conceptualizes public space as an instrument of private choice regards the preferred setting for the good life as a market, a space where individual men and women, consumers rather than producers, choose among a maximum number of options and where the autonomous individual confronts his/her possibilities of ultimate being. This argument is definitively supplied in Locke's *Second Treatise of Government* (1960: 305–477) which argues that 'the great and chief end therefore of men uniting into commonwealths and putting themselves under government is the preservation of their property' (Locke, 1960: 395, ch. 9, par. 124). The identity of freedom with property, with 'possessions and a right to them' (ibid. 335, ch. 5, par. 36), is a concept that merges into modern liberal utilitarian arguments. It has been enlarging worldwide at a rapid pace in the post-Cold War period under the liberalization movement, and holds that political community is an instrumental rather than an intrinsic good, and that the idea of public life and participation has no concrete reality beyond the inherent natural relations of the market.

Locke's particular understanding of natural law as individual self-preservation and property acquisition forms the basis of his argument that the contractual motive for civil society derives from the individual's need for encoding and enforcement of these laws of nature in order to ensure their pre-eminence over other codes of association. He imbues property with a pre-political validity which is the defining characteristic of humanness: 'Though the earth, and all inferior creatures be common to all men, yet every man has a property in his own person' (ibid. 328, ch. 5, par. 27). The aim of common existence is not to share in power or to be part of a community but to contain power and community and to judge them by how they affect the freedom of property ownership.

Thus to live well in this social vision is not to make political decisions as the ancients suggested, or to make beautiful objects by one's own labour as Marx suggested, but to make personal choices about possessions. The market within which ownership and consumption choices are made, like the socialist economy, largely dispenses with politics. It requires at most a minimal state—not the regulation of common interests and political freedoms—along with a military to guard against external threats and a law-enforcement system based on contract to guard the rights of property. The laws of nature therefore suggest only a minimal state for human association.

This naturalization of the character of democracy—as with naturalization of other aspects of human experience—renders the form of political society immutable and beyond questioning since it eliminates conceptual clues as to its essential constructed reality in order to shield liberalism's existing form from broad social challenge. The appeals to an inherent naturalism which stands beyond debate in the political thought of utilitarian liberalism are deepened, albeit less palatably, by significant contemporary implications in Hobbes's construction of human nature and his rationale for the civil state. In the *Leviathan* (1991), Hobbes claims that human life comprises the perpetual pursuit of desires, and that man's natural condition is one of incessant competition oriented towards a 'war of all against all' (Hobbes, 1991: 88). The consequence of this competition in the state of nature is 'a general inclination of all mankind, a perpetual and restless desire of power after power that ceaseth only in Death', and its primary cause is 'because [we] cannot assure the power and means to live well . . . without the acquisition of more' (Hobbes, 1991: 70). The realities of history, no less in the present than in the past, continue to vindicate Hobbes's uncomfortable hypothesis as to the character of brutality, injustice, tyranny, and persecution arising wherever democratic civil society has been absent or inattentive. Yet it is less a matter of engaging Hobbes on the correspondence of his theory of man's natural condition with human history, than on the grounds of his solution to the inevitability of such a fate. His political state for deliverance from a fate of mutual self-destructiveness is a government empowered to do all that is necessary to bring into being and keep a civil peace—but nothing more.

The core of civil society, therefore, is a state that exists to enforce a minimal set of laws demarcating property rights and civil discipline (Gray, 1993; Oakeshott, 1975). Hobbes's notion of the importance of adjudicating property rights does not emerge from some belief in the identity of freedom and property as Locke proposes, but in order to keep the common peace and security:

The distribution of the materials . . . that is to say, in one word property, belongeth in all kinds of commonwealth to the sovereign power. For where there is no commonwealth, there is a perpetual war of every man against his neighbour. . . . Seeing therefore the introduction of property is an effect of commonwealth . . . which we call law and define justice by distributing to every man his own. (Hobbes, 1991: 171)

The source of freedom in the Hobbesian minimal but authoritarian civil state is the condition in which individuals can pursue their private appetites: 'Felicity [happiness] is continual progress of the desire, from one object to another; the attaining of the former, being still but the way to the latter . . . . That the object of man's desire, is not to enjoy once only, and for one instant of time; but to assure for ever, the way of his future desire' (Hobbes, 1991: 70). Thus the good life which creates the most opportunities for the freedom to perpetual pleasure can only be accommodated by the potential of the commercial market. In the late-modern form of liberal utilitarian reasoning which may be called 'liberalization', there is no final or higher good than progressive, that is, ever advancing ways to satisfy desires, and there can be no political context other than the minimal civil state whose essence is the market-place instrumental to that end. With the historical acceleration of entrepreneurial capitalism into monopoly capitalism, this conceptual foundation has become structurally fused to the globalization of commercial and democratic practice, thereby assuming considerable formative influence on the policies, trade agreements, and political arrangements of worldwide liberalization.

The value of the citizen, the individual member of such a state, is as consumer or entrepreneur, the latter being the artiste of independence who competes to supply whatever all the other consumers desire or might be persuaded to desire. New technological innovation is designed to allow enterprising market suppliers to track consumer preferences or desires, and their aim is to increase their market power and maximize both their own options and the options of consumers, but most of all, to enlarge their assets. Competing with one another, they maximize every-one else's options as well, filling the market with objects of desire (see Chapter 7 for discussion of development of these ideas in the competitive order of the information society). The market, in other words, fixes the meaning of public space and common welfare, and is preferred over the idea of a political community and the cooperative economy because of its promise of plenitude and increased ownership.

The issue of justice is highly problematic for a market-centred socio-legal order. The theory overlooks the fact that individuals come to the marketplace with highly differentiated economic assets—some with virtually none at all. Not only is it illogical to assume every individual can compete successfully in commercial production, the assumption is even less rational under the conditions of late modernity and the globalization of the marketplace where the conditions of competition no longer describe the behaviour of individuals but the rivalry of large-scale entities. The market, therefore, is not a good setting for the non-commercial association and organization that supports the structures of civil society since the social basis of mutual assistance would undermine the social basis of competition. As Walzer observes, 'I cannot help someone else without reducing my own options and compromising my drive to desire' (Walzer, 1992: 95). Individuals and entities have no reason, in this paradigm of public space, to accept any limitations on their potential for proprietary accumulation for someone else's sake. A concept of public space which devolves on realization of market freedoms is not equipped to support the idea of non-commercial ends such as political community and social solidarity. Indeed, arguments in support of this theory of freedom, which contains no concept of political space, hold that social justice is a 'myth' and the notion of 'society' illusory (see Hayek, 1982; Nozick, 1974).

All the same, this view of public life has to confront the reality that the successes of commercial production, the good life of property ownership and consumer choice, do not account for the needs, interests, and inclusion of all members of community. The market-choice theory of public space is unable to incorporate or implement in its socio-legal structure the essential premise of public space, which is universality of thought and law and the public-interest foundations of constitutional society (see discussion of the participatory paradigm in Chapter 4 and its public interest regulatory approach in Chapter 6). Large numbers of individuals drop out of the market economy or live precariously on its margins because universality of participation cannot be guaranteed from barriers built into the competitive structures of competition (see further analysis of this problem in Chapter 7). Conceptually, however, the reality of wide inequalities in property is consistent with this doctrine of a natural right to property and natural necessity of desire, even though it is also irreconcilable with Locke's view of the right of the majority to rule. As MacIntyre (1966: 159) observes, an essentialist proprietary theory of democracy is unable to explain the contradiction that to give the rule to the majority will be to give the rule to the many whose interest lie in the abolition of the right of the few to the property the minority has acquired. The private-choice theory of public space can only hold sway if it is assumed that the majority of citizens in a democratic social order will accept, and benefit from, oligarchic government controlled by proprietary power, which privileges by law and public policy—in the name of each citizen—the interests of owners of large-scale property.

Participants in this social order are not conceived to be active in the state other than to articulate claims for enforcing, regulating, and guaranteeing the contractual basis of market relations. Thus, in its ideal form, democracy that sees itself primarily as the processes of private choice is difficult to reconcile with the socio-legal basis of public space grounded in citizen participation. Defence of the market-based paradigm (Johansson, 1991 for a survey of the literature; de Jasay, 1990; Gray, 1989; Buchanan, 1975; Buchanan and Tullock, 1962; Hayek, 1948) as the only valid path to democracy interprets citizenship in economic terms, a view which increasingly supports public policies in a number of spheres, from information and education to the transformation of citizens into consumers who must then seek out the party or programme that most persuasively promises to strengthen their market position. Participants in a market-choice public space need the democratic state but have no ethical relation to it. Instead, they seek its capture for gaining advantage with the buying or not buying of what they make, sell, or consume. Since the market has no political boundaries, commercial ownership, production, and consumption inherently transcends state control. The state is required for determining rules of fair play, but there is no loyalty to political community guaranteed by the state, which brings the political order into continual conflict and struggle with the basic universal principles of guaranteeing a free society.

As Barber (1984: 253) observes, the reality of the pre-eminent value placed on private choice in the marketplace has been a major historical obstacle to achievement of democratic experience: 'the giantism of the modern, monopolistic multinational corporation [is] the liberty-corroding heir to the independent, small-scale firm', suggesting that market entities today stand outside, and to some extent against, every political community. For them, the practice of political liberty in public life, the value of public space, deliberation, and public debate on matters of common concern and political solidarity is, by and large, irrelevant to the more pressing concerns of consumer preferences, the dismantling of trade barriers, and the flow of global investment. Since the conditions of the international marketplace can now be guaranteed and regulated in the global arena, even the democratic civil state becomes irrelevant, at most, an anachronism. The intractable paradox, therefore, of the utilitarian private-choice paradigm of public space is that, by its own logic of the meaning of freedom as property and desire, this version of the democratic state along with its members whose identity is defined by consumption, threatens to enact its own effacement in the face of historical realities favouring the transnationalization of the market.

To the extent that international liberalization has incorporated in its discourse and policies this articulation of selfhood, which is also a framework of freedom most favourable to commercial culture, conceptions of political liberty deriving from justice and common interest are rendered historically problematic. This is because alternative conceptions of these basic requirements of human experience are at variance with the central features of the modern order and more especially its distinctive understanding of individualism, its acquisitiveness, and its elevation of the values of the market to the status of public space, an arena of human association which is meant to facilitate the conditions and practice of political liberty (Arendt, 1973; see elaboration of this concept in Chapter 3). The requirements of political community are at odds with information liberalization which constitutes the basis of the information society because growth of international information networks and enhanced services is not aimed at ensuring public conditions for the deliberation or imagination of relations among the inhabitants of a political community. As a set of institutional arrangements of communication, in which the idea of society is constructed as an aggregation of consumption choices executed without any genuine consensus regarding the ends of political association, the commercial content of the public spheres of transnational media and information networks can but render the nature of political and public obligation to the meaning of democracy systematically unclear. MacIntyre calls this condition 'a rejection of the modern political order' (1984: 255), referring to the erosion of the political enterprise for progressive emancipation of social groups from all spheres of domination, a process of ideas and political transformation that began in the seventeenth century constituted by the information revolution of print media.

For liberal internationalism, the wholesale adoption of a Lockean notion of civil society and identity in the policies of the information society—such as examined later in the EU policies for telecommunications, content ownership, cultural production, and information rights, or as emerging in multilateral trade agreements for elimination of public-interest regulation for audiovisual, satellite, telecommunication, or the Internet—may lead to a design of global information space with characteristics fundamentally opposed to the requirements of a democratic public sphere. These developments are evident in many industrialized nations such as the USA where the public realm of modern information systems has become a narrative and deliberative world in which a particular kind of vocabulary consecrating the self has created a historical disjuncture with the idea of political community. What users of new information infrastructure and service in European or other regions can therefore expect to possess may be no more than the fragments of a conceptual scheme of the possibility of society (MacIntyre, 1984). If this should be the case, as Tocqueville (1990) anticipated in the pathologies of modern atomism, then in the culture of the transnational information society democracy would become imaginary. The basis of this claim is that the particular character of a market-driven, monopoly-oriented, technologically determined public sphere generates a set of social conditions under which audiences and users are powerless to detect the disorders of political thought and practice. They are powerless both before the disorders of science to address the basic human problems of common existence, and in the face of the domination of content of the public realm by a single form of commercial expression and industrial culture projected through universalization of the consumption-driven being (Ferguson, 1992; Bauman, 1991).

The significance of this monological state of rights and self-interest, of individualism and utilitarianism, is not merely at the level of private belief. This late-modern condition has succeeded in establishing a social order only through fundamental transformation of institutions and social arrangements. The actions and policies of government and all other social institutions, such as schools, the law, economic entities, answer only to this standard of value: the primacy of private interest (Taylor, 1989a, 1989b). Thus, adopting a private-choice approach to the regulation of information systems offers regulatory and structural legitimacy to organize society by the standards of private, not associational or common ends, with the inevitable consequences for public space, the construction of consensus, and the practice of political self-determination.

Media policies under this system of thought concern themselves largely with protecting rights of media ownership and are thus rapidly subsumed under ownership laws or proprietary rights (Porter, 1993b), the most important and defining category of laws for this type of civil society (Oakeshott, 1975). Moreover, liberalization of economies in East Asia, Latin America, and in the post-socialist states of Eastern Europe indicate the emergence of a model of civil society which leans more heavily in the direction of a Hobbesian state. That is to say, emerging forms of civil society offered as alternatives to declining totalitarian orders are engaged in the production of laws and policies guaranteeing private property and contractual liberties but not necessarily political and information rights of participation, expression, press freedom, association, dissent, and so on (Gray, 1993). This enlargement of liberalization forces further fixes the central values of economy and society in favour of fortifying the international socio-legal guarantees of proprietary rights but without a corresponding expansion of information and political rights. The international reorganization of state and civil society compels nations through powerful supranational regulatory systems to abandon alternative assumptions of the organization of a free society in favour of policies of deregulation, privatization, and exclusively market-based criteria of public reasoning and policy formation.

In the UK, for instance, a commitment to some version of a public-space concept for communications policies during most of this century, especially since the end of World War II, has been steadily dissolved at all levels of public information systems, both audiovisual and telecommunications (Scannell, 1992; Curran, 1991; Garnham, 1990; Smith, 1989). Elsewhere in the European Union, this view has been inscribed into the information-society design of policies and laws for restructuring and regulating the information industries despite the explicit discourse of information liberalization which professes social, political, and cultural goals necessary for political legitimation (Venturelli, 1993; Servaes, 1992).

Despite the contemporary historical power of this paradigm in shaping the international order, it should be recognized that a maximization of a private-choice approach to public space is a singular form of rationality. It is unable to conceptualize inequalities of access to social goods and information, and unable to articulate a set of principles for democratic political association. It ignores one of the central questions of late modernity: given that there is no alternative to the market, what degree and kind of public intervention in markets do information rights and justice require? This question informs the analysis of information-society policies undertaken later in the book.

PUBLIC SPACE AS PRACTICES OF THE SELF

Conceptually intermingled, but nevertheless distinct from a Lockean–Hobbesian basis of public space, is another instrumental paradigm which regards the civil state as a vast store of assets to service contending projects for the political protection of subjective identities. The state is an instrument of predation, the arena within which a legal war of all against all is fought out by rules and laws specifying not only property rights and contractual liberties, but every type of private right and personal freedom. Individuals and collusive interest groups engage in lobbying and colonizing regulatory authorities, legislative bodies, and the judicial system to mould these rules to suit their own interests on the assumption that if they do not alter the legal and regulatory framework to their advantage, their competitors will amend it against their interests. Individuals and enterprises must organize collusively so as to capture the democratic state, if only because they know that if they do not, others will. What they seek from government, Gray (1993) argues, is not equal freedom under the law but particularistic political recognition and legal privilege. They seek political endorsement not of common values emerging from public deliberation in which citizens are allowed opportunities for participation on issues of common concern, but of their private values and interests. Although this view could also be articulated from the perspective of Locke's oligarchic individualism, this discussion will attempt to address the philosophical basis of another form of individualism from which the inflation of the rhetoric of private rights can be said to emerge: namely, from a particular but influential vein of Kantian thought directed towards the defence of the ultimate sovereignty of subjectivism (see defence of this reasoning in Rawls, 1993). It should be made clear that Kantian political thought on the 'principle of publicity' addressed in the preceding chapter is distinct from his moral defence of subjectivity because the latter is conceptually tied to his theory of metaphysics and must be set aside altogether in the exposition of his theory of public reason and public freedom which must necessarily account for the basis of political, not atomistic, identity. This obligation does not inform Kant's theory of the radical subject who constructs universal norms from private reason alone.

The paradigm of a private rights-based theory of public space sets out from the assumption that a chronic, low-intensity civil war on personal rights is the natural condition of a free society (Gray, 1993). The significance in terms of public space is that the moral validation for private rights as the final end of a good society derives from Kant's construction of the rational hence free being who utters the commands of morality to herself, and obeys no one but herself. The absolute sovereignty of the subject emerges from Kant's 'categorical imperative' in the *Foundations of the Metaphysics of Morals* (1990: 22–62), by which he constructs the individual as a morally autonomous entity, able to abstract universal principles or maxims of social relations from private reason, and who is obligated to no authority external to herself. The categorical imperative states: 'Act only according to that maxim by which you can at the same time will that it should become a universal law' (Kant, 1990: 38).

This power of the individual will to endow itself with moral sovereignty releases it from obligation to the political order because we are each empowered a priori by reason to give ourselves our own laws without taking into account associational concerns, the achievement of consensus, or public debate on common ends. Individual members of civil society, therefore, stand outside the social order and have no duty other than to personal, pre-political claims against the state. If the market-choice paradigm is modified by Kantian subjectivism, then you arrive at the conclusion that the purposes to which the public world is instrumentalized are found within us. These purposes are: self-preservation (pursuit of happiness or property or both) as prompted by assumptions of natural instincts and processes, but carried on under the control of far-sighted calculating and generalizing reason.

As Taylor (1993) observes of this philosophical system, reason in a rights-based theory of freedom is no longer defined substantively, that is, in terms of a public notion of the good which deliberation and debate among social groups brings about, but formally, in terms of procedures the private subject should follow in rationalizing private rights and actions to social ends. Thus freedom takes on a new meaning, entailing breaking loose from any external authorities in order to be governed solely by one's own reasoning procedures, the 'absolute worth of the [private] will alone, in which no account is taken of any use [existing conditions]' (Kant, 1990: 10), social, political, cultural, or otherwise.

In a 'search for and establishment of the supreme principle of morality', Kant (1990: 8) puts forward a rights-based deontological theory based on universal rights that are not public but private, and which if followed will be moral regardless of the ends: 'The good [subjective] will is not good because of what it effects or accomplishes or because of its competence to achieve some intended end. . . . Usefulness or fruitlessness [either in a personal sense or in terms of the common interest of political society] can neither diminish nor augment this worth' (Kant, 1990: 10). Self-interest is morally valid, but only by the right rules. The state is there not to facilitate the practice of political self-determination but to prevent individuals from infringing on each others' rights and to defend and enhance the sphere of private rights. Kant's regard for the laws of democratic society, therefore, are from the perspective of hindrance. They are 'statutes and formulas, those mechanical tools of the rational employment or rather misemployment . . . [which] are fetters of an everlasting tutelage' (Kant, 1990: 84).

The condition of liberty for Kant arises far less from the form of political community than by the private immanence of reason. 'If only [private] freedom is granted,' he writes, 'enlightenment is almost sure to follow' (Kant, 1990: 84). It is the role of government, therefore, to 'divest the human race of its tutelage and [to] leave each man free to make use of his reason in matters of conscience' (Kant, 1990: 88). Thus conscience, the inner private world of the self, replaces citizenship while the vocation of private reason and subjective practices substitute for public life and political participation. Apart from the utterances of private reason to serve as the basis of public opinion, this framework has little to offer in terms of a concept of public space or even political space. Accordingly, so long as information policies are centred on the question of private rights and the diffusion of personal and subjective communications media and practices, there is no conceptual foundation on which to articulate a socio-legal basis for the design of public space and political practices in the structures of modern information networks and the production of content.

The moral rationale for subjectivism in Kantian thought assures the notion of human dignity derived from private reason a new importance, since human existence is now removed from the context of obligation by its own status as a sovereign reasoning being demanding the use of rational control. The imagination of this subjective essentialism has pervaded social thought and cultural practice in late modernity despite the realities of rampant irrationalism in practices of the self, because the idea of human dignity can be invoked from Kantian moral categories to transform such practices axiomatically into ends in themselves. Thus the good life socially translates into our freedom to be disengaged from political society, from common welfare, and to indulge our private desires or 'emotivism' as MacIntyre (1984) calls it, without social compunction.

The question for a rights-based theory of democratic relations is whether a theory of atomism, however morally worthy, notwithstanding its potential for reprehensible social and political uses, holds potential for imagining broad participatory inclusion in society and economy and in the construction of public space. After all, the requirements of justice, citizenship, and widespread access to public space are supposed to distinguish democratic society from other forms of polity such as oligarchy, authoritarianism, and totalitarianism. The question arises, to what political fate would the information age be drawn in the trend towards privatization of all reasoning and communication practice, whereby issues of common concern and political community are removed from the political sphere and placed in the private sphere of subjective tastes, preferences, and interactions? In so far as democracy requires the public participation of individuals in the preservation of the political order, the argument here is that, as with the private-choice paradigm of public space, the logical orientation of rights-based freedom is the evacuation of political, that is, common reasoning from significant spheres of associational human experience.

The collection of private rights with respect to conscience, speech, and autonomy from state authority has served as the historical standard for the ideal of freedom. Yet under a rights-based theory, these rights have been subjected to certain social and political uses whose consequences have not always furthered the interests of a democratic political community (Gray, 1993), which is obliged to guarantee the conditions of citizenship in order to guarantee political society itself. In so far as any social or legal entity under this paradigm can assimilate to itself the moral sovereignty of private rights (Porter, 1993*b*), the rights-based theory gives rise to media laws, information policy, and jurisprudence increasingly tilted against guarantees of citizenship practice or the rights of individuals to knowledge, public reason, and constitutional community (see critical legal analysis of free-speech jurisprudence in Streeter, 1990; and Unger, 1983).

For this reason, policies for the information society, which rationalize the promise of revolutionary advancements in individual freedoms brought about by accelerated technological innovation, focus on liberalization of media ownership, not only under the necessity to protect ownership rights, but under a process granting a growing *moral equivalence* between the individual rational being and the individual corporate or institutional entity (Porter, 1993*b*). Kant's idea of human beings as ends in themselves, therefore deserving of dignity and respect in their public speech, has become transposed to special interest groups, corporate, institutional, or bureaucratic beings as ends in themselves deserving of dignity and respect in their public speech—which is increasingly commercial rather than political, as Habermas (1989) points out in his critique of the modern democratic public sphere. The current historical trend, therefore, is for artificial entities somehow to absorb more and more of the status of the individual human citizen and therefore more and more of the private rights originally intended in the Enlightenment origins of modern democratic thought for the emancipation of individuals from forms of domination.

This tension is apparent in media policies within the EU, where freedom of expression is acknowledged as a necessity for individuals to actualize their liberty as citizens (see discussion of information rights in the EU in Chapter 8), but placed within communications regulations which are tilting increasingly in favour of artificial individuals and their rights of media ownership, consolidation, vertical integration, multimedia monopolies, and transborder alliances (Nesvold, 1996; Porter, 1993*a*, 1993*b*; Tomlinson, 1991). Communication policies for the information society appear to be shifting away from the rights of individual citizens to receive substantive knowledge and information about their surrounding world in order for them to practise their freedom in the first place (Curran, 1991), while the rights of proprietors of the public realm, content monopolies, cultural industries, and global infrastructure oligopolies are being released under liberalization proposals to new heights of autonomy from regulation and from public accountability. This is also why media laws of the new post-socialist states contain so many ambiguities regarding free speech. They pay ample homage to its necessity, but when applying Western models of public space, become confused and politically fragmented over the issue of how to translate laws favouring freedom to own, buy, and sell media enterprises into the realities of freedom of participation, information, and knowledge for their citizens (see analysis of policies for tele-communications, content ownership, audiovisual production, competition, and free expression in Chapters 4–8). Hence we find long lists of exceptions, in the form of economic, industrial, and cultural exceptions for consolidation of the competitive order of liberalization (Johnson, 1993; Jakubowicz, 1992).

Thus information policies defining a reconstituted, liberalized public space for democratic societies are caught between an ownership discourse and a rights discourse, with the increasing tendency of the two to converge in the permanent fixing of public policy to favour proprietary rights of media consolidation and corporate rights of speech. The privatization of law and rights has strengthened the power of communications entities in the processes of rights extraction while weakening the power of individuals to claim their public and political rights of information and participation in the design of the information system (see further discussion in Chapters 5 and 8). Communication laws therefore cannot conceive of how to apply the category of public interest, even when that seems to be the intention, as with policy visions for an information highway (Commission of the European Communities, 1994*a*; US Government, 1995*a*, 1993; *New York Times*, 12 January 1994; *Financial Times*, 13 January 1994) which plead for the common good but without providing the principles for the application of the public interest to the information society. This dilemma is evident also in the European vision for an advanced information infrastructure in the Community (Commission of the European Communities, 1993) that regards the enterprise more as a public works undertaking than a project to facilitate political self-determination and common interest among a plurality of social groups—the latter being the normative purpose of democratic public space (Habermas, 1989; Aristotle, 1981; Arendt, 1975).

PUBLIC SPACE AS INSTRUMENT OF RADICAL INDIVIDUALISM

The third private mode of public space in a free society is less influential in terms of historical reality, but significant in terms of a modern intellectual struggle to present an alternative social vision. Critical legal studies and critical theory are intellectual manifestations of a broader debate over the meaning and reality of civil society in advanced industrialized democracies. As self-conscious reflections on the place of the individual in the late-modern age, the general movement distinguishes itself from preceding approaches in the following ways: far from rejecting individualism or being indifferent to legal protections for basic human rights as in a Hobbesian civil state, critical approaches seek to solidify these values more deeply in the structure of society; and instead of choosing either to reject or embrace fully the privatism of the market or the self which holds a formative power on contemporary liberalization policies, these approaches prefer to see subjectivism reconciled to the founding ideals of individualist thought.

Civil society is thus re-articulated as the legal, institutional, and economic realization of individualism's philosophy and prophecy implicit in contemporary legal and political doctrines but absent in their corresponding practices. Employing different forms of justification, a critical individualist paradigm of public space attempts to unmask the halo of naturalness and necessity that enshrouds the canonical forms in which democratic society is ordered and shielded from scrutiny. It advocates a civil society more closely representative of the ideal of radical subjectivism which implies a rearrangement of the fixed order of society to liberate the self from social, political, legal, and economic constraint. As Unger (1983) observes of this reconstructivist programme:

It pushes the liberal premises about state and society, about freedom from dependence and governance of social relations by the will, to the point at which they merge into a large ambition: the building of a social world less alien to a self that can always violate the generative rules of its own mental or social constructs and put other rules and other constructs in their place. (Unger, 1983: 41)

To achieve reconciliation between individualism's political practices and its political ideals, Habermas (1989; 1987; 1984; 1979) advances a significant theoretical project for civil society in which he retools Kant's idea of freedom grounded in reason to reinvigorate the moral grounds of democratic relations. The central propositions of Habermas's project comprise: first, purification of the public sphere of civil society by restoring reason and open disclosure (Habermas, 1989: 181–235); and secondly, defining the procedures of discourse ethics which establish rules of reasoning for arriving at common consent among sovereign individual beings (Habermas, 1987: 69; 1979: 97). In this attempt to reconstruct the Kantian concept of freedom, Habermas makes no serious departure from Kant's theoretical focus on the sphere of individual social action, in the definition of the political order. What may be considered substantive, perhaps, is Habermas's attempt to shift discussion from the entrapments of a monological perspective of the subject which dominates Kant's theory of individual reason and rights, as well as Locke's theory of self-interest, to the notion of 'intersubjective relations' (Habermas, 1987: 62).

A theory of society based on the atomized individual is thus partially transformed into a theory of society based on the dialogical individual oriented to mutual understanding of the other. Further, a theory of political freedom derived from Kant's (1990: 28–30) 'categorical imperative', that is, the test of the universality of moral maxims, and from Locke's (1960: 329) natural necessity of property ownership, is transformed into a theory of freedom derived from the rules of un-coerced argumentation in an undistorted public sphere. Thus civil society is still largely conceptualized by the categories of personal contingencies, private relations, and ethical procedure, and not by social outcomes or participation in the production, ownership, and distribution of information in the public sphere of political community. It should be stressed, however, that this view of public space is distinct from the preceding rights-based approach of irrational absolutism in claims upon the state. Habermas insists on the value of private reason and distinctive modes of rationalization legitimate to intersubjective relations (the 'lifeworld'), on the one hand, and institutional relations (the 'systems world'), on the other. The differentiation of forms and contexts of rationality is a recognition he regards essential to the very possibility of civil society (Habermas, 1987: 186) in late modernity. In this sense, Habermas reclaims the validity of modern reason from the legacy of despair in Weber's (1946: 196–244; 1930: 180–1) account of the devastating consequences of instrumental reason, or rationalization for the authentic conditions of a free life.

This portion of the Weberian legacy is best understood when contrasted with Marx's (1978c, 1978d) theory of modernity which demonstrates how the universalization of capital-exchange relationships leads to conditions of exploitation, scarcity, and the intensification of economic crisis. Despite the grim prognosis, and following the dialectics of Hegel (1952a), the theory also holds that processes of capital accumulation carry the seeds of their own negation, which conceptually permits the emancipation of humankind to be prefigured in the dynamics, the crises, and the logic of capitalist social development (Marx, 1978d, Grundrisse: 291–2). Clearly, the notion of liberation implicit in Marx's critique of modernity owes a great portion of its analytical power to Hegel's (1953) philosophy of history on the creation of unity through reconciliation of opposites and the ultimate synthesis of the dialectical progression at the end of history: the state of universal freedom. Since a Hegelian theory of reconciliation between the individual and community is absent from Weber's critique, he concedes little, if any, emancipatory hope in his explanation of modernity, both in terms of its processes and in terms of its ultimate consequences. Modernity as the process of advancing rationalization signifies for Weber (1946: 123, 184–6) an increase in formal rationality in all spheres of social experience but without bearing the seed of its own negation as capitalism does for Marx. Thus the absence of an immanent utopian orientation in Weber's assessment of reason has left a difficult theoretical legacy to critical philosophers like Habermas who wish to reclaim its virtues in the interest of preserving modernist emancipatory development.

The critical approach to public space is also advanced by Keane (1991; 1988) who describes it as inherently indeterminate, therefore open to perpetual self-invention by the subject. Keane dismisses the idea of consensus over public goods since this would threaten the requirement of systematic uncertainty essential to the subject's self-construction. In fact, these arguments regard the civil state's role in guaranteeing certain public goods as 'ideology'. Keane writes: 'to defend democracy in this sense is to reject every ideology which seeks to stifle this indeterminacy' (Keane, 1988: 47). Elsewhere, however, Keane argues that communications media are defensible as a public service (Keane, 1991: 116) in order to 'serve as the primary means of communication for citizens living, working, loving, quarreling and tolerating others within a genuinely pluralist society' (Keane, 1991: 150). He favours the 'decommodification' (Keane, 1991: 153) of communications in order to liberate the subject as so-called 'empty signifier', to its indeterminate or contingent practices of the self. Keane's approach, therefore, is an extension of rights-based theories which construct civil society as an aggregation of private sovereignties, with the important distinction that his defence of radical subjectivity converges with a developed critique of free-market liberalism.

Unger, Habermas, and Keane represent three main currents of thought in the radical democracy movement and, while distinctive in many ways, share certain key features regarding the normative foundations of public space and membership in political community. One common feature is an intensification of the moral category of the subject and its autonomy from any constraint on discretionary rights. Another is an attention to the problem of theorizing interpersonal discourse, the sphere of experience where the immunity of the subject from social obligation must be tempered by the need for relations outside itself. For those occasions, Habermas has developed the procedures of dialogics that are ethical in so far as their validity is deontological—that is to say, the rules of intersubjective relations impose a certain duty or a condition upon discrete subjects. In order for a norm to claim validity, the subject's absolute autonomy from history and culture in the zone of self-actualization must be scaled down within the intersubjective experience to meet with the consent of all affected in their role as participants (Habermas, 1990).

Because of this theoretical advancement in individualism's recognition of personal associations within the larger context of private autonomy, as compared with Lockean–Kantian concepts of insular private freedom, critical theories are able to articulate a concern for public space in their attention to it as a feudal sphere (Habermas, 1989: 195) of oligarchic structures, irrational relations of social power, and political domination. Consequently, Keane proposes the 'decommodification' of communications media, Habermas the intersubjective use of private reason, and Unger the 'destabilization rights' of the subject to disrupt established institutions and social practices (Unger, 1983: 38). Thus a radical subjective paradigm of public space is the only one of the four privatist modes explored in this chapter which can articulate a challenge to the social legitimacy of the market in the determination of public space.

But in terms of a political understanding of the civil society and the production of the socio-legal order, critical individualism perpetuates its root tradition of defining the state negatively, that is, defending the absolute claim of the subject to autonomy from the political sphere. Civil society has a single purpose: to provide an environment conducive to the practice of passionate individualism, the liberation of the individual into newer forms of subjective excitement. Practices of the self within political and social surroundings free of domination either by state or market is the overriding virtue, while self-invention is the only duty. In other words, critical individualism, like its more liberal counterparts, still cannot articulate the notion of political community—though it can recognize communal claims (Unger, 1983: 38). Habermas's procedures for achieving mutual consent notwithstanding, ideas of justice or common welfare are implausible if they arise from any category beyond private reason. Though public policy in this way of thinking may drop market metaphors and choose not to invoke supply-side assumptions of a free market, yet its articulation must remain confined, as with Lockean and Kantian bases of democratic reasoning, to questions concerning subjective rights and entitlements. Keane's argument for a public-service approach in communication cannot, therefore, be reconciled—despite his critique of commercial media—with his theory of democracy as radical subjectivity.

The political foundations of this general approach bear some debt not merely to liberal sources of individualism but also to Marx's theory of individualism. The discussion here will address just a few key aspects of his theory of history relevant to the analysis of concepts of public space. It is argued that Marx seems to share in common with Locke several categories by which the question of freedom is problematized, including a disdain for the state and a high regard for pre-political human life which they both hold up as more 'authentic' (Marx, 1978a: 149–55). They also share an emphasis on the sanctity of the individual's labour and thus both articulate labour and ownership theories of freedom, or notions of liberty that are tied to proprietary relations. In *The German Ideology* (1978a), Marx defines the preferred setting of the free life as the cooperative economy where we can all be producers, that is, artists, inventors, and craftsmen (Marx, 1978a: 150 and 157). The picture Marx paints, Walzer (1992) observes, is of creative men and women making useful and beautiful objects, not for the sake of production of objects, but for the sake of creativity itself, the highest expression of our ontological condition as man-the-maker. He writes: 'The mode of production must not be considered simply as being the reproduction of the physical existence of the individuals. Rather, it is a definite form of activity of these individuals, a definite form of expressing their life, a definite *mode of life* on their part. As individuals express their life, so they are' (Marx, 1978a: 150, emphasis in the original). This equation of the conditions of cultural production and cultural expression with the essence of human freedom is interesting of itself. Yet it is also reasonable to argue that Marx and Locke regard the economy as the substance, boundary, and constitution of civil society, with the key difference that while Locke regards private property as the essential, perhaps sole condition of human freedom in the state of nature, Marx regards private property as the source of the division of labour and thus the eventual alienation of individuals from authentic conditions of production in his account of the state of nature (Marx, 1978a: 160).

Given this construction of the notion of freedom, it could also be said that both Marx and Locke view the civil state in instrumental terms. As Marx sees it, the state ought to be managed in a way that sets production free, following which politics simply ceases to be necessary (Marx, 1978a: 160–1). The disappearance of the state would apparently require its replacement by some administrative agency necessary for economic coordination of production, and perhaps within some regulatory structure that is non-political; the implication being that the individual producer, as also the consumer-entrepreneur in a radical individualist or private-choice paradigm of public space, is freed from the burdens of citizenship. Thus Marx's conception could be interpreted as radical anti-politics because the free life requires a worker-controlled factory where men and women make decisions and make things without any socio-legal and constitutional basis for defining how a concept and system of justice, the political resolution of conflict, political self-determination and information rights, or participatory common interest would apply. The vision of a cooperative economy is set against this romantic background: a non-political state and regulation without participation, deliberation, or conflict. This effacement of the conception and structures of a public world, and therefore disregard for the value of political freedom, is woven into the very structure of critical theories derived from a convergence of Kantian and Marxian critical individualism tied to the notion of pre-political, radical subjectivism. It is one among many reasons why a critical individualist theory of public space cannot transcend the subjective and private categories of reason within which an approach to apolitical associational life is articulated.

In terms of information policy, critical paradigms of public space regard all sectors of civil society, including the system of public communications, from the standpoint of their instrumental potential in the liberation of the individual to a more authentic condition of selfhood, or of non-subjugation to visible and invisible constraints, social rights, and communal experience—though not necessarily in the sense of a political community. It is a paradigm of public space which focuses on the social and political conditions of the existence of a 'Subject', as Touraine (1992) has defined a critical theory of the radical subject. Principles of information policy emerging from this politics of the subject would advocate:

- media representation of social diversity in modes of subjective being;
- disengagement of communication systems from both state and commercial control;
- enhancement of a plurality of public-communication sources to reflect the plurality of subjective realities;
- and the general weakening of the power of reified notions of ownership in law and policy in the determination of communication structure and content (see Habermas, 1992, 1989; Keane, 1991).

PUBLIC SPACE AS CULTURAL COMMUNITY

One of the most powerful ways of apprehending public culture in the period of post-socialism and in late modernity is the idea of nation or community grounded in the essential and pre-existent 'nature' of a people. The building of community posited on archaic identities of 'blood' and 'cultural tradition' was recognized by the Romans as distinct from constitutional, therefore political, community. Lepsius

(1992) explains that, for the Romans, *natio* referred to peoples and tribes not yet organized in political associations, in order to distinguish communities of people of the same descent, integrated geographically and culturally but not yet politically integrated. Since the seventeenth century, *natio* has been used interchangeably with the nation of the citizen, a meaning which does not include a concern for common ethnic properties but with the relations of citizens who believe and enact some concept of civil society. In seeking an explanation for modern occurrences of the supposedly pre-modern tendencies to xenophobia, ethnic conflict, and the imagination of a common cultural history, recognized analyses of cultural and national identity (Smith, 1992; Hobsbawn, 1990; Gellner, 1983) do not seem to make the Roman distinction.

But as Hayden (1991) and Bowman (1992) have determined in their study of ethnic persecution in the states of the former Yugoslavia, there has not been sufficient recognition in intellectual thought that the nationalisms we see today are neither manifestations of a will to overcome traditional modes of organization as Hobsbawn (1990) suggests in his theory of nationalism as the process of dissolution of tribal identities, nor are they an attempt to re-establish the historical condition of pre-existing cultural rituals as Geertz (1973) suggests. Both explanations locate modern nationalism within a progressive context of the quest for communal liberation and freedom. Instead, as Bowman (1992) points out, and Anderson (1983) has theorized, mobilization of imagined identities provides, not a return to the world which existed before modernity effaced it, but a route to yet another modern 'alternative', albeit anti-democratic, community—this time constituted by narratives of sameness and common descent, and often by perceptions of persecution by an external antagonist.

It is argued that the contemporary study of new structures in international relations has for the most part failed to recognize that the notion of national identity as citizenship completely parts company with the idea of identity in an imagined pre-political community integrated by descent—though both may be modern in conception and practice. While the community of citizenship in civil society and that of membership in nationalism have sometimes fused as catalysts, yet the democratic nation state has not always forged a historical and constitutional link between *ethnos* and *demos*, nor can *demos* be reduced to *ethnos* (Francis, 1965). Citizenship has rarely in its earliest articulation been conceptually tied to ethnic national identity (Habermas, 1994) because the term 'freedom' has completely different meanings for each. For *ethnos*, that espousal of distinct states for supposedly distinct 'peoples', 'freedom' implies collective self-assertion for a particular collectivity not generalizable to other social groups. For *demos*, 'freedom' is political liberties of participation, self-determination, and deliberation in the public realm of constitutional civil society; liberties that are universally conferred upon all social groups, not the preserve of selective groups, and exclude in principle any connection between ethnic or religious ascription and one's political status as citizen.

Thus cultural notions of public space implicitly incorporate the legitimation of defensive violence against threats to narratives of cultural self-construction, sustained by the reification of progressively essentializing notions of culture derived from the dynamic construction of cultural origins. This modern tendency has continuously confounded the modern philosophy of freedom because there has been little serious attempt to distinguish nationalist movements for statehood or public policy, from democratic movements for statehood or public policy. Patterson (1991) argues that private freedoms, whether for individuals or distinct groups, have been historically founded not upon the dignity of human self-determination, but upon the social deaths of others. In the last decade of the twentieth century, nightmare scenarios of social death, of slaughter and population transfer, are being acted out from nebulous markers of cultural identity filled out by the imagined common history in one discourse of public space, endangered by the imagined common history in others.

The problem with the notion of information policy as cultural policy or cultural self-defence is that the sovereignty of the ethnic nation state to preserve its imagined cultural legacy against hostile forces has very little to do with arguments for a politically self-determining community arising from universal civil liberties and the conditions of open communication and access in the deliberations of public life. There is no conceptual connection between nationalism and citizenship because the idea of citizenship is not based on sharing the same ethnic or cultural origins. Rather, citizenship's political culture depends on the creation of a constitutional community of guaranteed political liberties and open public communications. In a participatory paradigm of public space (Chapter 3), one's ethnic, religious, or racial identity becomes irrelevant to one's identity as a citizen. The problem, of course, is that not only the contemporary resurgence of xenophobia with its romantic appeals to the *Volk*, but also democratic theories of public space based on maximization of choice, private rights, or critical subjectivism as the highest social goods, are all equally unable to translate into political reality the ideals of participatory democracy oriented to public not private ends (see more discussion of the nationalist–culturalist model of regulation in Chapter 6).

Thus the success of France in the GATT negotiations (*New York*

Times, 1993) in gaining a temporary 'cultural exception' for trans-national trade in audiovisual programme production and transmission, while applauded by many for inserting non-economic recognition into the meaning of communication in global negotiations, and while significant as a counter-discourse to the supposedly 'natural' impera-tives of the global market, nevertheless fails as an alternative paradigm for a political public sphere oriented to democratic ends. While notable in its attempt to provoke an international debate on the structure of public space in the information society, the collectivist paradigm remains bound to the untenable arguments of cultural self-defence, making it difficult, therefore, to differentiate from arguments for the preservation of reprehensible cultural traditions such as the domination of women, children, or other groups. Consequently, the cultural-exclusivity approach to the information society remains problematic from the normative standpoint of what is required in information policies to facilitate common interest among a plurality of social and ethnic groups, deliberative citizenship practices, equal and open access to public space, and the need of citizens for substantive know-ledge of social, cultural, and political matters. The conflict between liberalism and cultural collectivism regarding the valid grounds of content regulation neither fully nor accurately represents all meaningful options in the design of the public sphere. The debate in multilateral and bilateral negotiations over the legitimacy of cultural policy in the infor-mation sector may constitute a false opposition with respect to the inter-ventionist role of the state in guaranteeing the conditions of public space. As discussed at more length in Chapters 6 and 7, liberalization is no less disposed to instrumental exploitation of the power of the state in enlarging the proprietary interests of the cultural industries than is culturalism or nationalism in regulating the conditions of cultural pro-duction.

Similarly, reforms of the press and broadcasting in Eastern Europe may indeed be undertaken to provide legal guarantees for free political speech in the public space of post-socialist civil states, but these laws have also chosen to engage in policies espousing the preservation of shared ethnicity and nationalist solidarity. Poland's version of *l'excep-tion culturelle* is codified in a broadcasting law passed in 1993 stipu-lating that both public and private programmes must adhere to a 'Christian value system' and 'should not promote activities that violate the law or the interests of the state nor opinions that conflict with morality and the public good' (quoted in Johnson, 1993: 13). In Hungary, nationalists mobilized to push for policy requirements to increase religious broadcasting as well as programmes to preserve Hungarian culture (Pataki, 1992). And in Russia, Slovenia, and other states, the equation forged between nationalist discourse for inscription of the 'pure nation' into the laws and policies of representative democracies, on the one hand, and the ostensible spread of movements for democratic reform, on the other, has made it difficult to disentangle anti-democratic concepts of 'public space as cultural community' from the modern promise of common citizenship, human rights, and political self-determination for all.

Attempts to rationalize a nationalist discourse in communication policy must confront the possibility that inter-ethnic peace may be inseparable from the challenge of defending the basis of political culture within a globally restructured social environment which recognizes only realism and liberalization (see Chapter 7). Analysis of the information society must proceed from the recognition that the potential for enhancement of peaceful relations among nations and communities in the post-socialist period will emerge, not so much from the dismantling of trade barriers, creation of common currencies, privatization and deregulation of economies, or, for that matter, from the hope for an enlightened regard among ethnic groups for each other's fundamental right to exist. Rather, the stability of civil societies is conditional upon the creation of a genuine form of common citizenship—not merely codified in law but also actualized by access to and participation in the political and technological arrangements of shared public space. This can only be constructed on the socio-legal guarantees of conditions of public participation in the broadband or multimedia domain. The project of constructing an information society with revolutionary capacities would require the extension of diversity of content production, distribution, and consumption to all social groups, as well as conditions favouring diversity of forms of expression. It would be necessary, in short, to design a policy framework that is not merely favourable for cultural or information industries that own and operate the information system and have a monopoly over its content and accessibility. The democratic political process can only be accountable if the public sphere is both representative of differences in points of view regarding the conditions of social life as well as structured, regulated, and organized to facilitate the emergence of common interests. These are not the aims which inform a culturalist–nationalist paradigm of public space.

Ultimately, therefore, the struggle to determine the form of public space in the name of cultural identities, private choices, private rights, or critical subjectivism leaves the citizens of the information society in reality with only a single mode of public space to choose from: namely, a model of public space which facilitates private reason, personal and exclusive privilege, and the recognition of subjective claims.

BEYOND PRIVATE MODES OF PUBLIC SPACE:

There is a pressing need to conceptualize alternative political foundations for information policy in a liberalized information environment. This chapter has attempted to challenge prevailing conceptualizations and to demonstrate, by exposition of their philosophical premises, that the development of human potential and the deepening of the structures of democracy, at least in the European context, can have no historical reality outside the particular constitution of public space by virtue of which common citizenship, human rights, private freedoms, and the idea of justice are possible in the first instance. The structure of this space which political freedom necessarily requires, its capacity to facilitate a deliberative environment through the reactivation of political agency in the 'public sphere', is both the conceptual and empirical challenge of information policy.

The concept of a public sphere for the information society is not, it is suggested, completely identical with the concept advanced by Habermas (1989, 1987, 1984). The historical validity of his argument for the public sphere has already been contested (Fraser, 1992; Benhabib, 1992; Curran, 1991), yet the normative and conceptual validity remains to be addressed. As argued in the preceding elaboration of principal paradigms, the theoretical problem of Habermas's public sphere for associational life is that he grounds his conception in a procedural theory of 'intersubjective' rather than public reason, principally because he is constrained by the monological and procedural liberalism of Kant's moral philosophy. Habermas has tried to address this problem, of course, by expanding Kant's universality of the monological conscience to a dialogical notion of communicative relations (1990). It is argued here that this is inadequate since such an approach to human emancipation continues in the pre-political, procedural, and ultimately subjectivist domain. The notion of public space that needs proposing in a theory of information policy ought to be closer to the idea of 'political space', a substantive, not just procedural or interpersonal space between individuals, where citizens can act collectively and engage in common deliberation about all matters affecting the political community. It is anachronistic to limit one's understanding of this space to the village square, the proverbial town hall, or dialogical experiences. Certainly, this space could possess many forms, but today its predominant mode is technological, industrialized, and global.

Regardless of the form or structure of political space, the principle of emancipation and political liberty which derives from this space should remain unaltered. Ultimately, it may be argued, human freedom cannot be actualized under the realities of a dysfunctional, distorted, and inaccessible public or political space whose structures and realities exclude the development of knowledge, deliberation, the enlargement of public opinion to include all major social groups; and the constitution of public identity in the practice of citizenship that necessitates transcending subjective, even interpersonal, interest and private reason.

The grounds of an alternative conception of public space are addressed in the next chapter. Here it is suggested there are three important categories of consideration which ought to be accounted for in any paradigm for a genuinely democratic public sphere.

Justice The distinctive feature of the identity of citizen, as opposed to that of consumer, producer, owner, or communal member, is its constitution within a web of egalitarian–participatory relations based on justice, not merely equality. The difference between a citizenship of justice and a citizenship of equality is fundamental to the distinction between information policies whose aim is to advance a participatory public sphere and policies that seek to facilitate the proprietary interests in ownership, competition, and consolidation of the information sector.

As we know from the history of liberal democracy, equality can be addressed by legal procedure or recognition. Yet having achieved recognition or equality under the law, the actually existing conditions of inequality may persist even while legally defined away through codification. This is not to say that any critique of the codification of the rights of man amounts to an unqualified endorsement of the view of human rights as nothing but the right of self-interest (Marx, 1978*b*) and symptomatic of bourgeois individualism. Articles 10 and 11 of the French Declaration of the Rights of Man (1789), for instance, declare the right of free communication of thought and opinion as one of the most constitutive rights of political freedom, which do not easily bear the interpretation of them as institutional egoism or a mode of private property (Marx, 1978*b*). As Lefort (1981) argues, Article 11 at least makes it clear that 'the right of man, one of his most precious rights, is to go beyond himself and relate to others, by speech, writing and thought. In other words, it makes clear that man could not be legitimately confined to the limits of his private wants, when he has the right to public speech and thought' (ibid. 58–9). Lukes (1985) also notes that these rights codified in the French Declaration are passed over in silence by Marx since they do not lend themselves to his interpretation.

Nevertheless, Marx's views of capitalism's justice provokes serious reflection, for while the positive, world-historical significance of human-rights equality is unquestionably necessary for any possibility of freedom, it is certainly not sufficient. As pointed out earlier in this chapter, the logic of Lockean and Kantian paradigms of freedom that form the philosophical foundation of democratic laws and policies, tend to result in practices of privatism where rights are typically the basis for claims by private interests to be treated in special ways. The consequence for information policy is the monopoly of the meaning of human rights by private institutional interests over the rights of citizens for adequate knowledge, information, and public speech. There is thus a considerable distance between the citizen's right of equality of access to public space in speech, thought, and expression, and the right's actualization.

Thus, contrary to Locke's and Kant's assumptions, equality cannot be pre-political; in itself it has little meaning external to political association, with the fundamental moral basis of such association, as Aristotle points out, being justice. Aristotle's definition of politics, not only as the essence of human experience but as fundamentally contingent on justice or ethical reasoning, develops from a concept of public space, public life, and information conditions:

Obviously man is a political animal . . . But nature . . . has endowed man alone among the animals with power of speech . . . [which] serves to indicate what is useful and what is harmful and so also what is just and what is unjust . . . It is a sharing of a common view in these matters that makes a . . . state (*The Politics*, 1981: 1253ᵃ7–17).

For a concept of public space in the information society, the implications of this argument are that political identity and self-determination are made possible by access to opportunities for deliberation and public reasoning, which is nothing less than the negation of the unjust and the affirmation of the just. What the ethical nature of public communication enables, then, is the 'sharing of a common view', without which society itself would not be possible. Thus justice is the central feature of political community in this vision. It is 'the arrangement of political association' (Aristotle, 1981: 1253ᵃ39), of the emergence of common interests, signifying that Aristotle understands the terms of the good society not merely by shared history, cultural meanings, symbols, and rituals, but by the terms of the virtues of justice. The second important argument Aristotle makes on the relationship between political association and justice is that he links the problem of justice to the problem of equality. Political justice 'is found among men who share their life with a view to self-sufficiency, men who are free and either proportionately or arithmetically equal, so that between those who do not fulfil this condition there is no political justice' (Aristotle, 1962: 1134ᵃ25–30).

Not only does political justice enable associative life, even the qualities of that life, according to Aristotle, are inseparable from access to political community, communicative competence, and the conditions of public life—all of which are matters of justice. Access to the public sphere and the competence to practise political liberty in that space is in fact the citizen's claim on lawgivers, namely, an issue of political justice (Aristotle, 1962: 1103^{b}4). Thus justice is the condition by which equality is realized for it seeks to aim higher than procedural guarantees. The original problem of justice, therefore, is not entirely as Rawls (1971) would define it. Seeking to deny the category of political justice because it derives from association as opposed to the separate lives of individuals, Rawls endorses the moral values of Kantian atomism, stresses equality as the baseline for the good society, and ends up by supplying a rationalization for existing thought on justice, as a term identical with the meaning of codified rights in law and policy. The contrast between the procedural justice Rawls offers and the idea of political justice is the difference between a theory which holds there is no such thing as social justice and a theory which is based on the premise that citizens have a fundamental claim on lawgivers for social action to address the requirements and functioning of public opinion and consensus formation.

In a democratic society, political justice in associational terms necessitates formulating legal codes which emphasize principles and procedural rules within a framework of public policy that facilitates the resolution of actually existing human needs in education, communicative competence, health, work, and other fundamental terms of membership in democratic community (see discussion of the development of rights in modern society in Dahrendorf, 1994; Marshall, 1950). These needs must be addressed not merely by codification or even at the minimum threshold of human survival, but by public policy and political action, and at a level that ensures the conditions under which all social groups have access to public space and possess communicative competence in the practice of deliberative political participation.

The notion of political justice, rather than just equality, or rights, provides the only conceptual hope for a universal ground of value by which important conditions and needs in democratic life can be identified, and the only philosophically defensible position from which to ask what the social and political arrangements of the information society would propose to do about them. Would the restructuring of European media under information liberalization ensure that citizens of democratic societies have increased opportunities for enlargement of participatory practice in the production of a diversity of non-commercial expression and associative relations, and be capable of addressing their conditions of information and knowledge for self-determination and collective will-formation? Will these conditions be addressed in a minimal way in the policy design of the information society, as privatist paradigms of public space would for the most part prefer, or will it be possible for citizens to make authentic, non-distorted choices for their well-being in public life? These questions simply cannot be addressed by a vision of the public sphere stemming from a restricted view of information rights emphasizing the procedural recognition of equality.

Civil Society The second important consideration in any alternative theory of public space is the question concerning the mode of civil society relevant or necessary to the information society. In what sense of civil society do we mean a participatory public sphere? While the international ascendance of the liberalization movement has delegitimized all alternative forms of social organization and left modernity with no effective competitors, the forms of civil society which supply its social foundation have deteriorated, in terms of democracy, to a point where the increasing privatization of law, public life, and political dissent, as well as a corresponding de-politicization of the technologically dependent public sphere, represent serious challenges to the structure and development of non-commercial expression and associative relations. These qualities are not merely at the minimal threshold beneath which civil society is so impoverished it would not be functioning at all, but at a somewhat higher threshold, envisioned by both pre-modern and modern democratic ideals. Below the minimum threshold of civil society, conditions favouring opportunities for imagination, diversity of expression and cultural forms, broad representations of social reality, conflict over conceptions of the good, effective non-commercial social networks, along with avenues for critical reflection and opinion formation, cannot be sustained.

From a normative standpoint, conceptions of civil society may be examined in any paradigm of information policy for a capacity to address the second threshold, the one that ought to concern us most when we argue for a participatory and influential public sphere. For we do not want democratic societies to make their citizens capable, as Nussbaum (1992) warns, only of the bare minimum. The move from a minimal civil society, as presented in the Lockean paradigm, to a self-determining community is supplied in a participatory framework by the capacities of civil society to construct, defend, and enhance a multiplicity of public spheres—weak and strong, political and cultural—with diversity of choices for self-definition allowing individuals and social groups the chance to influence the political order and transform their social and political contexts.

To answer in what sense of civil society do we mean such a concept of the public sphere it is necessary to examine the modes of civil society that are meaningful to a progressive construction of the information society. It is suggested that the cause of democracy can be advanced only from a more powerful understanding of civil society as communicative relations. If the essential possibility of civil society resides in the idea of vigorous public spheres capable of penetrating, fragmenting, decentralizing, and influencing political and economic power in the cause of human freedom, then a stronger sense of civil society would require at least two things: first, the most widespread and developed conditions of critical communicative competence to resist and defend the system of public spheres from normative depreciation and systematic distortion; and secondly, a stronger societal claim on public policy to regulate the conditions under which information industries and networks are maintained free of powerful, unequal, and oligopolistic domination.

Such a theory of civil society must be firmly rooted in the recognition:

(a) that private, individual, subjective rights of any kind are meaningless without institutional and socio-legal guarantees of information rights whereby citizens may participate and deliberate through a universalized public realm accessible to both content production and distribution (Montesquieu, 1989; Aristotle, 1981, 1962; Hegel, 1952*a*);

(b) that securing private rights is not the only goal of political community—justice and the common welfare are of equal if not greater value since they are prerequisites for securing rights in the first place and in fact delimit them so that all citizens may enjoy these rights equally under the law (Preamble to the US Constitution; Hamilton and Madison, 1961; Tocqueville, 1990); and

(c) that the freedom of citizens requires not merely the legal codification of such rights, but the actual conditions for practising their political liberties in the public deliberations of civil society, the only grounds on which the information society could claim legitimacy (Montesquieu, 1989; Aristotle, 1981, 1962; Arendt, 1975; Tocqueville, 1990).

Public Goods The conditions of the public realm necessary to the functioning of a democracy are conditions held in common among all members. In democratic theories drawn from utilitarian and ethical liberalism, republican, or communitarian thought, these conditions are termed 'public goods' or 'public interest', constituting thereby the essential mandate of the state in a political society. Thus the final consideration offered in this chapter regarding an alternative paradigm of public space is the problem of articulating the fundamental terms of common existence in institutional arrangements and in the definition of the role of the state for guaranteeing the public interest. Any call for an information society with a transnational socio-legal basis, as is increasingly likely for cyberspace, must face the test of a civil society that is universal to all members of the political community on at least three criteria of public goods. First, public goods are goods in those categories deemed necessary to the functioning of democracy. Certainly, the quality of the information environment which makes citizenship possible in the first place would easily qualify for the status of public good. Secondly, public goods which must be provided to all or to none, such as universal education, infrastructure access, and public-library services, or public catalogues of content in cyberspace that are accessible without proprietary barriers, are the responsibility of the policies of the state. Once again, it would be difficult to justify the exclusion of information industries and networks under this criterion of democratic goods, for that would mean justifying vast inequalities in access to, and quality of information, in the same way that inequalities in clothing and consumer products may be justified by free-market determinants. Thirdly, goods passing the test of necessity and universality would still not qualify as 'public'—that is, the responsibility of law and policy—unless these could not be supplied in a universal, accessible, and qualitatively adequate form by the private sector (for a more detailed discussion of the public-service model of information regulation, see Chapter 6).

Democratic states cannot deny the first two criteria to public communications since that would imply a rejection of the ideals of democracy. However, the third criterion involves intense debate in contemporary policy. In global relations, the ascending value of the market, on the one hand, and private rights and liberties, on the other, have allowed information infrastructure and content to be excluded from a public-goods status under the third criterion (see analysis in Chapters 4–8; also, 'Global Telecoms Agreement', World Trade Organization, 1997; Braman, 1990). This is because standards of substantive adequacy of information in a free society can be reduced to considerations of technological innovation and commercial exigencies in the production and distribution of information services.

CONCLUSION

This chapter has tried to argue that the problems of information policy for the public sphere of the information society are very much problems of theory. In the exposition and critique of paradigms of public space it was pointed out that challenges to realizing broad-based participation in the production and distribution of expression in contemporary public space are deeply connected to flawed conceptualizations of citizenship, common welfare, justice, and the meaning of civil society and the state embedded in their privatist theories of political practice. Modern history has shown that the right to vote, the rule of law, contractual liberties, and private interests can all exist, without, in fact, the existence of democracy. Membership in political community does not necessarily bring with it the actual experience of information rights and participation. Partly this is related to the ungovernability which afflicts democratic states caught up in the integrative vortex of contemporary transnational liberalization. We may have created a technological world whose imperatives we can no longer control and whose emancipation from all human will and purpose may have rendered it extremely difficult for us to govern ourselves, to remain our own political masters.

The challenge of the information society under various ideologies of the public sphere relates to the progressive depoliticization and privatization of information infrastructure and information content, and to the redefinition of political expression as the public airing of private interests which in turn allows public goods to be redefined as private assets. Our public interests as citizens, as Arendt (1975) observes, are quite distinct from our private interests as individuals, and therefore the public interest cannot be automatically derived from the private interest. Indeed, it is not the sum of private interests, nor their highest common denominator, nor even the totality of enlightened self-interests. The interests of the world, Arendt argues, are not the interests of individuals: they are the interests of the public realm, the realm of state action and citizenship action. As citizens we share that public realm and participate in its interests but the interests belong to the public realm. This is a substantive distinction from atomist, individualist, procedural, and minimal theories of the public realm.

The next chapter will attempt to construct a framework for a participatory paradigm of public space which is then applied to the analysis of some key policy initiatives for the information society.

3

Participatory Public Space:
A Post-Liberal Framework

Introduction

The previous chapter has demonstrated the intellectual sources of ambiguity in the construction of modern public space. It was argued that limitations in each paradigm regarding the meaning of civil society, the state, the individual, information rights, and political community are situated at the heart of constraints and contradictions of modern information policy, reflected in the institutional arrangements for democratic practice in the information society. Bobbio (1989*a*) observes that democracy is not a concept which can be made to mean whatever we choose it to mean, even though that has often been the historical experience not only with the liberal democratic model but also with more authoritarian models. A plurality of forms of democracy does not in any sense diminish the requirements of key principles and conditions to be present in each: in essence, conditions and procedures for arriving at collective decisions in a way which secures the fullest participation of all citizens possibly affected (Cohen and Arato, 1992; Habermas, 1990; Bobbio, 1989*a*). Aristotle's famous distinction (*The Politics*, 1981) between good and bad forms of political society endorses the principle that conditions furthering collective decisions involve broad participation, thereby opposing forms of governing for the common good against forms favouring the good of those who govern. His argument upholds one of the core burdens of political society, namely, that '. . . either we must say that those who do not participate are not citizens, or they must share in the benefit' (ibid. 190, book iii, ch. 7, par. 1279^{a}22). This vision of rights of inclusion in public deliberation for 'all those possibly affected' is echoed more recently in Habermas's (1990) discourse ethics and in his notion of rules of validity in public discourse (discussed later in this chapter).

The significance of communication, as a system of participatory structures for knowledge and deliberation, to the legitimacy of democracy was introduced in Chapter 1 by means of Kant's 'principle of publicity'. The principle was then contrasted in Chapter 2 with private choice and subjectivist as well as unitary paradigms of information and public space. This chapter will attempt to develop the theoretical framework of public space in terms of structures guaranteeing conditions of public freedom, thus expanding on Kant's principle to explore the conceptual system from which such a framework may be drawn. It is held that the 'principle of publicity' is not an obscure kernel of progressivism in an otherwise inherently liberal construction of the term 'democracy' whose central tenet is the primacy of the private in all matters of society and public policy. Rather, it is argued that liberalism's tenet is more a departure from the substantive body of reflection on the essence and basis of freedom, and thus exists outside of and even against, a broad tradition of progressive thought. The utilitarian and proprietary focused roots of the liberal democratic model and its marginalization of public space as political, cultural, and social space should be regarded as a somewhat particularistic and not defining mode of what we mean by and hope for democracy. The retrieval of the normative foundations of democratic legitimacy and the place of communication in that substantive system of thought will be explored here in order to develop an adequately grounded theoretical framework for analysis of the socio-legal basis of information liberalization.

This retrieval and its development for communication policy is a departure from the principal schools of communication theory which have largely drawn from three broad traditions

(a) liberal assumptions of negative freedom within social scientific aggregations of private preference in the determination of mass or public opinion on a range of political–cultural attitudes and habits (Lazarsfeld *et al.*, 1948; Katz and Lazarsfeld, 1955; Berelson, 1959; Schramm, 1983);

(b) pragmatic solutions of organic solidarity through ritual, symbolic, and communal bonds in modernity's mass-mediated public space, as a counterweight to liberalism's endemic atomism (Dewey, 1927; Carey, 1988); and

(c) neo-Marxist critiques of modern media of mass communications as the ideological production of social relations (Hall, 1980; Horkheimer and Adorno, 1972; Schiller, 1976; Golding and Murdock, 1979; Williams, 1961).

The concerns and focus of contemporary communication theory have therefore left unaddressed underlying conceptions ordering the institutional and policy arrangements of the modern political order outside the liberal versus Marxist parameters of the virtues and vices of the market. These parameters were critically assessed under the relevant modes of public space in Chapter 2. The place of public freedoms and rights of communication, as evolved under diverse traditions of political theory on citizenship, civil society, and the basis of the role and legitimacy of a democratic political order, have largely been assumed in communication theory rather than problematized or explained. Communication studies have therefore encountered difficulty in conceptually justifying, even identifying, the normative grounds of information policy and the socio-legal construction of the public realm other than by liberalism's highly constrained and defensive articulation of a welfare-state obligation to counterbalance the worst inequities of the market.[1]

At the same time, the problem of communication for modern democracies has remained somewhat underdeveloped in political theory, generally marginalized to the procedures and processes of contemporary political campaigns[2] and rarely to the question of how political society is fundamentally ordered by particular modes and structures of public communications. The question of public space, as demonstrated in the previous chapter, has been inconsequential in liberal political theory and it is only lately that political theorists such as Habermas (1989), Benhabib (1992), Cohen and Arato (1992), among others, have attempted to reconnect the conditions of the public sphere to the development of liberal democracy. Even so, the problems of public policy, the relations of citizens and other social actors to structures of public communications, and the political/policy design of the information society are by and large overlooked even in recent emphasis on a discourse model. This chapter will argue that the 'principle of publicity', the meaning of public space and of democratic legitimacy, is threatened with abstraction and symbolic irrelevance from the failure of modern theorizing to account for its actualization and generalization under the rapid rise of global communication networks and their attendant social and political forms. An approach to public space will be advanced here on the basis of holding together elements in a tradition of thought which emphasizes participatory and public freedoms.

PUBLIC SPACE, COMMON INTEREST, AND PARTICIPATORY RIGHTS: THE ELEMENTS

To address gaps in communication and political theory, this chapter will explore the development of the participatory concept of public

---

[1] For 'media imperialism' arguments, see Schiller (1976); Hamelink (1983); Galtung and Vincent (1992); Gerbner *et al.* (1993); for technological determinist arguments, see Pool (1990); Branscomb (1994); for legal positivist arguments, see Fowler and Brenner (1982); Smolla (1992); Frohnmayer (1994); and for the defence of liberal justice, see Rawls (1971); Nozick (1974).

[2] For a comprehensive survey, see Swanson and Nimmo (1990), *New Directions in Political Communication Research.*

space as the basis of democratic legitimacy, then use this philosophical foundation to construct a normative framework for the analysis of information policy. The theory is developed from two categories of emancipatory ideas: first, from the work of Aristotle and Arendt; secondly, from the thought of Hegel, Kant, and Habermas. On the basis of a foundation of non-liberal democratic theory emerging from both traditions on public freedoms, a mode of public space will be constructed and defended which can be broadly contrasted with that of either liberalism, collectivism, or subject-centred critical theory. Key areas of difference between a participatory framework of public space and paradigms explored in the previous chapter are summarized as follows.

First, the perspective advanced here does not imagine a state-less civil society, or associational life vastly alienated from the state. As argued in the last chapter, the dismantling of the state pursued by both market-centred and collectivist reasoning promises to return us to a Hobbesian condition of anarchy and hardly to Locke's or Marx's vision of either a rational balance of aggregate self-direction or a rational consolidation of collective self-direction. Secondly, Chapter 2 has emphasized the danger of anti-political tendencies commonly accompanying the celebration of civil society either as capitalist competition or socialist co-operation. For this reason, a participatory concept is inherently opposed to theories of anti-politics such as the anti-politics of *laissez-faire*. Thirdly, this view of public space is neither communitarian, as in moral/social communitarianism,[3] nor a euphemism for a theory of cultural-nationalism which was critiqued in the previous chapter's discussion of public space as cultural community.[4] The principle of participatory rights should not be contingent on organic loyalties arising from a priori moral or religious consensus, or perceptions of shared blood, history, and culture. Fourthly, a view of public space as public freedom holds that individual rights cannot be disconnected from the liberty of political society, and thus provision of widespread deliberative conditions favouring the emergence of collective will-formation in the public interest, or on issues of common concern, paradoxically, as Skinner (1986) describes it, but also historically, has constituted the only means of ensuring the personal liberty of individuals. This understanding informs the political theory of Machiavelli (1961) who, while regrettably often recognized solely for supplying the rationale for modern international realism, also insisted upon the public service route to individual liberty in the paradox that citizens of a free society can

---

[3] See Etzioni (1993); Walzer (1990); Taylor (1989b); MacIntyre (1984).
[4] See Smith (1979); Anderson (1983); and Hobsbawn (1990). See analysis of culturalist/ nationalist model of regulation in Chapter 6.

only hope to enjoy their liberty if they do not place that value above the pursuit of the common good.[5] In short, this perspective argues that both private liberty and common welfare are contingent on widespread structures of knowledge and participation in the public space of democratic society, without which there can be no legitimacy for the democratic state, and no possibilities for determination of the terms of justice, the public interest, or the protection and pursuit of personal freedoms.

This approach to public space will be elaborated first by focusing on the relation between political liberty and the public interest or common good as developed from classical thought predating modern liberalism, and largely obliterated by the latter's historical ascendance in late modernity. Following exposition of the meaning of public space in neo-Aristotelian thought, an attempt is then made to connect key elements of that tradition to a non-liberal emancipatory approach emerging from modernist and contemporary political philosophy.

THE AUTHENTIC PUBLIC REALM: AN EXCAVATION

The act of excavation, of return to the original problem of modern freedom, is urged by Heidegger in *Being and Time* (1985) in his call 'to reconceive the possibilities which the "Ancients" have made ready for us' (ibid. 40). This possibility is articulated by Aristotle who begins his main account of democracy in *The Politics* (1981) with the statement that 'A basic principle of the democratic constitution is liberty' (ibid. 362, book vi, ch. 2, par. 1317^{a}40). Identifying freedom as the defining characteristic of democracy, Aristotle proceeds to describe the political arrangements which follow from this underlying idea. Such arrangements would be designed to secure the widest possible dispersal of participation, therefore power, among citizens (ibid. 363–4, book vi, ch. 2, pars. 1317^{b}17–1318^{a}3).

The idea pinpoints what could be argued as the central question in Aristotle's political analysis: the distribution of power. The question surfaces in his discussion of equality (ibid. 250, book iv, ch. 4, pars. 1291^{b}30–8) which, as already addressed in the preceding chapter, can be held to flow from a notion of political justice. It also flows from the crucial concept of citizenship as participation in judgement or deliberation (ibid. 169, book iii, ch. 1, par. 1275^{a}22), which is grounded in Aristotle's extended defence of the value, not of oligarchic collectivism, but of collective decision-making (ibid. 201–9, book iii, ch. 11). His belief in the value of collective judgements, as against innumerable

[5] For further discussion of Machiavelli's contribution to political liberty, see Skinner (1986).

private opinions aggregated together, is augmented by the consideration that the value of participatory common judgement of the *demos* will be greater than that of any individual or group of individuals, however wealthy or economically powerful (ibid. 202, book iii, ch. 11, par. 1281ª39). This favourable judgement of collective will-formation indicates that Aristotle saw the character of the citizen body as the determinant factor from which political society emerges. His defence of common deliberation in the creation of consensus makes it clear that the distribution of power among citizens through provision of conditions favouring participation is of fundamental importance to democratic legitimacy.

In *The Politics* (1981), Aristotle also argues that the man who is isolated, who is unable to share in the benefits of political association, or has no need to share because he is already self-sufficient, is not part of the polis, and therefore must be either a beast or a god. By this he would seem to refer to something beyond the instrumentality of the state, to the individual's material self-sufficiency. He means, rather, that 'man is a political animal in a sense in which a bee is not, or any other gregarious animal' (ibid. 60, book i, ch. 2, par. 1253ª7). Starting from this premise of man's place in the natural order, Aristotle sets out to elaborate the distinguishing characteristic of human life which then necessitates certain conditions of the political order:

Nature, as we say, does nothing without some purpose; and she has endowed man alone among the animals with the power of speech . . . [which] serves to indicate what is useful and what is harmful, and so also what is just and what is unjust. For the real difference between man and other animals is that humans alone have perception of good and evil, just and unjust, etc. It is the sharing of a common view in *these* matters that makes a household a state. (Ibid., emphasis in the original)

The power to communicate thus gives the power to articulate justice. A common deliberation on the problems of justice gives rise to a common view. And a common view allows the possibility of political society: 'The virtue of justice [arising from participatory practice] is a feature of the state; for justice is the arrangement of the political association, and a common [i.e. shared] sense of justice decides what is just' (ibid. 61, book i, ch. 2, par. 1253ª29). Strauss (1973) describes this approach to the political order as a 'regime', a specific manner of life, the form of life as living together, which he argues the ancients saw as whole, not fragmented as in its modern form. 'Regime', Strauss explains, 'means simultaneously the form of life of a society, its style of life, its moral taste, form of society, form of state, form of government, spirit of law' (ibid. 34). Aristotelian political ideas are guided by the question of the best regime submitted to the following test: where the good man is identical with the good citizen, which can only be in one case, you have the best regime. In other words, this conception is highly dependent on the ideal, meaning, and practice of goodness, which Aristotle calls 'virtue'. Virtue is a quality indispensable to citizenship, therefore to the state, and is derived, not from blood or descent, but from habituation, in other words, from education. Strauss rightly observes that this knowledge is not supplied mysteriously by private conscience, as Rousseau (1973) held, but by social and political conditions conducive to communicative and moral competence.

Retrieval[6] of the Aristotelian concept of *phronesis* or ethical knowledge—distinct from *episteme* or scientific knowledge—that is dependent on ethos, the cultural and historical conditions current in a community, is held here to be indispensable to the development of a normative foundation of information policy and law. While for Mouffe (1988), the concept of *phronesis* implies a renunciation of all pretence to universality, it will be argued here that Aristotle's concept of knowledge as inherently ethical requires an essentialist anchor which he supplies in terms of the essence of human life—the political (*The Politics*, 1981: 59, book i, ch. 2, par. 1253ª1). Further, as observed already, Aristotle situates the political within a notion of action as communicative praxis or deliberative citizenship that would place the burden of defending particular principles and structures of public space upon the polity.

A definition of politics as fundamentally ethical—'the good'—thus establishes ethical reasoning in political action into the definitive human purpose: it contains and explains all human experience in terms of a higher principle, the common welfare of the community (*Nicomachean Ethics*, 1962: 3, book i, ch. 1, par. 1094ª). In *The Politics*, the idea of being-as-communal is expressed as a theory of society constituted by discourse ethics whereby the central feature of the state, 'the arrangement of political association' (ibid. 61, book i, ch. 2, par. 1253ª29), arises from a shared sense of values, not just of cultural meanings, symbols, and rituals, but about the virtues of justice. Aristotle's attempt to establish the necessity of communication to a theory of citizenship grounded in the necessity of ethical reasoning retains considerable relevance for the emancipatory context of late modernity.

Aristotle's theory of ethical praxis for civil society has lately been

---

[6] An important synthesis of Aristotle's ethical theory is furnished by Gadamer (1975) who was among the first to turn to Aristotle's model of *phronesis* as a form of contextually embedded and situationally sensitive judgement. An Aristotelian approach to practical reason therefore accounts for historical context, as does Marx with his attention to historical critique, and this could be contrasted with Kant's ethical theory based on abstract generalizability of private conscience, and context-free procedures.

revived (beginning with Gadamer, 1975) by critical theorists, postmodernists, and humanists who seek separate confirmations for differentiated post-socialist philosophies. To begin with, an emphasis on the communal, the associational interest as prior to individual interest is very different from the liberal idea emerging from Locke (1960) of aggregate individual interests constituted by calculus alone—instead of by common deliberation over the collective welfare. For instance, in the US Declaration of Independence, the authority of government is based on the protection of individual 'rights', whereas in *The Politics*, authority of the state comes from pursuit of collective decision-making in the common interest. Thus the Aristotelian position on political legitimacy is consistent with Rousseau's (1973) social contract as the rule of justice residing in the sovereignty of collective self-determination; with Marx's (1978a) analysis of the ideal cooperative association without government; and with principles of inclusion for public dialogue based on general interest argued by Habermas (1990; 1989; 1984) in his approach to the public sphere.

Though the polis exists prior to the individual in the *Nicomachean Ethics* and *The Politics*, the state is not held to coerce individuals; rather, reminiscent of Hegel's (1952a) view of the civil state, the individual can only achieve individual happiness through political society emphasizing values of liberation and self-determination. Human activities are not regarded as conceived in isolation, yet Aristotle's theory is still very much a theory of the individual—of the subject as moral actor. This possibility renders his theory appealing to a postmodernist vision, especially since he insists on a plurality of the good: 'men should derive their concept of the good and of happiness from the lives which they lead' (*Nicomachean Ethics*, 1962: 8, book i, ch. 5, par. $1095^{b}15$). This notion of the contingent, the contextual, and the conventional, by which judgements of social morality are based on historical conditions, renders social virtue a matter of practical reason in place of transcendent wisdom.

Aristotle's kind of rationality is deemed proper to the study of human praxis by some postmodernists such as Mouffe (1988) who call for the application of practical, not metaphysical, reason in the pursuit of the reasonable over the demonstrable. This is contrasted with the notion of Kantian subjective reason which requires a universality extended by private conscience and regardless of social context. By elevating to the rank of supreme principle the rule of universalization, Kant, Mouffe writes, 'inaugurated one of the most dangerous ideas which was to prevail from Fichte to Marx: that the practical sphere was to be subject to a scientific kind of knowledge comparable to the scientific knowledge required in the theoretical sphere' (ibid. 13). Thus the Aristotelian notion of *phronesis* is considered far more adequate by a few post-modernists than the Kantian analysis of judgement to grasp the kind of relation existing between the universal and the particular in the sphere of human action.

It should be emphasized, however, that in opposition to this argument of the radically contingent character of all value, any return to Aristotelian thought would actually disallow the rejection of rationality *qua* rationality. Instead, there arises a demand for broadening the conception of reason beyond minimalist versions both in orthodox Marxist positivism as well as liberal positivism in order to make room for the 'reasonable' and the 'plausible' and to recognize the differentiation of rationality under various historical conditions. But while Aristotle's notion of practical reason, ethical knowledge, and the political as communicative ethics in public space, is both historical and culturally contingent, contrary to Mouffe (1988) and Laclau's (1988) assertions, it develops its explanatory power from certain claims of essential human nature as social and political being, realized in the distinctive domain of ethical reason as communicative praxis. 'Being', therefore, is hardly the empty entity nor is politics the empty signifier that postmodernism claims for the Aristotelian vision.

No doubt, human good and human happiness are culturally and socially specific and, as such, there is difficulty in generalizing social action, political, policy, or individual action from the arguments in *The Politics*. Yet the classical tradition of freedom may rightly hold that by elevating the subjective element in Aristotelian political philosophy to the level of the dominant, any hope for collective ethical praxis with regard to broad participation by citizens in the public realm, as well as any hope for influential modes of emancipation from domination—not simply the 'language games' of radical contingency—will be difficult to achieve.

Laclau (1988: 35) may argue that 'the discourses of equality and rights need not rely on a common human essence as their foundation', yet, as both Nussbaum (1992) and MacIntyre (1984) indicate in their separate ways about Aristotle, you must admit to an understanding of a common human essence to have a normative view at all. Reference in the *Nicomachean Ethics* and *The Politics* to common interest has no private meaning, for Aristotle's virtues are virtues for citizenship—the characteristics of individuals active in public life who ask, how can humans best live together? To say that we are 'by nature political' (*The Politics*, 1981: 59, book i, ch. 2, par. 1253^{a}1) is to argue that it is our nature to have culture. Nature does not here mean 'necessity', since it contains the concept of choice in its application to social action. Without this association of culture, we cannot 'become' in terms of final causes, which implies that without culture, we are no longer. The primacy of the subjective is, therefore, not considered in Aristotelian arguments as a relevant political concern.

This comprises a forceful justification for the liberty of community to pursue its own goals brought about by widespread deliberative participation; for the unity of human life; for the necessity for justice in social relations; and for political participation as the foundation of associative being. From the standpoint of public communications and public policy, this approach has a clear significance.

In so far as Aristotle insists that participation in society requires virtue of the individual and virtue is a 'habit' not linked to natural necessity but is socially derived, the polity bears a common interest in furthering both communicative competence among its citizenry and structural opportunities for knowledge and deliberative inclusion. This is because the 'habit' of virtue, prerequisite to one's social being, occurs from ethos, 'education', the cultivation of sufficient capacities for ethical knowledge, and practical reason (*Nicomachean Ethics*, 1962: 33, book ii, ch. 1, par. 1103^{a}15). Not only, then, does the ethical nature of speech make society possible, as noted, but the individual's access to associative life, and the qualities of that life, are related to communicative competence, in the sense Habermas (1990) advocates. Inequalities in communicative competence, factors affecting the universal rights to education, or barriers in access of public space result from the structural and public conditions of the information environment. This is underlined in Aristotle's argument that 'Lawgivers make the citizens good in inculcating good habits in them, and this is the aim of every lawgiver' (ibid. 34, book ii, ch. 1, par. 1103^{b}4).

In the most explicit sense, therefore, political participation which constitutes the highest form of a free existence in Aristotle's theory of liberty, is a condition of the social and political constraints of the information system, while the defining character of society represents a condition of the broad distribution of forms of communicative action in public space allowing participation in deliberation and judgement.

CITIZENSHIP AND THE PUBLIC REALM

The most significant effort (Benhabib, 1992) in the twentieth century to recover Aristotelian political thinking on the principles of the political realm is furnished by Arendt's important theoretical work, *The Human Condition* (1958). The discussion here will address the form in which Aristotle's approach to collective will-formation and deliberative participation rights for all citizens is incorporated into the modern challenge to articulate a non-liberal alternative for the foundation of a free society. Arendt's views are taken up before those of Hegel and Kant because it is relevant to examine the relative continuity of principles from Aristotle to Arendt before reflecting on the place of Aristotle's theory of freedom in the Hegelian–Kantian debate whose logic presses for a somewhat distinctive conceptual path to the problem of liberation.

Arendt places great emphasis on political action in the public realm and maintains the Aristotelian distinction that freedom has significance only in public rather than private contexts. The opposition between public and private realms is necessary to maintenance of public space for broad participation, Arendt argues, but in modernity the boundary and the realms themselves have become distorted. What ought properly to be private has been made public, while other areas that ought to be public have been assimilated by private interests and concerns. Thus Arendt is concerned with retrieving and identifying conditions of an authentic public realm.

The standards of authenticity as elaborated in *The Human Condition* (1958) include the notion that a public space of information and participation must be the focus of universal attention (ibid. 45); that is, it is space pushed to the centre of common concern, or space on which common attention is focused. The argument implies that when individuals are drawn together to be informed, to gain knowledge, to reflect, to take action, to interact, to enter into dialogue, to express opinions, to try to influence public policy, to propose initiatives, or to deliberate on matters of common concern or the collective interest, they constitute a public arena. It is a view which underscores Aristotle's support for space for widespread participation in judgement and collective decision-making.

Another standard for establishing authenticity is the elimination of distortions in the public realm created by parties furthering their own private interests, airing or promoting their private preferences, or having their economic interests given public attention (ibid. 63). Thus the privatization of the public realm since the rise of the market economy in the sixteenth century, and its taking over by essentially private concerns administered on a national, now international, scale (ibid. 27), is a process which holds for Arendt a perversion and steady delegitimization of political society and the cause of freedom itself.

The inherent artificiality of public space comprises the third principle of its authenticity. Opposing Locke's (1960) view[7] of the spontaneous and natural condition of civil society, in *On Revolution* (1963) Arendt argues that political association is a human achievement arising from

---

[7] See discussion of Locke's attempt to naturalize the social conditions of liberty, provided in Chapter 2.

struggle and political action to further the cause of freedom against tyranny and therefore cannot be a gift of nature (ibid. 141–214). For this reason, public space does not arise spontaneously as a product of natural social evolution but, like political society itself, must be constructed, maintained, and guaranteed as a tangible space of relations where freedom, as Aristotle argued, can be enjoyed. This implies that, for Arendt as for Aristotle, public space is a cultural artefact needing to be guarded and passed on—that is, regulated by law and policy in the common interest as a public-interest responsibility of government.

There is fundamental conceptual consistency between this view of the artificiality of the public realm and the Aristotelian notion of equality or justice. The principle of equality between citizens encoded as a first principle in the constitutions of modern democracies is an extremely artificial affair. Equality is not a natural condition guaranteed by rights inherent in nature (which is the liberal assumption: see Chapter 2). As Arendt remarks in *The Origins of Totalitarianism* (1973), those who had been deprived of citizenship by the Nazis and thrown into a kind of state of nature were not able to appeal to natural rights. On the contrary, they found that while they were outside a body politic, existing in Locke's apolitical natural association or Hobbes's state of nature, they had no rights at all (ibid. 290–302). Thus Aristotle's essential point that political liberty and equality are conditions of political association and not derived from conditions external or autonomous to such association, is defended by Arendt in her argument that equality is not a natural human attribute but an artificial one that can be conferred only by access, and the terms of admission to the public realm (*On Revolution*, 1963: 23).

Canovan (1985) argues that Arendt's stress on the artificiality of political life is directly opposed to all versions of the nationalist or cultural essentialist blood-and-soil theory—discussed in more detail in Chapters 2 and 6—that political institutions must be an expression of the natural identity of a *Volk* (see discussion of Herder in Chapter 6), together with other modern ethnic activist deductions that only those who share the same blood can be political equals. Arendt's position on a non-communal concept of citizenship anchored in the principle of access to public space is also opposed to organic or pragmatic communitarianism advocated as a solution to the systematic alienation and value crises of modern industrial societies (see approaches to communitarian democracy in Dewey, 1963, 1927; Carey, 1988; Etzioni, 1993). Arendt's position is equally contrary to utilitarian liberalism's antipolitical theory of natural rights and its profession of the natural workings of the market as substitute for an authentic public realm accessible to all regardless of relations to property, economic production, and social power.

A fourth standard of authenticity in Arendt's thought is the stress on *spatiality*, the actualization and embodiment of sharing common space—'a house where freedom can dwell' (*On Revolution*, 1963: 28)—in which public concerns can emerge without conditions of visible or invisible domination, distortion, and appropriation. For freedom to be possible, it is not sufficient to have atomistic individuals voting in isolation, polled separately on their expressions of private sentiments and preferences, or citizens inserting themselves in a public space whose structures favour fragmented, anonymous, and disconnected acts of communicative engagement (ibid. 253–8) linked to technological devices and networks such as the Internet which record their preferences and private tastes and opinions with increasing and systematic efficiency. This conception is quite different from the liberal view that 'the public' are a mass of unassignable individuals who do not know one another and do not form a group (see development of the primacy of atomism in Locke, 1960; Mill, 1974; Lippman, 1922; Lazarsfeld *et al.*, 1948). Rather, Canovan (1983) argues with respect to Arendt, it is spatiality itself, the space between individuals and social groups where common affairs can be disclosed, knowledge gained and debated, which unites the members of a political community, instead of some quality inside each individual or cultural group, or inside the mysterious workings of the competitive market economy. Authentic opinion arises only when there is communicative competence, the 'habits of virtue' Aristotle emphasizes for citizenship, which is a factor of universal education, and when citizens have opportunities to confront one another in some mode of public space, that is itself a factor of the terms of admissibility to public space.

Thus, for Arendt, public opinion or collective will-formation, the baseline of democratic legitimacy, is formed *between* people rather than inside the conscience of each one of them (as in Kant's defence of subjectivist conscience in the *Foundations of the Metaphysics of Morals* (1990)), or than in their separate acts of self-interest (as in Locke's (1960) proposal of the primacy of private self-direction to serve as the basis of political theory).

Clearly, the distinguishing feature of this system of thought on public space is its ability to articulate a concept of public interest within a democratic context—without resort to unitary moral or totalitarian values as rationale for the common good, and without resort to undermining the principle of plurality in notions of the good which a democracy necessarily must sustain. Arendt's concept of the public interest is thus neither organic nor privatist. Political thinkers such as Rousseau

(1973), impressed by the problems of deriving a public interest from private interests, have turned to more organic notions of a community possessing a single general will but without accounting, as Aristotle does, for structures of public space and deliberative opportunities for judgement and knowledge by which the general will might be democratized. Arendt's view is also unlike Rousseau's since, from her perspective, the people can only share a common interest if it emerges from actual and widespread participation in the public realm, so that there is room for articulation of differences, and for democratic creation of consensus. Thus the public interest both for Aristotle and Arendt is tied to freedom of admission to public space and to the furthering of free activity itself.

Arendt recognizes, as Aristotle could not, that in a mass representative democracy most people do not participate in politics and that it is quite possible for individuals to have no more comprehension of the public interest other than on the basis of their own private interests. For this reason, her theory of public space strongly emphasizes the need to defend the public realm against privatization in the interest of the continued legitimacy of political society (*On Revolution*, 1963: 280–4). Since her theory holds that commonality emerges from participation in communicative arrangements rather than by aggregation of discrete opinions or private acts, her arguments imply a conceptually well-developed normative foundation for public policy in democratizing the structure and terms of admission to the technical, legal, and economic institutionalization of public space.

Concluding this discussion rooted in neo-Aristotelian thought on the participatory principles of public space, the fundamental arguments for guaranteeing public communications in the common interest of a democracy are as follows: first, as Canovan (1985) notes, since public freedom is something that needs a public location, physical or temporal, and can only happen in a public space, then if individuals or social groups are not present in such a space—prevented by whatever forms of structural barriers, social, commercial, legal, or procedural—they are simply not privileged with freedom.

Secondly, the public realm cannot be philosophically defended as the space for the resolution of private interests, be they enlightened or not, but is inherently a space for the democratic discovery and construction of the public interest of a civil society which regulates its affairs by means of constitutional laws and procedures. Such a theory of public space thus necessarily translates into a theory of citizenship that is primarily participatory.

Finally, the possibility of reactivating broad and inclusive possibilities for judgement depend upon the creation of public spaces in the information age of late modernity with diverse modes for knowledge and deliberation in which members of modern democracies can test and enlarge their opinions. Where appropriate public spaces exist, these opinions can in fact be challenged, enlarged, and transformed through a process of communicative action. Such action in public space is indeed crucial to the formation of opinions that can claim more than subjective validity. While individuals certainly hold personal opinions on many issues, both personal and social, they can only form valid representative opinions by enlarging their standpoint to incorporate those of others. Thus the capacity to form valid opinions, or 'judgement' according to Aristotle, requires public spaces where individuals can test and purify their views through a process of engagement and debate. Judgement can only be exercised and tested in public, in the free and open exchange of the public sphere, and thus, to be valid, depends on the presence of others. Arendt therefore furnishes the premises of standards of validity in judgement which Aristotle assumes: namely, that it depends on the ability to think 'representatively', from the standpoint of everyone else.

An element of Arendt's approach to public opinion works its way into Habermas's (1990) discourse ethics (taken up later in this chapter). In this respect, as Benhabib (1988) explains of Arendt's theory, the cultivation of enlarged thought 'politically requires the creation of institutions and practices whereby the voice and the perspective of others . . . can become expressed in their own right' (ibid. 47). The creation and cultivation of public space guaranteeing to everyone the right to knowledge, opinion, and political action is therefore essential, this perspective holds, to the development and maintenance of a free society.

PUBLIC FREEDOM AND THE SOCIAL ORDER

The relation between public space and modernity's emancipatory ideals has already been introduced through the political philosophy of Kant (1991*a*) as part of an unrealized project derailed both by modernity's social forms which were precisely, even scientifically, identified by Marx and Weber (see Chapter 1), and by modernity's underlying operative assumptions of negative liberty, definitively supplied in the utilitarian liberal thought of Locke and Hobbes (see Chapter 2). This section will address the tension and dialectic between the negative freedom of modern liberalism raised in Chapter 2 and the positive freedom of Aristotelian participatory citizenship elaborated in the preceding section. Analysis here will approach the problem in terms of recent attempts (Habermas, 1990) at redeeming not only the legacy of Kant but the thought of Hegel. Hegel's own efforts to synthesize negative with positive freedom have been judged unsuccessful (Cohen and Arato, 1992; Taylor, 1985) on grounds of conceptual flaws in his metaphysics of *Geist* or Spirit (Hegel, 1953). Nevertheless, a modification of his political theory to discount the relevance of *Geist* to the modern political order, as may be done with flaws in the subjectivist metaphysics of Kant's (1990) moral philosophy, is argued here to be crucial to revitalization of the democratic project. Marx certainly thought so, but as Taylor (1979) observes, Marx's attempts at modification distorted the coherence and potential of Hegel's political philosophy on the normative basis of civil society, thus releasing indignation at Hegel's conception of the state while mistakenly, it is argued, ignoring his theory of freedom.

It is held, therefore, that weak conceptual elements in the Hegelian framework relate to a theory of public freedom and of public space, and by developing this dimension of neo-Aristotelian political thought within Hegel's fundamentally emancipatory ideas on the institutional arrangements of civil society, a conceptual structure emerges that is crucial to principles governing democratization of civil society in the information age. Since such an insertion cannot be direct without being facile, the means selected for recovering the Hegelian framework involve the evolution of the 'principle of publicity' from Aristotle to Kant to Habermas in order to demonstrate key areas of contradiction and affinity arising inherently from the Kantian–Hegelian debate on the political legitimacy of civil society.

It will be argued that a theory of public freedom defended by Arendt and Aristotle, along with the 'principle of publicity' articulated by Kant, demands a reconceptualization of modern civil society and institutional arrangements under which public space could hold forth opportunities for widespread judgement and collective will-formation. This issue was raised in the discussion in Chapter 2, namely, that in order to move beyond private models of public space, a post-liberal framework for democratic civil society must be identified within which principles of public freedom in the information structure of society could be actualized. It is held here that Hegel's conceptualization of the relation between principles of freedom and the organization of civil society provides a significant approach to the problem of constructing political and socio-legal foundations for the organization of public space in the information society. It will be shown that reconciliation between Hegelian and neo-Aristotelian thought around the issue of principles and policies of the contemporary public realm is fundamental to recovery of the processes of democratic enlargement in modernity.

The dominant debate in contemporary political theory between the defenders of liberal principles of private rights, on one side (Hayek, 1982; Dworkin, 1978; Rawls, 1971), and advocates of conceptions of public goods and civic virtue (Taylor, 1985, 1979; MacIntyre, 1984; Walzer, 1983; Sandel, 1982; Arendt, 1963), on the other, is generally argued in terms that seem to preclude any attempt to confront how the cause of modern democracy is to be advanced given this division, or at bringing the two together along common dimensions central to that cause. To do so, it will be necessary to challenge the liberal interpretation of civil society as 'the private sphere', as well as challenge the communitarian equation of democracy with a substantive, therefore unitary, and ascriptive moral conception of the public good. As argued in Chapter 2 (see discussion of public space as instrument of private choice, subjective rights, and radical individualism), the former leads to a misapprehension of rights as arising from nature, thus fundamentally apolitical and a guarantee solely of the private autonomy of individuals over every and all terms of associational life; whereas the latter is clearly incompatible (see discussion on public space as cultural community in Chapter 2) with the principle of plurality of forms of life which is inseparable from self-determination in modern civil societies.

It is the counter-thesis here that the problem of rights and common welfare can only be resolved from a conceptual interrelation between a neo-Aristotelian theory of public space and a Hegelian approach to the institutional organization of civil society. The defence and expansion of both private rights and participatory public freedoms depend on the democratization of modern public space accomplished only by further democratization of the institutional organization of contemporary civil society. These goals can no longer be achieved from liberalism's and communitarianism's conceptually inadequate foundations that have clearly approached the limits of their forms of rationality. Such limits are visibly demonstrated in the global liberalization movement as a substitute political theory and the only alternative it can provide to cultural or communal collectivism.

While Hegel is often taken to task for rejecting the modern understanding of democracy in terms of popular sovereignty, it is argued here that his assumption that popular sovereignty would mean the rule of the mob (Hegel, 1952a: 1–36)—also echoed in the ambiguous support of popular sovereignty in Hamilton *et al.*, *The Federalist* (1961) and in Tocqueville's (1990) suspicion that tyranny had a popular basis—arises from failing to account for a theory of public space based on broad participatory rights in the manner conceptualized in Aristotle's and Arendt's approach to the public-space foundations of common welfare and collective will-formation. Nevertheless, Hegel supported the principle of public freedom and the autonomy of civil society which he attempted to secure and supplement by differentiation from the state through a concept of institutional guarantees (Hegel, 1952*a*: 122–55).

Enlarging on Kant's (1991*a*, 1991*b*) recognition of the participatory basis of political legitimacy which is limited by the atomism in Kant's historically acontextual theory of private conscience (see Chapter 2), Hegel perceives clearly that the central principle of modern civil society is not merely the private sphere of property and moral freedoms, but also the public realm of associational conditions and the structure of public institutions. This sphere is 'freed from personal opinion and contingency . . . recognized, guaranteed, and at the same time elevated to conscious effort for a common end' (Hegel, 1952*a*: 154). Hegel's theory of civil society (ibid. 122–55) is thus directly connected to his theory of freedom in the notion that the public realm and public institutions ought to constitute an embodiment of the principles of universal freedom, 'the actuality of the ethical Idea' (ibid. 155). He is thus able to conceive a set of institutions that mediate between private and public realms, between egoism and public-mindedness, and between individual and common life both within civil society and between civil society and the state. This significant element is missing from liberalism's conceptual foundation. The demands and privileges of citizenship, and the public practice of judgement and self-determination, are less abstract in Hegel's work than the moral responsibilities and freedoms of private conscience in Kantian liberalism, as well as less impoverished than the non-political forms of freedom, political identity, and justice in utilitarian liberalism. Hence the irreconcilable dualism of public and private is not assumed in Hegelian political theory at the same time as the integrity of each sphere is provided with a philosophical basis.

Nevertheless, Hegel did not develop the concept of public space for deliberative practice, rights to knowledge and information, and participation in common judgement in a sufficiently democratic direction (see Marx's *Critique of Hegel's Philosophy of Right*, 1970). No doubt, Hegel recognizes the voluntary associations of civil society as:

the firm foundation not only of the state but also of the citizen's trust in it and sentiment towards it. They are the pillars of freedom since in them particular freedom is realized and rational, and therefore there is implicitly present even in them the union of freedom and necessity. (Hegel, 1952*a*: 163)

But this is precariously close to liberalism's reliance on private initiative as the only valid form of public practice and as the only type of social action that bears value. Cohen and Arato (1992) therefore argue that the status and role of public opinion in civil society is ambiguous in Hegel's work. However, his position cannot be entirely assimilated to the liberal conception of private rights as the institutionalization of the absolute autonomy of private individuals from public interference, because the sphere of public participation within civil society and thus the political identity of otherwise private persons is more explicitly grounded in Hegel's thought (Cohen, 1989; Pelczynski, 1984) than in the apolitical negative freedom of private individuals and the articulation of civil society as a predominantly private sphere in the thought of Locke (1960). Still, this dimension of the terms and characteristics of public identity is far less developed in Hegel's text than in the preceding exposition of a neo-Aristotelian approach to public space.

The second major problem with Hegel's political theory is the unresolved tension between authoritarian and republican dimensions in his model of the civil state (Hegel, 1952a: 123–55). Again, it is held here, this arises from the underdevelopment of a model of public space in his political framework by which public freedom is narrowly thought to reside in the institutions of state bureaucracy rather than in the conditions of universal admissibility to the public realm whose structures are guaranteed by public policy to be free of distortion and barriers.

Despite constraints in Hegel's idea of the meaning of public freedom within civil society and also within the civil state, Hegel's insistence on the primacy of institutions of public discourse such as public corporations, legislative institutions, and public opinion within the state as the basis of political legitimacy shifts the meaning of his theory to rationality, universality of principle, and democratization in the determination of common welfare. For this reason, Hegel's theory cannot simply be reduced to collective authoritarianism as is sometimes the liberal charge (see discussion on this point in Cohen, 1989; Pelczynski, 1984). Had he not feared mass public opinion he might have developed a model of political society in the way Aristotle did, as organized around communication space, while also retaining the principle of public freedom appropriate to a plurality of forms of life not present in ancient thought.

DISCURSIVE VALIDITY OF COMMON INTEREST

Habermas's discourse ethics tries to achieve this balance between Kantian liberalism and Hegel's concern for the need for common political identity by returning to Arendt's stress on deliberative public space. Central elements in this theoretical system have been critically dealt with in the previous chapters. Habermas (1990) explicitly considers his efforts to formulate a theory of public communication as universalistic moral theory in the Kantian tradition. The question that has been raised (Fraser, 1992; Cohen, 1989; Benhabib, 1989) is whether discourse ethics provides an alternative theory of democratic legitimacy to traditional and neo-contractarian theories. This issue will be addressed here from the perspective of the form in which it returns us to the original problem of liberation and legitimacy while at the same time emphasizing Hegel's emancipatory question of the standard of freedom embodied in the institutional organization of democratic society.

As explained already in earlier discussion, discourse ethics (Habermas, 1990, 1984) aims at rationally motivated consensus among private subjects on the validity of norms raised for public discussion in any area of public policy, cultural practice, social life, or other human experience. The ethic articulates the standard for distinguishing between legitimate and illegitimate notions of the good, public interest, or common welfare. Notions of the good or the common interest are considered to be legitimate if all those possibly affected would, as participants in an actual discourse, arrive at an agreement that such a norm should come into or remain in force (Habermas, 1984: 19). Thus for conditions of public space to produce valid social outcomes there must be ensured: first, fully public communicative processes unconstrained by political or economic force; and secondly, public space must be public in terms of universal access in order for all those possibly affected to be admitted to deliberative expression or the experience of real knowledge. Participation in public space on equal terms for all potentially affected is clearly a principle which draws from neo-Aristotelian theory of public freedom, but discourse ethics also draws heavily from the procedural ethics of Kantian liberalism in the concept of procedural rules regulating the organization of communication for ascertaining the common interests (ibid. 21).

Most political theory on the social contract resolves the question of legitimacy and the general will in representative or virtual terms and by principle alone (see this demonstrated in Rawls, 1993; Mill, 1974; Rousseau, 1973; also see the debate on this problem in Hamilton *et al.*, *The Federalist*, 1961). This delimitation has forced individuals in modern democracies to be resigned to unequal access to the public realm rationalized on the grounds of representative exigency, with the general will or common interest reflected in codified principle alone within constitutional law. Thus the principle of free expression while codified in laws on human rights is rarely extended in practice to most individuals in the public space of modern democracies, with its historical form emerging in large part as subordinate to a different class of rights concerning property.

Habermas's approach instead insists on actual conditions of public discourse extended to all potentially affected and real structural–procedural possibilities for universal participation in judgement, knowledge, and deliberation on any matter of common concern. For only under such actual conditions can individuals know that the political community as such is convinced in public (not private) of something. Since his approach suggests the significant historical implication that the institutional organization of public space ought to reflect the principles of public freedom, Habermas's discourse ethics may be interpreted as consistent with conditions Hegel establishes for the correspondence between emancipatory ideals and historical context (Cohen, 1989)

Moreover, Habermas achieves a partial convergence with Hegel's philosophy of freedom by formulating the Kantian categorical imperative (see analysis of Kant's categorical imperative in Chapter 2; also, Kant, 1990) along lines compatible with liberal procedural rules of argument. Accordingly, norms of the public good held in common by a community do not indicate their validity by mere virtue of collectivism. The first premise for validity in notions of the good, that is, consensus on common ends, is that it can only be ascertained by establishing a connection with structural conditions and processes of public space in the creation of collective will-formation.

The other premise for validity in discourse ethics concerns communication content. Habermas (1984: 19–24) maintains that consensus emerging from public space must not only conform to procedural rules of universal access and structural conditions of actual possibilities of deliberation and knowledge but, as with Kant's (1990: 28–30) categorical imperative, should be generalizable interests. The difference between the categorical imperative and the discourse-ethic imperative was mentioned in the last chapter as a difference between monological and dialogical reason. Kant requires that generalizable interests conform only to a maxim extended from one's private conscience, whereas dialogical reason requires maxims to be generalizable from actually achieved consensus among interacting individuals.

By this reasoning, the choices of public policy, or the direction of political society, must satisfy the condition that the consequences and effects which result from collectively achieved judgement could be accepted by all those affected or concerned. Of course, this principle requires actual knowledge and deliberation in the public sphere in which the needs, interpretations, and interests of all social groups get a fair hearing and in which it becomes possible to discern whether there is indeed a common interest which could become the basis of values and norms in public-policy choices. The guiding question required by the second premise of validity is: does a given norm really express general rather than particular interests, and public rather than private interests?

Thus Habermas's reliance on a historically contingent concept of the general interest in his discourse ethics connects him not only to Hegel's emancipatory theory of the social basis of freedom, but also to Arendt's stress on the necessary relation between public space and the fate of political society. Arendt (1958) has made the compelling argument that only in a public space can a public opinion and consensus on the public interest emerge. In addition, by connecting Kant's moral theory to his political theory, discourse ethics also offers one form of developing and operationalizing the 'principle of publicity'. The problem of the general interest is thus crucial to democratic legitimacy as it is to the idea of political community itself.

This is recognized under liberalism's democratic theory, but as abstract principle alone since no solution seemed to present itself in reality other than representative government and confinement of participation to voting rights. Thus to avert the likelihood of authoritarian rationalization of social solidarity, modern democracy turned to the lesser of the two evils: an abstract doctrine of the common good governed by the general reality of private interest. By making the conditions and processes of collective identity 'rational' as well as participatory and universal through the concept of discourse in public space under rules of validity, Habermas's theory improves on the liberal dilemma by suggesting an empirical socio-legal test of the necessary institutional arrangement for achieving common interest without authoritarian implications: that is, the test of the institutional organization of the public realm.

IMPLICATIONS OF THE DELIBERATIVE MODEL

Institutional Guarantees of Public Space

The conceptual foundations of public communications and democratic legitimacy developed in the preceding discussion suggest that a participatory theory of public space does not prescribe a particular theory of the good, as has sometimes been the criticism of the neo-Aristotelian approach (Benhabib, 1992; Wolin, 1983) because it was deficient in accounting for procedures and standards for democratizing access, participation, and the processes as well as results of consensus creation. Yet the conception also clearly leads to a specific organizational model of political practice that is primarily grounded in non-discriminatory public communications for increasing numbers of individuals and social groups in democratic society. Obviously, no single model of democratic institutions flows from such a theory because it would be just as relevant to corporatist democracies, social-welfare democracies, or those lacking constitutions, as it is to more federalist, centralized, or constitutional republics. But the framework does maintain for all forms and modes of democracy, as supported by the terms of Hegel's and Habermas's contextually grounded emancipatory emphases, that public space should and does have a link to an institutional level of analysis (Cohen, 1989). It would thus be misleading to conceive of democratic legitimacy without the actual democratization of access to structures of public space and of processes of consensus formation on the common good; that is, the framework would invalidate the claim of a democratic order without socio-legal and institutional guarantees for the empirical organization of the public realm.

Failing in this actual reorganization of public space in the information age—not merely by codification of negative rights of expression—history would indeed prove Marx's critique of modernity (see discussion of his view in Chapter 1) that democracy is merely another form of domination and democratic legitimacy is simply an ingenious way of justifying domination. A participatory theory of public space must be able to indicate at least the minimum conditions on the level of organization and regulation of the institutions of public communication. By the conceptual foundations developed here, democratic legitimacy requires at minimum the establishment of the rules of access to the infrastructure and to the means for production and distribution of expression in public space, as well as conditions of participatory practice on the level of organization.

The most obvious example in liberalism of the institutionalization of deliberative opportunity is the creation of the legislative-parliamentary public sphere (Cohen, 1989). However, this confines the public sphere in thought as well as in practice to formal political representation, to exclusive participatory rights, and is therefore oligarchic and unequal but justified on grounds of pragmatic constraints in the management of modern democracies. The contradiction that the majority of individuals have no genuine opportunity to participate in the political society except in the most passive way has been rationalized by the political uses of Locke's doctrine of implicit legitimacy—the doctrine of every modern state which claims to be democratic. Locke writes: '. . . every Man, that hath any Possession, or Enjoyment, of any·part of the Dominions of any Government, doth thereby give his *tacit* Consent, and is as far forth obliged to Obedience to the Laws of that Government, during such enjoyment, as any one under it' (*Second Treatise of Government*, 1960: ch. 8: 392, emphasis in the original). Thus it follows that even if citizens are not consulted and have no means of expressing their views or gaining real knowledge on a given topic, they are nevertheless held to have tacitly consented to the actions of government (see discussion of this problem in Pateman, 1985). It is also evident why modern democracies have no alternative but to fall back upon a doctrine of this kind. For, relying on Locke's civil oligarchy as civil society, they have nothing to ground their legitimacy upon but tacit consent, which today is given the name 'public opinion', in the passive recording of private attitudes by aggregate, non-deliberative polling methods.

The concept of public space elaborated here argues instead that democratic government and the democratic state were from the beginning of their conceptualization supposed to be penetrated by the principle of accountability to a valid consensus formed in the public sphere—though these claims have hardly been adequately realized (see discussion of this point in Chapter 1). And it is for this reason that rights of free press and individual rights of expression were inserted into constitutional guarantees (see debate on this question in Hamilton *et al.*, 1961: *The Federalist*, no. 84: 575–87). The possibility of participating—not by passive and monological polling—in public opinion, judgement and consensus formation, and in genuine knowledge and deliberation, hence, in the influence of public decision-making and the choices of political community, is considerably restricted. Participation is restricted through segmentation of, for example, the voter's role, the struggle among particular interests of power, and a deformed public realm of commercial expression, proprietary monopoly of infrastructure and content, and industrial culture, where the possibility for information and knowledge diminishes with each new advancement in technological innovation and the information revolution.

The participatory theory of public space holds, therefore, that to proceed from the level of contemporary existing institutional arrangements in order to develop the necessary minimum democratic legitimacy is extravagantly wishful at best. If one proceeds from the standpoint of public space rather than the political system, as Aristotelian thought originally proposed but inadequately realized, and from the standpoint of Hegel's necessary correspondence between principles of public freedom and the institutional organization of society to reflect those principles in actual forms and practice, a way beyond the liberal antinomy of public/private interests opens up.

Similarly, just as the approach to public space suggested here has implications for the institutional organization of democracy, so too it has implications for the liberal principle of rights. The conceptual foundations of the theory advanced here highlight the requirement of rights as socio-legal forms enjoyed only if participatory opportunities are genuinely available in the public realm. Both democratic legitimacy and the rights themselves are validated not only at the level of the constitutional origin of rights, but also at the level of accessibility to

structures of public space necessary to their actualization. With indus-
trialization of information and cultural expression, the chances for
assembling in the village square were closed off some time ago. Where
individuals assemble in thought, attention, and gratification is not the
town hall but the electronic, digital, broadband or broadcasting networks governed and managed by the information industries. The
question arises, from foundations elaborated here, what chances exist to
assemble, associate, learn, gain knowledge, and articulate and confront
publicly on the terrain of an information civil society? At issue, therefore, is the relationship between the practice/assertion of rights and the
socio-legal guarantees of information rights in information policies and
laws.

Undoubtedly, rights in the liberal sense presuppose the positivization
of law (Unger, 1983), since it is argued that rights are stable only when
embodied in constitutions and legal codes. But a perspective grounded
in an undeformed and functioning public space points to the structural
conditions of possibility for effective self-determination in which rights
are historically embedded. The low-intensity civil war of all against all
on the question of the private rights of particular constituencies has
been assessed in Chapter 2. Undeniably, this has been the inevitable
logic of liberalism's philosophical foundation, that a competitive
struggle over the extension of private rights grows over time and the
problem of the common interest eventually shrinks to the problems
of proprietary relations. Though this process may be immanent in
liberalism, it has become exacerbated by the failure of the modern state
to ensure a genuinely participatory public realm so that the practice of
public freedoms can be realized under existing constitutional provisions
of liberty of expression (see Chapter 8) and rights of ownership of
expression (see Chapter 5). Thus the institutionalization of deliberative
structures in the public space of the information society, in societal and
cultural public spaces and not merely the legislative public sphere of
elected representatives, is paramount to a recovery of this crucial class
of fundamental rights.

Finally, the class of rights securing the integrity and autonomy of
private interests has been undergoing a fully developed expansion in the
processes of modernity, and yet those rights having to do with free communication (assembly, association, and public expression) have failed to
enlarge themselves since the onset of the industrial age and accompanying decline of face-to-face communities. Instead, the public space of
industrial democracies is governed by a government/industry consensus
to maintain it predominantly for commercial voices and the enlargement of proprietary interests for private exploitation, with the result
that commercial expression has been gaining larger protections in

liberal jurisprudence and public policy than the political-expression rights of citizens (Streeter, 1990; Horwitz, 1989; Unger, 1983). From the point of view of the foundations advanced here, the rights of communication are the most fundamental since they are constitutive of self-determined participatory practice itself, and hence, the key institution of modern civil society that ought to be the obligation of all, especially the burden of public policy, is the public sphere.

While Aristotle's and Arendt's approach to public freedom presupposes rights of public freedom but not the private class of liberal rights, and Hegel's approach endorses both with qualifications, it is evident that Kant's moral as well as political theory and Habermas's discourse ethics logically presuppose both classes of rights. But by basing private rights not on an individualistic ontology as classical liberal thought has done, but on the theory of communicative relations, a participatory theory of public space has strong foundations for emphasizing the cluster of rights of communication. In this framework, even private rights assume a more enlarged justification: they are affirmed because of the need to reproduce authentic autonomy of individual thought in cultural life without which deliberative participation would not only be impossible, but have no rational basis. Indeed, as pointed out earlier (see Chapter 2), individual rights exist in theory only, beyond the parameters of political society. Accordingly, while both classes of rights are preconditions of a participatory public sphere that seeks rational, knowledge-based, truth-centred legitimacy of the democratic social order, under liberalism only one pillar has developed and the other has become deformed or effaced (Habermas, 1989; Arendt, 1958).

THE MODE OF CIVIL SOCIETY

Some have argued that Habermas's discourse ethic is compatible with the different historical models of democracy (Benhabib, 1992, 1989; Cohen and Arato, 1992; Cohen, 1989). The foundations developed here hold that while a plurality of forms of democracy are not incompatible with a participatory theory of public space, there nevertheless remains to be addressed the question posed earlier in Chapter 2, namely, in what sense of civil society do we mean such a notion of public space? On the basis of the conceptual system emerging from examination of Aristotle, Arendt, Hegel, Kant, and Habermas on the issue of public freedoms, two aspects of civil society are implied.

First, the sphere of formal representative democracy (government and the state) and the sphere of society (the economy, culture, and private life) share but one critical institution that mediates between them: the institutional infrastructure of public space. Any mediation must be real, not illusory or deformed, or else knowledge and participation with respect to the direction and choices of political society will be severely limited, thus rendering illegitimate the democratic social order. This implies the central responsibility of public policy to ensure the establishment of a public sphere whose structures do in fact perform the function of mediation to make possible widespread participation in judgement and the exploration of consensus on common interests. The theory of public space advanced here suggests, therefore, there is no connection between civil society and the civil state without a fully democratized public sphere.

Secondly, the mode of civil society posed by the terms of this theory suggests radical democratization in a variety of differentiated and alternative forms of public communication or a plurality of public spaces. This is in order that the constitution of the public realm is neither dominated or governed by a single logic, such as commercial expression, nor by a handful of proprietors, such as conglomerates, oligopolies, monopolies, public or private, while furthering the emergence of institutional differentiation, diverse forms of participation, and alternative reasonings and conceptualizations of the social order. As it was observed in Chapter 1 of Marx's (1974) critique, if democracy is confined to one sphere only, to the legislative procedures of representative democracy and periodic voting alone, while oligarchic forms of governance and unaccountability prevail in the economy and in social and cultural life, then the democratic forms of the first sphere cannot but be progressively undermined. The renewal of alternative publics is thus intrinsically tied to the renewal of the public sphere itself and to the elimination of built-in processes of exclusion (Curran, 1991). A civil society characterized by the plurality of forms of public space contains, therefore, the promise of more meaningful and actual participation on several levels otherwise eliminated in the design of information policy.

This returns full circle to Kant's articulation of participation and publicity (see Chapter 1) as the locus of the principle of democratic legitimacy. The participatory theory of public space is thus incompatible with forms of civil society based on domination, oligarchy, or systematic inequality. The theory militates for further democratization of the institutions of civil society that are at present based on such relations and hence in severe opposition to the political promise of modernity. Accordingly, the question of the public sphere migrates back to the sphere from which it first emerged in Aristotle, Kant, and Hegel—that of civil society— taking the meaning of democracy to a post-liberal model.

TOWARD ANALYSIS OF THE INFORMATION SOCIETY

A participatory theory of public space thus begins with the normative standard for information structures and one of the tasks of such a framework is to explain what it would mean for real people living real lives in democratic societies to engage in practices of public freedom in the public realm of the information age. Why it should be important that citizens be allowed to engage in practices of knowledge and deliberation and what place such a practice has in political society has been addressed in the preceding elaboration of the conceptual basis of this theory. Participatory public space is supposed to accomplish a rationalization of public-opinion and will-formation because, as Aristotle maintains, it is only in rationalizing the process through which individuals come to believe their democratic context to be legitimate that they can reconcile justice with the social order. Rationalism in this theoretical perspective is introduced not as a rational plan for society but as a process of rationalizing the consensual foundations, the common interest, of society. The framework here will outline what is required of information policy to allow public space to be structured in a manner which makes it possible for individuals to engage in the practice of consensus formation.

Drawn from neo-Aristotelian and neo-Hegelian traditions of thought on the problem of human freedom, the participatory theory of public space, advanced here for purposes of assessing the policies of the information society, is held together by the following elements.

The participatory public space test proposes to replace the liberal private rights/private-choice test of public communications in structure, policy, and law. For the test to be truly democratizing, it cannot be undertaken as a rhetorical experiment to invoke an ideal world, or to justify existing practices and tendencies in technological innovation, global competition, or projects for wealth creation. The test fails if it amounts to policy visions of a revolutionary change in information diffusion (often attributed to revolutionary innovation in communication technology) without corresponding public-policy provisions in reality to ensure that the real emergence of an information democracy will not be left purely or mostly to the governance and non-accountable structures of marketplace rivalries among large-scale content and infrastructure monopolies. By insisting that the test must be undertaken in fact, we ensure that liberal principles of freedom of public discourse encoded in constitutional law do not take the form of paradoxical co-existence with oligarchic governance of public communications in practice, but are institutionalized and reflected in real structures and socio-legal arrangements. Social and political institutions cannot maintain their legitimacy entirely through the exercise of social power or strategic manipulation, as Weber (1946: 78–9) observes on the exercise of power by modern states. Hence the test is consistent with Hegel's idea of reconciliation between principles of freedom and the proper embodiment or objectification of their form in political community in order for the latter to qualify for legitimacy.

The test specifies the goals of information policy: it functions to establish the democratic legitimacy of social-political institutions and common interests or norms only if citizens would freely consent to them. However, as established in the theoretical foundation of this framework, genuine consensus is possible only if there exists (a) broad access to the public realm; and (b) the content of the information system offers the potential for real knowledge and deliberative engagement. Thus access and content serve as the test of free consent and their existence in reality answers the question of legitimacy of the political order. Chapters 4 and 7 will address the problem of communication policies in the European Union with respect to infrastructure access, while Chapters 5, 6, and 8 will address the information policies concerning the problem of content in terms of content ownership, audiovisual and cultural regulation, and information rights.

In policy terms, the participatory public-space framework establishes the validity of information policy in the presence of provisions requiring that admission to the public communication network is non-discriminatory to all voices, commercial and non-commercial; and that adequate space on the network, regardless of technology, is reserved for un-distorted-substantive fora of information, dialogue, and debate. While these may assume many communication forms, not all forms of public communication contribute to real knowledge and deliberative opportunity. By the terms of Kant's 'principle of publicity', and the standards of Aristotle's participation in judgement for collective will-formation, communication is more or less knowledge-producing and more or less conducive to participatory expressions of judgement, to the extent that its forms and content provide diverse representations of social reality, and not just social fiction, fantasy, or ideology.

This is not to say that the forms must exclude entertainment—which is the predominant cultural form of the modern multimedia public sphere permeating both fiction and non-fiction—merely that space be ensured for production and distribution of non-commercial, non-industrialized expression that is transparent with respect to the social reality of the modern political order. Otherwise, neither information nor deliberative practice will have a rational basis and consent, consensus, and legitimacy would be annulled. This is just as true for political expression as it is for cultural expression. In effect, such a problem describes the crisis of contemporary democratic politics, namely, the vast alienation of individuals within liberal democracies—reflected in declining voter turnout and public participation—from the democratic process and from political institutions (Dahrendorf, 1994; Turner, 1992; Habermas, 1973). Members of political society necessarily require real knowledge of their social, cultural, and political environment in order to make reasoned judgements regarding their own welfare and that of political community. For the 'force of the better argument' to prevail, for participants, viewers, or users to be 'convinced by reason' (Kant, 1991b: 85), there must be set conditions to ensure carriage of a substantive diversity of opinion, argument, and discourse forms in the public sphere as well as conditions to ensure these are immunized in a special way against repression of voices and inequality in programme representation. Thus if public policy fails to address the content of public space, citizens cannot build better foundations for their opinions or their life plans, or for institutions and norms of their society, and thus cannot be said to enjoy freedom.

Since participatory public space is the institutional form of democratic will-formation, its normative test leaves the structures of public communications with the 'task of supplying reasons why an existing political order deserves to be recognized' (Habermas, 1987: 188), for without such a process, the shared background to the social world would fall apart. This test replaces the liberal test of public space as a marketplace of ideas governed by elite entities, individual, institutional, or corporate, whose interests compete with each other for domination. Instead, public communications are required to guarantee conditions with the potential to lead to the construction of common understandings among a wide range of social actors. The test fails, therefore, if the opening up of the information infrastructure to participation through democratization of media access for both commercial and non-commercial voices is excluded from the policy framework.

Accordingly, key policy issues identified by the test for scrutiny under the terms of the framework in the remaining chapters include:

- the principles and criteria for minimum conditions of non-discriminatory access by individuals, social groups, and content providers to the information network (Chapter 4);
- positive content regulation—not negative, for that may lead to curbs on the range of voices—to ensure adequacy of information services so they are neither predominantly commercial nor predominantly for entertainment (Chapters 6 and 8);
- rules regarding ownership of content and infrastructure and forms of consolidation which affect participation in provision of programmes,

and which may structure access to features of the information infrastructure (Chapters 4, 5, and 7);

- the structure of proprietary rights or intellectual-property rights
  governing who owns information and the creation of a balance
  between the interests of three principal social groups—the cultural
  industries, creative labour, and the public—in deciding who benefits
  from production and exploitation of content (Chapter 5);
- rules regarding governance, accountability, and public-interest
  standards in development and functioning of the multimedia public
  sphere, including the need to address the decline of the public-service
  model of regulation and its displacement by the converging interests
  of the liberalization and nationalist models (Chapters 5, 6, and 8);
- the implications of privatization of law, privatization of the state,
  privatization of constitutions, and privatization of public goods in
  emerging policies for the information society (Chapter 6);
- construction of the competitive order of the information society in
  regulation of the distribution of market power as concerns tendencies
  to monopoly or oligopoly, reflected in the terms and application of
  competition law to multimedia cultural industries (Chapter 7);
- finally, provisions to ensure that the public and constitutional information rights of citizens to expression and information are given
  priority over private rights of the information industries to be free
  from obligations to the public-opinion-formation process, to cultural
  diversity, education, and other constitutional functions of public
  space (Chapter 8).

Together, these issues inform the analysis of the policy design of the
information society undertaken in the following chapters. They point to
the essential policy question of a participatory framework of public
space: how can the structure of public communications be demo-
cratically justified when the social conditions in which participation,
expression, knowledge, and deliberation are carried on and judgement
and consensus generated do not exist? It is also incumbent on any
analysis of information policy to explain and ground the implicit
normative view that guides the inquiry and directs it to consider certain
elements of the socio-legal basis of the public realm but not others.
What a normative theory of communication policy can do is to clarify
the universal core of the normative principles by which the analysis proceeds. The study which follows accepts this challenge with respect to the
construction of the information society in the European Union.

4

Telecommunications and the Political Design of the Information Infrastructure

THE ORIGINS of information liberalization in the European Union are expressed in policies for harmonizing regulation of the information infrastructure, especially telecommunications. The significance of these origins lies in clarifying the basis for the construction of the information society, since they establish a set of key instruments for redefining relations between the state and the public realm, thereby radically shifting the source of its governance and power. Employing new mechanisms for liberalization, de-monopolization, universal service, and competition (the last is taken up more fully in Chapter 7), the EU's regulatory approach towards the information infrastructure is transformed into arguments and provisions of technological necessity and improved competition. This emerging shape of an information society is examined in this chapter as revealed first in the origins, arguments, and provisions of information-infrastructure policies and their market-access theory of public space.

WHO GOVERNS THE PUBLIC REALM?
SOURCES OF TRANSFORMATION

Industrializing economies in the nineteenth century attempted to answer the problem of governance of the communications sector through criteria of national security via projects of nation-state building but also from growing recognition of the actual functioning of markets under large-scale capital formation, production, and distribution. As enacted by the 1890 Sherman Antitrust Act,[1] competition law in the USA, for instance, implicitly recognized, albeit in a limited sense (Hawley, 1966), that the unencumbered free market does not always work according to the processes of economic rationality assumed in its eighteenth-century idealization by Adam Smith (1986). In contrast, it was not until the beginning of the 1980s that the European Union (EU or the Union) started to draw on its constitutional power under the founding 1957 Treaty of Rome (Commission of the European Communities, 1993c) to

[1] For a brief history of the Sherman Antitrust Act, see Weaver (1980).

develop competition rules in the nationally segregated public-communi-cations sectors of Western European countries. In the post-war period, these sectors were governed by various agencies of the nation state subject to national regulatory systems drawn from the nationalist/culturalist model and the public-service model (see discussion of these models in Chapter 6). These models had in common an emphasis on universal service and strong public-interest regulatory standards. The Union, or European Community as it was then known, was beginning in the 1980s to experience intense liberalization pressures led by the USA and the UK under their respective Reagan/Thatcher political regimes and by the US-led, growing liberal international economic order whereby the General Agreement on Tariffs and Trade (GATT) rose in significance within international policy to ensure globalization of labour, production, and capital in an increasing number of sectors of the modern economy. In seeking to assimilate the infrastructure of public space in telecommunications networks and services, and in audiovisual networks and services to its sets of competencies, the Union was limited to instruments of policy for achieving a competitive single market grounded in the 'Five Freedoms of the Common Market' (see Pinder, 1991). These are: economic rights for free movement of labour, entrepreneurial domicile, service transactions, goods, and currency.

Accordingly, EU-wide policy for the first time began to re-examine the fundamental organization of public space in member states and in trans-European communication structures, with the legitimacy of national public operators of communications networks falling under the scrutiny (Ungerer and Costello, 1990) of the European Commission. The political attack on public-telecommunications monopolies launched in Great Britain and the USA in the early 1980s under the Thatcher and Reagan political regimes which led to the privatization of British Telecommunications and the divestiture of AT&T, now crossed over into EC policy. This took the form of a seemingly innocuous question that redefined at one stroke the meaning of public space, hence the meaning of the liberal state, and the communication rights of citizens. Put simply, it asked how the Union could overcome certain bottlenecks to the expansion of free trade created by the communication technology and power of the public operators of communications networks, and what to do about their network infrastructure and basic services in order to attract and better serve the interests of transnationally oriented large-scale economic actors? While the rationale for information-infrastructure policy (see, for example, the Bangemann Report, Commission of the European Communities, 1994*a*) professed commitment to Community common interests such as competitiveness, education, employment, culture, and democracy, the actual provisions of EU policy and law largely reflect the competing private needs and requirements of global and transnational communications entities (Esser and Noppe, 1996) over market share and conditions of investment. This is consistent with the public-policy approach to the information infrastructure developed in the USA.

To formulate a response to these questions and to assimilate public communications to the competence of the European Commission, several initial legal and political hurdles had to be overcome. First, there is no specific mandate in the founding EC Treaty (Commission of the European Communities, 1993*c*) dealing with public communications, in contrast to areas such as transportation or the environment.[2] Competition provisions in the Treaty establishing the European Community (ibid.) covered only the control of anti-competitive agreements (Article 85), monopoly abuse (Article 86), and application of all Treaty rules to the public sector (Article 90).[3] Up until the early 1980s, these provisions were thought to have only limited application to common European policy in telecommunications, broadcasting, other public communications systems, and to public utilities in general. However, the Court of Justice of the European Communities[4] (ECJ or the Court) ruled in 1985 to assimilate communications policy to the competition provisions of Articles 85 and 86 of the founding Treaty with the British Telecommunications decision (in *Italy* v. *Commission, 1985*) and in 1991 widened application of Article 90[5] to cover the communications sector with the Court's landmark judgments in the so-called terminal equipment (*France* v. *Commission*, 1991) and services directive (*Spain* v. *Commission,* 1992) cases.

Furthermore, at the beginning of the 1980s, the Community was still confronted with the difficult political choice of reconciling the general free-market philosophy exemplified in the founding Treaty, with the public-service philosophy of social organization in certain member states, such as France and Germany, in seeking to create or maintain public-statutory monopolies within central areas of society and economy. This dilemma has seldom arisen within the USA, except for rare instances of legislative debate which failed in every attempt to establish the meaning of the public interest in communication law (see

---

[2] See Articles 74–84 and Article 130*r*–130*t* of the Treaty of Rome (Commission of the European Communities, 1993*c*).   [3] Cited in Appendix.

[4] The Court of Justice of the European Communities, based in Luxembourg, is the supreme arbiter of Community law. The Court has three main roles: first, to rule on the legality of the Community's legislation or acts of the Community's institutions; secondly, to rule on alleged breaches of the Treaty by the member states or Community institutions; and thirdly, to rule on questions of Community law referred to it by the national courts. The Court is assisted by a Court of First Instance, which deals with appeals, among other issues, against European Commission's antitrust decisions (Sbragia, 1992; Elling, 1990).

[5] Cited in Appendix.

historical record in Kahn, 1984; also discussion and analysis in Horwitz, 1989; and Rowland, 1986). These debates questioned the contradiction between private-sector domination of basic communication services such as telecommunications and broadcasting, and the general public-interest goals of advancing education, information, and diversity of ownership inherent in the constitution and in antitrust law. Political and judicial interpretations of competition law and public-interest policies in the USA have not, in general, developed in the direction of maintaining minimum obligations of common welfare in the regulation of the market and the private sphere, except in the most vague and inapplicable terms (Streeter, 1990; Horwitz, 1989; Kohlmeier, 1969). This historical trend continues unbroken into the next phase of technological and economic change, evident in the absence of any public-interest goals other than supply-side objectives written into the 1996 Telecommunications Act (US Congress, 1996*a*).

In seeking for a way to supply real market-opening mechanisms that would alter the fundamental classification, therefore regulation, of public space in European states, but without denying politically the opposed set of public-interest principles underlying existing national-communication policies, the Community chose to adopt a strategy of harmonizing legislation (Commission of the European Communities, 1989 and 1987) as an indirect way of questioning the market power of public-service monopolies. This legislation has fundamentally shifted the categorization, meaning, and policy approach towards what counts as public space in favour of the demands of multinational users of communication networks and services for propelling national and international information liberalization policies to service expansion of their marketing, production, and investment operations (Esser and Noppe, 1996; Mosco, 1996; Boyle, 1996). For transnational communications industries, success in achieving their aims at the European level is not sufficient. As the EU has discovered, despite the substantive restructuring of the organization of European democracies implied in the restructuring of the public realm, harmonization of European communication policy fails to satisfy the demands of the transnational communications industries. For this reason far greater information-liberalization pressures have emerged externally from the GATT and now the World Trade Organization (WTO) to extract more dramatic restructuring in favour of sweeping away all non-commercial public-interest objectives in communication policy (see World Trade Organization, 1997; US Government, 1995*a*; US Congress, 1994*c*; Nicholas, 1990; Feketekuty, 1988; international arrangements for the global information infrastructure are discussed further in Chapter 7).

Above all reasons for rationalizing the restructuring of European communications, the EU has pointed to changes (Commission of the European Communities, 1994*a*; 1994*b*; 1990*a*) made imperative by the independent forces of technological upheaval which necessitate that Community policy underlines competition and liberalization as paramount principles of information regulation. Policy choices thought to be implicitly necessitated by accelerating technological innovation are most frequently attributed to convergence of information and telecommunications technologies, and to the emergence of optical fibres[6] and digitalization[7] which together foster the creation of a multitude of enhanced telecommunications, information, and multimedia services. At the same time, both EU and US public policies link the forces of technological innovation to new economic forces capable of providing these services more competitively and efficiently through the private, commercial sector than through the public-service sector. Such competition, it is argued, by the mere fact of being private, promotes the most efficient allocation of resources to take full advantage of the new technologies. Thus the imperative of information-technology innovation suggests an imperative of competition and liberalization in the organization of the public space of liberal democracies. The approach becomes all the more important for its correspondence with the inter-state commerce goals of the European Single Market[8] which argue that only a fully competitive environment would impart real advantage to the terms of union between member states.

[6] Fibre-optic cable is a bundle of hair-thin glass strands capable of carrying, as pulses of light, digitized information containing more than a hundred thousand telephone conversations, thousands of video channels, or a combination of both, simultaneously. Digital compression technologies and optoelectronic technologies may further increase the carrying capacities of fibre-optic cable to include an almost unlimited amount of data; for instance, tens of millions of conversations. Existing copper (telephone) wire would have to be replaced with fibre-optic cable to permit delivery of advanced digitized information to the home (for a more complete explanation, see US Congress, 1994*d*).

[7] The new way of storing or transmitting voice, data, or video. The information is converted into binary code (ones and zeroes) and travels as electrical impulses in a discrete pattern. The information is converted into its original form (voice, data, or video) by electronic devices at the site of reception. Transmission can be accomplished through wire or through the air. Unlike existing analogue transmission, the digital format allows simultaneous transmission of multiple voice, data, and video signals and, depending upon the medium of delivery, is not as subject to signal degradation. Compact discs, high-definition television, and emerging personal-communications services (portable, wireless services) are digital (for a more complete explanation, see US Congress, 1994*d*).

[8] The Single European Market has been created through a rolling programme of 279 legislative measures which the Community agreed to adopt and implement by the target date of 31 December 1992. The package of measures originate in the European Commission's White Paper on completing the internal market (Commission of the European Communities, 1985) adopted by member states in Milan on 28 and 29 June 1985. The aim of creating a Single European Market through the removal of all barriers to the free movement of people, services, goods, and capital within the EU is not new. The obligation to remove such barriers dates back to the inception of the Community itself, but the political effect of the 1992 date was to give new political impetus to the process.

In response, therefore, to these developments and to a particular perception of their meaning emerging in advanced industrialized democracies, the European Commission[9] (the Commission), which administers, initiates, monitors, and enforces Community policy within the scope of the powers delegated to it under the Treaty, undertook in the mid-1980s a far-reaching policy review whose outcome was the 1987 Green Paper on telecommunications (Commission of the European Communities, 1987). This in turn led to the adoption of Community legislation designed to open the national telecommunications markets, both for terminal equipment and for the provision of enhanced information services, by providing first, a framework for increased liberalization and privatization through the abolition of the statutory public monopolies previously enjoyed by the telecommunications industries in each member state, or more precisely, the abolition of exclusive rights attaching to them from public-interest rationales developed over the course of nearly a century; and secondly, by the growing application of Treaty competition rules to the communications sector.

This chapter will examine the democratic problem of access to the public realm (as developed in the normative framework for policy analysis in Chapter 3) emerging in policies governing the infrastructure of the information society. The issue of infrastructure access will be addressed in terms of the origins of liberalization, de-monopolization of public service, and the redefined boundaries of universal service. The paradoxes of competition law emerging in the information society are taken up in Chapter 7, while the problem of access to content in the European Union's approach to a common information space is addressed in the following two chapters (5 and 6) as part of the second test of free consent and therefore legitimacy of the organization of democracy. The relation between policies of liberalization and the construction of public space by political principles of broad access will be explored and developed empirically within key instruments of recent jurisprudence, policies, and laws for communications infrastructure within the Union. In the first part of the chapter, case law establishing the scope and meaning of Commission competence to regulate public space will be examined, together with emerging policy design of the information infrastructure. In the second part, the application of

---

[9] It is important to note that, under the Community's legislative and policy-making structures, in the majority of cases, policy and formal legislation is finally agreed by the ministers of the member states, meeting in the Council of Ministers (the Council). Proposals for such policy and legislation, however, may only be made by the commission, taking into account the opinion, and amendments of such proposals made by, the European Parliament. The Council may not initiate legislation itself, while in all but exceptional cases, the Commission may not adopt binding legislation. It is just such an exception, provided for in the field of competition policy, that has been of key importance in the liberalization of telecommunications.

liberalization in Community information-society policies to the structure of public communications will be considered by standards of validity of democratic public space (as developed in Chapter 3). The chapter concludes with rationalizations supplied by EU policy-makers drawn from interviews, along with an assessment of emerging information-infrastructure regulation which forecasts the forms and modes of the organization of the public sphere in the information age.

THE ORIGINS OF LIBERALIZATION

It is in the British Telecommunications (BT) case (*Italy* v. *Commission*, 1985) that the pre-political validity of market-based rules as paramount criteria of communications policy become legally 'naturalized'. This notion of a natural validity to supply-side policies for the information sector is implicit in the Court's judgment on this case, according to supporters of this view (see praise for the Court's judgment in Ungerer and Costello, 1990, Kohnstamm, 1990, Long, 1990, Delcourt, 1991, Scherer, 1991, and in the Commission's interpretation of the implications on its own legislative authority, Commission of the European Communities, 1994*a*, 1993*a*, 1991*a*, among other documents). The Commission's initial decision, applying the Community's competition rules, found that BT was abusing its monopoly position in breach of Article 86 of the Treaty by curtailing the activities of telex agencies based in the UK. These agencies, by using state-of-the-art technology, were able to undercut significantly the tariffs charged by BT for international telex transmissions. BT introduced regulations or schemes which, complying with its international obligations within the International Telecommunications Union (ITU), obliged such agencies not to charge below the prevailing rates applied by BT for such services. As a result of complaints, the Commission issued a decision finding that BT was abusing its dominant position over its UK communications network.

The Commission's decision was challenged by a number of member states concerned about the application, for the first time in Community or European history, of competition rules to a public communications network. The action was led by Italy and the subsequent case established the terms of future use of competition rules in the telecommunications sector, indeed setting the stage for re-categorization of communications industries in all media sectors, from satellite and cable to broadcasting and audiovisual production.

Four aspects of a new approach resulted from this case. First, the Court found that public-sector entities are 'undertakings' within the meaning of Articles 85 and 86[10] if they carry out an economic activity, irrespective of whether or not the undertaking itself is of a 'commercial nature'. Secondly, Italy claimed that BT schemes of tariff compliance considered abusive by the Commission actually constituted the exercise of BT's regulatory power given it under statute, which could not be subject to competition policies since these might effectively annul the explicit aim of existing law of guaranteeing the principle of public service. Hence, to avoid seeming to annul existing law but simultaneously seeking to uphold the constitutional mandate of the Commission and its prerogative to extend inter-state commerce principles into re-categorization of newer and newer areas of society and economy, the Court did not say BT's rules were not of a regulatory nature but that their content was the result of commercial activity.

The Court's ruling on commercial activity is central to the logical progression by which the public service and nationalist models of public space in European democracies (see exposition of these models in Chapter 6) were reclassified and transformed into a new structure. The ruling demonstrates how this displacement was achieved by legal and policy exposition, a construction of grounds in the Treaty, by arguments and concepts that steadily disallowed non-commercial criteria in the determination of the public realm, other than on welfare-state terms of supplementary justice for marginal social sectors. The developing legal-policy discourse pointed to growing legitimization for assimilation of all structures of public communications to private governance.

In order to ease the Court's dilemma on future cases concerning public-sector entities in communications, the Commission later issued the terminal equipment and services directives (Commission of the European Communities, 1998a and 1990a, respectively) which require the separation of regulatory and operational activities, thus divesting these entities of their regulatory function (see further discussion later in this chapter).

Thirdly, Italy argued that statutory monopolies were compatible with the Treaty on the basis of Article 222,[11] which states that the effects of the treaty are neutral as regards the member states' choice of property ownership, that is, neutral with respect to the state's choice of placing an activity in the public or the private sector. Thus member states, under the Treaty, should be free to create public-sector entities in areas deemed essential to the public interest. Accordingly, it followed that BT had the right to protect its area of operation and competence by preventing activities intended to undermine the public-sector servicing of a socio-economic need (in this case, telephony) designated in the common interest by law and policy. The Court rejected this argument, holding

---

[10] Cited in Appendix.   [11] Ibid.

that BT's monopoly rights concerned the provision of a network and not the provision of services over that network, thus leaving the question of compatibility of BT's public-service monopoly with the Treaty to one side. This ruling on the scope of a public-service entity's 'rights' evaded the direct question of consistency with constitutional provision. Its long-term implication seems to be a reduction in the legitimacy of non-commercial alternatives to proprietary domination of this sector as apparent in emerging approaches to organization of public space in the information society.

Finally, this legal realignment of the meaning of public communications in economy and society overrode Italy's defence of public service in the argument that the disputed BT rules, which had been introduced to restrict the activities of international telex agencies, did not constitute an abuse under Article 86 since they were designed to prevent an improper use of the BT network, over which the operator had been granted exclusive rights in the public interest of universal service. In particular, Italy claimed that the telex agencies wanted to circumvent normal tariffs by using special equipment and advanced information technology to transmit a high volume of messages over a very short period. The Court rejected this argument on the basis that a counter- or other public interest, namely, the fostering of new technology allowing rapid information transmission, could not be regarded as an improper use of the network. In essence, the Court held up the 'technological necessity' argument as a pre-eminent public good for the public realm over existing policy approaches emphasizing national and public-service interests.

In the Court's view, therefore, the abusive nature of BT's conduct lay not in the economic, possibly commercial operations of a public-service entity or in the condition of monopoly over a communications network, but in the attempt to constrain the use of new information technology thereby limiting a form of technical development whose logic favours the Community's constitutional goal of competition. This goal, specifically identified in Articles 85 and 86, and its mechanism, the rationale of technical necessity identified by the Court in the BT case, together have since become the cornerstone of all Community legislation of public communications, appealed to in many of the Commission's policies for the construction of common information space in the European Union. Significant elements of the policy design have emerged in a number of initiatives which can now be considered historical in light of the dramatic shift in thinking and approach to the public realm they have provoked.

CREATING A EUROPEAN INFORMATION POLICY

The 1987 Green Paper on Telecommunications

The Court's ruling and the Commission's action against BT, along with pressures from the global economy and multilateral trade agreements, as touched on above, gave rise to a detailed reconsideration of all aspects of the Community's public communications systems, beginning with telecommunications. Owing to protection provided by Article 222 for the basic doctrine of public service, namely, the freedom of political societies to protect activities in the common interest from the effects of market forces, the Courts in the British Telecommunications decision left open the question of whether, in principle, the statutory monopolies granted over telecommunications equipment, services, and infrastructure could be compatible with the Treaty.

Yet in elevating the logic of 'technical necessity' to a pre-eminent public good, the Court made it possible for the Commission to circumvent the constraint of Article 222 by claiming pressures of technological evolution as a rationalization for the global review and political resolution of telecommunications policy in the EC. In effect, not only the operations of public-service entities could now be delimited by technological-innovation arguments, but also their very existence could be challenged if such arguments were to be framed in a way that established 'technical necessity' as a higher public interest in Community policy and law. If the existence of such entities and the structure of public space they bring about could then be shown to present obstacles to the development of information technologies, it would comprise a legitimate legal and constitutional basis for legislating their abrogation, regardless of Article 222.

This approach first surfaced and found expression in the Commission's 1987 Green Paper on the development of the common market for telecommunications services and equipment (the Green Paper, Commission of the European Communities, 1987), which forecast the meaning of a common policy towards the telecommunications sector in particular, but also in general towards the entire communications structure of European public space, as analysed in this and succeeding chapters. Significantly, in order to employ the technological argument in a manner most effective to undermining the status of public-service operations, the Green Paper chose to highlight, not the structure of the network itself, but the problem of the development of telecommunications services and equipment. It argued that such development was necessary for the industry to take full advantage of the technological and economic evolution of the world market which is becoming increasingly more transnational and competitive. Quite strategically, at the same time that it advanced the validity of technological pressures, the Green Paper inserted a political acknowledgment that the 'role of Telecommunications Administrations in the provision of network infrastructure must be essentially safeguarded in order to allow them to fulfil their public service obligations' (Commission of the European Communities, 1987: 15).

In devising a policy method to lay down a path of eventual decline for public entities in communications, the Green Paper accepted, on the one hand, that a combination of economic and legal considerations, together with a possible public interest, had led member states to reserve to one or more telecommunications administrations[12] the right to provide the basic network infrastructure and telecommunications services. On the other hand, however, the Green Paper holds that such monopolies should henceforth be narrowly defined by being subordinated at the very least to the following additional tests (ibid. 70–2, 74):

(a) *efficiency*—this criterion imposes economic and technical rationality upon the underlying legitimacy of the mode of public space despite evidence that cost-based efficiency is problematic and that costs are, by and large, politically determined (see Hills, 1993; 1990; 1986);

(b) the Treaty's *competition rules*—which justify separation of regulation from operation as a first step in the application of such rules; and

(c) *removal of hurdles to technical innovation,* not only in telecommunications, but in all information-related fields, including satellite communications, mobile, broadcasting, cable TV, and Internet networks—a criterion which could supersede at any time the national legal status of public entities whenever the notion of 'obstacle' or 'hurdle' to technical progress can be invoked.

Similarly, the Green Paper acknowledged, on the one hand, the two most significant non-commercial public-interest criteria prevailing in the organization of communications for over a century: universal service and equal access. Telecommunications administrations are granted the power to draw on sufficient public funds in order to operate a network that is 'national' and 'public', in the sense that it should cover the whole of the national territory and be accessible to anyone within those bounds (Commission of the European Communities, 1987: 139–40). On the other hand, these goals are, first, removed from the political, national, or cultural goods grounds from which they arose and recast as

[12] 'Telecommunications administrations' describes the structure common to most EU member states, namely, of a government department with overall responsibility for telecommunications (and usually postal) services, as well as the public telecommunications operator providing the network and services under that department's control.

goals for advancing the creation of a 'common information market' (Commission of the European Communities, 1987: 141). In other words, universal service and equal access, as indispensable principles of liberalism's public space as a free marketplace of ideas, is reduced here, reflecting the American historical context (see Streeter, 1990), to the problem of freedom of commercial information, by which 'enhanced exchange and free flow of information . . . are closely related to the development of trade and the operation and promotion of business information services' (Commission of the European Communities, 1987: 139–40). On the other hand, universal service and equal access, as the status of public entities themselves, become substantively constrained in so far as the Green Paper does not accept them as grounds to justify a grant by member states of monopoly rights in the provision of telecommunications services. While connection to the network may be governed by universal service, the Commission's argument suggested that henceforth access to information services—in voice, text, graphics, or video—must be determined by the marketplace according to the economic power of participants. By holding back the application of universal service and equal access from information services and placing the latter under market imperatives, the Green Paper effectively cancelled the empirical foundation of the universal rights of admission to public space even while accepting the principle in theory.

At the very outset of the communication-liberalization movement, therefore, European policy had impaired and enfeebled the one public-interest achievement liberal democracy had been able to institutionalize that is compatible with the Hegelian test of the social forms of policy and law institutionalized within actual conditions of participatory public space (described at the end of Chapter 3). The political success of this trend, not only in the European Union but far more in the USA and the GATT and WTO, can be attributed to arguments advancing instead the cause of competition which is one of two substantive public interests—the other being contractual or ownership rights—explicit in the maximization of choice mode of public space elaborated earlier (see Chapter 2). Among other things, Chapter 2's exposition of Locke's and Hobbes's utilitarian liberalism attempted to show that the cause of market competition and that of proprietary rights are not only the substantive ends of a civil society defined by the terms of a private sphere, but that they are also its moral ends.

As such, from within the categories of this ontology, these ends are placed beyond the bounds of dispute, assumed on grounds of faith, and as moral claims play a fundamental role in the ideology of liberalization. Given the emerging dominance of this thought in Europe since the early 1980s and its worldwide expansion in the post-Cold War period, it was not necessary for the Green Paper to offer proof that the exigencies of competition—however that may be defined—are more moral or more superior public interests for democracies than, say, information sufficiency or universal rights of admission to the public realm. Nor could any challenge to the rational premises of competitive rivalry as an organizing principle for communications succeed without also challenging the coherence of the entire system of thought in which the Treaty is grounded. Indeed, a challenge of that nature would undermine the very democratic legitimacy of social orders constituted by utilitarian liberalism. This is why alternative views of the public interest articulated from within the premises of this system are rendered fallacious—at best irrelevant, more often normatively invalid. This may suggest why attempts to account for non-commercial public-interest standards of regulation—such as for protection of children in US communications history—have failed in practice (Mosco, 1990; Streeter, 1990; Horwitz, 1989; Rowland, 1986), or why movements to impose alternative normative criteria on grounds of cultural self-determination in EU communications legislation (Commission of the European Communities, 1989) have been vehemently opposed by the international liberalization regime.

As the Green Paper set in motion an argument for a shift from public-service grounds of operation to competitive grounds in the provision of telecommunications services, thereby invalidating the regulatory authority of the state, the inherent rationality and validity of the proposition went largely unchallenged. It was, in fact, endorsed as a 'progressive' and an ethically superior policy shift by the USA (Center for Strategic and International Studies, 1994; US Congress, 1993; Darnton and Wuersch, 1992; among many such instances). Once competitive grounds have displaced public-service grounds, the discourse of competition (though it has scant basis in actual implementation) must necessarily take over as the regulating principle of information space. And since the market access theory is constructed on the assumption of conditions of pure competition (however unrealizable), it becomes the responsibility of political authorities to apply competition laws limiting monopoly abuse, paradoxically suggesting new forms of state intervention (see discussion in Chapter 7).

Given that public-service communication entities in Europe have been dominant operators and providers, the strategic importance of the Green Paper's conceptual rearticulation of the basis of communications systems became evident. Competition rules could now be politically employed as the instruments of restructuring. The dangers of public-sector monopolies in communication markets emerged as the primary concern of liberal democracies and it was concluded that the application of the Community's competition rules to dismantle the public-service entities should be strengthened (Commission of the European Communities, 1987: proposed positions H and I, p. 184; Sepstrup, 1991; Negrine and Papathanassopoulos, 1991; Duch, 1991; Ungerer and Costello, 1990; Lanvin, 1990).

As the Green Paper was generally hailed by the private-sector international communications industry, the Commission set out a work programme for its implementation in 1988 (Commission of the European Communities, 1988*b*), approved by the Council of the European Communities (member-state governments) that same year (Commission of the European Communities, 1988*c*). Building on the mandate of the Council Resolution (ibid.), the Commission adopted two directives[13] liberalizing first, the supply of terminal equipment (the 1988 'terminal equipment directive', Commission of the European Communities, 1988*a*), and secondly, the provision of telecommunications services (the 'services directive', Commission of the European Communities, 1990*a*). These are examined next for the path they open to a particular form of the information society, with an emphasis on provisions in the services directive.

De-monopolization of Public Service

In order to open up the supply of terminal equipment to commercial competitors and to harmonize telecommunications equipment standards, the Commission's terminal equipment directive (terminal equipment directive, Commission of the European Communities, 1988*a*) was adopted under Article 90[14] of the Treaty which permits application of Treaty rules to the public sector. Among other things, this statute attempted to:

- remove the special and exclusive rights over terminal equipment (telephone, faxes, etc.) that is, limit rights to import, market, connect, bring into service, and maintain terminal equipment which, in general, had been granted to public-telecommunications organizations (PTOs) (ibid., Article 2);
- limit restrictions on certain specified requirements which could be imposed on terminal equipment and on its suppliers, in the interest of

---

[13] A Commission directive is a binding legal measure which sets out specific goals and provisions which the member states must implement into their own law by a specified time limit, usually eighteen to twenty-four months after adoption. The member states of the EU are generally free to decide how they implement the measure, for example, through primary or secondary legislation or by administrative regulations (Sbragia, 1992). In most cases the power to adopt a directive rests with the Council, acting on a proposal from the Commission. However, in the field of competition policy, Article 90(3) of the Treaty gives the Commission the power to remedy structural competition problems by adopting directives. Both the terminal equipment and the services directive were adopted under the Article 90(3) procedure.

[14] Cited in Appendix.

the protection and interoperability of the public-communications network (Commission of the European Communities, 1988*a*: Article 2);
• require telecommunications equipment to be approved by an independent body, and the publication of network technical specifications necessary for commercial competitors to manufacture interconnection equipment (ibid., Articles 5 and 6).

Thus, initiating the de-monopolization of public service entities, this directive is also significant for its choice of Article 90 as the constitutional grounds of communications liberalization. A directive under Article 90 made it possible for the Commission to avoid the need for formal Council approval where the necessary political consensus was lacking for such fundamental restructuring of the public-service organization of communications. It also demonstrates the first instance of Commission use of competition rules to suppress a statutory monopoly (see Communication to the Council, Commission of the European Communities, 1993*e*) rather than simply regulating the manner in which the monopoly is operated. More noteworthy, the directive in its recitals establishes 'technical necessity' as a legal basis of liberalization, indicating technological progress in terminal technology and the need for users to be allowed a 'free choice' of the full benefit from such technologies—adequate rationales for commercialization of communications:

Several Member States have, in response to technical and economic developments, reviewed their grant of special or exclusive rights in the telecommunications sector. The proliferation of types of terminal equipment and the possibility of the multiple use of terminals means that users must be allowed a free choice between the various types of equipment available if they are to benefit fully from the technological advances made in the sector. (Commission of the European Communities, 1988*a*: recital 2)

The political significance of permitting competitive forces out of 'technical necessity' caused the French government to challenge the Commission in the terminal equipment case (*France* v. *Commission*, 1991) in the European Court of Justice on four grounds:
(1) the Treaty cannot be used to prohibit public monopolies *per se*, but only to remedy their possible abusive conduct;
(2) the directive amounted to the exercise of legislative power reserved to the member states;
(3) the Commission should have used the more stringent enforcement procedure (a set of juridical steps) under Article 169 of the Treaty against member states, instead of introducing market-opening legislation under the simpler procedure allowed by Article 90; and
(4) the Commission had failed to comply with an essential procedural

requirement set down in Article 173 of the Treaty, namely that the directive be adequately reasoned which it was not.

France's arguments were formulated around challenges to the Commission's misuse of procedure, lack of competence to act in this way, and infringement of essential procedural requirements. The principal issue for France was whether the effects inherent in the mere existence of exclusive and special rights on public-service grounds was sufficient for the Commission to invoke Article 90. Reflecting the traditional view of Article 90 as non-contradictory to public service (discussed in the Communication to the Council, Commission of the European Communities, 1993e), France argued that as Article 90 presupposed the existence of such public-service rights, the Commission could only intervene against the way rights were used by the public-service entities and not against the rights themselves.

The Court, however, procedurally countered all of these objections and upheld the Commission's use of Article 90 by requiring that assessment be made on grounds of competition or free movement of goods and services flowing from exclusive public-service rights, rather than from assessment of the specific conduct of the right holder. The Court also rejected any suggestion that the Treaty allowed or could be used to protect, the mandate of public service entities *per se*. It further rejected the French argument that the Commission was making industrial policy, which is supposedly the preserve of the Council of Ministers acting under Article 100a of the Treaty, which provides the legal basis for legislation designed to open national barriers by introducing harmonized standards of regulatory conditions—meaning, one set of public policies for all member states in specific domains. Last, but not least, the Court declared the directive as a legitimate normative act, as are nation-state laws and legislation, thus meeting the French charge of insufficient reasoning. As normative acts embodying the collective will and the common welfare, laws and legislation must be more generally reasoned than any specific decision enforcing competition rules against an individual, member state, or undertaking.

In addition to supporting the Commission's use of Article 90 for restructuring the public realm, the case also reveals two further aspects of information-society policy. First, the Court's opinion seems to be firmly coupled with global liberalization trends towards multilaterally agreed-upon rules affecting national laws and policies and everyday life for individuals and social groups in a steadily growing range of social, cultural, economic, and political sectors. By allowing the Commission to use its powers of harmonization of multinational policy and law in the EC under Article 100a—similar to trends at the global level—in order to remedy what it may view as a breach of the Treaty flowing from the inherent condition of public-service monopoly under Article 90 (and not necessarily an abuse of power linked to specific acts), the significance of harmonization to the causes of 'technical necessity' and competition became instantly available to international proprietary interests in the communications industries. Harmonization in communications policy has, since the terminals equipment directive, evolved into a primary policy instrument (as seen in Commission of the European Communities, 1994*a*, 1994*b*, 1993*a*, 1990*a*, and 1989) for suppressing or removing obstacles (technical, political, social, cultural, or regulatory) to the creation of a single framework for conditions of private contractual rights in the European Union's transnational structures of communications. These obstacles are since thought to result from variations between the national regulation of member states (see status report on EC telecommunications policy, Commission of the European Communities, 1994*c*) even though the regulation may not itself conflict with the Treaty. In other words, alternative approaches to the policies of public space indicating alternative terms and conditions of associational/political life—be it cultural, participatory, or market-centred—could now be reorganized towards supply-side conditions tilted solely in the interests of large-scale private international investors for access to this sector.

The terminal equipment case (*France* v. *Commission*, 1991) also upheld the requirement in the directive for the separation of regulatory and operational functions by public-service entities through establishment by member states of independent national regulatory bodies along the lines of the Federal Communications Commission (FCC) model of separation in the USA (prior to the directive, PTOs could approve terminal equipment for connection to their network as well as regulate prices and other conditions of sale). In market-access policies for other industrial sectors, this separation is regarded as fundamental to the introduction of competition. As argued in more detail later (see Chapter 7), while the directive served as a first step towards de-monopolization of *public* entities, it was unable to address the problem of monopoly as such. The results call into question the normative grounds of the competition principle with respect to real motives in anti-monopoly regulation upheld by the forces of liberalization.

Finally, it seems clear in this case that the approach to competition in communications taken by the Court closely parallels the notion of competition recognized by the US Courts and the Federal Communications Commission (FCC)[15] in their efforts to coax the market to behave by the ideal premises of its theory (best articulated and defended by

[15] For a good discussion of this US approach, see Horwitz (1989).

Smith, 1986; Hayek, 1982, 1948; and Schumpeter, 1947). In so far as competition goals prioritize market freedoms over other categories of freedom such as human/civil rights and political freedoms, they tend to draw on contractual law (see Chapter 5) which is biased in favour of existing arrangements, assimilating the legal constitution of society to the domain of private law, whose philosophical basis, as pointed out in Chapter 2, is drawn from Locke's *Second Treatise of Government* (1960). The effects of this direction in the European Union's legal order is deeply significant for all aspects of future arrangements and possibilities for public space in the information society, and will be taken up at greater length later in the book (see in particular, Chapter 5). For the present, it is sufficient to note that the very first communications legislation in the Community, and its corresponding case in the ECJ, fundamentally transformed not only the legal grounds of policy and law (for a juridical analysis of European law, see Koopmans, 1991; and Elling, 1990), but indeed the entire socio-legal tradition for conceptualizing the relation between communications and the social order (see discussion later in Chapter 5).

This orientation is expanded and more firmly established by the telecommunications services directive (Commission of the European Communities, 1990*a*) and the services directive case (*Spain* v. *Commission,* 1992) which sought to remove special and exclusive rights over the provision of most communications services, and by the open network directive (Commission of the European Communities, 1990c) for promoting 'equal and fair' access to the network infrastructure and existing services. Since telecommunications services were projected at annual growth rates of nearly 8 per cent,[16] the services directive assumed particular importance for the Community's approach to the information industries. It had three explicit aims:

(a) the abolition of special and exclusive rights, meaning, more accurately, elimination of public monopolies, or situations of exclusivity enjoyed by an entity, from the discretionary award of those rights by a member state;

(b) the abolition of restrictions on the use of liberalized services and on their tariffs; and

(c) the separation of regulation from operation. 'Telecommunications services' were defined to include all services for the transmission and connection of signals over the public network (services directive, Commission of the European Communities, 1990*a*: Article 1.1).

---

[16] A study carried out by the Commission estimated the value of the European tele-communications-services market in 1990 at 88 billion ECU (see Commission of the European Communities (1991*b*), 'Telecommunications: Issues and Options 1992 to 2010', a study conducted for the Commission by Arthur D. Little, October 1991).

Citing incompatibility of exclusive rights of operation in communications, not only with Article 90[17] of the Treaty, but also with Article 59 (prohibiting restrictions on freedom to provide services within the Community) and with Article 86[18] (prohibiting abuse of market position[19]), the directive made illegal all special and exclusive rights in telecommunications services (i.e. public-service provision). An exception was granted for basic voice telephony[20] services though this too was purely temporary. The Council of Ministers was later urged by the Commission to reconsider its initial political fear of dismantling one of the essential pillars of public interest in communications, and as a consequence the last remaining basic public service in telecommunications was finally subjected to de-monopolization and market competition, taking effect in the year 1998 (see Commission of the European Communities, 1995a; 1993f).

The intent of the services directive, therefore, was to render the very concept of telecommunication services legally incompatible with exclusive rights granted by political societies on the grounds of common interest, even if those rights attempt to guarantee conditions of the public realm through universal provision of minimum information services. In short, the question of legality was no longer to be rooted in the distinction between notions of good and bad forms of public communication, that is, between forms that are held in common to be beneficial (such as in areas of culture, education, public opinion formation, or social needs) and forms that are not so held. Rather, the distinction drawn from now on was essentially between information services that are commercial and those that are distorted by the public-service model. Non-commercial forms of communication, regardless of benefit judged by collective will, were quite simply placed, for the first time in European democratic history, on implicit yet *de facto* illegal footing.

This argument regarding the illegality of public-service communication services was attributed in the services directive to the following inherent effects of exclusive rights, that is, of non-commercial communication rights of provision and access. The directive asserts:

(a) such rights reinforce monopoly over the communication network by promoting abuse of dominant position over services provided through the network (services directive, Commission of the European Communities, 1990a: recital 15);

---

[17] Cited at Appendix.

[18] Ibid.

[19] The manner in which the services directive employs the constitutionality of provisions in the Treaty of Rome to support anti-public monopoly legislation is enumerated in recitals 13 to 17 (services directive, Commission of the European Communities, 1990a).

[20] Also excluded from the services directive were telex, radio mobile, paging, and satellite communications.

(b) non-commercial communication rights exclude or restrict commercial competitors' access to communication markets thereby infringing upon consumer freedom of choice (Commission of the European Communities, 1990*a*: recital 16(*a*));

(c) they oblige commercial service providers to be at the mercy of the holder of the exclusive rights (ibid., recital 16(*b*)).

All three premises of the illegality argument oppose public service to commercial organization of communications in a framework that renders them fundamentally irreconcilable to one another. Thus if commercial rights are a public good, public-service rights cannot occupy 'goods' status, suggesting that these two categories of rights cannot co-exist without rendering incoherent the legal reasoning of liberalization. The domain of public service is essentially non-commercial, a domain organized to facilitate the communication needs of civil society which is neither necessarily nor entirely identical with the interests of the private market. This condition is made apparent by Hegel's (1952*a*) eminently anti-Lockean, three-part distinction between the state, society, and the economy (see discussion of significance in Pelczynski, 1984). The implications of arguments in the services directive would appear to deny that civil society requires forms of communication other than commercial forms. In effect, this effaces recognition of civil society as a social reality and submerges it beneath the private rivalries of the market economy. Such a conceptual move marginalizes the connection between civil society and the state, making it possible through public policy to erode the existence of public/political freedom as a reality independent of commercial freedom, as well as the potential for participatory structures of collective will-formation to allow for actual democratic legitimacy.

If the concept of public service is placed on an illegal footing by the logic of the services directive, and the information needs of civil society are erased as ends and goods in public policy, how then can one make the case for exception, albeit temporary, for the extensive public-service provision of voice telephony? The answer to this question is the key to understanding the manner in which the century-long concept of universal service in communications is redefined to prepare for the reality of the technical and economic imperatives of the information society.

In view of this exception, the Commission risked challenge to its entire legal reasoning for the elimination of public service through liberalization of telecommunications services. A strong legal basis for abrogating the public-service information sector to the level of Community competence had to be found. The basis was identified as Article 90(2)[21] of the Treaty which requires public-service undertakings to be

---

[21] Cited in Appendix.

submitted to Treaty competition rules except where application of such rules would 'obstruct the performance, in law or in fact, of the particular tasks assigned to them [the undertaking]' (Treaty of Rome, Commission of the European Communities, 1993c: 197). Exemptions from competition rules for public services are first, finding a 'service of general economic interest' (ibid.), granted to a PTO that constitutes those particular tasks, and secondly, proving that application of competition rules would obstruct the actual performance of the particular assigned tasks.[22]

BOUNDARIES OF UNIVERSAL SERVICE IN THE INFORMATION SOCIETY

In the social and political environment of the information society, the concept of universal service will take on a higher significance because access to the telecommunications network is the route by which individuals gain entry to new information services that make possible participation in society and economy. The telecommunications infrastructure is therefore important not merely for access to basic voice telephony but as the gateway to the information, knowledge, data, and cultural forms in video, text, voice, and data essential to the terms and conditions of social, cultural, and political life. Access and availability of these enhanced service—not merely a voice connection—in homes, communities, and public institutions such as schools, libraries, and government agencies, will become the grounds of differentiation between social groups and geographic and economic sectors, thus restructuring the hierarchy of dependencies in the organization of the social order. The information society carries the potential for creating new social divisions, slowing down or undermining political progress and citizenship. These divisions may arise not just within nations but between nations. For this reason, it is a critical task to examine the emerging approach to universal service in information-society policies.

While the origins of universal service in modern communications history can be associated with the strategic interests of the nation state for consolidating power in national security, territorial governance, and domination of a critical sector of social control (see argument in Garnham, 1997), it is also the case that a nationalistic model of the public sphere has developed alongside a public-service democratic

---

[22] In the terminal equipment directive, the possibility of exception granted in Article 90(2) was dismissed by the Commission with the statement that the necessary conditions for exception did not exist and that removal of special and exclusive rights would not block the performance of tasks of general economic interest (see terminal equipment directive, Commission of the European Communities, 1988a: recital 11).

model whereby access to communications and plurality of information sources to serve the public-opinion-formation process, education, and culture has evolved as part of the fundamental development of the meaning of citizenship in a modern democratic polity (see discussion of this model in Chapter 6).

In the early phase of information liberalization in the EU, the 'particular tasks' of a 'service of general economic interest' for voice telephony were defined in the services directive to consist of 'the provision and exploitation of a universal network, i.e. one having general geographical coverage, and being provided to any service provider or user upon request within a reasonable period of time' (services directive, Commission of the European Communities, 1990a: recital 18). The particular task of voice telephony was thus equated with the non-commercial, political obligation of 'universal service' which has deep historical roots in all modes of political society, and hence in the communications environment of each member state. Ensuring the continuity of universal service throughout the Community was not a matter of debate. In terms of the Commission's policy and political challenge, it was not only that the Community could not liberalize voice telephony without eliminating universal service, but the fact that it was forced to make a political concession on universal service in order to ensure that member states would adopt the services directive. Yet, the directive itself does not actually offer the legal guarantee of voice telephony as a universal service, even though this is the type of concession individuals and states within the Community initially believed had been set aside from marketplace forces (Bauby and Boual, 1994; Caby and Steinfield, 1994; Mansell, 1993; Darnton and Wuersch, 1992; Kohnstamm, 1990).

What precisely happens to universal service under EU law? Under definitions in Article 1 of the services directive, the information network comprises the particular tasks of a service of general economic interest, and thus includes the entirety of the 'public communications infrastructure which permits the conveyance of signals between two defined network termination points by wire, by microwave, by optical means or by other electromagnetic means' (services directive, Commission of the European Communities, 1990a: Article 1). In other words, the 'general economic interest', which defines the limits of universal service, applies to the infrastructure, that is, to the physical network, but not to the services provided over it, not even to the service of voice telephony provided over the public communications network. Thus universal service is limited to the universal network and no more, in effect making the actual condition of universal service an impossibility or an incoherent idea.

Subsequent development of Community policy in relation to universal service attempts to wrestle with and re-rationalize these inimical tendencies in the services directive whereby voice telephony is granted as a universal service of the public operator but implicitly prohibited because the boundaries of universal service in the information society are defined by the physical network and not by any services over that network. But instead of remedying the untenable reasoning, the Commission attempts to fix the substantive contradiction into wider application for a future multimedia information society.

The directive on open network provision (ONP directive, Commission of the European Communities, 1990c), for instance, emphasizes that universal service obligations must be developed in line with basic principles of competition rules, in particular non-discriminatory access and transparency of cost-based tariffs, and be fully compatible with Community law (ibid., Article 3). In line with economic regularization tenets of the Treaty, the ONP directive's approach to universal service is essentially geared to eliminating trade barriers and harmonizing competition law in order to create standardized legal and regulatory conditions for transnational market participants. It strengthens protection of corporate-services providers and users gearing to compete over access to the network, rather than the interests of individuals and social groups to gain minimum terms of access, quality, and affordability in information services—not simply the physical network. The ONP directive subordinates, therefore, information rights to competition rights in its conceptualization of the problem of universal service and in so doing further channels the universal-service implausibility of the services directive. Such a reasoning path appears to employ the universal-service issue as a device to ensure political support for the dramatic shift of power from the public to the private sector.

These elements are fashioned by the Commission into a framework for developing universal service for the digital age (see communication of the Commission on developing universal service in a competitive environment, Commission of the European Communities, 1993g), then adopted in the Green Paper on information infrastructure (infrastructure green paper, Commission of the European Communities, 1994b: part 1 and 1995a: part 2). The two elements exist in an implausible relation to each other and the goal of EU policy is to develop an exposition and rationalization of that relation. The contradictory elements are first, the principal objective of information-society policy in the EU is to privatize all communications services, including basic minimum services such as voice telephony, and secondly, this sweeping liberalization in the EU can be accomplished 'whilst maintaining universal service' (Commission of the European Communities, 1993g: 5).

The European Court of Justice has supported these contradictory goals in its ruling (*Corbeau* v. *Régie des Postes*, 1993) that the grant of exclusive rights over information services, regardless of category, for public-service entities is not justified (thus supporting sweeping liberalization), except where necessary to ensure the performance of a task of 'general economic interest' such as maintenance of the physical network (thus enclosing universal service within the boundary of the engineered hardware and excluding from the principle the domain of information content). The Court does not explain how universal service for communication could have a rational meaning if the category of information itself was removed from consideration.

The Commission goes further in securing limits on the meaning of universal service by prohibiting member states from placing any non-commercial, public-interest obligations on communication industries, public or private, if such obligations lead to the creation of barriers to market entry (Commission of the European Communities, 1993*g*: 6). Since the Commission and the Court reserve the right to define by the terms of the Treaty what constitutes at any given time a 'barrier to market entry', EU policy upholding universal service as 'making available a defined minimum service of specified quality to all users at an affordable price' (ibid. 4) is assuming more the form of a rhetorical declaration rather than a policy guarantee of this fundamental information right in the information society (see assurances in, for instance, the Bangemann Report, Commission of the European Communities, 1994*a*). Moreover, the untenability of the two elements now implanted in policy, statute, and case law will make it exceedingly difficult later to accommodate, even in moderate terms, the demands of governments, citizens, and social groups, that is, of civil society, for democratic benefit from the information age.

The approach to public policy in the information age revealed in the principal statutes of terminal equipment, telecommunications services, and open network provision, provide one further and significant boundary to the problem of liberalization, public service, and universal service, pertaining to the limitations placed upon future policy or initiatives at the EU or member-state level. Should the purposefully erected cancelling-out mechanism for universal service be resolved at some stage by such means as judicial interpretation or national discretion, these defining statutes of the information revolution appear to have established the scope of permissible arguments on minimum information rights. These pre-emptive limits arise from Article 1 of the services directive (Commission of the European Communities, 1990*a*) which reserves until 1998 only statutory monopoly for voice telephony on highly narrow and specific terms. In fact, voice-telephony services may not be subjected to the universal-service requirement except where

'The commercial provision for the public of the direct transport and switching of speech [is] in real-time between public switched network termination points, enabling any user to use equipment connected to such a network termination point in order to communicate with another termination point' (Commission of the European Communities, 1990*a*: Article 1). Thus the question of determining which voice services carry the universal service obligation is not broad but rather prescribed with exactitude. No doubt, the scope of reserved services, that is, information categories assigned to non-market imperatives for the benefit of civil society without distinction, must be narrowly defined given that they are an exception to the general objective of communication liberalization. Nevertheless, the specific form in which services are defined as reserved until full-scale liberalization, established the meaning and potential of universal service for the information society, as evident in the Commission's proposed legal framework on communication infrastructure for the next century.

On the one hand, the Green Paper on liberalization of telecommunications infrastructure and cable-television networks in two parts (Commission of the European Communities, 1994*b*: part 1, and 1995*a*: part 2) had as its goal the task of balancing the residual public service needs remaining from the public-service mandate which commercial competition cannot address, such as the non-commercial needs of civil society, including education and information exchange, information rights of citizens, and democratic requirements of access to the public realm. On the other hand, the Green Paper demonstrated as its over-riding objective the construction of the information society by the terms and conditions of market processes. The infrastructure Green Paper stresses its responsibility to this end in the recognition 'that full scale network liberalization can only proceed after a satisfactory solution to this problem' (Commission of the European Communities, 1994*b*: 29), and that 'maintenance of universal service is an essential part of the infrastructure liberalization' (ibid. 30). Despite the exploration to provide a basic definition of the approach towards minimum conditions of information without distinction to all in the EU, the formulation of the universal-service problem in preceding statutes discussed here has already both delimited as well as resolved the issue, with little for the infrastructure Green Paper to do but to make the policy explicit.

Following nearly a decade of debate, therefore, universal-service policy is to mean voice telephony in real time only. The EU has experienced a rich debate in recent years over a more social approach to the information society than may be emerging in the USA, as evidenced by assurances of governments, the urgency of technological convergence and digitization articulated by communications industries, and in the

Commission's profession of an information revolution that will socially, culturally, and economically benefit all EU citizens (see the Bangemann Report, Commission of the European Communities, 1994*a*; the White Paper, Commission of the European Communities, 1993*a*; and Council resolution on universal service, Commission of the European Communities, 1993*g*). The appeal to social values scattered through these arguments seems not to have survived in the actual provisions of later policy. The infrastructure green paper guarantees no more for the democratization of information—which intelligent networks and multi-media-interactive contexts supposedly could potentially provide in an unlimited sense—than the same service mandated for universal provision a century ago as well as reserved by EU statute from commercial forces up to 1998 (infrastructure Green Paper, Commission of the European Communities, 1995*a*: section 5: 41–7). While '[T]he Commission reaffirms the fundamental importance of maintaining and developing universal service in the European union, on the basis of a common minimum set of services and infrastructure' (ibid., section 5: 41), the elements of 'minimum service' in the information society advance no further after a century than the 'obligation to provide a basic voice telephony service at an affordable price to all customers' (ibid.), which is but a nineteenth-century promise, though of considerable magnitude at the time.

However, even the concept of obligation is reduced to conform with the assurances offered to private operators and providers for a fully market-driven sector and thus to the true spirit of the temporary exemption to voice services granted under the services directive (Commission of the European Communities, 1990*a*). Communication competitors, both public and private, will not be 'obliged to provide service to customers whom they would otherwise have insufficient economic incentive to serve' (Commission of the European Communities, 1995*a*: section 5: 41); that is, private entities would not be asked to bear the burden for information services to uneconomic market sectors offering diminished rates of return. Rather, market players would be free to operate by profitability determinants and commercial rivalry, and thus the guarantee of basic voice telephony to all should be financed through 'other mechanisms . . . while ensuring compliance with competition rules' (ibid.).

Mechanisms for fulfilling constitutive commitment to citizens' participatory rights so that common consensus may arise on matters affecting political society and thus legitimacy be gained, is defined in the infrastructure Green Paper as 'targeted schemes for needy citizens and uneconomic customers instead of favouring general subsidies for [universal] access' (ibid. 82). While the precise form of the mechanism continues to evolve as the structures of information society are laid in place, once more the scope of options has already been decided in the preceding statutes and related initiatives. One option considered is to establish a fund for universal service to which operators who originate or terminate calls on the public switched network would contribute (Commission of the European Communities, 1990a: 84). The 'common fund' approach to universal service frees the communications industries from all non-commercial obligations, such as equality and adequacy of minimum service, and affordable tariffs, in order that they be governed solely by rivalry over the market share of high-end, more profitable users and thus gain incentives for technical innovation. A similar solution to the universal service dilemma of liberal democratic states is proposed in the US Congress (1995a: draft legislation for a tele-communications act of 1995, US Senate Committee on Commerce, Science, and Transportation).

Nevertheless, even if member states deem it necessary as part of their national information-infrastructure initiative to organize one or other universal service financing scheme, the Commission will retain the power to intervene to determine what, if anything, the scheme can cover (see Commission of the European Communities, 1997a; 1996a). National initiatives must be non-discriminatory, transparent, and objective even though it may be impossible to meet these standards since universal service is, by virtue of its basis in non-commercial democratic objectives and values of justice and social solidarity, necessarily interventionist. Thus the discourse of universal service as unfolding in the EU, as with that in the USA, eventually points to the progressive decline and delegitimization of effective universal service in information policy. Martin Bangemann, Commissioner spearheading the EU's approach to the information society in the European Commission, has made clear the minimalist concept that must apply in universal service:

There is no new definition of the universal service, we do not want to deal with that again. We stand by the voice telephone definition. It is the only telephone link which can also provide fax and Internet connections . . . That is the universal service, that is the official definition. We have not scheduled any obligation for Member States to finance the universal service in a particular way (Commission of the European Communities, 1996b).

A market-choice mode of public space (described in Chapter 2), evident in this political solution to policies of the information society, carries some significant implications.

1. Reflecting utilitarian liberalism's view that the essence of freedom is proprietary rights (see discussion of Locke (1960) in Chapter 2), the information revolution's approach to the good society is primarily

directed at strengthening rights of proprietorship and contractual freedoms in the multimedia age. Since contractual rights are essentially economic, the first principle governing state responsibility for development of the digital network is to guarantee more and more of an unconditional environment for the practice of contractual freedoms and proprietary struggles.

2. The underlying system of political thought revived as a global model for all societies in the post-Cold War period (critiqued by Bauman, 1991; Held, 1991; Wallerstein, 1989; and upheld by Lipset, 1994; Sakamoto, 1991; Fukuyama, 1989), holds that the public interest is best served when society, through the actions of the state, gives preference to the maximum extent under given circumstances, to the proprietary interests of the communications industries. Such action comprises the 'public interest', since the perspective assumes that all of society would benefit by wealth which flows from accumulation processes pursued by proprietors. Thus supply-side economics is a fundamental political and ethical tenet of the market-choice theory of public space, constituted by an unquestioned assumption which is not open to rational debate. Its approach to universal service reveals both the consistency of utilitarian liberalism's application of this assumption as well as the core tension which prevails in the problem of compatibility between the central (not peripheral) concerns of liberal, as against democratic, thought over the terms of social and political participation.

3. As universal service—which is a democratic concern—suggests a non-economic burden and as such an intrusion on commercial freedom, some method must be found, in the interest of political legitimation, for the state and communication proprietors to claim that universal service has been addressed without, in fact, addressing it all, so as not to constrain contractual rights.

4. The method logically suggested to achieve this result is not new but old and well developed in this century to force transient accommodation between liberalism's promise of contractual rights, on the one hand, and democracy's promise of public freedoms and political participatory rights, on the other. It is the only form of accommodation, the single idea to balance accumulation-legitimation needs, that utilitarian liberalism has evolved and cast up and to which there is provided no fresh alternative in the construction of the information society. This form is welfare economics or the welfare state which seeks to leave market processes largely unconstrained while the state subsidizes the actual cost of labour. It also allows a market-centred political order to claim a degree of humaneness through institutionalized state structures of paternalism and charity (Dahrendorf, 1994; Marshall, 1950).

Mechanisms for a universal service proposed in the EU, effectively releasing the communications industry from the political requirement of participatory structures of access and information provision, treats public-interest regulation in information-society policy as welfare economics. In place of public action to guarantee conditions of common consensus and public freedoms for all, the market-choice approach to universal service regards public policy as the agency of contractual-rights escalation at all levels while shielding this process through paternal upkeep of the dispossessed or of the most uneconomic social zones. Apart from devaluing the information rights of citizens from a political category down to a philanthropic category, the paternalistic solution transforms political problems of democratic deficit, which enlargement of information could address, into problems of social welfare in order that the hundred-year condition of universal-voice connection is maintained against the disequilibriums inevitably produced by competition among information providers and distributors over global market share. In casting the political need for expanded universal public freedoms into an issue of social benevolence, this approach to universal service does little to address the political rights—not just social-welfare rights—of citizens and the democratization of public space assumed in the concept of an information 'revolution'.

The final significance of the EU's approach to the problem of universal access to the public realm lies in the political implications inherent in the legal foundation of contractual rights. Since a more detailed exposition of this issue is taken up in Chapter 5, it is only necessary here to touch on the main theme. In so far as contractual rights define the boundaries of private law, the legal tradition within which they would be most privileged is common as opposed to civil law. This is because common law recognizes all law as private, that is, as relations between private parties. This study argues that as private relations are essentially of a contractual nature, the purpose of law, under the common-law tradition, is to regulate market forces with respect to property. Under civil law, however, contractual rights are less privileged since private law is but one, often secondary, classification of law which includes others not focused on questions of property relations (see Chapter 5). Thus common law may be regarded as largely contractual law based on existing structures of property and not on the question of the correctness or relevance of that structure for the common interest of civil society.

Once more, this is consistent with Locke's moral and political foundation for common law under utilitarian liberalism, since 'Government has no other end but the preservation of Property' (Locke, 1960: Second Treatise, ch. 7, par. 94: 373). The question of property precedes political society, that is to say, it is a pre-political, common-law reality, for the fundamental reason given for persons to enter the social contract and place 'themselves under Government, *is the Preservation of their Property*' (Locke, 1960: Second Treatise, ch. 9, par. 124: 395, emphasis in the original). It is for this reason, as argued in Chapter 2, that the market-choice theory of public space to which this political foundation gives rise sees contractual/property rights as the first principle of freedom. But it is also the reason that common law, the legal tradition embodying this theory, cannot alter proprietary structures already in place since they exist in the state of nature and are not governed by constitutional or political ends. Hence, contractual freedoms are not subservient to the public interest of political society.

The regulation of universal service as a project within welfare economics takes this path under the market-choice theory because existing proprietary structures take precedence over any other vision of public interest in the liberal democratic state. However, the political and social consequences of such a policy result in the deepening of prevailing structures and the powerlessness of government and civil society later to alter the system of arrangements or even to pose the question of their appropriateness on any grounds of common welfare other than proprietary grounds.

RATIONALIZATION OF STATE POWER IN THE INFORMATION SOCIETY

Clearly, the political thought of information liberalization, as this chapter has attempted to demonstrate in an exposition of policies, is to bind the public sphere to the civil society vision of Locke, Hobbes, and Smith—the logic and premises of which are elaborated in Chapter 2. The analysis here has also tried to argue that apart from its inherent incapacity to account for political democratization and public freedoms (see Chapter 2), the Anglo-Saxon conception of civil society is made even further problematic from major inconsistencies between the form of its institutionalization in public communications and the central elements of its own vision. Liberalization has challenged through public policy the organization of democracies by a root philosophical criterion of minimum state–maximum liberty of proprietary rights. Yet as argued more extensively later (see Chapter 7), the concrete provisions of information liberalization evident in these policies do not actually shrink the power of the state to intervene in economy and society; rather, they act to redirect state intervention, thereby channelling the power of government towards strictly proprietary imperatives and away from the non-commercial, political imperatives of civil society. How these irreconcilable directions are assimilated and explained in the debate over policies of the information age is also relevant. Drawn from extensive interviews, this section provides the voices of policy-makers speaking to the significance of reconstituting the public-communications industries of Europe in line with the assumptions, values, and interests of the liberalization model.

Two parts to 'intervention' have emerged from examination of the Commission's policies with respect to the reorganization of public space. First, the use of Article 90[23] of the Treaty to eradicate public service based on non-commercial criteria such as universal access, and an erection in the information sector of commercial structures and services based on proprietary-rights criteria. Article 90, in fact, has become a powerful constitutional tool to shape the information society in Europe since it now provides new power to the state sector to bring about change in the social and political basis of the public sphere. One has only to examine the large body of subsequent statutes and regulation flowing from the discovery of Article 90 in these early initiatives, to grasp the force of a state-directed information society and its impact on the evolving social order (see example in Commission of the European Communities, 1997). The other aspect of the increasing interventionist power exploited in the Treaty to shape the information society on proprietary grounds is the rationale of promoting competition policy derived from Articles 85 and 86[24] to promote particular market structures in cross-media consolidation and rivalry over the communications marketplace.

An adviser to Commissioner Martin Bangemann in charge of telecommunications, elaborates the parameters of the first type of intervention:

The Commission's role [in the information society] is to shape the regulatory regime so member states are more willing to abrogate their sovereignty to the EU in the telecoms sector. We must send a strong political message to heads of states [through the 'Bangemann Report'] that liberalization is absolutely crucial. True, it will be here in 1998 [to end public service in all communications services, including basic areas such as voice telephony]. But this is too late. We must move faster [with de-monopolization of public-service entities] to ensure interoperability of networks. To prepare for 1998, governments must free operators from social responsibility such as universal service and other social responsibilities. Tariffs should not need to pass a test of affordability but rather a test of being cost-based. The Commission has got to push organizational restructuring of telecoms operators to prepare for privatization.[25]

---

[23] Commission of the European Communities, 1988*a*: recital 11.
[24] Cited in Appendix.
[25] From interviews with Dr Detlef Eckert, adviser to Commissioner Martin Bangemann, DGXIII, Commission of the European Communities, Brussels, 19 April and 11 May 1994.

Despite the growing marginalization of social responsibility in communications policy, the question of universal service remains central to the legitimacy of public space in a democratic social order, even if it exists only rhetorically. Again, policy-makers suggest in their own words how the issue is likely to be approached in policies of the information society:

Of course, universal service still remains a key issue. But should it be extended beyond voice telephony? The answer is no. I don't see a universal obligation in the pay-per-services. So most if not all video services on the broadband network will be definitely determined by economic ability to pay. Private sector can provide the minimum universal service of voice telephony. The old assumption that private sector cannot provide universal service to all is wrong. There's no need for regulation because market will solve 90 per cent of universal-service needs. Competition is the solution to this problem. We are suffering from less competition and not too much. We [the Commission] disagree with the French [public service] view that universal service must be enforced by policy and law. The minimum standard for all should be determined by the market.[26]

Precisely this perspective emerges, as discussed earlier, in concrete action taken by the Commission in the infrastructure Green Paper (Commission of the European Communities, 1995a, 1994b). EU infrastructure policy holds that universal service in the information society should comprise no more than a minimum provision of voice telephony, thus effectively excluding all advanced information services from the broad access which the revolution has held forth to citizens of democratic states (Commission of the European Communities, 1997, 1996a, 1996b). As pointed out, access to such a level of defined minimum service advances the participatory potential of the public sphere no further than the level acknowledged in telecoms policy at the end of the last century. The challenge to public policy will be how to achieve democratic legitimacy for the view that universal-service goals beyond a minimum service of voice-telephone access will be met by the 'natural tendency of providers to search for mass markets',[27] that is, by the natural and autonomous processes of the invisible hand.

Thus the political aim of the first type of intervention, the removal of the civil state from guaranteeing democratic conditions of public space and from proprietary safeguarding of communications structures as a public trust has been compressed by liberalization into one powerful market-centred argument. 'The message is deregulate. You cannot stop human progress. If the Catholic church couldn't stop Galileo, then governments won't be able to stop things now' (Carlo De Benedetti, chief executive of Olivetti, the Italian computer maker, quoted in the

---

[26] Ibid.
[27] From an interview with Herbert Ungerer, head of regulatory division, DGXIII, Commission of the European Communities, Brussels, 3 May 1994.

Financial Times, 26 February 1995: 1). The premise of 'progress' here summons, of course, the technical-necessity reasoning that information-society policies are restructuring the role of the state and its relation to the social order in a positive manner.

Here arises the significance of the second type of intervention. In shifting capital into what proprietary interests regard as an 'innovation sector', that is to say, a sector where the rate of return on capital investment is higher than elsewhere in the market economy (Noam, 1995*a*, 1994), the use of the normative authority of competition arguments has been essential in transforming the non-commercial functions of public communications into commercial functions. To this end, Herbert Ungerer,[28] one of the principal architects of the 1987 Green Paper (Commission of the European Communities, 1987) that launched the liberalization movement in the EU, identifies the logical sequence of policy aims: 'So we lift all restrictions, create possibility of cross-structuring [cross-media ownership consolidation], and in the end we concern ourselves with competition or anti-trust.' Of these, the second is the most significant: 'Infrastructure by itself is not important [as a policy concern]—it's cross-ownership that's more important'.[29]

As evident in the rationalization, from the point of view of the proprietary aims of the international communications industries, the reasoning of liberalization and its effects are politically useful in coaxing market-opening changes in societies where the liberal model is not dominant. This merely underlines the intrinsic bias and paradox of competition policy evolving in the information-society debate: 'The AT&T divestiture experience of the US is an approach of the past—the old way of doing things. Concern with divestiture and antitrust is an outdated approach to telecoms regulation'.[30]

Also confirmed on close examination is the extent to which such policies favour by design the forces of convergence, consolidation, and cross-media ownership interests of global competitors as they seek to integrate the major content sectors—audiovisual, databases, computer software, and so on—with information infrastructure and information technology sectors.

Commission policies restructuring European networks are not the end of the story. In ten years, we won't have eighteen major European network operators competing with major global long-distance operators. The market niche for each will become too narrow. The result of Commission liberalization policies will be an inevitable process of mergers, buyouts of each other, and so on. A

[28] From an interview with Herbert Ungerer, head of regulatory division, DGXIII, Commission of the European Communities, Brussels, 3 May 1994.
[29] Ibid.
[30] Ibid.

major industrial battle is brewing among European network operators and service.[31]

Thus the approach to the role of the limited state is constituted not by policies of withdrawal but by redefinition of whom state intervention should serve:

Major role of intervention is to remove barriers. Decentralization is irreversible. But the information highway takes a common vision of the future. In order to have a common vision, you have to have Commission policies. They will help the market to benefit from technological research and turn them into assets through alliances on a global scale. We [the Commission] must move this process along.[32]

The discourse of policy-makers demonstrates that in the new information policy environment, the real struggle is undoubtedly for control over the network itself; but it is even more a rivalry among giant global conglomerates for dominance over the entire multimedia content/technology range in telephony, satellite, broadcasting, cable, computing, software, text, video, and data industries within single-capital structures. Effective support in public policy for such dramatic vertical integration of capital for dominance in the information society abolishes most antitrust limits on proprietary ownership with respect to forms of convergence in capital, information sectors, and technologies. In essence, the civil state is caught up in an intense conflict among proprietary interests, not over regulation of competitive market entry, but over the precise terms of oligopolistic freedoms in the shaping of public space.

CONCLUSION

This chapter has examined the European origins of liberalization in the public space of the information age. Policies harmonizing regulation of the information infrastructure were assessed in terms of key instruments redefining state intervention for shaping the public realm by liberalization, de-monopolization, and universal service. A radical transformation seems evident in the Community's regulatory approach towards the information infrastructure driven by policy arguments of technological necessity and unshackled competition rationalized by claims to normative standards of liberal utilitarianism and its market-choice theory of public space.

[31] Interview with Peter Johnston, RACE Programme, DGXIII, Commission of the European Communities, Brussels, 24 March 1994.
[32] From an interview with Spyros Konidaris, ACT Programme, DGXIII, Commission of the European Communities, Brussels, 25 March 1994.

It should be evident from these trends that, in contrast to the enhanced freedom of consumer choice the information society is supposed to bring about, the multimedia digital age is far from being designed to function as a demand-led environment. Rather, as is consistent with the political conceptions of Locke and Smith, it is proprietary-oriented towards large-scale capital concentration and thus very distinctly supply-led. The orientation in granting liberty to the private sector for unlimited economies of scale seriously contradicts the terms and arguments of liberalization's own theory, namely, that it was supposed to deliver a competitive commercial structure rather than a monopolistic one.

The problem of public communications has been addressed here from the standpoint of infrastructure policy. The next two chapters will examine the path taken in information-society policies for ownership and regulation of content, as with intellectual property rights and audiovisual policy. As recognized to some extent by both industry and policy-makers[33] and as argued in the following chapter, the resolution of conflict between proprietary rights and citizens' rights to content production and distribution will determine the real potential of the information age, both for economic growth as well as for the fate of political community.

---

[33] Cited at note 16 above.

5

Redefinition of Intellectual Property:
The Control of Content

Introduction

At a G7 (group of seven wealthiest industrialized nations) ministerial conference on the information superhighway, the president of the European Commission articulated the principal rationale for the liberalization of public space. In his concluding address he noted: 'What we are aiming at is to construct a truly shared vision of human enrichment . . . For the benefits to be fully realized, competitive conditions will have to be fair and markets more open' (Chair's conclusions, G7 Ministerial conference on the information society, 25–6 February 1995, Brussels, Commission of the European Communities, 1995b).

The emergence of liberalization, and its political uses of competition, as a collective movement on a world scale, invoking a vision of unprecedented transfer of knowledge through modern communication networks to individuals worldwide, can be traced, as argued earlier (see Chapter 2), to the ideological revival of Locke's late-seventeenth century theory of limited government and to its paradoxical justification of a form of political authority based on proprietary—in place of divine or democratic—power. Locke's (1960) defence of the liberal social order, constituted in the contractual socio-economic relations of a market society, has been so successfully reconstructed by the liberalization movement of the post-Cold War period (see critique of globalization in Bauman, 1991; Held, 1991; Meehan, 1993; Bauby and Boual, 1994), that in terms of depth and degree of influence, 'liberalization' may be regarded as one of the major social movements of the modern age. The others, as Wuthnow (1989) has documented in his study of ascendant ideological structures and the social basis of their transformative power, are the Reformation, the Enlightenment, and European socialism.

Like other powerful social movements and ideologies of the modern age, the process of liberalization poses a different principle of social organization, or another way of putting individuals, societies, and nations into relations with one another. This restructuring inevitably involves a redistribution of dependencies and hierarchies, or a reconstruction by different means (apart from war, colonial invasion, or strategic sabotage) of social, political, and economic power. The means in this case, as relevant to the historical logic of liberalization, is preeminently information—a monopoly over its technologies, content, networks, and cultural forms.

Apparent in the dramatic redistribution of power from the public to the private sector is one significant feature of information-infrastructure liberalization: it appears to be brought about, enforced, and extended by the instruments of state action, that is, by public policy. The arguments of liberalization are at once revolutionary in the context of the prevailing and alternative theories of democratic organization that have evolved in the last two centuries, but the paradigm is also rendered ideological by a set of anachronistic post-feudal assumptions of economy and society originating in the thought of Locke and Smith. These assumptions effectively defuse the subversive implications of participatory citizenship inherent in the idea of a public sphere accessible to all social groups and comprised of a substantive diversity of content in ideas, expressive forms, opinion, information, and representations of social reality. Liberalization of communication serves the liberal theory of market choice and contractual liberty so well because it is fully as much a defence against content which enables participatory public freedom (see framework outlined in Chapter 3) as it is an attack on a public-space model that promotes cultural–nationalist xenophobia and totalitarian control (see discussion of public space as cultural community in Chapter 2).

Thus it is in the policy and legal approach to content or expression—its ownership, production, distribution, and regulation—that the information liberalization movement can best be apprehended as a theory of property rather than a revolution to 'enhance democratic principles and limit the spread of totalitarian forms of government' (US Government, 1995a: 6–7), or to 'add huge new capacities to human intelligence and . . . build a more equal and balanced society' (Commission of the European Communities, 1994a: 7–8).

The aim in this and following chapters is to examine the liberalization of content as revealed in information policies for intellectual property rights (IPR), audiovisual policy, and information rights that together comprise the core of the construction of the information society. The socio-legal analysis of information-infrastructure policy in the preceding chapter moves here to content and will attempt to demonstrate the policy mechanisms whereby content liberalization sweeps away constraints on proprietary accumulation by altering notions of competition in a way that would inhibit rather than stimulate the diversity of ideas, expressive forms, opinion, and representations of social reality in a multimedia digital environment.

The political analysis of copyright provided here treats the content regulation mechanism of IPR law as a struggle between distinct socio-legal concepts of intellectual property in order to redefine information policy and to reconfigure the state's obligation in balancing the interests of creators, exploiters, and the public for enlargement of the public domain. These opposed concepts of proprietorship over intellectual property in the intelligent network domain reflect differing theories of political constitution, citizens rights, authorial rights, ownership, and contractual relations. Obstacles to a balanced political development of IPR are assessed in terms of privatization of law, the state, and public goods. Thereafter, the political or constitutional rights of creators and citizens as against the economic interests of large-scale rights holders are addressed in an examination of the approach to each model of IPR emerging in the design of the information society. Discussion will explore the differences concerning economic and constitutional ways of thinking about the role of monopoly of content ownership in the promotion of the diffusion of expression. The ascendancy of corporate rights holders in achieving an IPR regime which gives priority first and foremost to their interests over the interests of all other social sectors in the intellectual property system is addressed here in relation to the struggle to determine the legal foundations of information regulation in the European Union. Attempts to bring the diverse legal foundations of democracies into symmetry in the multilateral regimes are taken up, and this is followed by assessment of the workings of these new forces in the liberalization of European copyright law.

Intellectual Property and the Nature of Content

The political and social meaning of intellectual property can be regarded as a relation between the structure of IPR and the structure of content, or rather, the relation between property rights and speech rights. It may be argued that the diversity and nature of expression is contingent upon the socio-legal model of IPR which prevails in society, while the approach to IPR can be said to determine precisely which mode of expression dominates the public realm. Hence, achieving information diffusion by means of legal mechanisms for claiming property rights over expression would constitute the cultural policy of the state because the approach to intellectual property, and the groups which benefit in any given construction, play a decisive role not only in who benefits economically from the exploitation of content, but in determining which cultural forms shall be produced and distributed at any given time. For this reason, among the most significant illustrations of content liberalization as a theory of property and as a cultural policy determining who has power over expression in the public domain is the political conflict over intellectual property rights.

IPR laws for the information superhighway cover rights of ownership in information content ranging from film and video to satellite/cable retransmission, computer software, and digitized databases, but their implications for the organization of political society far exceed the juridical domain. It is a policy arena that, if properly understood, seriously contradicts Lockean theory on its central claim as a theory of democracy. While intellectual-property issues have assumed considerable importance in the information-society debate, a large portion of the discourse (see Wilkinson, 1994; Kurlantzick, 1994; *International Media Law*, 1994; Ehrlich, 1994; Moebes, 1993) appears oriented towards legal summaries, technical exposition of statutes and case law, and a focus on procedural issues in law and policy-making which render it difficult to raise questions regarding the validity of structures of power, authority, and benefit under existing arrangements. To understand the socio-legal significance of intellectual property rights in shaping and naturalizing the information age, it becomes necessary to explore unexamined premises in its diverse conceptual foundations concerning production and diffusion of expression.

Examination of multilateral treaties, national laws, and EU legal instruments[1] shows that current intellectual-property debates in the West draw on several IPR models and concepts, containing in their separate frameworks and objectives some crucial distinctions and aims. These set forth the fundamental terms of the international debate over proprietary development of public space: namely, the debate over laws privileging the contractual-economic rights of large-scale content rights holders, or the constitutional–political rights of citizens and the general public, or finally, the rights of individual creators. Bias towards any of these three sets of interests in a transnational or international IPR regime, or the particular form in which they are balanced, defines the political, cultural, and economic structure of expression itself. This is especially relevant to the multimedia intelligent network domain of the information society in which technologies of storage, distribution, and reproduction of information are not necessarily limited by geography or national regulations, thus creating pressure on national IPR traditions to favour the contractual interests of corporate rights holders in ever-extending rights to monopoly over expression.

Public policy in the European Union is caught between fundamentally

---

[1] Analysis of intellectual property is based, among other documents, on a scrutiny of the Berne Convention (1971), the Rome Convention (1961), the US Constitution, the French Declaration of the Rights of Man, the European Convention for Human Rights (1950), and a collection of constitutional and legal instruments of the European Union referred to specifically in the text all through this section.

opposed sets of reasoning in many areas of information policy as demonstrated in the analysis of infrastructure liberalization (Chapter 4). But in the area of intellectual property, the nature and resolution of the policy conflict has profound implications (see Koopmans, 1991) for the potential of ideas and expression in the public sphere and therefore can be said to play a central role in determining the evolving structure of political community.

UNDERSTANDING INTELLECTUAL PROPERTY: THE EXTENSIONS OF EXPLOITATION

The bias towards large-scale proprietary interests and supply-side provisions is rooted in the deep structures of liberal assumptions and thought, and informs the development of information policies on content ownership. Rationalized in the *Second Treatise of Government* (Locke, 1960), liberalism's theory of property, assumes, or it might be said, conjectures, that the property-holdings of private parties are equal (ibid., ch. 7, sections 94 and 111: 373 and 387); except, however, when the right to proprietary enlargement through participation in society or the market can be facilitated by the state or by public policy. The transformation into exchange value of all property through the invention of money, Locke argues, makes possible the expansion of private interests through expansion of property: 'Find out something that hath the Use and Value of Money, amongst his Neighbours, you shall see the same Man will begin presently to enlarge his Possessions' (ibid., ch. 5, section 49: 343). Within the political foundations of utilitarian liberalism, the consent to monetarization of property and its expansion under contractual arrangements implies, therefore, the development of social and economic inequality and the emergence of two classes in the state of nature: those who accumulate material possessions of land, capital, and other forms of valorization of goods and services, who buy or contract to possess the labour of others; and those who own only their person and their labour and who sell or contract to relinquish the latter. Such enlargement of property through monetarization of increasing domains of human life is not, according to Locke, a transgression of the state of nature:

[i]t is plain, that Men have agreed to disproportionate and unequal Possession of the Earth, they having by a tacit and voluntary consent found out a way, how a man may fairly possess more land than he himself can use the product of . . . . This partage of things, in an inequality of private possessions, men have made practicable out of the bounds of Societie, and without compact, only by putting a value on gold and silver and tacitly agreeing in the use of Money. For in

Governments the Laws regulate the right of property. (Ibid., ch. 5, section 50: 344)

It can be said, then, that the prejudice towards private or contractual law emerging in information policies assumes that consent has been given to commoditization of creative labour because all individuals may eventually benefit from this development. The state of nature that the proper form of civil society ordains and institutionalizes implies general consent to supply-side public policies. Although proprietary arrangements, by means of contractual processes in the market, are very unequally distributed, it is supposed that great wealth can be generated and the poorest day-labourer in a liberal market is better off than a chieftain among primordial social units (such as American Indians) where enlargement of property through commoditization was originally unavailable to property-holders (ibid., ch. 5, section 41: 338–9). Given the social relationships of the market economy, only one legitimate socio-legal system and mode of the state is suggested: a contractually centred, proprietary-directed civil state. The rationale for entering civil society is derived directly from the market and its private-law legal order that ensures the protection and expansion of property. It is a socio-legal order which thus gives further justification to, and is expressly designed to preserve, the social inequalities of the market economy.

The relation between exploitation of content and proprietary enlargement sums up the political conflict confronting liberalization among opposed approaches to content property rights in the information society. Under information liberalization, intellectual property rights comprise the predominant growth domain in exchange-value transformation and thus form the foundation of proprietary expansion in an information economy. This is recognized and argued explicitly in the design of an IPR regime for the information society (Commission of the European Communities, 1996d, 1995c; World Intellectual Property Organization, 1996; US Government, 1995b).

The real challenge to the supply-side economic-incentives model of copyright is often thought to come from nations outside the West with totalitarian state authority where individuals enjoy no formal, constitutional guarantees of political and civil rights, even if they do enjoy certain economic and social rights. Yet apart from recourse to a national-sovereignty argument, these states cannot appeal to some independent basis of democratic legitimacy in global trade negotiations in defending their legal order or any distinctive national tradition of intellectual property rights. The real challenge to the international IPR regime is from within the system of democratic and constitutional values that are being undermined, even abrogated, by the policies of the information society.

The US–China intellectual property rights dispute illustrates the case (see *Financial Times*, 13 February 1995: 15). Since the level of political rights in China is lower than in the USA, the disparity allows for a discursive construction whereby what is essentially a property issue concerning the interests of corporate creations, large-scale rights holders and exploiters, is transformed into a class of moral issues threatening the moral dignity of authors and creators in the Western tradition (see discussion below of this second approach). China's admission to the multilateral trading system is made contingent on a profound moral necessity of permitting, not freedom of political action for its citizens, but freedom of rights of proprietary expansion in information products for multinational entities (see discussion in Boyle, 1996).

Rather, the substantive challenge to liberalization's defence of an economic-incentives IPR model arises from competing approaches in the West itself that recognize higher levels of political and information rights for individual creators and the public—in addition to the information right of free speech—than the contractual–proprietary framework growing in significance under supply-side information policies affirmed by case law and state activism. Examination of the problem of intellectual property rights in the European Union reveals that any standard of IPR which departs from the economic-incentives approach favouring corporate content monopolies is a more serious obstruction to the validity of proprietary expansion in the global economy than the complete absence of individual rights in non-liberal regimes such as China. This is because political rights that are more extensive and constitutionally protected under a human-rights or public-access IPR model, confer upon human citizens (as against legal entities) inalienable and exclusive rights of participation, information, and the right of ownership to one's creative labour, and thus form barriers or hurdles to proprietary expansion. It is this distinction between the constitutional–political foundations of IPR that discriminate in favour of political or human rights and those of supply-side liberalization initiatives which discriminate in favour of contractual rights of the cultural industries, that lies at the heart of the political struggle between separate paradigms of democracy and public space in determining the social basis of the information society.

The outcome of this struggle for expansion of property-holdings in the domain of ideas and expression is embodied in these separate approaches and, in many respects, will determine the real revolutionary and participatory potential of the information society.

Socio-Legal Concepts of Intellectual Property

The importance of intellectual property rights in the West is rooted in the information revolution of the Enlightenment and in the rapid diffusion of print technology in this period of the eighteenth century (see Eisenstein, 1983). British copyright law, for example, dates to the Statute of Anne enacted in 1709 (republished in Brown, 1978: 851), while in the USA, copyright is grounded in the US Constitution (1787). An examination of these legal traditions makes it apparent that one of the aims of the state in awarding property rights and monopoly rights over ideas and expression is a powerful assumption regarding 'incentives'. The incentives model of copyright is intended to motivate innovators and creators to release the products of their creative labour to the public in exchange for limited monopoly interests. The granting of monopoly rights in expression of ideas and opinion therefore restricts the information marketplace since it creates barriers to the use and exploitation of the creative expression of others. On the one hand, the interest of the democratic state is served by the increased production of knowledge and information which the economic stimulus brings about, while on the other, creators are rewarded for their labour by the grant of monopoly. Yet this comes at a cost since the 'free marketplace of ideas' which is assumed as the natural condition of the minimum liberal state, is transformed by the incentives rationale for IPR into a market-place of exclusive and pre-emptive information monopolies that hinder free flow and open access to the public and to new market entrants. This contradiction between property rights as a precondition to wealth creation in information and ideas in a free market, and unhindered information as a precondition to the functioning of the free market whereby all participants compete equally in a perfect information environment, is among the defining socio-legal ambiguities of political and economic liberalism and modern information policy.

If the tradition of intellectual property has been shaped by concepts of a relation between the level of property rights prevailing at any given time and the level of creative production in society and economy, it has also been shaped by notions of 'authorship', 'originality', and the romantic vision of unique individual spirit or genius (for an early con-tribution to legal thought on authorship and originality, see Fichte, 1793, quoted in Woodmansee, 1984: 445). The debates over copyright in the eighteenth century as provided in the account of the rise of intellectual property in Germany by Woodmansee (ibid.) show a grow-ing linkage between romantic authorship and property rights by virtue of the internalization of an ineffable source of inspiration in the product of creative effort (see discussion also in Boyle, 1996). The eventual legal consequences of this debate are institutionalized in the moral and human rights of creators which are guaranteed by some republican constitutions such as the French and the German constitutional and copyright tradition discussed below.

The third significant socio-legal concept in intellectual property is associated explictly with the public sphere itself, or the 'public domain' as commonly referred to in IPR law. This concept takes into account not the economic incentives for rights holders or the moral and constitutional recognition of the contribution of creators or 'authors', but the continual enrichment of the public domain to allow citizens in a free society access to increasing dimensions of knowledge, information, ideas, and cultural forms. The democratic constitution is served by guaranteeing the public-opinion-formation process a socio-legal foundation which is oriented towards enlarging the content base of the public sphere, while the information rights of citizens irrespective of economic power is reinforced by a second legal basis, the other being the free expression right as a fundamental human right. The best known constitutional formulation in the West for defending and promoting the public domain through the mechanisms of IPR is evident in the US Constitution. Power is given to the state: 'To promote the progress of science and useful arts, by securing for limited times to authors and inventors the exclusive right to their respective writings and discoveries' (US Constitution, 1787: Article 1, Section 8, Clause 8).

This power to intervene in the marketplace of ideas, in society and economy, by granting legal privileges in expression and innovation for a 'limited time' is designed to serve a larger social good in promoting the 'progress of knowledge'. In most democratic countries, such socio-legal notions of limited monopoly rights over information—without which rights holders have an absolute property right—emerge in provisions for 'fair use',[2] in 'public access' or 'public domain' rights (Boyle, 1996; Jaszi, 1996), or in the legal imposition of compulsory licensing. In short, the state is confronted with the difficult challenge of designing an IPR regime in a fine and precarious balance of interests between the incentive model, the author or moral-rights model, and the 'fair use' model to achieve protection for the public domain. Any shift in the balance and bias of the IPR will result in transformation of the public domain, or possibly even its elimination by inversion to a legally induced private domain .

How the information society addresses this challenge is explored by examining, in turn, the place of each of these socio-legal approaches and their relation to one another in the construction of the emerging IPR regime in the information society.

---

[2] See discussion of 'work-for-hire' and 'fair use' doctrines in US copyright law in Branscomb (1994) and Patterson and Lindberg (1991).

Obstacles to a Balanced IPR Regime in the information society

Regardless of a democratic constitution's emphasis on justice, liberty, and the common good, its social development within a liberal civil state which recognizes only pre-political, contractual rights as the basis of the polity has rendered it increasingly difficult in the modern age to achieve a balance between the three IPR models and between constitutional and economic rights. Some of the obstacles to a balanced information policy in intellectual property can be described as follows:

Privatization of Law First, the fundamentalist tendencies in international liberalization tend to subsume constitutional and social relations under private law which, as Bobbio (1989*a*) observes, makes it difficult to address the needs of political society, or *res publica*, as 'a thing of the people' when 'people' means not just an aggregation of individuals but a society held together by common interests. The privatization of law can be defined as the formal sanctioning of a policy system whereby a set of pre-political conventions or norms established among private parties to regulate their reciprocal relations through, for instance, bilateral agreements and contracts, becomes increasingly independent of public regulations arising from common concern. Since public policies in the new liberalization model treat both the social and political question of human experience as a private matter between contracting parties, then only private interests assume legitimacy in the definition of public interests. Thus the social order resembles evermore Locke's state of nature as a state of natural law where private self-interests form relations on the basis of liberty of proprietorship, and the reason for the social contract (Postema, 1989), for consent to polity in the first place, is to formalize these relations through a system for contractual enforcement.

Privatization of the State A second obstacle to a balanced IPR approach is that, since private law appeals, not to the authority of political society and public law, but to the state of nature of private ownership, it legitimizes only institutions of property and contract and undermines the public-interest function of the state. The bonds that unite the state to its citizens are transformed into contractual bonds, and by definition to private and revocable conceptions of the civil state (see discussion of Hegel in Chapter 3). The compression of recognizable claims to a contractual domain translates social and political issues into economic values, and is thus governed largely by market relationships. This, too, is consistent with Lockean–Hobbesian utilitarian and proprietary-based liberalism and its extensions by Smith's justification of liberty through criteria of commercial freedom.

Privatization of Constitutional Law The third social obstacle emanates from the growing subordination of the class of law and policy that is termed constitutional, public, civil, or general interest, to private socio-legal forms. Since contract is the typical form in which individuals govern their relations in the state of nature where a public power does not as yet exist, then constitutional vision, public policy or statute must assume a subordinate role in jurisprudence to pre-existing arrangements and precedence. The production of public law in the general interest assumes a lower order than natural conventions cumulatively codified in case law. This approach to determining public goods or the organization of society must then necessarily adopt a form of reasoning whose premises are always individual circumstances—the peculiarities of a case—rather than principles of common interest. The reasoning of private law (Llewellyn, 1960) seldom accounts for the fundamental social and political implications which may be embedded in particular sets of arrangements, but rather serves to project private interests as universal interests (for an illustration of this device, see its defence in Ehrlich, 1994; Samuelson, 1994; Moebes, 1993; Llewellyn, 1960).

Privatization of Public Goods Finally, a successful, democratic approach to IPR in the information age is impeded by the growing emphasis on procedural approaches to the construction of policy and law in a liberal social order, as against the substantive approaches that are constitutionally based. As a result, it becomes increasingly difficult under radical liberalization of economy and society to question the correctness or justice of the outcomes of public policy, as, for example, in information policies concerning competition, telecommunications, free expression, or intellectual property. The ends and outcomes are no longer the issue; the question rather is whether decisions were arrived at by some directed set of codified procedures (Postema, 1989; Llewellyn, 1960), as may be established by regulatory authorities. While regulatory institutions continue to struggle with reconciling the substantive ends of public-interest policies with the pressures of international liberalization to favour the contractual, proprietary, and procedural transformation of societies, it is not clear whether such national efforts can entirely prevail under international trade law (see discussion in Chapter 7).

Consistent with unacknowledged normative assumptions in the concept of civil society formed in Lockean liberalism, procedural approaches to policy and law may subsume the 'good' under the 'correct rules' but are nevertheless founded upon some fundamental concept of the good. Taylor's (1993) discussion of procedural ethics suggests that procedural approaches to the regulation of society misconceive the specific nature and logic of what is the common good because they assume that the 'correct' can be decided independently of assumptions about the 'good'. Thus the defence of procedural justice, as offered, for instance, by Rawls (1971) and Dworkin (1978), elevates a rule-governed social system, ostensibly in order to preserve freedom for a plurality of the good, yet by so doing institutionalizes one specific form of the public good over all others: namely, the public good that privileges inequalities of a contractually defined and proprietary-governed civil society. In the design of an IPR system, the bias towards proceduralism prevents any rational challenge to the democratic/consti-tutional basis whereby domination of content by monopoly ownership either ought or ought not to be allowed, inevitably causing an inherent bias in information policy towards large-scale rights holders.

ECONOMIC RIGHTS OF EXPLOITERS: THE INCENTIVES DISCOURSE

An effective, functioning IPR regime that retains a rational, democratic balance between the three principal concepts and aims of copyright law is blocked by growing privatization of the public interest under liberalization, yet further consolidated by the policies of the information society. These policies (Commission of the European Communities, 1996d, 1995c; US Government, 1995c; World Intellectual Property Organization, 1996; GATT, 1993) now favour the economic rights of third-party exploiters, who are the corporate entities or content industry which hold the rights to large catalogues of content and are the principal beneficiaries in the exploitation or commercialization of expression. By elevating the incentives model in the IPR triad of aims and directing the incentives towards these entities, the information society has recast the political rights of the public, the moral rights of creators, and the constitutional rights of both, as largely subordinate if not marginal interests. Several mechanisms are employed in this recon-struction, including strengthening the position of corporate entities as parties to the IPR contract in extracting rights from creators, or by extending the term of protection for corporate rights holders which depletes and diminishes the public realm, or by closing provisions for 'fair use' of expression by individuals for private, non-commercial purposes. The former subordinates the interests of creators by failing to recognize their non-economic rights in their own creations, while the latter developments diminish public-access rights and the information basis of civil society in the immediate and long term.

Thus IPR, as the power of the democratic state to intervene in the general interest of enriching the information basis of the polity, gradually turns into, or is deposed by, contract law which can annul this basis. Freedom of expression, public-access rights to serve the opinion-formation process, the constitutional rights of creators, and other communication rights essential to a functioning public realm are reformulated as economic values revocable by contract. This trend then renders it necessary to assign what were intended as political rights to the content proprietors or the communications industry. Since privatized law and public goods cannot under such IPR frameworks make a political distinction between human citizens and artificial or legal entities, the communications rights of the latter become equivalent to the former but without accounting for the economic power differential. The tendency then under current proposals for the information society (Commission of the European Communities, 1996*d*, 1995*c*; US Government, 1995*c*; World Intellectual Property Organization, 1996; GATT, 1993) is for private-communications entities to seek more and more of the free expression, that is, political rights, of individual citizens and to push for reclassification as producers, rather than mere carriers and distributors, of ideas and expressive forms in order that the negative freedom prohibiting government from regulating expression applies as extensively to the industry as to the individual. But since private entities hold a monopoly over production and dissemination of expression, any elevated protection for their human rights as communication rights carries enormous historical and social implications.

The disenfranchisement of political society implied in the IPR regime of the information society (ibid.) exaggerates the already existing limits of information liberalization in addressing the public interest. There may ensue declining rational grounds to argue the common good, the need for participatory structures to ensure the formation of the general will, or for more democratization in the selection of ends or goods the community as a whole must pursue—beyond private contractual processes. Thus the ability of citizens to govern themselves through the participatory structures of the public realm is a problem that becomes inadmissible to the enforcement of economic agreements. The question of a public interest is an absurd and unreasonable one in the emerging IPR regime (see Boyle, 1996; Elkin-Koren, 1996; Hamilton, 1996; Jaszi, 1996; Reichman, 1996*a*), thereby endangering the capacity to sustain processes for the determination of the general interest.

However, the policy agenda of the information society continues to profess broad societal benefit (see Commission of the European Communities, 1995*a*, 1994*a*; US Government, 1995*a*, 1993), even though the actual provisions of recent initiatives (Commission of the European Communities, 1997, 1996*a*; US Congress, 1996*a*) remain confused over identifying the public interest in the areas of universal access, culture, education, and information in the public domain.

Among the effects of the tilt in incentives for the content industry in current IPR is that conditions already prevailing in the unregulated sphere of private-market relations become more binding on political society than rational approaches to ensure by law or public policy the incentives for achieving content diversity and access which may require a demand-side approach grounded in constitutional rights. As argued in discussion of the participatory standard of public space (see Chapter 3), the socio-legal basis of the public sphere lacks legitimacy if it fails to incorporate the rational grounds of public freedom. The issue for the digital revolution from this tilt concerns the ascendancy of industry arguments (see Commission of the European Communities, 1994*e*, 1994*f*, 1993*i*; International Chamber of Commerce, 1992; US Congress, 1993; US Chamber of Commerce, 1995) that without a more favourable property-law climate for monopoly in immense inventories of content—such as software, audiovisual programs, databases, and texts—unconstrained by considerations of creators' rights or public-access rights, the information society may arrive much later, if at all. As a result, the principal goal of copyright is a race to provide the industry with the incentive to bring modern societies the benefits of the information society, while the industry itself will settle for nothing less as the price of its participation. The audiovisual and film industry, for instance, have persuaded governments that extending their relative position in the new IPR regime should form the core of the new incentives vision.

One of the great secrets of the [US] dominance in the world is [its] ability to put into a film enormous resources. The most talented people in the world cost money. . . . Unless we are able to protect what we own in our libraries, we will be unable [to do so] in the future, in the year 2010, and thereabouts, when the new technology has avalanched through this whole landscape, not in this country but around the world, then we are doing a terrible economic injustice to the Treasury of the United States.[3]

This parallels technological determinist views that communications industries should be allowed an unconstrained market environment before the social consequences of their uses and arrangements are taken into account through regulation. As Horwitz (1989) points out in his study of American communications deregulation, the case for liberating technology to work out its forces independent of human will, state action, or the general welfare of civil society has governed US public policy since the Radio Act of 1927,[4] and can be seen in the

---

[3] Testimony of Jack Valenti, Motion Picture Association, at the US Congress Hearings on H.R. 989 Copyright Term Extension Act of 1995 before the Subcommittee on Courts and Intellectual Property, 104th Congress.

[4] Radio Act of 1927, Public Law 632, 69th Congress, 23 February 1927; reprinted in Kahn (1984).

Communications Act of 1934,[5] then through the accumulated decisions of the independent regulatory agency, the Federal Communications Commission, and in recent statutes such as the Telecommunications Act of 1996 (US Congress, 1996*a*). The technological-necessity argument for releasing private-communications proprietors from public obligation now forms the centrepiece of most proposals for the information society (US Congress, 1995, 1994*b*, 1994*f*). The same reasoning also applied in the approach adopted by the UK government (British Broadcasting Act of 1990, ch. 42: part I, ch. 3) to permit satellite broadcasting a regulatory-free environment, and occurs in major components of the European Commission's information-society policy initiatives (Commission of the European Communities, 1995*a*, 1994*a*, 1994*b*, 1994*g*) which are premised fundamentally on 'nurturing technology' by market mechanisms preconditioned on release from short-term public accountability.

The consequence of this reasoning in IPR and most information policies is to extend the immediate structures of the information industry effectively into the long term. Once new content monopolies and communications technologies have evolved within a certain structural environment whose governance is solely by proprietary and commercial criteria, defended by IPR laws and information society statutes, a communications system emerges which is essentially irreversible and intractable to policy. Governments must validate existing structures and future public attempts to pose the question of the appropriateness of the IPR system by other goals and standards is far less likely to lead to subsequent reversal.

Prevailing institutional arrangements under US communications legislation[6] obstructed succeeding public-policy initiatives challenging the legitimacy of the private appropriation of the spectrum that had already arisen in a regulatory-free environment. Congress was compelled on each occasion simply to endorse legally the existing set of arrangements (Horwitz, 1989; Rowland, 1986). This history is reflected in emerging information-society policy proposals (Commission of the European Communities, 1995*a*, 1995*b*, 1995*c*; US Congress, 1996*a*, 1995, 1994*b*, 1994*f*) which reserve a narrow notion of information services and infrastructure in the broadband environment for public-service exploitation, while the rest is awarded for commercial development, despite the revolutionary vision for the information superhighway initially articulated by the European Commission (Commission of the European Communities, 1994*a*) and by the White House (US Govern-

---

[5] Communications Act of 1934, Public Law 416, 73rd Congress, 19 June 1934, reprinted in Kahn (1984).

[6] Cited at notes 4 and 5 above.

ment, 1993). In the Telecommunications Act of 1996 (US Congress, 1996*a*) even further reductions of public-interest criteria find their way into legislation.

In the European Union, the ascendancy of the economic-incentives model for stimulating monopolies in content over public access and creators' rights may constrain the development of content diversity in ownership and substance to serve political, educational, and cultural innovation. EU public policy for the multimedia age renders comprehensive broadband-network evolution problematic because it would favour the strategic consolidation of the communication industry justified by arguments of economic incentives and technological necessity. This may create zero options in retrospective regulation seeking a balance between proprietary interests for commercial development, on the one hand, and the public interest in cultural, social, and political applications of the digital broadband network, on the other.

The rise in the incentives concept of content ownership has other social costs. For example, rights of authors and creators to the products of their creation can no longer be granted from a political or constitutional recognition of their claim, but only from fair compensation for the extraction of their implicit rights. Creative labour is converted to 'work for hire'[7] or a source of commercial innovation. This is regarded in the new policy environment as a more efficient, hence rational, way of stimulating expansion of the content sector. It is rationalized (for examples of rationalizations, see Branscomb, 1994; Samuelson, 1994; Moebes, 1993; Patterson and Lindberg, 1991) on the grounds that the incentives model serves the 'public interest' better than a more politically grounded rights protection—which is valid only if one assumes that all of society benefits from supply-side public policy and law. From the perspective of corporate rights holders who benefit from exploitation of works, it is also essential to circumscribe the scope of the contractual environment itself. Not only is all information and cultural production in the information society now funnelled through contracts between investment capital and creative labour, but even the outcome of this contractual arrangement is assured by the new IPR system so that the economic rights of creators are irrevocably exchanged or extracted.

As a result, incentives to creators for irrevocable rights in their creations that would stimulate a diversity of non-commercial speech and cultural forms, and the constitutional basis of the public sphere in guaranteeing free flow of opinion and ideas unrestricted by information monopolies or other forms of authoritarian barriers, becomes inherently incompatible with the contractual and exploitation process promoted in the emerging IPR regime. While this regime may serve to

[7] See note 2 above.

proliferate commercial forms of expression, ideas, and information—which promotes industrial culture, standardization, and harmonization of ideas—it would be unable to serve the development and enrichment of the public sphere in the production of the more diverse, non-commercial forms essential to the functioning of real democracies in the information society.

Thus the information age, through this anti-political copyright framework, possesses only a restricted potential to generate deliberative, participatory forms of programming, to promote diverse representations of social reality, offer a substantive diversity of cultural or educational multimedia forms, or conceive more accessible sources and structures of information-technology application (in software or hardware) premised on political, as against proprietary, rights of public freedom for creators and users.

It seems apparent, then that the problem of copyright in the information age has little to do with establishing a socio-legal foundation for enriching the public sphere with greater levels of diversity of expressive forms in a multimedia environment, the so-called 'democratization of information' offered by the public policy of the information age. Instead, the problem has become how to erect a legal system that transfers greater levels of proprietary control over expression to large-scale rights holders whose monopolies of content may grow even larger (see Jaszi, 1996). The challenge for liberalization processes with respect to copyright is to transpose to the content-production domain of the multimedia network a certain kind of contractual-law edifice that guarantees proprietary enlargement, therefore a type of Lockean rationale for information inequality, under the guise of the information revolution. To that end, it will be necessary for the liberalization movement to enforce a global intellectual-property rights regime, as with the GATT (1993) Agreement on Trade-Related Aspects of Intellectual Property Rights (TRIPs)[8] which in essence extends the economic-incentives model to the global level (see further discussion in this chapter), where it becomes legally binding on nations—even developing countries for whom it may be quite detrimental in terms of content needs in educational and social development (see Blakeney, 1996; Gana, 1996; Hamilton, 1996).

---

[8] See TRIPs section, Annex 1C , in the General Agreement on Trade and Tariffs in the Uruguay Round of Multilateral Trade Negotiations, MTN/FA, 15 December 1993, UR-93-0246.

RIGHTS OF CREATORS AND CITIZENS:
CULTURAL POLICY AND THE PUBLIC INTEREST

The boundaries of social relationships fixed by law and public policy under an economic-incentives-based IPR system are necessarily premised on inequality (in content ownership, information power, and cultural participation) because the inequalities of contracting parties in the market mirror the inequalities in natural society, that is, in society prior to taking into account the socio-legal basis of political association. In effect, the civil state itself is inconsistent with many conceptual elements of liberalization, which advances a form of social organization whose principal aim is to guarantee contractual and property rights. Conversely, a system of law which assumes political association would have to be constituted in some form of public-interest socio-legal approach to the production of information and ideas. In the social construction of the European Union, forms of public-interest law and private law are in continual conflict owing to the incorporation of diverse legal traditions. A serious assessment of EU policy reveals that the privatization of law is gaining ground, especially with respect to the area of information policies in intellectual property.

Vico (discussed in Bobbio, 1989a; MacIntyre, 1984; Foucault, 1972; Arendt, 1958) explains that public-interest law, by which he means Roman law, proceeds from the premises of the political organization of society. European public-interest law is rooted in a Roman–Germanic legal tradition (Elling, 1990; Koopmans, 1989; Kapteyn and van Themaat, 1989; Hartley, 1988), developed in modernity by means of the constitutional state (Bobbio, 1989a). Its form of reasoning rests on the distinction that Hegel (1952a) makes between the state, society, and the economy; that is to say, it distinguishes the society of the citizen and of the public interest from that of the burgher who takes care of his or her own private interests in competition with others. Hegel's objection (see Bobbio, 1989a; Pelczynski, 1984) to governance of civil society by private law is based on two illegitimate aspects of the institution of contract as a foundation of the state. First, the bonds that unite the state to its citizens are not economic but permanent and irrevocable, whereas the contractual bond can be revoked by the parties; and secondly, the institution of contractual rights is an inadequate conception of political association because it offers no basis for general will-formation and the articulation of common interests. This critique is echoed in Marx's (1978c, 1974) identification of bourgeois law with private law.

In contrast, in most Western nations, public-interest law, just as theories of constitution and constitutional forms, is founded not on the nature of things but on the value of public reason. The socio-legal tradition of public interest, with roots in Roman-Germanic public law, Hartley (1988) and Lasok and Stone (1987) argue, is a systematic body of norms or principles concerning the political–moral rights of citizens and the basis of their political constitution. Resistance which the law of property holds against the state's legitimate authority to delimit absolute contractual liberty is mitigated by public law's emphasis on the irreducibility of the common good to the sum of private welfare (Arendt, 1975) and by conceptual and rational approaches to the general welfare. As Arendt (ibid.) has observed, a free society has ends which cannot be reduced to the sum of the aims of the individual interests that compose it (see Chapter 2). In public policy terms, the logic of public-interest law requires the state to guarantee the conditions of political society in the common interest, that is, to make state action or regulation legitimate in spheres that bear on certain fundamental processes of political association. These spheres include, for example, the maintenance of a public realm to ensure public freedom for citizens and universal access to minimum human needs as with education, social needs, and public utilities. According to Hegel (1952*a*), progressive epochs can be identified as those in which public-interest law reverses the complete absorption of civil society by proprietary relations of contract.

French and German constitutional approaches emerge from this tradition (Bauby and Boual, 1994; Koopmans, 1991; Kapteyn and van Themaat, 1989; Hartley, 1988; Lasok and Stone, 1987; Usher, 1981) separating private law from public law, and applying constitutional principles to social and political problems in which individual creators are granted some irrevocable moral rights in their works (see earlier discussion). This human-rights approach to IPR has several significant implications for the regulation of public space that stand in opposition to the tendencies of the economic incentive model.

First, the human-rights approach to IPR proceeds from constitutional guarantees which regulate political claims, as against the contractual conventions in the state of nature that regulate proprietary claims enshrined in the economic-incentives model. Thus the category of citizen is a moral one and cannot be made equivalent to the rights of legal or artificial entities. For this reason, the human-rights-based IPR is logically oriented to subordinate any unconstrained extractive agreements to political guarantees of constitutional rights in speech, conscience, expression, participation, social inclusion, and so on (Meehan, 1993; Koopmans, 1991; Lasok and Stone, 1987). Contractual liberty is one among a collection of citizen rights but it does not occupy the summit in a hierarchy of rights as information-society policies and the liberalization project seem to suggest. Thus the rights of the communications industry in a public-interest tradition are not afforded the same degree of negative freedom under free-expression provisions, as are the communication rights of human citizens. And since the communication rights of the latter exceed the contractual claims of the former, the state is obliged to require a socio-legal mandate for provision of knowledge, ideas, and information in cultural, social, and political matters from the proprietors of the public sphere—the so-called 'non-commercial obligations'.

Secondly, the emphasis on a substantive approach to the common interest in the public interest model has led to development of non-discriminatory, common-carrier, universal-access standards in an array of social sectors, ranging from health and education to public utilities and infrastructure (Bauby and Boual, 1994). In other words, its form of constitutional reasoning leans towards a public-service culture often derided as interventionist or *'etatism'* by liberal states, especially in reference to resistance against the information liberalization model (for an example of this tone, see Samuelson, 1994; Moebes, 1993). Liberalism's disapproval of public-interest law as less democratic than natural contractual freedoms upheld by procedural, private law is intensified under contemporary information liberalization, but does not arise solely from the historical context of the restructuring of contractual relations on a global scale common to late modernity.

Hobbes satirized public-service forms of legal and political reasoning for the common good, as irrational in comparison with the natural right to the absolute freedom of private interest, 'there being no Obligation on any man, which ariseth not from some Act of his own' (*Leviathan*, 1991, ch. 21: 149–50). Even so, a public-interest socio-legal system is misapprehended when reduced, for instance, to the 'peculiarities' of French cultural and historical circumstances (termed 'Colbertisme', 'Napoleonic law', or the 'Jacobin state'; see instances in Casey and Wu, 1994; Caby and Steinfield, 1994; Center for Strategic and International Studies, 1994; and discussion of the interventionist state in Chapter 6) in the debate over a regulatory system for the information society in the European Union. Historical peculiarities notwithstanding, the doctrine of public interest and a human-rights IPR model rest more on the political and conceptual assumptions of constitutionally based regulation, than on the legitimacy of pre-emptive extractive agreements beneficial to owners of large-scale content in the market which motivates the critique of 'Colbertisme'.

A logical potential exists in the conceptual system of public-interest law for questioning either distortions from excessive ownership consolidation, forms of bias in technological development and access, structural monopolies in cultural production, or the growing absence of content diversity. It permits modes of reasoning which ask what type of social order should information-society policies bring about. Civil society may not be bound, necessarily, to deformations from *de facto* appropriation of public space by proprietary-contractual processes in the natural world, that is, in the market.

Under a public-interest, human-rights approach to IPR, current proposals to extend the term of protection of large-scale rights holders (Commission of the European Communities, 1996*d*, 1995*c*; World Intellectual Property Organization, 1996; US Government, 1995*c*; GATT, 1993), would not be judged socially desirable in so far as extending protection for expression made for hire, and expression by corporate authors is concerned. Instead, the approach would make a better case for prolonging the intellectual property rights of individual creators and authors. Thus cultural policies can be said to be embodied in this model to ensure that creators and their heirs, rather than corporate rights holders, obtain real opportunities to benefit from any extension of the term of protection. The inverse approach, favoured by an economic-incentives IPR model, would be regarded by the human-rights concept as a social cost in the form of an unjustifiable subsidy to cultural industries (Reichman, 1996*b*).

However, since the economic-incentives model has become dominant through such initiatives as US copyright initiative (US Government, 1995*c*), EU copyright initiatives (Commission of the European Communities, 1996*d*, 1996*e*, 1995*c*, 1991*d*), and international IPR initiatives (World Intellectual Property Organization, 1996), the principle of corporate creation and corporate authorship has effectively displaced the human-rights IPR model (Reichman, 1996*b*) for the information society and for the global information infrastructure. The subsidy to the cultural industries legalized and institutionalized in the information-society IPR regime is especially beneficial to the international audio-visual industry, but at the expense of individual creators (Boyle, 1996; Elkin-Koren, 1996; Reichman, 1996*a*) and the public sphere where freedom of information is legally undermined through national and international IPR laws.

The Public Interest in European Law

The problem of enlarging the sphere of political society in Europe along transnational lines is related not merely to the issue of constructing pan-European institutions and the processes of establishing democratic legitimacy, or to achieving mutual consensus among nation states in a growing range of sectors, or to constructing a common information space and infrastructure. It is also a problem of determining which concepts of law and regulation or which theories of political association should apply to the role of an already existing 'legal-constitutional suprastate' (Habermas, 1994; Meehan, 1993; Lange, 1993; Lepsius, 1992; Tassin, 1992; Pinder, 1991). The difficulty of deciding on concepts of policy is not wholly restricted to the question of reconciling diverse legal traditions but involves: first, recognizing the consequences for a social order of applying a certain model of policy in specific sectors of economy and society; and secondly, distinguishing areas of fundamental conceptual irreconcilability that, when combined in a single policy approach, would render it impossible to achieve an integrated legal framework.

This is the experience of US information policy which, in attempting to combine constitutional principles of public interest and the political rights of citizens for access and information within a utilitarian economic-incentives information-policy framework that confers increasing recognition to corporate creations and contractual rights, has spent the better part of a century discovering these irreconcilable concepts make it exceedingly difficult to define the basis of the public interest except on a rhetorical level (Porter, 1993b, 1989; Horwitz, 1989, 1986; Krasnow *et al.*, 1982; Rowland, 1982). Proposals for information-society legislation appeal to the public interest as a politically useful reference in mobilizing support and legitimizing policies which then propose, in the name of the public interest, even greater proprietary governance over information networks and content (see instances of public-interest arguments in US Congress, 1996a, 1995, 1994b, 1994f; US Government, 1995a, 1993; *Congressional Quarterly*, 1994a, 1994b).

Is the European Union having more success in achieving an IPR balance between economic-incentives and human-rights approaches? The most important constitutional foundations of EU law comprise the 1957 Treaty of Rome (Commission of the European Communities, 1993c) and the 1992 Treaty of the European Union, the Maastricht Treaty (Commission of the European Communities, 1993b). In terms of historical analogy, the Treaty of Rome in its basic form may be described as a more developed version of the US Interstate Commerce Act (1887), at least in so far as each legal system sets rules and competencies for trade across state lines, without explicit provision for human rights on a political or civil basis.

In Europe, however, the conditions of the social order have increasingly become the objective of policy and law (Newman, 1996; Habermas, 1994; Meehan, 1993), and the European Court of Justice has assumed the task of establishing and developing the essential elements of a new socio-legal order by means of case law (see Shapiro, 1992; Koopmans, 1991; Hartley, 1988; Schwarze, 1988). At the very outset, therefore, important gaps in the constitutional provisions of the European Economic Community have made it necessary to resort to precedence for establishing rules and authority in areas left silent by the Treaty. At the same time, the Court of Justice has consistently held (Arnull, 1989; Hartley, 1988; Lasok and Stone, 1987) that the Community legal order is founded on legal principles, not merely procedures, thus ostensibly offering a public-interest doctrine of rational and comprehensive approaches to the construction and maintenance of constitutional community (Hartley, 1988) whereby rulings in individual cases may be annulled by the terms of normative public-goods principles inferred from the treaties.

The conflict of legal conceptions with regard to the role of public policy and the parameters of competencies in regulating the spheres of economy and society, therefore, is built into the legal foundations of the Union. This is because the provision of rights is restricted to the scope of commercial freedoms which compels the Court to make inductively reasoned judgments on matters not covered by the Treaties on a case-by-case basis, a process that tends to validate existing social arrangements among contracting parties. At the same time, however, the Court, in keeping with a public-interest approach, is engaged in interpreting and extrapolating a number of underlying principles in the treaties through analysis of their provisions and basic elements (Brown and Kennedy, 1994). This method enables the Court to determine the primary implicit grounds of union among member states embodied by the Treaty, and to deduce the corresponding freedoms and rights that can be inferred from those grounds to which citizens and artificial entities must necessarily be entitled (Kapteyn and van Themaat, 1989; Koopmans, 1989; Lasok and Stone, 1987). In this manner, the Court has extended 'market freedoms',[9] that is, commercial liberties in the integration of national economics, as legal principles in their own right which must be observed by Community regulations and by national legislation. But it has gone further to infer comprehensive maxims of non-discrimination on grounds of nationality, race, religion, or equal protections in social rights, or political rights of voting in European-wide elections now guaranteed under the Maastricht Treaty (Commission of the European Communities, 1993b: part II, Articles 8, 8a, 8b, 8c, 8d, 8e, pp. 121–3). These are rules which amount to general principles of citizen rights not unlike the ones provided under a national democratic constitution.

[9] The freedoms of the market the Court has identified are as follows: free movement of goods, freedom of exercise of professional activities, free movement of workers, freedom to capital movement and of payments throughout the common market (see Kapteyn and Themaat, 1989).

Thus public-interest approaches form a significant source of legal principles in the EU. The development of this concept is closely allied to and extended from, a distinctive process of comparative method which identifies 'general principles common to the laws of the Member States' that is explicitly referenced within the Treaty of Rome (Commission of the European Communities, 1993*c*: Article 215, par. 2: 382). Such 'common' principles are therefore thought to exist, and considered by this provision as a source of Community law. Koopmans (1991) notes that the comparative method to seek out common public-interest principles has frequently been followed by the Court's case law in very diverse areas.

Among the most important categories of common principles that could prove problematic for the liberalization movement launched in the mid-1980s are the civil and political rights constitutionally guaranteed by the legal systems of some member states. It has not seemed to matter that the Treaties themselves do not contain any explicit provision for human rights, for the Court has revealed through public-law methods of deduction and inference with regard to comprehensive rational frameworks, as well as by comparative methods of identifying common principles, that the constitutions of member states and the provisions of the 1950 European Convention on Human Rights (henceforth ECHR: see *European Convention on Human Rights: Collected Texts,* 1987) ratified by all member states, furnish a set of minimum standards for regulation in the European Union (Kapteyn and van Themaat, 1989; Hartley, 1988; Koopmans, 1989). Appeals to constitutional protections of human rights and civil liberties drawn from the constitutions of member states and from the ECHR place limits on the validity of retroactive rulings or precedence, on the grounds that these may be harmful to the political and civil rights of EU citizens (see further discussion on this trend in Chapter 8). Court decisions arrived at in cases involving contractual arrangements may, therefore, be considered subordinate to a teleologically oriented public-interest protection of human rights.

This aspect of Community law has significance for the regulation of the public realm since human rights of freedom of expression determine the course and character of state action and place such action in a hierarchical relation with needs and necessities in social and economic sectors. Article 10 of the ECHR, for instance, is a more extensive free-speech right than the First Amendment to the US Constitution, in so far as it is both a negative and a positive right (see more detailed discussion in Chapter 8), in which freedom of conscience, or the liberal prohibition on the state to intervene in the thought, opinion, and speech of individuals, is combined with the right to be informed. The positive right constitutes a legal basis for the regulation of communications industries

and information providers to supply content that serves opinion formation, education, culture, or other public-information goods. This is part
of the basis by which the public-service tradition of communication
regulation has evolved in some European states with written constitutions, such as France, as well as in those without written constitutions
but articulating public-service principles through statutory practices,
such as the UK.

The adoption of a constitution by the European Parliament (see European Parliament, 1994) would probably combine this negative freedom
from interference in speech with positive rights of reception and information (ibid., Title VIII, par. 5: 36). Proposals for a European constitution are indicative of a growing human-rights movement within the
European Parliament (European Parliament, 1994, 1989*a*, 1989*b*), the
Council of Europe (1993), and to a large extent within certain direc-
torates of the European Commission itself (Commission of the European Communities, 1993*j*, 1990*d*). The human-rights and citizens-rights
trend in Europe (see Newman, 1996, Meehan, 1993) places political
rights of information and deliberation at some odds with the relatively
more extensive proprietary rights or market freedoms in capital, goods,
and labour that are explicitly guaranteed by the Treaty of Rome.

It is becoming apparent, therefore, that a human-rights framework
evolving in Community law and policy would furnish the European
Court with a clear basis on which to grant the European Commission
authority to regulate communications industries so as to ensure rights of
information and participation for citizens, as against the negative speech
right of freedom from regulation for artificial entities or private communications enterprises common in the USA. The free-expression right
in the ECHR, as it is more extensive than the US First Amendment,
would provide the Court with the legal mechanism to invoke the provision for annulment that exists in the Treaty of Rome (Robertson and
Merrills, 1993) in order to abrogate the binding authority of case law in
the service of a more comprehensive political right, namely, the right to
be informed.

Yet the danger for the protection of political rights of participation
and information in the European Union is that the reality of information liberalization through statutes strengthening the basis for the
privatization of law, the constitution, and the public interest has already
overtaken (Koopmans, 1991) the potential of constitutional rights that
may in future be implemented through public-interest concepts.
Initially, in the Community of six member states, as Kapteyn and van
Themaat (1989) and Koopmans (1991) point out, the impact of public
interest and administrative law was pervasive. It reveals itself in the text
of the Treaty of Rome, especially in the provisions of Article 173 for

annulment of Community decisions and Court rulings (see Commission of the European Communities, 1993c: Article 173: 338–9) which are similar to those developed by the French Conseil d'Etat as forms of '*excès de pouvoir*' leading to annulment under French civil law (Hartley, 1988; Lasok and Stone, 1987; Usher, 1981). Annulment would allow the state and the courts to approach the problem of constitutional rights on deductive, comprehensive grounds as against ad hoc, inductive, or case-by-case grounds. The French public-law tradition is also mirrored in some common legal principles of other founding states such as Belgium, Luxembourg, and Italy. The German public-law tradition, as it derives from Roman–Germanic civil law, has not presented a serious contradiction. In fact, the integration of the German public-interest tradition has strengthened the appeal to constitutional principles (Hartley, 1988).

From the accession of the UK in 1973, the common-law tradition entered into the Community and, as Koopmans (1991) and Lasok and Stone (1987) argue, it has gradually grown in importance. The Court has increasingly limited itself to the contractual circumstances or facts in a case and has attempted to infer rules from those circumstances. These procedures elevate the importance of precedent as binding on Court decisions over general rules deduced from constitutional principles. The Court has started to rely explicitly and more openly on its earlier case law and it is not uncommon, Arnull (1989) observes, that earlier cases are more often used as the sole argument, examples being: 'it is established case law that . . .'; or, 'as the Court already held in its judgment of . . .'.[10] Thus Community law has been constructing a socio-legal system in which the regulation of economy and society is decided by cases referring to earlier cases as well as by a gradual process of extending deductively determined constitutional principles on earlier rulings and the interpretation of EU statutes.

Nevertheless, the cumulative effect of individual opinions has conferred the same moral/political human rights upon legal entities as are granted to citizens, penetrating Community law (see Meehan, 1993) and making the Court's decisions more sensitive to contractual and corporate rights. This development allows private proprietary interests an increasing degree of recognition in hearings, process, and contractual claims and an expansion in competition claims advanced by competing entities as players in the marketplace (Arnull, 1989). In other words, the emphasis has shifted from public-interest problems of Community building—such as the general effectiveness of competition rules and the

---

[10] For an example of such common-law arguments employed by the Court, see *Commission v. Ireland*, 113/80, 1981 ECR 1625. This judgment quotes earlier case law on four different issues.

constitutional scope of Community law—towards the economic, proprietary rights of commercial institutions accused of anti-competitive behaviour (Meehan, 1993; Koopmans, 1991; Arnull, 1989; Lasok and Stone, 1987).

The intellectual strength of the comparative method, that is to say, the potential for participatory guarantees for citizens inherent in the search for 'common principles' among constitutions of member states, is vastly diluted by the privatization of law and the public interest, thereby constraining the future competence of EU institutions to bring about Community transformation on constitutional grounds of political and civil freedoms. At the same time, as the significance of the EU's legal system steadily grows (Meehan, 1993; Koopmans, 1991; Kapteyn and van Themaat, 1989; Arnull, 1989; Hartley, 1988; Lasok and Stone, 1987) in terms of binding obligations on national laws and national courts, the power of Community law to become generalized implies a profound pan-European trend towards declining public-interest regulation and towards the ascendancy of contractual rights in all member states. The 'harmonization' of national laws by this approach may restrict the responsibility of states to guarantee citizens' political rights of deliberation and participation, and the authority of governments to ensure these rights through real access and substantive information in the public realm.

In so far as information liberalization has handed more rights to legal entities, represented in the form of contracting parties and proprietary claimants, the rise of this information policy in the European Union suggests a shift towards the political arrangements of the USA where contractual rights have, through the binding power of precedent (Schwarze, 1988; Schwartz and Wade, 1972), considerably curtailed the application and meaning of the US Constitution in the protection of political rights of information. The construction of a European legal edifice under the liberalization of the economy and society, particularly in the information sector, may ultimately submerge the potential of public-interest concepts to apply uniform standards of citizen protection in political, civil, and social rights. It may also undermine the ability of a future EU political constitution, such as the one proposed by the European Parliament (1994), to guarantee that the information society serves democratic progress at a European level in educational, information, and cultural applications.

Decline of the Human Rights of Creators

As discussed, challenges to the liberalization of intellectual property and its agenda for transforming content into the predominant form of wealth creation or gold, so to speak, through fixing the contractual meaning of copyright, arise not from systems granting lower political and contractual rights, as in the case of China, but from systems that subordinate contractual rights to more extensive political rights. This is the difficulty the European Union faces in an approach biased towards corporate rights such as is favoured in the USA. It is a difficulty the EU confronts in the attempt to reconcile the tradition of private law and a supply-side IPR framework under liberalization pressures, with the public-interest, human-rights IPR framework.

The human-rights approach to copyright originates in its constitutional form from the French Revolutionary Decrees (see French Declaration of the Rights of Man, 1789) and is incorporated not only into French and EU law, but also into the legal system of most EU member states, including Germany, Belgium, Denmark, and Italy (for an account of the development of this tradition in the Community, see Dietz, 1978). In contrast to the utilitarian, two-part IPR formula for public-information rights, on the one hand, and economic incentives for rights holders, articulated in the US constitution, on the other, the French political-rights tradition constitutionally guarantees authors and artists exclusive rights to control the exploitation of their own creative works (Porter, 1992; Hartley, 1988; Lasok and Stone 1987; Dietz, 1978). It is an approach which embodies an ethical dimension of moral and not just economic rights, thus rendering copyright equivalent to other human rights as a fundamental liberty conferred on human citizens from which they cannot be alienated by other categories of law such as private law pertaining to contracts. The immediate departures from the US tradition are obvious: first, the human-rights status makes this form of copyright less limited for creators, hence more exclusive; conversely, the limitation is transposed from constraint on creative labour to constraint on the exploiter by subordinating contract law to constitutional human-rights protection, that is, to political rights which may not be contractually removed; and finally, since human rights as political or moral rights are conferred only on human citizens and cannot be assigned to artificial citizens, the model does not recognize as equal both parties to a work-for-hire or contract-to-exploit agreement in the way they would be so recognized under an economic-incentives IPR system.

As a result, the human-rights model grants more extensive protection to creators, exceeding governance by economic regulation such as competition law or contractual law, while simultaneously subordinating the latter to a higher standard of constitutional protection whereby the copyright is invested in or attached to the creator, and to that end, is perpetual and inalienable (Lasok and Stone, 1987; Dietz, 1978). Since creators cannot assign a moral right, that is to say, they cannot waive it through contractual agreement, the corporate investor, employer, or third party—in most cases cultural industries—may develop or exploit creative labour by the creator's temporary waiver of the exclusive right, but proprietary entities are neither entitled to, nor can they own, the right. Copyright laws both in Germany and France stress the individual creator's inalienable moral rights of entitlement or exclusivity over economic rights of exploitation of his/her creative works by third-party entities (Moebes, 1993; Porter, 1992).

This does not mean that creator's rights cannot be exchanged. For creative expression to be transformed into exchange value to generate proprietary expansion in the information age, cultural production must necessarily derive from the exchange of the creator's rights by legal contract. The key distinction, however, in a human-rights IPR approach is that, while creators may be alienated from their economic rights on contractual grounds, they cannot be alienated from their moral rights of entitlement in the work or else such a right would not fall under the class of civil liberty. As Harris (1995), Corbet (1994), and Williams (1992) explain, residual rights of entitlement which remain after the economic right has been extracted in a contract with large-scale rights holders include:

(a) rights of paternity, or the author's absolute right to assert that he or she is the creator of a work, allowing the creator to place his or her name on the creative work even after the economic right has been extracted;
(b) rights of integrity, or rights protecting a creator from harmful substantial changes being made to his or her work without permission, although this right is not absolute and applies only if changes are prejudicial to the creator's honour or reputation;
(c) rights of pursuit, or the right to seek legal action against the exploiter over use of the creative work, even where the economic right has been legally assigned to the private entrepreneur.

Since these rights are moral and therefore inalienable, they cannot be contractually removed by a third party and would therefore constitute an exclusive right. This exclusivity runs counter to the form of exclusivity corporate rights holders would wish to claim, without which content cannot be monopolized. The conflict over exclusivity presents an obstruction to proprietary enlargement in a key area of wealth creation and accumulation in the information society. As such, the human-rights IPR approach may, perhaps, comprise a more serious threat to information liberalization than totalitarian, non-liberal legal systems. This is because the latter bear no democratic legitimacy in international trade and hurt their own nations more by acting as obstacles to participation in multilateral arrangements than they obstruct or deprive the economic interests of exploiters in liberal states—although this is precisely what is vociferously argued by the International Intellectual Property Alliance representing the interests of the content industry (see testimony of the alliance, US Congress, 1996*b*), and by information-society policy proposals (see US Government, 1995*a*, 1995*c*, 1990; Commission of the European Communities, 1995*c*, 1994*a*, 1994*e*). In shaping the global IPR agenda for cyberspace, cultural industries have claimed immense losses from piracy in developing countries for purposes of strengthening their strategic position in the extension of the term of corporate rights to monopoly of expression at the expense of public-access rights (see World Intellectual Property Organization, 1996; Blakeney, 1996; Boyle, 1996, Jaszi, 1996).

For the economic-incentives IPR model, the struggle to prevent a higher standard of political rights for creators, or of information access for the public, means that a coordinated foreign and trade policy must be devised within multilateral trading agreements such as the GATT (1993), in order to institutionalize the rights of exploiters and efface, by making largely nominal, the rights of public domain or public access and moral rights of creators (see concern of the International Association of Audiovisual Authors and the European Federation of Audiovisual Producers in *European Report*, 1996*a*; for a justification of this international strategy, see US Government, 1990).

On political grounds, this counter-strategy implies an unprecedented direction in the development of liberal democracies. The history of modern liberal democracy does not record where a civil liberty has been removed from the status of constitutional protection. Rather, as Lefort (1988) and Arendt (1963) have argued, the history of democracy from the time of the Hellenic period, and particularly since the American and French revolutions, has been to add and enlarge the sphere of constitutionally guaranteed civil and political liberties through gradual stages in the universalization of information rights. The conceptual underpinnings of the logic of the democratic revolution over time is also defended in Kant's discussion of universal history (1991*a*; 1991*c*) as well as Hegel's defence of universal thought and law and the theory of international civil society (1952*a*, 1952*c*).

Yet under the economic-incentives IPR regime of information liberalization, rights of creators and public-access rights or citizens are being targeted as obstructions to global competition in the development of the information society (see defence of this notion of obstruction to liberalization in Samuelson, 1994; Branscomb, 1994; and Moebes,

1993). These political and human rights are cast as contrary to 'the public interest', because the benefits of supply-side public policy are steadily gaining political validity as undisputed assumptions in global relations (see the applications of this assumption to support liberalization in, for instance, Commission of the European Communities, 1995*a*, 1995*b*, 1994*a*, 1994*b*; U. S. Congress, 1995; US Government, 1995*a*).

Just as it was shown in Chapter 4 that the question of exclusivity in public-service rights was constructed as one of the primary enemies of the information age—the other being so-called 'constraints' on technological innovation, and both serving as grounds for undermining the public interest and public-service paradigm of communication in the EU—so, too, human rights, in so far as they embody the principle of exclusivity, constitute a danger to the liberalization movement and are targeted for dismantling (see advocacy of this necessity in US Government, 1995*c*, 1990; Branscomb, 1994; Moebes, 1993). As arguments in this chapter have attempted to reveal, the contemporary global trend in intellectual property-rights law suggests that under policies of the information society, human rights or political rights are gradually being cast as trade barriers. This is indeed a profound paradox for liberal societies that see themselves as democratic, but as exposition of information-society policies shows, it is hardly a paradox for liberalism itself given its underlying conceptual system. Such a conclusion can be further supported by an examination of the copyright regime evolving at the international and the EU level.

DESIGNING A GLOBAL INTELLECTUAL-PROPERTY REGIME

The difference between the economic incentives and human-rights foundations of copyright is a useful way to organize the problem of copyright in the multimedia world. The meaning of the disparity has less to do, it is argued, with so-called 'cultural differences' which advance understanding no further than conventional 'grammar of civilizations' arguments, so often employed to explain the status quo and to avert rational challenges to prevailing circumstances. The cultural peculiarity argument monopolizes trade negotiations on both sides of the Atlantic in the area of copyright, but also dominates in scholarly and legal assessments of the US–European copyright division (examples are Branscomb, 1994; Samuelson, 1994; Moebes, 1993; Koopmans, 1991; Arnull, 1989; Hartley, 1988; Lasok and Stone, 1987; Dietz, 1978). It could be suggested instead that the difference is more significant if regarded from the perspective of a conflict over the meaning and legitimacy of democracy in terms of political rights and freedoms, a form of explanation that is of greater relevance to the well-being of individuals regardless of cultural or ascriptive affinities, than is the cultural differences argument.

The realities of this difference are not new to international debate. For more than a century now, at the transnational or international level, the division between these separate concepts of IPR has been incorporated, albeit in a contradictory manner, into multilateral agreements. The Berne Convention for the Protection of Literary and Artistic Works (1886, revised 1971) administered by the World Intellectual Property Organization (WIPO), for instance, appears to balance the concerns of artistic labour, or creators, with the concerns of corporate rights holders or commissioning entities. Yet in the history of the Berne Convention's application by its 100 members, as Porter (1992) and Harris (1995) point out, the form of accommodation to both traditions has amounted to favouring the inherent social interests of the corporate rights system at the expense of the cultural policies of the human rights system. The reference to moral rights in the Berne Convention takes the following form:

Independently of the author's economic rights, and even after the transfer of said rights, the author shall have the right to claim authorship of the work and to object to any distortion, mutilation or other modification of, or other derogatory action in relation to, the said work, which would be prejudicial to his honour or reputation. (Berne Convention, 1971, Article 6bis)

This provision grants rights of paternity and integrity but not rights of pursuit. The real issue, however, lies not in the provision itself but in other elements of the convention which effectively cancel out, barring nominal recognition, the human rights of creators. These elements include the following:

1. As Harris (1995) and Kurlantzick (1994) observe of the convention, member countries to the convention are obliged to include in their own legislation the rights provided in the convention as a minimum standard of protection, but they may choose to raise that level. Moreover, the convention is based on the principle of national treatment which means that protection is given according to the law where protection is claimed. It appears, therefore, as a result of these provisions, that unequal treatment of creators' rights is almost structured into the international agreement since Berne members are allowed to practice a diversity of levels and classes of protections for creators. This compares unfavourably with rights of cultural industries or third parties since Berne, as also the GATT (1993) agreement, affirms a single standard protecting the exploiter in the extraction of the economic right through universal economic-incentive guarantees of the contractual

arrangement. This universal framework of protection for corporate rights holders is further consolidated by subsequent modifications to the WIPO treaties (see World Intellectual Property Organization (WIPO), 1996)

2. Porter (1992) notes that although Article 6bis recognizes the author's human right of paternity and integrity, nowhere does the Berne Convention define criteria for 'author' or 'authorship'. This omission, coupled with ineffective legal mechanisms to enforce the Berne Convention's recognition of authors' rights, demotes the moral right to a nominal liberty in national and international law. Countries such as the USA or UK may recognize such a class of rights in principle but are compelled to incorporate these rights into national copyright laws. Imperfect implementation mechanisms for Article 6bis opens significant loopholes for member countries such as the USA which may, with no human-rights provision for creators in their copyright statutes (Harris, 1995; Kurlantzick, 1994; Moebes, 1993), claim that their laws are in compliance with Berne since it is up to each country to decide how to implement the convention. The USA has gone so far as to assert (US Government, 1990; see support of this in Branscomb, 1994), in the export of its copyright tradition to the GATT level, that contractual liberty in and of itself is a uniform protection for creators and exploiters alike, making any additional protection for the former unnecessary.

The GATT Agreement on Trade-Related Aspects of Intellectual Property Rights (TRIPs: see GATT, 1993), a more recent devolution of an international IPR agreement, requires all parties to the work-for-hire contract to comply with the Berne Convention. However, in part II of the agreement, the GATT TRIPs releases third parties, and thus national copyright laws, from compliance with Article 6bis of the Berne Convention which at present constitutes the only multilateral provision for a creator's moral rights:

Members shall comply with Articles 1 through 21 of the Berne Convention (1971) and the Appendix thereto. However, Members shall not have rights or obligations under this Agreement in respect of the rights conferred under Article 6bis of that Convention or of the rights derived herefrom. (GATT Agreement on Trade-Related Aspects of Intellectual Property Rights, 1993, part II, section 1, 'Copyright and Related Rights', Article 9, 'Relation to the Berne Convention', par. 1)

In other words, as applied to the information society, emerging multilateral agreements on copyright subvert the nominal liberty granted to creators under Berne, thereby removing a civil liberty in the internationalization of liberal democracy (see WIPO, 1996).

Moreover, there seems to be strong transatlantic support for implementation of the TRIPs agreement (see GATT, 1993), now adminstered by the World Trade Organization. Both the EU and the USA have argued that the economic-incentives approach to IPR embodied in TRIPs will encourage job creation and stimulate incentives for the information economy. Under TRIPs, the economic incentive approach to IPR will become binding international law, and illustrates the general argument (Lopatkiewicz, 1995) that the model of information liberalization imposed on nations worldwide is a specific model exported under the liberalization-enlargement initiatives proposed by the international-communications industries. Another example includes the FCC's proposal to force deregulation and liberalization on the public communications systems of other nations, especially EU member states, through requirements of reciprocal evidence of 'effective market access' to US communications industries as a condition of allowing increased foreign ownership in the US domestic market (US Government, 1995b). Thus global-liberalization initiatives in information policies that are harmonizing the socio-legal foundation of public space appear to be creating a legal symmetry through disestablishment, among other things, of constitutionally guaranteed political and civil rights, and a systematic restructuring of the terms of legitimate competence and authority of the role of democratic government.

Finally, Article 14bis of the Berne Convention formulates a complicated definition of the ownership of rights in audiovisual works, specifically film, which, Dworkin (1993) and Porter (1992) argue, was designed to accommodate both the American and European IPR traditions. The provision has been described as 'the most obscure and least useful in the whole Convention' (Dworkin, 1993: 153) because it leaves member states free to define authorship in their own way, thus leaving the meaning of author and consequently author rights to arbitrary, prejudicial forces. But when clarification was subsequently attempted, a revision emerged in favour of expanding the rights of cultural industries but not those of individual creators. This occurred in the 1961 Rome Convention for the Protection of Performers, Producers of Phonographs, and Broadcasting Organizations which extended the rights of phonograph producers and guaranteed neighbouring rights to performers, phonograph producers, and broadcasting organizations. Porter (1992) notes that only the category of performer could be counted as creative worker, the others being employers. In an international environment whereby creative labour or authors are finding their moral rights vitiated from an absence of enforceable mechanisms and steady erosion of provisions, it is also becoming possible to render such rights further ineffectual by extending them to other classes of claimants. For instance, 'performers', an ever-enlarging classification which now includes many types of workers, not just creative workers, have been able to gain the modest moral rights available to authors under the 1996 Protocol to the 1961 Rome Convention (see World Intellectual Property Organization, 1996).

Under more recent international initiatives for the Global Information Infrastructure (GII), even further revisions and extensions of rights for corporate rights holders may historically expunge the human-rights IPR model from the information society of the next century. For instance, in the interest of international harmonization, both the EU and the USA are cooperating on extending more protection for databases and the digital transmission of works, which are new categories of property rights, and this is reflected in attempts to modify the Berne Convention (World Intellectual Property Organization, 1996). The reason is because the TRIPs adds a significant number of new or higher standards than the WIPO treaties such as the Berne Convention (1971) where the latter is silent or where it is thought to be inadequate to the needs of corporate right holders in the information society. Modification of the Berne Convention is therefore for the purpose of converging these two systems into a single information-policy system for the GII.

The trend in international agreements for IPR, therefore, is an expansion and elevation of IPR protection for the cultural industry, accelerated implementation of IPR, targeting, sanctioning, and penalizing of violations in the assertion that foreign violations are costing firms billions of dollars (see World Intellectual Property Organization, 1996; see analysis in Boyle, 1996; and Jaszi, 1996). New areas of rights grant to computer programs and databases the same level of protection as literary and artistic works, in short constructing new and growing areas of exclusive monopoly rights (see World Intellectual Property Organization, 1996; see analysis in Boyle, 1996; and Jaszi, 1996). Developing countries, but also many developed nations, will be forced under this framework to transform fundamentally their legal and juridical systems, ranging from laws governing the production to those governing the enforcement of IPR law (Blakeney, 1996; Gana, 1996; Hamilton, 1996).

While it is important to achieve some global framework for content ownership in the information society, the real question it seems is precisely what type of framework is needed by democracies to sustain a functioning and expanding public sphere and which model best serves the long-term interests of participation and progress. The current economic incentives approach aggressively pursued for swift implementation is far from progressive. It may worsen and perpetuate the dependence of developing countries upon content produced in industrialized regions (Blakeney, 1996; Gana, 1996; Hamilton, 1966), because the framework does not allow creative innovation to be employed for national development or public-access exploitation, such as 'fair use' of proprietary content. Instead, the emerging IPR framework gives all rights to commercial exploiters which amounts to thwarting the goals of competition in advance of information-sector development. This is so serious that one day history may judge this approach to have been an act of imperialism that worsened the dependency cycle (see discussion of the inherent imperialism of these initiatives in Hamilton, 1996). It is an approach that will ultimately eradicate the public domain on which democracy is so utterly dependent. Third-party copyright owners, or the international content industries, under the TRIPs and under proposed revisions to the Berne Convention may gain absolute control over the use of cyberspace. It is a model of the information society that will paradoxically restrict diversity of information and cultural dynamism even as societies experience an explosion in technological innovation.

This effect can be demonstrated in one particular element of the new international IPR laws. Under the new treaty revisions for the Berne Convention, most countries would be required to curtail severely the public's right to use public-domain materials stored in 'databases'. The most potentially anti-competitive intellectual property right created may emerge from the resulting legal constraint of the information society. The database right is being pushed by large publishing companies lobbying hard to obtain *sui generis* (one of a kind) property right to monopolize database content (World Intellectual Property Organization, 1996). This has the potential for creating private monopolies on data and document sources that have traditionally always been in the public domain in democratic societies. Exploiters have sought to restrict the public's right to use information without even the very limited types of safeguards for public access that exist in current copyright law. Should the citizens of an information society enjoy less access to information and knowledge than citizens of modern industrial democracies have thus far achieved over the course of the last few centuries?

Such a trend signals the growing assimilation of content production and distribution, and therefore of expression in general, to the pre-eminence of contract law over constitutional law. The implications of organizing the content of the information society around the terms and conditions of intellectual property law centred on the economic incentive contract can be summarized as follows:

(1) this direction in information policy elevates the interests of one
    particular social sector over all others in the information age of the

twenty-first century, namely, the interests of content monopoly industries;

(2) by strengthening the rights of large-scale proprietary interests over information production and distribution, IPR law of the information society will erase even that very marginal space that has been allotted till now to public-access rights of citizens to information and knowledge, or fair-use rights;

(3) these directions de-emphasize the rights of creators, ranging from their economic rights to their moral as well as constitutional–political rights

Clearly, the information society should be strengthening the democratization of information by expanding public-access rights in accordance with the potential of the new interactive broadband medium, rather than moving backward by parcelling out the public realm to concentrated proprietary governance. The supranational regulatory and legal design of intellectual property will affect not only who benefits economically in the information society, it will fundamentally alter the nature of content or expression itself—its very mode, form, and diversity.

One might argue that the intellectual property debate goes to the heart of what we mean by 'universal access' and 'information diversity', or 'pluralism', and of our inability in the information society to implement these ideas which form the rationale for the information revolution in the first place. These new international proposals for intellectual property laws, if implemented, will turn the information superhighway into an information toll road with the structure of knowledge defined exclusively by economic-incentives criteria and proprietary power. This radical privatization of the public domain is unparalleled in history, in effect reversing the direction of modernity from the gradual expansion of information participation among social groups over time, to gradual contraction. Not only will public-access rights and fair-use rights be cut back, individuals will be denied the right to use information for associational purposes in order to organize and participate in society at large. Even reading a document in cyberspace could become a copyright violation if the current trend in international IPR law continues on its present path.

There is immense pressure being brought to bear at the multilateral level on most countries. The outcome will be legally binding with enormous consequences not only for countries with alternative copyright traditions, but also for developing countries and their chances for real benefit from participation in the global information economy.

LIBERALIZATION OF EUROPEAN INTELLECTUAL PROPERTY RIGHTS

The European Union has been faced, as argued, with reconciling the constitutionally grounded public-interest approach to copyright with the contractually oriented economic-rights concept of IPR. But in addition, as the preceding analysis demonstrates, it has been necessary to assimilate to European law modifications to international agreements like the Berne and Rome Conventions and the GATT (1993) TRIPs agreement, with their combined logic biased towards third-party rights. The EU has thus been forced to deal with a set of serious complexities in regulating content-ownership rights in the construction of the information society.

This tension is evident in a collection of information policies which attempt to define the Community's IPR framework. Predictably, there is some entanglement among legal and political concepts of IPR, as addressed in the preceding discussion. It is difficult to assess whether there exists any consistency in the Community's attempts to balance the human rights, public interest, and economic incentives approaches alongside the hybrid multilateral tradition of the Berne Convention, and the biased, singular model embodied in TRIPs. Yet it is safe to conclude that the logical trend and general pattern of EU information-society policies seem to be moving in tandem with multilateral tendencies emerging in international IPR regimes for the GII as defined in the TRIPs agreement and in recent modifications to the WIPO treaties such as the Berne Convention. The basis of this trend unambiguously fortifies and extends the economic rights of content monopolies and cultural industries by simply ignoring the political, constitutional, and human rights of creators and citizens.

An example of this pattern may be observed in the term of protection offered to creative labour in the economic contract. The longer the term for individual creators, the lower the exploitative rights of third parties to the contract. Many EU member states have afforded longer terms of protection, both in the interest of the economic rights and moral rights of creators, than the minimum term of fifty years required by the Berne Convention and more recently the GATT (1993) TRIPs agreement. The Commission's statute on the term of protection of copyright (Commission of the European Communities, 1993k) attempts to establish a common term of protection in the Community, choosing the standard of the maximum of all those granted by individual member states. Thus, the directive (ibid.) affords protection to the creator for life plus seventy years (ibid., Article 1, par. 1); protection of an audiovisual work of life plus seventy years from the death of the last of the principal directors, the author, the composer (ibid., Article 2, par. 2); and protection for neighbouring rights of performers for fifty years after the date of the first performance (ibid., Article 3, par. 1).

This is a departure from economic-incentives IPR regimes which Kurlantzick (1994), Samuelson (1994), Branscomb (1994), and Moebes (1993), among others, have criticized from the US perspective, because it raises the level of protection to seventy years following death of the creator from the fixed term of fifty years currently provided in countries such as the UK (Dworkin, 1993) and USA. A second disagreement with governments of both the UK and the US (Kurlantzick, 1994; Samuelson, 1994; Moebes, 1993) derives from the Community's decision to grant comparable creator's rights to film directors and performers which expands the club, so to speak, of who counts as an author. The criticism holds that not only will the film director join the ranks of authors but so also will a number of others involved in the film-making process (Kurlantzick, 1994; Dworkin, 1993).

On these grounds it appears then that the Commission has acted in fairness towards authors by strengthening the rights of creative labour through protection for life, plus an extension of seventy years after the creator's death, and an extension of creative rights to film directors and to performers. Predictably, the Commission has faced strong international opposition to these proposals from the international content industries who own the rights to important copyright works and see the central source of high compensation levels in the information age to be intellectual property. However, it is also the case that the Commission's decision on precisely seventy years was undoubtedly influenced by higher moral-rights protections in France, and also in Germany, which has long allowed the seventy-year protection (Corbet, 1994; Dworkin, 1993), as well as by the immense practical difficulties in constructing a lower European term of protection to life plus fifty years. Political demands for authors' rights in Europe are relatively more prevalent than elsewhere, as in 1994, for instance, when the German federal government announced (World Congress of International Performing Rights Societies, 1994) it would advocate an international copyright law capable of giving authors sufficient protection to cover future technological developments in digitized forms of their works.

Fairness to authors notwithstanding, the logic of the directive harmonizing the term of protection ought to be of very little concern to proprietary parties and corporate rights holders for at least two reasons. First, the directive awards a common term of protection thus making it easier for copyright proprietors to forge pan-European distribution strategies for programme marketing—whether film, audiovisual, software, databases, or text—in the certainty that higher level of protection in some national laws will be abolished and made illegal by the directive and by emerging international law. Secondly, the common term protects only the economic rights of authors but does nothing to affirm the inalienable life term of their human rights of paternity, integrity, and pursuit. Moreover, the directive allows third parties to legally extract the economic right thus guaranteeing a contractual structure for the information society biased towards the cultural industries. The legal alienation of creators from their creative labour would, by virtue of European law, supersede any contrary national constitutional structures guaranteeing their human rights because of the transnationalization of content exploitation.

Though Dworkin (1993: 155) concludes that the directive 'marks yet another shift away from traditional common law copyright principles', in reality it endorses the sovereignty of private contractual guarantees of economic rights of exploitation advocated by an economic incentives model, and thus plays a significant part in facilitating proprietary enlargement over intellectual property in the era of the information revolution. But this does not answer the question of how European law has been able to abrogate its public-interest tradition and arrive at this juncture in the information policies of liberalization. Part of the answer is in the groundwork laid by legal and policy instruments which preceded the term of protection directive.

Thus the second area in which the ascendancy of corporate rights concept of IPR is apparent is in the use of Treaty (Commission of the European Communities, 1993c) provisions which allow intellectual property rights to be asserted under the claim that national laws threaten to hinder the free movement of goods and services prohibited by Articles 30 and 36[11] of the Treaty of Rome. It has fallen to the European Court of Justice to decide how to balance the constitutional human rights of authors with Treaty rules of freedom of commerce. Corbet (1994) documents the number of instances in which the Court has actually precluded the exercise of the creator's right where it acted as a barrier to the import and distribution of parallel foreign products. But the more significant conceptual solution the Court offers is a distinction between the validity of the grant of intellectual property rights—which Article 36 could also conceivably protect under the state's right to protect 'industrial and commercial property'[12]—which are inviolable if guaranteed under constitutional political and civil liberties, on the one hand, and the practice of those rights, or their 'exercise' which could be limited by the anti-monopoly provisions of Articles 85 and 86 (see discussion of these competition provisions in Chapter 7).

---

[11] See Appendix.
[12] Cited at note 9 above, the 'industrial and commercial property' provision in Article 36.

In the previous chapter it was shown that, in fact, these are the very same provisions wielded against public-service communications entities in the EU by placing in the hands of private commercial entities and the Court the instrument that renders illegal the practice of exclusive rights. In seeking the common interests of the single market and disallowing market segregation by large-scale exploiters, the Court may have unintentionally implicated a subordination of authors' rights to the larger good of effectuating freedom of commerce in content ownership (see Corbet, 1994; Williams, 1992; Koopmans, 1989; Lasok and Stone, 1987; Usher, 1981).

It appears, accordingly, that an author's exclusive moral right in a creative work can be abrogated if the exercise thereof restricts freedom of commerce through constraints on third parties in their freedom of contract, that is, in their freedom to exploit expression. Consistent with liberalization's assumptions of inequalities necessary to the supply-side organization of civil society, and in the absence of an explicit ruling on the relationship between property rights and political rights in the area of expression, the Court may have cast the right to transform expressive forms into exchange value to be a more extensive right than the political–civil right of protection against alienation from creative property in one's labour.

The third legal area of development in the direction of economic incentives is represented in the Community's attempt to establish new rights that do not exist in any other copyright regime, including until recently even the Berne Convention—although, as addressed above, new rights for corporate monopoly owners of databases have now achieved codification in international law. The rental and lending rights directive (Commission of the European Communities, 1992*a*) provides authors with the right to authorize or prohibit rental or lending of their works (ibid., Article 1, par. 1). However, these new rights do not derive from the class of moral rights since they are completely transferable, and can be assigned or extracted for a remuneration (ibid., Article 4, paras. 1 and 2). Thus they would appear to strengthen the economic rights of authors, though not necessarily at the expense of exploiters. This development has been supported by the German and French governments and by other member states over the objections of the USA and UK (see Mosteshar, 1994; Samuelson, 1994; Corbet, 1994; Jorna and Martin-Prat, 1994). Yet authors and performers as well as third-party exploiters alike have welcomed the new rights (Mosteshar, 1994; Porter, 1992).

Clearly, the directive aims to take account of new forms of exploitation driven by innovations in copying and distribution technology based on digitization, compression, and intelligent networks that could potentially deprive all rights owners—whether individual or corporate—from potential compensation. However, it is equally clear that creative labour can be required to waive any moral right in the assignment of their rental or lending right. It is only the right to 'equitable remuneration' that cannot be waived by the author or performer:

Where an author or performer has transferred or assigned his rental right . . . that author or performer shall retain the right to obtain an equitable remuneration for the rental. (Commission of the European Communities, 1992*a*: Article 4, par. 1)

and

The right to obtain an equitable remuneration for rental cannot be waived by authors or performers (ibid., Article 4, par. 2).

Thus not only is there no provision for protection of moral rights in the duplication of artistic works in the digital age, but even further, the directive affords exploiters, that is to say, audiovisual producers, publishers, or broadcasting organizations, broadly the same rights as creative labour (ibid., Article 2). This reinforces the exploitation side of the copyright contract, as compared with the constitutional human rights and public-interest tradition which tends to discriminate in favour of political rights of human citizens over commercial rights of artificial entities. In a similar way, the interests of the multinational exploitation industry is reflected in yet another directive.

The fourth development in copyright law pertinent to these shifts is action the Commission undertook to issue transnational guarantees of large-scale content ownership rights through legal instruments designed to accommodate the interests of the international film producers and satellite broadcasters. From the perspective of the international content industry, the directive on copyright issues related to satellite broadcasting (Commission of the European Communities, 1993*l*) is strongly justified because, as argued by the broadcaster CBS, Inc. (quoted in US Government, 1990: 27), broadcasters and networks hold copyrights in much of their programming, including news and public affairs programming, sports broadcasts, and a significant number of entertainment programmes and made-for-television movies. Representing the interests of multinational broadcasters, CBS has further noted that 'the unauthorized resale or retransmission of these works infringes on these copyrights and deprives networks and broadcasters of potential income' (ibid.).

The aim of such a directive, therefore, is to create legal certainty in the Community for transnational broadcasting, thereby facilitating the free movement of copyrighted works throughout the EU by means of satellite broadcasting or cable retransmission. The directive holds that the initiative serves the purpose of facilitating higher levels of remuneration for satellite broadcasting because 'broadcasts transmitted across frontiers within the Community are one of the most important ways of pursuing Community objectives which are at the same time political, economic, social, cultural and legal' (Commission of the European Communities, 1993*l*: recital 3).

Among the inhibitions to transnational communication, or the creation of a 'common European space', is thought to be national IPR systems (Moebes, 1993), many of which grant constitutionally protected human rights to creators for their works. The measures in the directive on copyright related to satellite broadcasting address these obstacles in terms of the interests of third-party retransmission rights. Any satellite broadcast originating in an EU member state is now regarded as an act of broadcasting for copyright remuneration purposes, regardless of the technology used, once it constitutes communication to the public (ibid., Article 1, par. 3). The directive actually creates a 'broadcasting right' that allows the author to authorize or prohibit satellite broadcast of the copyrighted work (ibid., Article 2), and a minimum level of harmonization of laws regarding copyright in satellite broadcasting is mandated to all member states (ibid., recital 21, Article 14, par. 1), ensuring that the interests of third parties will be safeguarded regardless of the broadcaster's member state. Finally, the right to broadcast protected works by satellite may only be acquired in the country of establishment of the broadcaster (ibid., Article 3).

The underlying principles at work in the directive follow an identifiable pattern. There is very little in the directive for creators' rights, moral or otherwise. The statute is a clear example of privileging contractual arrangements for expansion of proprietary monopolies of content in the guarantee of their transnational exploitation. The adverse consequences devolve to the general public whose interest in a real diversity of content may be harmed by legal structures permitting concentrated content holdings in a few multinational capital structures. It is obvious that national content industries or small-scale rights holders may be unable to compete transnationally, except by acquiring rights or licensing arrangements for similar forms of commoditized expression and/or by becoming integrated into collaborative alliances with large-scale rights holders. This implies the construction of competition barriers in content production, distribution, and access in the public sphere. By encouraging forms of collaboration among content providers who seek to develop transnational distribution networks, the directive has an effect similar to that raised in the previous chapter regarding the realities of infrastructure competition under liberalization: namely, the creation of a governance structure over public space with built-in barriers to universal and participatory access in representations of social reality and real choice in ideas, information, and knowledge.

For these reasons, it is argued that the directive on copyright protection for satellite broadcasting and cable retransmission (Commission of the European Communities, 1993*l*) inherently favours multinational distributors of programming and broadcasting over smaller or national distributors, more specifically over European audiovisual and broadcasting industries. The former can afford to construct comprehensive international-distribution networks for carrying immense acquisitions of creative works, known as 'catalogues', integrated with strategies in other media. However, European independent national programming and broadcasting distributors cannot effectively license satellite broadcasts in coordination with national release patterns in other media, given their limited catalogue of intellectual properties and cross-border distribution structures.

In another example of the design of an IPR regime in the EU, the Community recognizes that the onset of a new information age would be impossible without the proliferation of software innovation upon which the development of everything, from the intelligent network itself to all information services, is wholly dependent (see Dixon and Self, 1994; Branscomb, 1994; Mansell, 1993). The Community has consequently produced a statute affording copyright protection for computer programs—the so-called 'software directive' (Commission of the European Communities, 1991*d*). Since the Berne Convention (1971) does not recognize protection for computer programs, the directive (ibid.) assimilates software to the category of 'literary and artistic works', thus invoking the same rights (ibid., Article 1, par. 1), provided software creations are original 'in the sense that it is the author's own intellectual creation' (ibid., Article 1, par. 3). Similar protection followed shortly thereafter in the GATT (1993) TRIPs agreement. The software directive also sets forth a statement of principles in the lengthy recitals to advance copyright protection in the networked world which ostensibly aim to protect the economic rights of individual creators. Yet the reality of software development is that it evolves in a highly concentrated industry (Ehrlich, 1994; Mansell, 1993) with large holdings of copyrighted software properties, and thus the extensive protections granted in the directive would serve to consolidate and extend further the domain of proprietary governance of software development, licensing, and distribution across networked public space.

There are obvious similarities, therefore, to the economic-incentives IPR approach. It may be evident, in fact, that the purpose of the directive is to bring European law into conformity with US copyright protections (see account of US approach in Ehrlich, 1994; Samuelson, 1994; Dixon and Self, 1994), since the tendency of the directive is to promote relatively harmonized laws on protection of software programs between the EU and the USA. Samuelson (1994) praises the directive's attempt to bring about harmony in EU–US law in a number of important respects, such as the fact both laws now adopt copyright as a form of legal protection available for software innovation, either for authors or legal entities, and that both laws consider programs to be 'literary works', the highest category of intellectual property in terms of protection. Both laws aim to protect 'expression' in programs, but not the 'ideas' and 'principles' underlying them (Commission of the European Communities, 1991*d*: Article 1, par. 2), and both protect programs for the life of its author plus fifty years or fifty years from the time the program is first made available to the public if the creator—as is most often the case—is a legal entity (ibid., Article 8, par. 1).

In the areas of disagreement, however, the USA, through bilateral negotiations and the GATT's multilateral mechanisms, has been successful in seeking changes to EU law (Corbet, 1994; Dixon and Self, 1994; Ehrlich, 1994; Samuelson, 1994; Dworkin, 1993) to make Community law conform even further with the economic-rights restrictions. Central aspects of the software directive that make it problematic for liberalization's promotion of contractual principles over public-interest constitutional principles, include:

1. Commercially significant rules regulating the terms of licences in contracts within the software directive allow both licensees as well as owners of copies of programs to make copies and modifications to the code of computer programs (Commission of the European Communities, 1991*d*: Article 5, pars. 1 and 2). This has been opposed by the software industry which successfully lobbied the US Congress to make these privileges available only to owners of computer programs, and to no one else under US law (see discussion in Dixon and Self, 1994; Samuelson, 1994).

2. Reflecting a public-interest approach, the law of the Community is largely fixed by the text of the statute or directive (Kapteyn and van Themaat, 1989; Hartley, 1988; Dietz, 1978) by the assumption that the state should approach its responsibility to civil society in a rational and comprehensive way by application of constitutional norms and principles. This IPR initiative has been developed, in part, on the assumption that IPR law should not be subject to the influence of private conventions, practices, and arrangements in the marketplace or be continually in a state of indeterminacy to be resolved entirely by content proprietors or individual cases.

Yet Dixon and Self (1994), Samuelson (1994), and Ehrlich (1994) observe that US and EU copyright laws for software are undoubtedly in harmony in a number of important respects. From the perspective of arguments in this chapter, the most significant harmony arises from the adaptation of Community law to a rigorous tightening of proprietary, economic-rights protection for works that are already owned—through work-for-hire agreements—by commercial entities but few by individual authors have been affected. Clearly, this direction strengthens and enlarges oligopolistic tendencies in the development of advanced information services, which are completely software dependent (Dixon and Self, 1994; Dworkin, 1993).

The final evidence of an evolving pattern under a proposed European IPR regime is the way it mirrors the effects of 'harmonization' initiatives also evident in telecommunications liberalization (see Chapter 4) by serving as a euphemism for the dismantling of public-interest structures in information policy. The database directive (Commission of the European Communities, 1995*d*), the Green Paper on copyright (Commission of the European Communities, 1995*c*) and a subsequent blueprint for a copyright statute in the EU (see communication of 20 November 1996, Commission of the European Communities, 1996*d*) formalize the erosion of the public interest and a human rights IPR model. The initiatives achieve this through rhetorical recognition of the model at the same time as they construct concrete provisions allowing the economic-incentives model to supersede in effective application through a complex system of loopholes on the premise that 'the existing legal framework [in Member States] will need readjustment' (ibid. 8). Accordingly, the initiatives argue for an IPR design that provides new rights to content exploiters such as publishers (see database directive, Commission of the European Communities, 1995d) or extends protections for corporate rights holders as in reproduction, on-demand information services, distribution, and digital broadcasting, but elects not to act at all to extend constitutional moral rights of creators (see Commission of the European Communities, 1996c): 'There are indications for a need to reinforce or introduce moral rights protection for, at least, authors and performers in the Information Society. . . . However, the time is not yet ripe for concrete harmonization' (ibid. 28).

Public access and fair-use rights to maintain freedom of information in the public sphere meet the even worse fate, perhaps, of being revoked in the information society. Even scanning of digitized materials, the equivalent of scanning a newspaper, magazine, or book, would be made unlawful in the new IPR regime:

The majority of rightholders . . . are against providing any kind of private copy exception [the fair-use right] or any other limitation in the digital environment. . . . Accordingly, rightholders may enjoy, without limitation, an exclusive right to authorise or prohibit acts of reproduction [and] . . . private copying may become a fully restricted act. (ibid. 11–12)

While current information policies reserve the right to remain 'flexible' in the application of the economic-incentive IPR approach, the mere fact that the cultural industries are granted accelerated rights to monopoly of expression in the information society, without a corollary balance in enhancement of public-access rights and human rights of creators, implies a public sphere of the digital era characterized by feudal structures of information concentration that constitute a legally sanctioned permanent drain on the public realm. It is difficult to imagine how flexibility in IPR laws to address these structural barriers to information production and distribution at some future date in the twenty-first century could restore a balance once oligarchic controls are in place.

CONCLUSION

This chapter has examined the political implications of the rise of the economic-incentives IPR concept as an ordering principle regulating ownership rights over content in the public sphere of the information society. A last reflection concerns the Treaty (Commission of the European Communities, 1993c) itself which does not govern the rights of authors since it does not govern the political rights of citizens of the European Union. The Treaty only regulates the activities of legal corporate entities, both public and private. Authors or creative labour, that is, human citizens, are not governed by the competition policy of the Treaty. Instead, it is the capitalist undertaking, meaning exploiter or third party, which acquired ownership/exploitation rights from creative labour through contractual processes, that falls under Community legal jurisdiction. This authority is not necessarily harmful to the interests of private undertakings, as might be supposed by the political assertions of liberalization arguments. On the contrary, as demonstrated in this chapter, Community governance over free movement of capital, goods, labour, and services across national borders is oriented towards protecting more and more of the contractual freedoms of enterprises, and thus renders inviolable contractual agreements that allow the extraction of the exclusive licence to exploit creative expression, provided the creator is 'equitably remunerated'.

The regulation of contractual processes in intellectual property requires, therefore, the application of private-law procedures to protect private entities as parties to the contract. In short, European law derived from the Treaty, while formulated on public-interest concepts, has laid an extensive groundwork for inherent discrimination in favour of protecting corporate rights holders in proprietary expansion over content.

Once more, the socio-legal reality of information liberalization in IPR has demonstrated that the mode of the information society appears to be the result of the activism of public policy. Accordingly, the forms of public policy chosen by the state and their tendencies to favour certain structures of ownership is becoming central to determining which social groups benefit or are vastly enriched by proprietary control over advanced information technologies, intelligent networks, and the content they will carry. It is also evident that the range of policy options open to the state may no longer derive from autonomous deliberation on constitutional values that should, by the standards of political society, be incorporated into law. As observed in the case of the EU, terms and standards of intellectual property rights are being forced by international agreement because networks are global, but more because the historical context of the multilateral political environment is essentially the context of liberalization and of the regimes which support it.

The USA, for example, views EU statutes limiting the exploitation of authors' works as a form of unnecessary government interference in contractual freedom (see the US view discussed in Branscomb, 1994; Ehrlich, 1994; Samuelson, 1994; Moebes, 1993), thus setting the stage for a struggle between creative freedom and contractual freedom. Liberal regimes are also in conflict with the European Court's interpretation of the Berne Convention (1971) and with the growing influence of the European Convention for Human Rights (ECHR, 1950) on Community statute creation and judicial interpretation. Despite the growing application of liberalization to the structure of public space in the EU, the opposite tendencies of public interest law and the incorporation of human rights from the ECHR into European law set the stage for a deepening conflict in other areas of the public realm. Even as the EU confronts the ascent of the economic-incentives IPR model prejudiced in favour of contractual rights, the appeal to moral rights, human rights, and political rights continues to constitute a strong legal foundation for arguing that any future political integration should prioritize guarantees for the fundamental constitutional rights of citizens in the public sphere.

The problem of expression in the expansion of liberalization's mode of social organization is explored further in the second area of content regulation that is of critical importance to the form of public space brought about by the information revolution: the conflict over audiovisual policy.

6

Audiovisual Battleground and Conflict of Regulatory Models

IN THE struggle to establish control over the basis of content regulation, the public/private distinction in information policy defines the boundary between political society and the market or between a constitutional as opposed to 'natural law' basis of association. The analysis of information infrastructure and content-ownership policies attempted to disclose how the naturalization of the market in information policy and its ascendance in governance over the public realm implies the undermining of the body politic. It was further argued that the political future of the European Union will in large part become a product of the approach to the information society and to the emerging form of common European public space that reconfigures the democratic social order and redefines the relation between the state, citizens, and the economic market. Since this framework appears to favour a particular policy environment, it raises certain questions regarding the capacity of civil society to sustain conditions of collective will-formation even as information technologies proliferate and time and space are made irrelevant in the production and distribution of ideas. It was suggested that current information-liberalization pressures at the international level and their unexamined assimilation to EU policy and law indicate that the information society for European citizens essentially constitutes a systematic dismantling of the public-interest paradigm of modern democratic development.

The political reality and significance of this historical change is now taken up in the context of competing conceptions of European public space emerging in a third area of policy central to the construction of the information society: audiovisual content. An attempt is made to further clarify the issue of content by assessing the struggle over audiovisual policy as a crucial component in the policy framework of the information society. Information policies for the European audiovisual sector are examined through the conceptions of public space explored in Chapters 2 and 3 which compete with liberalism for dominance in the EU. These are: the public-interest or public-service model and the nationalist or culturalist model. Based on earlier discussion of models of public space, this chapter will examine the struggle between these concepts of regulation over a class of expression, audiovisual content, which dominates the modern public sphere.

Against liberalization, these two historically important models—the nationalist/culturalist model and the public-interest/public-service model—are engaged in a complex process of opposition and collaboration. In its attempts to deal with the effects of the transnationalization of audiovisual programmes and the concentration and consolidation which characterize this sector, the EU has tried to balance three models of regulation and address multiple aims for the information society: to create a single market in audiovisual programmes by expanding the proprietary and commercial potential of the European audiovisual industry; to develop a notion of European cultural identity borrowing the nationalist/culturalist model from member states; and to preserve some form of public interest or public service in order to balance the proprietary market forces unleashed by the competitive order of information liberalization. The tangled structure of these policies is examined to determine if, by confounding regulatory models, the EU is better equipped to address the social, political, and cultural needs of the information society and to manage the effects of liberalization upon the public sphere.

PUBLIC INTEREST AND THE SPIRIT OF REGULATION

While the application of a liberal model to the European information sector is demonstrated in the two previous chapters, it is also necessary to examine the public-interest/public-service model,[1] (henceforth referred to interchangeably), both in conceptual origins (see also Chapters 2 and 3) as well as in forms of assimilation to the information-society framework. In the category of audiovisual content, a reigning expression of the modern public realm, the fate of this model makes it possible better to apprehend the stakes posed by a construction of Europe according to the terms of information liberalization and its transformation of the foundations of political society. Within the EU, audiovisual policy, for instance, has evolved as a powerful site of conflict, not only between rival political and social interests but also between the liberal, nationalist, and public-service theories of how the European Union ought to develop.

The public-service concept has always been a contentious problem for

[1] The terms 'public interest' and 'public service' are used interchangeably in this discussion since they reflect variations in national terminology sharing a number of common conceptual roots with respect to the role of the state. For analysis of common European notions regarding public interest and public service, see Bauby and Boual (1994).

the liberal paradigm, manifest in many areas of economy and society. Since the early 1980s, the growing integration of the global economy and the liberal political arrangements which sustain it have challenged the very essence of the public-service paradigm of democracy. For instance, Collins (1994) as well as Morgan (1989) characterize the audiovisual problem and telecoms liberalization in Europe as a conflict over two views of the role of the state, one advocating intervention (*dirigisme*) in the market and the other eschewing it (liberalism). But as was shown in the case of telecommunications and intellectual property, this construction of the problem does not adequately recognize that liberalization may have been mischaracterized as a non-interventionist conceptual and regulatory system similar to the way in which it is often misapprehended as a theory of open and perfect competition. As suggested all along, just as liberalism has been oversimplified as a minimal theory of the state, so *dirigisme* is frequently reduced to a peculiarity of French history which is a caricature that obscures serious examination of the arguments advanced, and of the nature of resistance to liberalization. Consequently, the debate over the role of the state in the audiovisual sector does not in reality involve a choice between intervention and non-intervention but rather a choice between forms of intervention and which social interests ought to benefit.

During the industrial revolution, De Paepe (*Les Services Publics*, 1895, quoted in Mattelart, 1994) distinguished the so-called *dirigiste* theory of the state, or Jacobin centralism, from the public-service conception of political community. De Paepe argued that the public or universal characteristics of a utilitarian activity, guaranteed for all citizens by social contractarian obligations of the state, is an entirely different theory of society when compared with the consolidation of feudalistic power in a non-democratic state expressed in the notion of *dirigisme*. To achieve this universal condition in a concrete sector of fundamental need or necessity, the state is obliged to remove it from the marketplace of proprietary conflict, or else the activity:

> ... wouldn't exist if one waited for private initiative, either because it would be diverted from its true destination or because it would constitute a monopoly that would be dangerous to abandon to private interests. [Thus] public service should be doubly public: in that it is accomplished by the direct or indirect cooperation of all; in that it has for a direct or indirect purpose the benefit of all. The true public service is thus at once public both by its subject and its object. (ibid. 49)

Of course, De Paepe may have had only the railways, post and telegraph, and the road system in mind, and not the information network comprising broadband communications, direct broadcast satellite, the

Internet, or the broadcast system. As a Belgian socialist active in the International Association of Workers in 1874, De Paepe, as Mattelart (1994) argues, was attempting to distinguish between authoritarianism and *laissez-faire*. Yet by defining public service as public at once in its subject and object, he posed the question of citizen participation in fundamental areas of membership. To this extent, as with the relationship of Lockean thought to the liberal social order, his conception was constructed on a set of socio-legal underpinnings that do not arise in a vacuum nor derive from feudalism or imperialism, but are closely aligned with well-developed concepts of political society. These foundations of a participatory public sphere were explored in some depth in Chapter 3.

But the public-service/public-interest idea, which De Paepe argued for as a modern alternative to liberalism's concept of society and which competes against liberalization in the European Union, can actually be better understood through political foundations in the thought of Montesquieu (1989) and Hegel (1952*a*). Public service can also be defended and developed through the ideas of Rousseau, Tocqueville, or Machiavelli. However, the significance of Montesquieu to the republican concept of the democratic revolution is central, as Lefort (1988), Furet (1981), and David and Spinosi (1973) argue, to any serious grasp of the distinction between the sovereignty of a free society (Montesquieu, 1989: part 1, bk. 1, ch. 3: 8) as a way of gaining freedom for the individual, and the sovereignty of one individual, one group, or even one people. It is a paradox which Machiavelli (1961) too emphasizes in his idea that we can only hope to enjoy a maximum of our own individual liberty if we do not place that value above the pursuit of the common good. In contrast to Locke's theory of a privatized civil society and a privatized, instrumental state (see discussion in Chapter 2), Montesquieu's notion of political society is one in which the sovereignty of the political rights of citizens is asserted or institutionalized, and cannot be disassociated from a government obliged to act in the name of the people. This de-naturalized theory of freedom, in contrast to the natural-law argument of liberalism (see Montesquieu, 1989: part 1, bk. 1, ch. 2: 6–7), regards political society not as that collection of individuals which Locke and Hobbes supposed, nor does it value social institutions, hence the state, as the instrumental means to private ends.

Rather, Montesquieu argued for a government by means of which the common good and the basic threshold of the terms of citizenship could be improved for all and not just for private proprietors. His definition of the civil state is constituted by, and preconditioned upon, the existence of a collective will, whereby the state cannot function 'unless all wills

are united. The union of these wills . . . is what is called the civil state'
(ibid., part 1, bk. 1, ch. 3: 8). Hence, the role of law or state policy in a
republic where the people as a body have sovereign power, 'should
relate to the degree of liberty that the constitution can sustain' (ibid.,
part 1, bk. 1, ch. 3: 9), and the totality of political liberties which the
state must take into account compose 'the spirit of the laws' (also the
title for his major work).

The social-political institutions and the whole framework of law and
regulation in a democracy cannot, therefore, be seen solely as devices to
secure the competitive private interests of individual parties. Instead,
such institutions and rules supply the necessary background against
which alone the ends and needs of individual liberty can be intelligible
(ibid., part 1, bk. 5, chs. 2–7: 42–51). Thus for Montesquieu, political
liberty is the criterion for judging a free society and not the criterion of
the level of protection afforded to existing private interests and claims in
the market.

Arendt (1963: 188) observes that 'among the pre-revolutionary
theorists only Montesquieu never thought it necessary to introduce an
absolute, a divine or despotic power, into the political realm', and this is
closely connected to the fact that a public interest concept of law is not
the Hobbesian or even Roman use of law as absolute instrument of
enforcing political authority. Rather, from Montesquieu's characteriza-
tion of public-interest law and regulation, the spirit of the law is a
'rapport' or relation subsisting between the collective will (the civil
state) and the political liberty of the individual citizen, as different
parties to the republican compact (Montesquieu, 1989: part 1, bk. 1, ch.
3; bk. 5, ch. 3). The rapport between government and the governed
amounts to no more than 'rules', *règles*, or principles of democratic
legitimacy (ibid., part 1, bk. 5, chs. 2–3: 42–4), supplying justified
legitimacy to those who govern in the name of citizens. When this
relation, which is a public relation, dissolves, so does the civil state
(ibid., part 1, bk. 8, ch. 2–10: 112–19). The publicness of the relation of
law and policy for Montesquieu is thus grounded in the relations of the
public realm which a free society must necessarily defend (Arendt, 1958:
202). In short, it is the absence of such a realm based on public
relations, as against private relations, that is the distinguishing feature
of tyranny (Montesquieu, 1989: part 1, bk. 8, ch. 2: 112–14).

Lefort (1988), Furet (1981), and Constant (1988, 1980) suggest that
this concept of civil society is far more useful to understanding
European differences over the role of the state than the simplistic, even
ethnocentric, charge of *dirigisme*. Thus the struggle in defining a social
order of a union of European states through a framework of laws and
regulations is more accurately revealed in the tension between the

public-service concept that the sole route to individual liberty is by way of a public-interest relation between citizens and the state, on the one hand, set against the liberal and nationalist models of social organization, on the other, than in any presumption of conflict between *dirigisme* and liberalism with respect to state intervention.

Hegel's conceptualization of civil society further contributes to the foundations of public service in this idea of democracy. As argued in Chapter 3, Hegel supported the principle of public freedom and the autonomy of civil society which he attempted to secure and supplement by differentiation from the state, not solely through the liberation of private competitiveness—as advocated by Locke, Hobbes and Smith—but also through a concept of institutional guarantees (Hegel, 1952a: 122–55). Hegel saw clearly that the central principle of modern civil society is not merely the private sphere of property and private conscience, but also the public realm of associational conditions and the structure of public institutions.

This sphere is 'freed from personal opinion and contingency . . . recognized, guaranteed, and at the same time elevated to conscious effort for a common end' (Hegel, 1952a: 154). Hegel's theory of civil society (ibid. 122–55, see also Chapter 3) is thus directly connected to his theory of freedom, in the notion that the public realm and public institutions ought to constitute an embodiment of the principles of universal freedom, 'the actuality of the ethical Idea' (ibid. 155). He is thus able to conceive a set of institutions that mediate between private and public realms, between egoism and public-mindedness, and between individual and common life both within civil society and between civil society and the state—an element of some significance which is absent in liberalism's conceptual foundation. The demands and privileges of citizenship, and the public practice of judgement and self-determination, is less abstract in Hegel's work than the moral responsibilities and freedoms of private conscience in Kantian liberalism, as well as less impoverished than the non-political forms of freedom, political identity, and justice in the utilitarian liberalism of Locke and Hobbes. Hence, the irreconcilable dualism of public and private is not assumed in Hegelian political theory at the same time as the integrity of each sphere is provided with a philosophical basis. Hegel's insistence on the primacy of institutions of public discourse such as public corporations, legislative institutions, and public opinion within the state as the basis of political legitimacy shifts the meaning of his theory to rationality, universality of principle, and democratization in the determination of common welfare. For this reason, Hegel's theory cannot simply be reduced to collective authoritarianism as is sometimes the liberal charge (Cohen, 1989).

A public-service/public-interest theory of democracy describes an important component of the French political tradition but also of several other states including, for example, Belgium, Italy, and Germany (Taylor, 1990; Lasok and Stone, 1987; David and Spinosi, 1973). The theory has evolved since the French Revolution, but especially in the period from the Industrial Revolution, as embodied in the corporatist organization of social sectors such as railways and utilities that are held to be basic to the common interest. While the public-service principle is constitutionally grounded in the French Constitution (1946), as in that of other member states, it is also provided for in constitutional provisions of the European Union (Article 2 of the Treaty of Rome, Commission of the European Communities, 1993*b*; Title 1, Article B of the Maastricht Treaty, Commission of the European Communities, 1993*a*) which underscore the role of Community law in guaranteeing the conditions of the general welfare.

As Bauby and Boual (1994: 11) point out, recalling De Paepe's century-old definition, the public-service principle rests on the recognition that certain social sectors must be exempt from sole governance by market processes in order to permit universal access to certain public goods and services that contribute to the minimum basis of equality in economic, social, and cultural relations. It is grounded in Montesquieu's cornerstone principle of equality under democratic or republican law (Montesquieu, 1989: part 1, bk. 5, ch. 5: 44–7) whereby the associational conditions of civil society, its self-regulatory conditions, are possible only if the law guarantees the minimum threshold of human need. The republican constitution requires, therefore, the obligation on lawgivers to maintain access to basic goods and services, or else 'inequality will enter at the point not protected by the laws, and the republic will be lost' (ibid., part 1, bk. 5, ch. 5: 45).

Civil society or associational conditions, as Tocqueville (1990) emphasized, can only escape destruction by being incorporated within the political organization of society. This is a fundamental departure from the liberalism of Locke for whom civil society requires no political basis whatsoever, thus casting the individual on to his or her own resources for every aspect of human need, even the most basic.

Drawing on Montesquieu's idea of the necessity for the political organization of civil society, Hegel later expressed scepticism of a totally autonomous, unregulated private sphere independent of the political order (Pelczynski, 1984). The common interest in fragmentation and diversification of power in civil society, and the empowering of citizens to foster their participation in the public realm, under the public-service theory, requires that minimum needs for health, education, basic utilities like water, electricity, communication, and so on, not be determined entirely by proprietary social power but be equally available to all. The criterion for application of public service arises if a collectivity, whether local, regional, national, or (today) European, determines that a public good or essential service for all, either existing or new, cannot be realized in an adequate or satisfactory manner by the private market (see discussion of the evolution of 'social citizenship' in Europe, in Dahrendorf, 1994, 1988; Meehan, 1993; Dyson, 1980). The essential characteristic of this good could proceed from a strategic common interest or a fundamental condition of equity or social cohesion and is mandated for all by an act of law or through processes of regulation.

The notion of public service is thus strictly tied to the idea of 'general interest', or a universal-service doctrine in such communication sectors as telecommunications, education, and broadcasting. There are at least three public-service principles that are held in common among EU member states (see Meehan, 1993; Bauby and Boual, 1994; Dahrendorf, 1994).

Continuity The regulation of an activity in the general interest implies its significance as a social or strategic good and thus necessitates it be regular and continuous.

Equality The notion of public service as universal is intrinsically allied to equality of citizenship, which reposes on the extension of constitutional guarantees, such as in the French Declaration of the Rights of Man (1789), for equality before the law. It is a principle which, by Montesquieu's and Hegel's standard, requires that the individual user of public-interest goods be placed in an equal position, without discrimination or special advantages. Among the regulations which follow from this, of course, is regulation of tariffs in sectors covered by public service, linked to the maintenance of neutrality of service with respect to all users. Whatever the respective characteristics of a public-service good, the obligation to provide a service to all at minimum cost logically removes the question of general interest or universal service from governance by processes of maximization of rate of return.

Mutability According to this public service principle, the domain governed by the service is adapted to historical needs and evolves both in range and quality. The notion of public service is not static, therefore, but prevails in a context of an evolving, dynamic jurisdiction.

Thus the attribution of governmental despotism which is inherent in the accusation of *dirigisme* does not adequately clarify an alternative conceptualization of democratic society based on a theory of political rights and public service and with considerably developed political foundations that stands in opposition to the premises of either liberalization or authoritarianism. The depiction of differences between the *dirigistes* and liberals in the European Union obscures, therefore, the true underlying debate over the actual aims of liberalization and the paradigms which oppose it. Among the nationalist, liberal, and public-service conceptions of the role of the state and the basis of union among peoples and nations in the Community, the first two indicate private modes of organizing public space (see Chapter 2), while the last bears many of the elements of a participatory concept of public space elaborated earlier (see Chapter 3). The distinction between a public-service conception and a nationalist or culturalist approach to communication is also significant, not merely in their fundamentally opposed assumptions regarding the identity of the body politic with an exclusive cultural form, but also for the ironic convergence between liberalism and nationalism which this difference reveals in the audio-visual sector. It is argued that, despite the ostensible divide between cultural and liberal conceptions of audiovisual production and distribution in the multimedia age, the forms of intervention identified by cultural theories of regulation are creating a paradoxical convergence with liberalization, thus further intensifying historical pressures on the public-service paradigm.

CULTURAL GOODS OR ECONOMIC GOODS?

Convergence of Nationalism and Liberalism in Audiovisual Policy

This discussion takes up the other significant hindrance to liberalization's competitive order which arises from assertions of cultural sovereignty or a nationalist discourse over the terms of production and distribution of audiovisual cultural forms. Despite appearances of profound irreconcilability between cultural and liberal conceptions of the audiovisual problem, the forms of intervention identified by cultural theories of regulation create a paradoxical convergence with liberalization, further eroding the political constitution of public space. The cultural conception of public space is discussed in Chapter 2 and the analysis now further elaborates its relation to audiovisual expression in the information society.

Notions of cultural collectivism as a basis for information policy may be opposed to market-based criteria. Yet the cultural approach itself may be inherently incapacitated in articulating a valid basis for participatory information structures that form the essence of the public-service tradition. The cultural–nationalist model emphasizes information content celebrating the exclusivity of the cultural bonds of the collective, but neglects advocacy for conditions of substantive participation in expression from a range of social interests as would be required in the universality principle of a public-interest approach. The emphasis on organic cultural bonds to delineate a cultural identity is accomplished at the expense of defence for widespread access to knowledge and information and for deliberative practices leading to common consent and common decision-making. In short, a cultural argument for public space is not necessarily a democratic one, in the same way that a market-choice argument for public space can exist in a fundamentally incongruous relation with the central requirements of political society. The relation between these two privatist modes of public space in the politically sensitive sector of audiovisual policy is addressed not only by the struggle between liberalism and nationalism, but in its concrete embodiments advanced by the respective positions of the USA and the EU over the legitimacy of audiovisual regulation in the information society.

Gellner (1983), Anderson (1983), and Taylor (1979) cite Herder's notion of the *Volk* (for a study of Herder's thought, see Clark, 1955) as the conceptual origin of modern nationalism. This approach advocates the community as an expressive, not a political, identity with a peculiar manner of expression that is unique, irreplaceable, frequently 'pure', and which requires to be sustained and handed down in some untainted, uncontaminated form. The expressivist conception of human association as articulated by Herder (see Taylor, 1979; Clark, 1955) thus defends the idea of culture as its own 'form' driven to some realization, which must be freed from external constraint—such as competing or alternative cultures—in order to discover the indefinable thread which guides it. The logic of this view of the public realm therefore suggests a purity of descent that must be defended against polluting cultural strains that are to be excluded and on occasion exterminated or stamped out, in order to release the forces of cultural self-realization or the unique form embedded within the expressive unity.

This was the reasoning articulated in the early stages of the European Community's justification for a transnational public realm in audiovisual production and distribution:

The audiovisual sector is of great importance to the cultural identity of peoples, regions and nations. It is also a rapidly growing sector of the world economy, significant in its own right and with considerable multiplier effects on other cultural sectors. (European Parliament, 1989a: 8)

Nationalist structures of reasoning earlier formed the political premise of the television without frontiers Green Paper (Commission of the European Communities, 1984) in a classical cultural syllogism:

European unification will only be achieved if Europeans want it. Europeans will only want it if there is such a thing as a European identity. A European identity will only develop if Europeans are adequately informed. At present, information via the mass media is controlled at national level. (Ibid. 28)

The 'unquestionable cultural significance' (Commission of the European Communities, 1993*a*: 120) of programme production and distribution has also been placed at the centre of information policy by a president of the European Commission:

. . . the culture industry will tomorrow be one of the biggest industries, a creator of wealth and jobs. Under the terms of the Treaty we do not have the resources to implement a cultural policy; but we are going to try to tackle it along economic lines. It is not simply a question of television programmes. We have to build a powerful European culture industry that will enable us to be in control of both the medium and its content, maintaining our standards of civilization, and encouraging the creative people amongst us. (Speech by Jacques Delors, European Parliament, 1985: 64)

The Community's emphasis on the creation of a European cultural identity, transcending national cultural borders, has been translated into a series of information-society initiatives to advance a shared culture through audiovisual forms. In the language of the EC, such policies 'will strengthen the Europeans' sense of belonging to one and the same Community' (Commission of the European Communities, 1988*d*: 52). Ministers of culture of member states have gone even further to propose expansion of transfrontier audiovisual distribution networks as 'one of the top priorities of a European cultural policy . . . part of the concept of a "people's Europe" ' (ibid. 49). The communication dimension of the single market later became a key rationale in the development of a 'European Cultural Policy' (Commission of the European Communities, 1990a: 52), and to this extent, as I have argued (Venturelli, 1993) along with Robins and Morley (1992) and Collins (1994), EU policy increasingly recognizes that questions of culture, politics, and identity are at the heart of the European project.

The momentum behind the expressivist conception of transnational association has been strong enough to cause a significant change in the Community's narrow economic mandate, gaining for the EU a gradual constitutional authority to shape the public realm as a cultural realm. Article 128 of the 1992 Maastricht Treaty on European Union provides legal grounds for the European Commission and other institutions of the EU, including the European Court of Justice, to intervene in the public sphere on cultural grounds. The political and regulatory significance of this provision makes it worth quoting in its entirety (emphasis has been added):

TITLE IX
CULTURE

1. The Community shall contribute to the flowering of the cultures of the Member States, while respecting their national and regional diversity and at the same time bringing the *common cultural heritage* to the fore.

2. Action by the Community shall be aimed at encouraging cooperation between Member States and, if necessary, supporting and supplementing their action in the following areas:
   — improvement of the knowledge and dissemination of the *culture and history of the European peoples*;
   — conservation and *safeguarding of cultural heritage* of European significance;
   — non-commercial cultural exchanges;
   — artistic and literary creation, including the *audiovisual sector*.

3. The Community and the Member States shall foster cooperation with third countries and the competent international organizations in the sphere of culture, in particular the Council of Europe.

4. The *Community shall take cultural aspects into account in its action* under other provisions of this Treaty.

5. In order to contribute to the achievement of the objectives referred to in this Article, the Council:
   — acting in accordance with the procedure referred to in Article 189b and after consulting the Committee of the Regions, shall adopt incentive measures, excluding any harmonization of the laws and regulations of the Member States. The Council shall act unanimously throughout the procedures referred to in Article 189b.
   — acting unanimously on a proposal from the Commission, shall adopt recommendations.

(Commission of the European Communities, 1993*b*, Maastricht Treaty, Article 128: 89, emphasis added)

These developments testify to the importance the EU attributes to the audiovisual sector as the most important of the cultural industries; an importance perceived relevant not only to the idea of audiovisual production and distribution as an agency of social cohesion (Commission of the European Communities, 1993*a*: 120–1), but also to the perception that programme production and the information industries are prime agencies in the regeneration of economic growth (Commission of the European Communities, 1994*a*: 11–14). It is evident here that Bell's (1973) liberal argument regarding the economic power of an 'information revolution' to recreate a new industrial age—'post-industrialism'—has been conjoined with the Community's notion of audiovisual creation as a cornerstone in the cross-stitching of self-proclaimed, exclusive national cultures into a unitary European identity. The Community's synthesis of liberalism and nationalism is best summed up in the declaration: 'The audiovisual sector has enormous potential to generate wealth and create jobs, as well as being essential to Europe's cultural life' (Commission of the European Communities, 1994b: 17).

According to Gellner (1983), the argument for the cohesive power of culture is classically nationalist especially when it presupposes that the body politic and an exclusive cultural form are congruent. That is to say, the formulation of cultural uniqueness employed to fuse the collective into a nation serves in fact to justify the legitimacy of social and political institutions, thereby substituting for the function of a participatory, deliberative sphere for achieving common consensus by democratic means. As Herder (cited in Clark, 1955) suggests, each collectivity constructed on the basis of cultural affinities must express its own inimitable path to humanness. Such an argument for human association does not, however, answer the question Hegel (1952a) attempted to raise: how can modes of social solidarity be distinguished on grounds of political freedoms that citizens enjoy as against the communion of blood, descent, language, religion, and other non-political ascriptive criteria of membership?

The idea of European cohesion is therefore framed in a nationalist matrix, ascribing to the circulation of audiovisual forms the strategic function of forging a sense of Europeanness as unique identity. The development of European audiovisual policy hence touches on the question of union as it touches on economic enlargement. Yet these separate aims obscure the profound difficulty in reconciling the Community's jurisdiction in enhancing the conditions of transnational commerce, with promoting the construction of pan-European nationalism. Former Commission President Jacques Delors may be credited with discovering a working concept which allows the tools of economic jurisdiction to be applied to the cultural sphere. In his speeches (European Parliament, 1985) and policy proposals (the Delors White Paper, Commission of the European Communities, 1993a), Delors identified the economic basis of cultural production, specifically audiovisual production, as a justification for state, that is, Commission intervention.

Now while the 1957 Treaty of Rome (Commission of the European Communities, 1993b) provides no specific grounds for Commission action in support of cultural policy, the Treaty could be construed as a basis for regulating cultural forms as commodities or services—that is, as activities conducted for a remuneration—thus legalizing any Commission instruments designed to create a 'common market' in audiovisual products. This approach led to the adoption in 1989 of a Commission statute establishing a single market in broadcasting, the television without frontiers directive (Commission of the European Communities, 1989) which regulates an economic activity whose form was judged as cultural. A Green Paper on broadcasting which preceded the directive by several years (Commission of the European Communities, 1984) justified Community authority over the structure of communication networks functioning as content or programming carriers in the public realm:

Contrary to what is widely imagined, the EEC Treaty applies not only to economic activities but, as a rule to all activities carried out for remuneration, regardless of whether they take place in the economic, social, cultural (including in particular information, creative or artistic activities and entertainment), sporting or any other sphere. (Ibid. 6)

Thus the debate over cultural and audiovisual policy is not a contest between *dirigistes* and liberals, that is, between interventionists and non-interventionists. Each of the three contending models of audiovisual regulation—nationalist, liberal, and public service—regard state action as central to the achievement of certain social and political ends. The real question and more accurate representation of the debate in the audiovisual sector is not whether but what kind of intervention is promoted by their distinctive and opposed formulations of the problems of an information society.

EUROPEAN CONSTRUCTION AND THE AUDIOVISUAL BATTLEGROUND

Asymmetries of Culture and Economy in Programme Distribution

The information industries are central to the debate among liberal, culturalist, and public-service models of European construction. Divisions in Community policy over the audiovisual sector exemplify the deep struggle at the heart of the political organization of the European Union. Proponents of cultural arguments and public-service arguments, each by separate justifications, are united against application of purely commercial criteria to audiovisual production and distribution, reflecting the promotion of particular forms of the role of the state and of integrating the Community. This dynamic characterizes the audiovisual battle as a 'debate over the paradigm of [a] European system of organization—can there be a common European?' (from an interview conducted for this study).[2]

---

[2] EU GATT negotiator for the audiovisual sector, DGI in the European Commission, interviewed May 1994.

The relationship between audiovisual policy and advocacy for a particular mode of civil society is true for liberalism as well, according to which public policy in the European Union should be aimed purely at securing the free circulation of proprietary assets, or a 'free market'. In the words of an American critic of the EU's audiovisual policy, 'The EEC is above all an economic community. Hence, the directive's objectives are mainly economic' (Wilkins, 1991).

The contrast between these competing visions of community is captured with unusual poignancy in the debate over the television without frontiers directive (Commission of the European Communities, 1989). Designed as an instrument to establish a single market in broadcast programmes while also incorporating culturalist mechanisms to promote European audiovisual expression, it has turned instead into a powerful tool of liberalization (Venturelli, 1993; Hoffmann-Riem, 1992; Robins and Morley, 1992; Servaes, 1992; Schlesinger, 1991). The television without frontiers directive is the European Union's most significant achievement in cultural policy yet it has been judged (Mulgan and Paterson, 1993; Siune and Truetzschler, 1992; Shaughnessy and Cobo, 1990) the most destructive to a European audiovisual industry. This is because it is held responsible for opening the public realm to the international audiovisual distribution network (Garnham, 1990), thus drawing European cultural production into the competitive order of transnational commercial broadcasting.

Advisers to the French broadcast regulatory agency, the Conseil Supérieur de l'Audiovisuel (CSA) hold the directive responsible for 'making competition for European productions very brutal because American productions are omnipresent'.[3] The Hollywood audiovisual industry has developed into an 'integrated strategic oligopoly against which few national producers in other nations can compete', according to Yves Mamou,[4] journalist for *Le Monde*. The Commission itself has come informally to admit that Hollywood domination of the European broadcasting market was essentially delivered by the television directive. The Commission itself has questioned the rationality of the sheer comprehensiveness of US audiovisual distribution in the European Union, Hollywood's largest overseas market: 'The US clearly has an overwhelming advantage in distributing over commercial broadcasting networks in Europe. But how about other cultures and languages in this world? Are smaller cultures and languages simply to die out? Is this the objective of transnational broadcasting?'[5]

How does an instrument of information policy for harmonizing the

---

[3] From interviews at the CSA conducted for this study, Paris, April 1994.
[4] Yves Mamou was interviewed for this study, Paris, April 1994.
[5] From an interview at the Commission conducted for this study, Brussels, May 1994.

European audiovisual market and furthering cultural cohesion suddenly become a powerful agent of liberalization serving the international audiovisual monopolies? Certainly, the instrument is worth examining to see how this effect was achieved. Following a three-year debate over its provisions in the European Parliament and the Council of Ministers, the European Community adopted the television without frontiers directive on 3 October 1989 (see Maggiore, 1990). As the first policy framework designed to address transnational broadcasting, it requires member states to ensure unrestricted reception of cross-border broadcast transmissions (the 'sender state principle'), and to refrain from limiting retransmission on their territory of any broadcasts that meet specific Community conditions (ibid.). Thus the overarching goal of the directive is the creation of a common market in television broadcasting which allows broadcast of audiovisual programmes to move freely across borders (Commission of the European Communities, 1989). The directive stipulates that member states have regulatory jurisdiction only over broadcasters operating in their country or making use of a frequency or satellite capacity within their state. Principal articles within the directive allow broadcasting services to contain both advertising commercials and sponsored programmes (within percentage limits), though on the condition of protection of minors and of the right of reply (ibid.).

But the most controversial regulatory measure of the directive is a mandatory programme quota which requires member states to oblige public and private networks to earmark at least 50 per cent of their total airtime for European audiovisual productions:

Member States shall ensure *where practicable* and by appropriate means, that broadcasters reserve for *European works*, within the meaning of Article 6, a majority proportion of their transmission time, excluding the time appointed to news, sports events, games, advertising and teletext services. This proportion, having regard to the broadcaster's informational, educational, cultural and entertainment responsibilities to its viewing public, should be achieved progressively, on the basis of *suitable criteria*. (Commission of the European Communities, 1989: Article 4(1))

The emphasis added above points to loopholes that have played a central role in abrogating the local content provision, thus tilting the directive towards the rights of transnational broadcasters to consolidate cross-border audiovisual markets while simultaneously weakening the power of member states to regulate these transmissions on anything but the narrowest grounds. 'Where practicable' is a loophole essentially rendering the provision rhetorical since practicality can easily be claimed as justification for wall-to-wall American programming.

Similarly, the absence of a working definition for 'European works' allows a wide variety of questionable categories, such as inexpensive talk shows and game shows, to substitute for production and dissemination of creative programmes intended as the real cultural objective of the provision. Finally, the wording of 'suitable criteria' invites the barest of standards to be ruled legitimate.

Nevertheless, it was not on account of un-enforceability that the directive gained notoriety on the international stage. Rather, it was the fact of the directive's existence and the idea of a quota at all that allowed the international broadcasters and audiovisual producers to oppose it as a trade restriction against foreign, that is, American films and programming. The international audiovisual producers were led by the Motion Picture Association of America and its president, Jack Valenti, and by the US government both alleging that the cultural motive of the directive was no more than a smokescreen for illegitimate economic protectionism (Reuters, 11 September 1989). For European audiovisual producers such as the European Film Companies Alliance (*Europe*, 1996), supported by members of the European Parliament, the single market in broadcasting without the quota provision would turn the directive into a 'Trojan Horse' for the Americanization of European cultural production (Roberto Barzanti, chairman of the European Parliament's Committee on Youth, Culture, Education, the Media, and Sport, quoted in Collins, 1994; see also Barzanti, 1990).

Examination of the directive as a whole, particularly the preamble, indicates that the quota provision in Article 4 was not simply appended to appease an isolated special interest, but reflects a comprehensive regulatory strategy to address the cultural agenda of 'common action to eliminate the barriers which divide Europe' (Commission of the European Communities, 1989: preamble), by employing a particular interpretation of competition law:

It is essential for the Member States to ensure the prevention of any acts which may prove detrimental to freedom of movement and trade in television programmes or which may promote the creation of dominant positions which would lead to restrictions on pluralism and freedom of televised information and of the information sector as a whole. (Ibid., preamble)

The 'acts which may . . . lead to restrictions on pluralism' refers, of course, to the domination of audiovisual production and distribution by imported programmes. The democratic value of pluralism in televised cultural forms appears to be applied to ensure 'the independence of cultural development in the Member States and the preservation of cultural diversity in the Community' (ibid., preamble). The goals of pluralism and diversity thus establish the rationale for the directive's cultural conception. Yet, the directive undermines its own rationale for public policy by structuring into the instrument the significant disclaimer 'where practicable' (ibid., Article 4(1), quoted above). The EU has thus left member states with no legal means to safeguard monopolization of distribution networks for European programmes, even where European audiovisual production may be promoted through national support systems as is the case in France. This default obviously works in favour of distribution of international audiovisual productions whose transnational market strategies and interests are inscribed into the framework for information liberalization.

The directive also defines certain terms which serve as additional loopholes, further derailing the cultural aims of audiovisual policy in the European Union. One of these, 'television broadcasting', is defined as 'the initial transmission . . . of television programmes intended for reception by the public' (ibid., Article 1(a)). This definition would essentially cover all programming destined to be viewed by a European public. The directive grants immunity to news and database services (see Article 4(1)), an exception which in retrospect seems not to have taken into account the recent dominance of international news production and distribution networks such as the Cable News Network (CNN). While the broad scope of the definition requires broadcasting to be regulated and conform to the directive's explicit cultural aims, the transformation of the cultural quota into a voluntary scheme through inherent loopholes permits all broadcasting, including foreign, to be shielded from higher content regulations at the national level by Community law. This translates into the imposition of universal reception requirements upon member states prohibiting them from regulating, preventing, or controlling foreign programming on public-interest grounds, whether cultural or constitutional. Once more, the information policy is biased in favour of international cultural industries that seek greater transnational governance over the information sector.

Secondly, the ambiguous nature of what counts as a 'European work' is caused by the complex but malleable provisions of Article 6 which allow the cultural quota to be satisfied if programming is composed of audiovisual works made in Europe. Since Article 6 fails to clarify differences between programmes produced outside Europe, those produced in Europe by the same international content monopolies or multinational audiovisual industry and indigenous European cultural production, the European content provision could be nominally satisfied by any substitution. The provision for 'European works' thus functions as another significant loophole, for a programme may assume this classification if it fulfils any one of the following requirements: it was produced by an established European producer; it was supervised and controlled by an established European producer; it was co-produced for the most part and controlled by an established European producer; it was produced or co-produced by producers established in 'European third states' that are party to the European Convention on Transfrontier Television of the Council of Europe (Council of Europe, 1989); it was produced in 'other European third countries' but mainly made with authors and workers residing in 'one or more European states'; or, it was co-produced outside Europe but 'made mainly with authors and workers who reside in Europe' (Commission of the European Communities, 1989: Article 6, 1(*a*), 1(*b*), 1(*c*), 2(*a*), 2(*b*), 2(*c*), 3, and 4).

Clearly, none of these provisions accounts for the crucial distinction between audiovisual programming integrated into the multinational production and distribution chain, and programmes that are independent of this structure. Since this is the only distinction that matters in the promotion of European cultural works in the public realm as against the predominant carriage of Hollywood cultural products by European broadcasters, the preceding requirements are quite simply irrelevant to their own professed aims.

In fact the co-production exemption (ibid., Article 6, par. 2(*c*)) which this definition of 'European works' allows has made it much easier for the international audiovisual industry to elude the cultural quota by collaborating, in part, with European producers and creators contractually, under work-for-hire arrangements (see account of this effect in the UK in Mulgan and Paterson, 1993). The advantages of such arrangements far exceed the time quota itself for they allow exclusive exploitation rights to audiovisual works that would otherwise have been forbidden by national copyright laws favouring the European creator (see Chapter 5). It is evident from this study's investigation that the co-production loophole in retrospect was not anticipated by European policy-makers since any debate, reservations, or misgivings on this provision are quite absent from records of either the Commission, the European Parliament, or European press reports in the period leading up to, and after, the directive's passage. Even considering the somewhat ambiguous definition of a European work, Article 6 reveals not the least intent on the part of the drafters to prevent non-European industries from producing programmes from within the Community with the same international content control. It is and has been an open-door for large-scale multinational-content monopolies to enter the European market (see Mulgan and Paterson, 1993). Indeed, licence to co-produce gives Hollywood audiovisual producers a significant competitive advantage as admitted in a comment by the vice-president of the European office of the Motion Picture Export Association of America (MPEAA, the overseas division of the Motion Picture Association of America):[6]

We feel American film companies are part of the audiovisual industry in Europe. We want to see a healthy audiovisual industry in Europe and we're spending on salaries, taxes, investments, production, marketing, advertising . . . Obviously, we qualify as European films and want a share of European subsidies that support European production.[7]

The co-production loophole demonstrates the profound European dilemma over the meaning of culture and the use of cultural sovereignty as a basis for organizing public space. In casting the circulation of expressive forms as a cultural issue, regulation of public space justified on grounds of cultural policy has decoupled creative production from the question of its economic dependency on large-scale proprietary-content monopolies. So long as creative participation and creative control remain European, the directive regards it as a secondary matter if the investment is foreign. Article 6 turns the issue not into a matter of European ownership of creative production, but into a question of the participation of European creative labour in the process of creating cultural forms in film and broadcasting. It further underscores the incongruous argument that the cultural and the economic are separate and unrelated classes of phenomena in the structure of public space or that either can be effectively addressed on purely economic grounds or purely cultural grounds (see rationalization of the inherent irrelevance of culture to trade in audiovisual services, in Donaldson, 1996; Kaplan, 1994). Yet, as will be addressed in the next section, this becomes the final solution as the cultural aims of the information society are steadily assimilated to the liberalization aims of constructing a European audiovisual market which satisfies the international audiovisual conglomerates.

It may be possible to envision a certain structure of a perfect information market whereby cultural monopolies in audiovisual forms do not inevitably dominate. But the competitive order of information liberalization has rendered this more an article of faith than reality. At no stage in the development and debate over these options is the understanding apparent that a cultural rationale would eventually become self-defeating and that a third approach must be found. At no level of public or governmental discussion was an approach conceptualized for guaranteeing information rights to cultural, political, social, and economic expression through the conditions of participatory public space. The socio-legal basis for an information-rights framework in the

---

[6] Frank Tonini of the MPEAA; from an interview conducted for this study, Brussels, May 1994.
[7] Cited at note 6 above.

information society could have been developed from existing constitutional provisions in the European Convention for Human Rights (1950), the Maastricht Treaty (Commission of the European Communities, 1993*b*), and from European public-service tradition oriented towards the preconditions of citizen participation.

Finally, the directive designates television broadcasting as 'in normal circumstances, a *service* within the meaning of the Treaty [of Rome]' (Commission of the European Communities, 1989: preamble, emphasis added). This has allowed the Community to propose in the GATT that broadcasting be exempt from GATT regulations since it is a service and not a tangible product subject to market-trading rules. However, the strategy has trapped the European Union in the same dilemma touched on above, namely, how to justify in the international arena the regulation of cultural production and distribution on grounds that it is a service and not a product. The EU argument divided programming from its structural context of distribution infrastructure and end-use technology (for example, direct broadcast satellites, cable networks, television sets, cameras, satellite dishes, fibre-optic cable, and so on) and raised other intricate questions. For example, is the broadcaster's use of creative labour—such as the services of software designers, scriptwriters, or directors—to be regulated separately from the use of the creative work such as the final script, the film, or tangible product?

These questions and the constitutional option of creating a participatory public realm have gone unanswered and untouched in the decade when the issue of cultural protectionism has come under scrutiny within the expanding international liberalization regime. Information policy has preferred to address this conflict on the technical level by engineering ever-newer mechanisms for imposing cultural policy on the content of the public realm, yet without ever clarifying the underlying issue of the normative basis of content regulation that is constitutionally justified on grounds of positive political rights of citizens, rather than the normatively ambiguous and constitutionally indefensible, nationalist grounds of 'cultural identity'.

Final solution of audiovisual liberalization: The Annulment of Culture

Liberal objections to the cultural sovereignty argument can be readily inferred. Smith (1993) and Donaldson (1996), for example, argue that regulation of information services on cultural grounds violates international free-trade laws by protecting 'inefficient' trade sectors from more 'efficient' international competitors. This undermines the 'theory of comparative advantage' (ibid.) that comprises the foundation of free-trade law, whereby each nation should be willing to undergo the

destruction of certain industries—or 'restructuring' as is often termed—
so that resources can be reallocated to more efficient industries (ibid.).
On these grounds of reasoning, the European audiovisual sector should
prepare for its own annihilation and resources should be shifted to other
industries that stand a better chance of being competitive in international markets—perhaps soap, widgets, or cheese. The theory
assumes, therefore, that the production and distribution of ideas and
expression must be subjected to the test of 'efficiency' and that other
criteria such as the needs of democracies for information to serve
public-opinion formation, education, culture, or the non-commercial
associational needs of civil society, are irrelevant, non-measurable,
'inherently subjective', and 'metaphysical' (see Donaldson, 1996: 147).
The implication clearly is that information rights to serve the aims of
democratic constitutions are non-admissible arguments in the regulatory framework of the information society.

But liberalization proponents are not the only opponents of European
cultural policy, however ineffective. The directive is equally criticized by
nationalist and public-service supporters. It has been fiercely resisted
by member states which perceive their languages and cultures to be
threatened by the internationalization of audiovisual markets and the
integration of Community markets in cultural expression that seems to
benefit only the international audiovisual industry (Rousseau, 1995;
May, 1994; Chalvon-Demersay and Pasquier, 1993). A mechanism
advocated and designed on grounds of cultural policy has been opposed
on the same grounds by those who view the directive as an instrument
of the transnational audiovisual industry and propose the Community
undertake alternate forms of intervention (Commission of the European
Communities, 1994*h*). The EU has in turn responded with policies
designed to promote diversity and fragmentation of culture as a protection against the unifying cultural forces unleashed by a directive
originally supported for that very purpose. These counter-unification
policies include, for instance, the MEDIA programme (Commission of
the European Communities, 1991*e*, 1990*f*, 1990*g*), and an audiovisual
production subsidy for individual producers in member states which has
emerged as an important element in Community action to buttress
indigenous cultural forms (Commission of the European Communities,
1994*i*; *European Report*, 1995*a*).

While EU audiovisual policy is marked by conflict among three rival
conceptions over the meaning of transnational community, its development is also marked by shifts in emphasis between rival cultural policy
goals: notably between the promotion of cultural unity and the promotion of cultural diversity. The opposition between unity and diversity is
not wholly identical to the argument between public-service supporters

and proponents of liberalization since the ultimate ends of each, and the approach to forms of state action to achieve those ends, differ considerably. The single element they do hold in common is a need for intervention, even under the liberalization model which ultimately seeks to reconstruct the role of the state by shifting public policy from non-commercial aims to entirely commercial aims. For instance, the television without frontiers directive has achieved the cultural integrative function it set out to create but only by facilitating, through a rich store of loopholes, much further domination of the audiovisual and broadcast markets by the multinational audiovisual industry originating primarily in the USA (Servaes, 1992; Robins and Morley, 1992). This may not be the form of common culture originally envisioned by the television initiative, yet a liberalized-content production sector structured in favour of the international audiovisual industry was the only type of 'unity' the directive and the EU has been able to deliver. Predictably, this has drawn the support of liberal internationalists within the EU and alienated both nationalists and public-service supporters.

This outcome has called up compensatory responses to the expansion of liberalization as an experiment in integration. To compensate for the decline in diversity of programming content, Community intervention in the audiovisual market has grown to defuse this threat. The question of diversity of creative forms serves both as a nationalist issue and a public-service issue for guaranteeing plural participation of ideas, information, and representations of social reality which may not be available through a commercially governed public realm.

When MEDIA was established in 1988, its mission was to promote production and dissemination of audiovisual works throughout the Community (Commission of the European Communities, 1991e, 1990g), with a specific focus on training, pre-production, multilingualism of programmes, and easier access to venture capital, among other goals. Thus MEDIA has supported, in a limited sense owing to modest funding, the circulation of films and television programmes made in the Community for the purpose of safeguarding cultural pluralism which was perceived to be threatened by the integration of markets, that is, by information liberalization. MEDIA can be said, therefore, to stand as a modest veto, ineffectual though it be, over cultural policies whose consequences are Americanization of audiovisual production and distribution, and the growing governance of the public realm by large-scale content monopolies. The significance of MEDIA has increased as a result of pressures from nationalist and public-service advocates in member governments and organizations demanding Community policy contain the ever-widening cultural gap between American and European productions distributed through programming networks (see suggestions in Commission of the European Communities, 1994*g*, 1994*h*).

These effects of the information society doubled allocation for MEDIA II (Commission of the European Communities, 1994*j*) which allows loans to support training, to 'develop programmes with a European dimension' or programmes 'to help preserve and enhance cultural identity' (ibid., section 1.2), and to further the transnational distribution of European programmes (ibid., section 3.4). These proposals emphasize the need for pan-European distribution networks to compete with the integrated distribution networks of Hollywood films, as suggested by the European audiovisual industry in evaluating EU policy in this sector (see Think Tank Report, Commission of the European Communities, 1994*h*).

Though these revised initiatives address some of the weaknesses of fragmentation of production and distribution in Europe and attempt to circumvent the constraints and controversies of the broadcast quota through direct public investment, MEDIA II nevertheless continues to replicate and extend the problems of the television without frontiers directive (Commission of the European Communities, 1989). For instance, the conceptualization of MEDIA is firmly within a nationalist rationalization, as is the 1989 directive, calling for safeguards to 're-establish cultural identity in the Member States' (Commission of the European Communities, 1994*j*: section 2.2), 'to help preserve and enhance cultural identity' (ibid., section 1.2), or 'promote Europe's cultural diversity' (ibid., section 2.3).

As argued earlier, this model of information policy results only in establishing boundaries of exclusivity, further isolating and dividing perceptions of uniqueness among various collectivities. Thus the initiative remarkably strengthens the position of large-scale international audiovisual producers and distributors which demonstrates that their particular creative forms are the only formulae that travel across such boundaries. Notwithstanding this complex structure of cultural initiatives and regulation, in the absence of a constitutionally grounded, public-service right for citizens to participate in the public realm of the information society, only a liberalization logic reigns.

Moreover, the MEDIA II initiative explicitly promotes the creation of new forms of concentration and consolidation in European audiovisual production and distribution while simultaneously objecting to such a structure in the US audiovisual industry. A policy which holds that 'cooperation between European producers . . . should be encouraged and reinforced' (ibid., section 2.4), thereby creating incentives for collaboration and integration, ultimately appears to lead to the same consequences generated by the television directive. As argued, the latter has unleashed forces of liberalization by allowing consolidation of distribution networks along transnational lines and crippling the legal authority of member states to regulate this growing form of domination of the public realm by a handful of broadcasters and programme suppliers. Since only the international film producers and broadcasters were organized along transnational lines, they were able to take immediate advantage of the favourable regulatory environment. In the case of the MEDIA II initiative, policies are undoubtedly tilted towards European-based consolidation through a programme of direct subsidy, even while ironically counter-charging that the US 'concentration in film distribution raises competition-policy questions'. Yet the support in information policy for European vertical integration is nevertheless still a support for an environment of proprietary consolidation in the audio-visual market, an approach which can easily be assimilated to the capital structure of the international audiovisual industry.

The logic of liberalization's theory of property rightly assumes that the competitive order of proprietary enlargement tends to favour the largest property holders, national origin notwithstanding. Hence MEDIA II, as well as the 1989 directive, is liable to generate powerful liberalization effects introduced paradoxically on grounds of cultural policy. The real deficit, therefore, remains in the participatory domain of societal and political need, suggesting diminished opportunities for further emergence in the European Union of non-nationalist, civil-society-based, public-service information policies and for the development of terms of common association among peoples and social groups.

Following a lengthy period of consultation over the gravity and nature of the loss of cultural identity in Europe, inviting the participation of European audiovisual producers, researchers, and policy-makers (see Think Tank Report, Commission of the European Communities, 1994*h*), the Commission in 1994 issued an audiovisual Green Paper (Commission of the European Communities, 1994*g*). The principal reason for exploring new forms of intervention, according to this proposal, is because 'if the European Union wants to strengthen its audio-visual policy, it must act quickly, otherwise it will be overtaken by the rapidly developing technology and the unavoidable liberalization of the industry at the international level' (ibid., introduction, p. 9). The crisis is created, the Green Paper argues, from a dramatic decline in the market share of European films and programmes since the passage of the tele-vision without frontiers directive in 1989 (Commission of the European Communities, 1989), which is precisely the opposite of the effect intended by the statute. Thus 'American films remain popular with their market share averaging nearly 80% for the European Union as a whole' (Commission of the European Communities, 1994*g*: 2.1.1.(i). 10).

These observations by themselves contribute nothing new to the problem since they merely reinforce earlier analysis in the years leading up to the directive's passage in 1989.

The proposal's departure from earlier attitudes to the cultural crisis in the audiovisual sector lies in its diagnosis of the causes of imbalance. The decline of the market share of European films is attributed, not to the decline in availability of European audiovisual products, but to 'the weakness of European distribution structures . . . and the failure to take account of market realities throughout the creation, production and distribution process' (ibid. 2.1.1.(ii). 10). This leads to the conclusion that the remedy appropriate to the scale of the problem is to reverse the 'fragmentation' or pluralistic competition among an array of producers, distributors, and creators—precisely the condition which the free-trade thesis values—and to promote by state action conditions favouring 'new forms of cooperation and strategic alliance to exploit their respective strengths' (ibid. 2.2. 13).

The only basis on which Europe can address the cultural sovereignty problem, then, is to allow private proprietors in audiovisual production and distribution 'opportunities and incentives to cooperate' (ibid.). The Green Paper goes so far as to hold up liberalization's model of proprietary consolidation in the international audiovisual market as a model form of collaboration in Europe: '[The] vertical integration of MCA and Matsushita, Columbia and Sony, Polygram and Philips, and Paramount and Viacom demonstrate that the most powerful operators on the world market must strive to acquire control of the most extensive programme catalogues (ibid. 2.2.3. 14). Echoing the rationale for liberalization's approach to a competitive order, the Green Paper connects liberty of communications—in culture, economic prosperity, and other benefits—to the consolidation of information monopolies identified with the emergence of the information society. Thus the solution to the cultural problem paradoxically devolves upon admitting the authoritarian premise of contingency within the liberalization argument: namely, that the information society will not arrive unless by the path of freedom of large-scale consolidation:

The convergence of the programme industry, broadcasting services, cable and telecommunications operators, the publishing industry and manufacturers of information and communications technology equipment is the cause of new products, new audiovisual services which are leading us into a new information society. (Commission of the European Communities, 1994g: summary, p. 42)

To bring about by state intervention new freedoms of consolidation in the public realm, the Green Paper suggests:

1. Shifting resources to large-scale private entities who would be more

likely, not so much to compete, but have a large enough capital base to engage in consolidation practices (ibid. 5.1.1.(iii). 30–1). Thus the form of competition to be promoted by public policy should be closer to the competitive order discussed earlier in this chapter, namely, a type of 'competition' which stimulates particular modes of strategic and structural change.

2. Tightening the time quota mechanism for majority European programmes in the television without frontiers (Commission of the European Communities, 1989) directive to remove loopholes, in particular the 'where practicable' loophole of Article 4, discussed above (Commission of the European Communities, 1994g: 5.1.2. 32–4). This effort later failed in the Council and in the European Parliament (Commission of the European Communities, 1996f; *European Report*, 1996b) as a result of enormous pressures from the international audiovisual industry and from member states opposed to cultural policy (ibid.). It was the only proposal in the Green Paper fiercely opposed by liberalization forces and nation states—either EU or non-EU—advocating information-liberalization policies (see US objections defended in Donaldson, 1996; Garrett, 1994; Shelden, 1994; Center for Strategic and International Studies, 1994). Yet the cultural quota, as argued, is already abrogated by a combination of loopholes—not just one—and by the entire structure of the directive which, as a collection of factors, makes possible foreign integration and collaboration with European industry effectively to efface the lines of what constitutes a 'European work'. Thus Hollywood audiovisual products can just as easily, under the growing liberalization environment, earn a European label through integration with European creative talent and private capital, but while ensuring continued information monopolies by retaining exclusive rights to exploitation. For the European citizen, this restructuring makes not the slightest difference to improving diversity of cultural expression in the substantive content of audiovisual programming itself.

3. Finally, the proposals advocate creating financial incentives through direct subsidy and other mechanisms for transnational consolidation of distribution networks, thus sanctioning the construction of monopolies of distribution (Commission of the European Communities, 1994g: 5.2.1 and 5.2.2. 35–7). This would be accomplished by shifting funds provided under the MEDIA programme for supporting audiovisual productions to supporting large-scale proprietors of distribution networks.

The audiovisual Green Paper is thus both an implicit and explicit admission that the liberalization-theory classification of the audiovisual sector as an economic service for purposes of inclusion in the multilateral trade framework is fundamentally correct. But it does not answer the question as to how the sector can continue to justify exclusion in the GATT. This dramatic *'changement de mentalité'*,[8] as the Commission describes it, is based on the recognition that economic consolidation in the private sector is a powerful tool of Community policy to achieve industrial and cultural policies. To use this tool, the Community must begin with the premise that the economic character of cultural production is the first and most important criterion of public policy, a premise that has also been the US approach all along (see justification of US view in Garrett, 1994). The Commission concludes that 'convergence of many industries needs policies to manage this convergence and to assure a maximum of concentration among many fragmented producers and distributors in the various member states'.[9] To achieve this, the EU will obviously need to abandon its conceptualization of audiovisual works as artistic creations of individual authors that comprises the basis of the cultural definition: 'The economic reality requires a shift from the European conception of authorship. For the global health of the industry requires a shift in concept of what is art, and what is the artist. Our way of doing things is not competitive.'[10]

This shift is necessary, according to Michèle Cotta, journalist for France 2—and one of the contributors to the Think Tank Report (Commission of the European Communities, 1994*h*) which led to the publication of the audiovisual Green Paper—because 'concentration of production is necessary'. The promotion of strategic concentration can only come about, if 'the French government abandons its old argument that audiovisual is a cultural not economic issue. So long as politicians treat audiovisual as culture and not as an economic industrial question, France will remain non-competitive. French [audiovisual] production cannot continue as "art" and "artistic expression" or it will die.'[11]

This argument could almost have been written by the US Trade Representative, an agency of the US government authorized to negotiate the audiovisual and cultural exception dispute with the European Union in the WTO. It demonstrates the way in which the cultural policies of the EU are necessarily reduced to the very paradigm they oppose.

The more the Community has adhered to its nationalist conception, the more it has been forced into the competitive order of the liberalization movement, and thus been constrained in its opportunities to engage with the potential of the information age. By skirting the normative

---

[8] From an interview with DGX conducted for this study, Brussels, April 1994.

[9] Cited at note 8 above.

[10] Cited at note 8 above.

[11] Michèle Cotta, journalist and commentator with France 2, the French public broadcasting network, and contributor to the Commission's Think Tank Report on the audiovisual sector. From an interview for this study, Paris, April 1994.

and constitutional, not just nationalist grounds of information policy in a participatory public realm, the Community's approach may have trivialized the cultural paradigm and inadvertently fostered a hostile environment against opposition to liberalization's competitive order. Dodging the constitutional and political-rights issue has ultimately clouded the central problem in the debate and deprived the cultural argument of its credibility. For reasons argued here, the study holds that the high-stakes international debate between liberalization's market sovereignty and nationalism's cultural sovereignty over the question of regulating expression may be a false argument, since the debate allows communities to imagine that the choices offered by each side are real and indeed exhaustive of the possibilities which are available in the information society.

While it is important to acknowledge the Community's endorsement of the cultural role of public broadcasting as a public service compatible with Articles 90-3 of the Treaty (see discussion of this in Porter, 1993*b*), it is increasingly apparent that no endorsement can ensure the fate of public broadcasting unless it is guaranteed a significant place on the digital spectrum along with other resources in the regulatory environment of the information society.

Closing the Cultural Loophole

In view of the struggle to determine the kind of intervention in the audiovisual sector that balances competing social interests, it is necessary briefly to examine the contentious attempts to revise the directive and tighten the cultural quota mechanism. While a content-based strategy runs through all three arguments for intervention, the nationalist and liberal approaches value public policy as an instrument of proprietary control over extensive programme catalogues, that is to say, over intellectual property rights to creative expression. Expansion in intellectual properties of audiovisual production is of course only possible if the regulatory environment creates opportunities for consolidation among and between industry sectors thus generating the surplus capital for enlarging catalogue ownership. In terms of nationalist goals, the only means of achieving cultural control is through proprietary control, while in terms of liberalization goals, the only means of achieving high rates of return on investment is through proprietary expansion. Hence the cultural-policy proposal of the audiovisual Green Paper calls for the same strategy as does liberalization, namely, that 'the audiovisual industry must rise to the challenges of internationalization and globalization' (Commission of the European Communities, 1994*g*: 4.6. 29).

The European Union's adoption of a cultural-policy approach towards audiovisual production, as shown, has ironically forced the Community into a form of intervention almost exactly isomorphic with that of liberalization. Thus the regulation of creative expression for the information society carries enormous stakes in proprietary power and governance for the European Union, precisely as it does for the international audiovisual industry. It is for this reason that, despite growing resistance in liberal member states including Germany, the audiovisual Green Paper proposed (Commission of the European Communities, 1994g) retention of the cultural-time quota for majority European works in any revision of the television without frontiers directive. This view is endorsed by the advocates of the nationalist conception in the European Parliament and in member states such as France, Belgium, and Italy (European Report, 1995b).

The amendment sought by culturalists following nearly four years of review of the directive (see results of the review in Commission of the European Communities, 1994k) proceeds from the recognition that the European television market has been considerably liberalized for cross-border commercial television, with double the number of channels since 1989 (ibid.), and that this situation is generally positive. Hence, no alteration in the liberal scope of the directive is advanced by any of the parties, leaving unchanged its application to point-to-multipoint broadcasting services, including pay-per-view, near video-on-demand, and home shopping—excluding new multimedia services to be covered by a separate Green Paper (European Report, 1995c). Instead, the amendments are described as largely technical, arguing for removal of the term 'where practicable' from Article 4 (see Commission of the European Communities, 1989) to close a loophole for carriage of a majority of European works. These disclaimers of the need for substantive revision further dilute the idea of change by offering a series of exceptions from the quota provision for new video services such as films, documentaries, drama, cartoons, and news, as well as setting a time limit on the time quota for ten years (European Report, 1995c).

Reversing directions even further, proposed amendments actually offer increased liberalization conditions for commercial multimedia services such as teleshopping by prohibiting any regulatory conditions on their operations and distribution, and creating more flexible rules for commercial speech, namely, advertising, than was permitted under the 1989 directive. Moreover, the framework for a revised approach would also prohibit public-interest obligations on any new interactive audiovisual services anticipated for the digital network (ibid.), on grounds of viewer choice and the fundamental freedoms or right to provide services enshrined in the constitution of the Community through Articles 52 and

59 of the Treaty of Rome (Commission of the European Communities, 1993*c*).

Concluding this section on the contest between market and culture over audiovisual regulation, it is relevant to take into account the opposition of the US government to the cultural restrictions in the television directive. In December 1993, confronted with the impending deadline for an agreement in the seven-year negotiations of the Uruguay Round of the GATT, the EU and US dispute over audiovisual classification as economic or cultural good threatened to derail the entire round of talks (Donaldson, 1996; Kaplan, 1994). Yet at the eleventh hour, the two sides came to an 'agreement to disagree' on the issue, leading to a suspension of the audiovisual category in the negotiations, or its temporary removal, and to the conclusion of the trade agreement on 15 December 1993 (see account of US position in Garrett, 1994 and Kaplan, 1994). According to EU negotiators for the audiovisual sector,[12] US willingness to suspend was from recognition that 'if the US wanted concessions in financial services and the maritime sector, it had to accept concessions in audiovisual'.

This negative agreement is regarded as purely temporary, however, as was admitted by negotiators on audiovisual policy within the French Ministry of External Affairs:[13] 'GATT simply now excludes audiovisual. But [there is] no permanent exception for culture. We've only bought time to organize ourselves against a new American attack which will come.' From the standpoint of the USA, challenges to cultural policy must come from many directions, not merely as a GATT matter. Accordingly, the US government turned its energies towards cultivating European industry in order to circumvent public policy through industry-to-industry 'cooperation':

US companies must make films that will count as European films. We need to identify how US-owned firms can get access to European subsidy programs, even though we regard all regulation as censorship. The cooperation between industries will eventually make regulation obsolete because it's going to be impossible to tell a US and European firm apart.[14]

The 'cooperation' strategy of transnational consolidation has become the official position of the Motion Picture Association of America (MPAA) which proposed to the European audiovisual industry a willingness to 'work closely with its European counterparts in order to help each [European] country build a busy, successful audiovisual industry, motivated by the fact that wherever the national movie/TV industry is

---

[12] From an interview conducted for this study, Paris, April 1994.
[13] From an interview conducted for this study, Paris, April 1994.
[14] From an interview for this study with officials of the US Trade Representative, Brussels, April 1994.

strong, film and television audiences grow larger, which is good for everyone competing in the marketplace' (from an MPAA press release responding to proposed revision of the television directive, quoted in *Europe,* 1995). Thus EU cultural policy whose form is liberalization is being assisted from outside the Community at all levels by a growing innovation in forms of collaboration.

The direction of Community policy for the information society as seen in the emerging proposals for the audiovisual sector seems to be progressively slipping out of the nationalist garments by which it was necessary to pursue an implicit but *de facto* endorsement of the competitive order of liberalization, while rejecting its premises in political discourse (see this strategy in the Bangemann Report, Commission of the European Communities, 1994a). These garments have now been exchanged for an explicit endorsement of liberalization policies, while retaining some cultural elements such as the purely symbolic quota provision. This approach maintains the idea of a nationalist conception for reasons of political legitimacy, but the direction is clear.

The analysis here demonstrates that at no stage in its evolution does Community audiovisual policy pose the option of preserving the public-service tradition of social organization that has been fairly well developed in the broadcasting sector during the decades preceding the emergence of the liberalization movement. It is equally clear from the investigation here that audiovisual policy has been of great importance within the Community, an importance extending beyond the economic value of cultural production relative to other sectors of the European economy. This is because policies on the structure of creative expression in the public realm are regarded by governments, industry, creative labour, and members of the European Parliament and Commission as a measure of commitment to certain versions of the general terms of union among peoples and communities. Cultural production is seen by liberalization supporters as linked to the expansion of private governance over the content sector—the sector with the foremost commercial potential in the information economy. It is regarded by culturalists as interchangeable with the meaning of political identity and common characteristics of lineage and ascriptive affinity. Finally, it is viewed by public-service advocates as central to the question of plurality of creative forms, information sufficiency, and participation for all social groups in the information age—and not merely to promote ascriptively defined cultural collectivities. Consequently, the mode of integration of societies, the competitive, social, and political order which emerges, is seen by all sides to depend in a very acute sense on the design of content and audiovisual policies.

Ultimately, the political struggle over managing the loophole ended in the death of directive with the European Parliament's decision on 12 November 1996 (*European Report*, 1996*a*) to abandon its long-standing demands for stricter limits on the number of Hollywood programmes shown on European television. Can it be said, then, that Europe has conceded its content industry? If so, on both economic and democratic grounds it has everything to lose in the information society since information content constitutes the core of the information economy, while the conditions of production, distribution, and access to expression constitute the basis of the public realm. More than any other single instance of failed information policy leading to the merger of a culturalist with a liberalization model in a formidable momentum for defeating information rights, the intense lobbying during this EP vote demonstrated the almost complete assimilation of the European commercial television industry by the international cultural industry, and the socio-legal acceptance of the liberalization theory of 'comparative advantage'. Clearly, the issue cannot be dismissed since there needs to be a comprehensive public-interest approach to the structure of content in the information society, without which European societies cannot expect political, cultural, or economic progress in the information age. Unfortunately, this cannot be addressed by shifting resources to more efficient sectors such as shoes, perfumes, and microchips as the comparative-advantage premise in the multilateral free-trade framework would seem to suggest.

It is evident from this study of audiovisual policy in the European Union that its evolving structure is a victory for the liberalization movement over the other two contending theories. In the politics of the information society, liberalization of audiovisual production and distribution appears to have established its own mode of unity of peoples and its own mode of intervention, regulation, and law. A further possible obstacle within the Community to audiovisual liberalization emerges from liberalization's own grounds of competition, and embodies a conventional movement to tame the market's reprehensible consequences but without in fact challenging its theory of property. This movement is the century-old concept of antitrust or competition law, and will be explored in the next chapter on the Community's dilemma in designing a competitive order for the information age.

Finally, the fate of public-service broadcasting, but beyond that, the very principle of public service in the multimedia, broadband network, has been shaped by the cumulative implications of European audiovisual policy. This place of public-service content distribution in the information society is an issue worth examining.

The Fate of Public Service Broadcasting

Noticeable in this audiovisual battleground shaped by liberalism and nationalism is the complete absence of any reference to public-service broadcasting. The television directive (Commission of the European Communities, 1989), for instance, makes no mention of a public service or general interest for the audiovisual sector. Although the purpose of the directive was to erect transnational regulation to induce the European-wide introduction of a dual broadcasting system in all member states—in other words, requiring a commercial system to coexist legitimately alongside public broadcasting—it did not address the question of how a public-service system could ultimately survive competition from private broadcasters and commercial programming. The issue remains conspicuous for its silent treatment in subsequent debates over revisions of the directive for the multimedia age (see preceding discussion).

The decline of audience share for public broadcasting throughout the European Union ever since the introduction of commercial audiovisual services by the television directive, has been dramatic (for accounts of share erosion in individual member states, see Contamine and Dusseldorp, 1995; Barnett and Curry, 1994; Achille and Miège, 1994; Sanchez-Tabernero *et al.*, 1993; Servaes, 1992; Prosser, 1992). The dual system has created in some instances, as in Germany, a loss in the vicinity of 50 per cent of viewers to private broadcasters (Bundschuh, 1994; Hoffman-Riem, 1992). Even so, none of the Commission's proposals (Commission of the European Communities, 1995*a*, 1995*b*, 1994*a*, 1994*b*, 1994*g*) for a common European information space and information society address even the most basic needs of a public-service programme-transmission sector. This has been interpreted by European public broadcasters as a sign of the Commission's weak support for public broadcasting and its funding basis,[15] since the particular strategies of public funding for audiovisual production that have been devised in the EU are not necessarily aimed at bolstering transmission of audiovisual programmes over the public network.

It could be argued that the problem for public-service content distribution under information liberalization is not Commission hostility directed specifically at the public-broadcasting sector through seeming neglect of legal protection. Erosion of guarantees for this service in the information society arises instead from the systematic effects of applying Article 90 of the Treaty of Rome (Commission of the European Communities, 1993*c*) in a particular form to the information sector. This was seen in the case of public undertakings in telecommuni-

[15] From interviews with public broadcasters conducted for this study, including: ARD, the German public network; France 2; the BBC; and the European Broadcasting Union, an organization of European public broadcasters.

cations, discussed in Chapter 4. The construction of new information policies grounded in Article 90 have precipitated the erosion of universal service as well as the essential legitimacy of public service in the telecommunications and advanced information-services environment, by forbidding member states from granting exclusive rights in any domain of public space—except, of course, to corporate rights holders in the ownership of ideas through exclusive intellectual-property rights (see Chapter 5). The approach to interpreting Article 90 is significant because, as addressed in Chapter 1, this provision of the Treaty is ambiguous on the question of public service in that it simultaneously acknowledges and constrains the jurisdiction of public entities. On the one hand, Article 90 requires public-service entities to be subjected to the general rules of competition, but on the other, bestows a legal and Community-level recognition to the concept of 'the general interest'. Given this important ambiguity, it could be said that Article 90 leaves open the possibility of supplying considerable unilateral legal authority to the Commission in constructing particular approaches to the meaning of 'competition' in the information market.

The audiovisual Green Paper (Commission of the European Communities, 1994g) and the Think Tank Report which preceded it (Commission of the European Communities, 1994h) attempted to update European audiovisual regulation by shifting the emphasis of public funding towards consolidated distribution networks for programme productions and away from small-scale individual film productions. This has been done, as mentioned earlier, to counterbalance the power of the multinationals through a strategy of emulating concentration and scale. Once more, the problem of public-service programme transmission or broadcasting in the multimedia digital environment simply cannot be discovered in the new proposals.

Thus the transnational regulation of broadcasting, while aiming for a common legal framework in programme transmission, has resulted in rendering public broadcasting into an anachronistic transition in the ultimate realization of the information society, following which it may disappear altogether. Similarly, regulation of information-sector ownership rules or media concentration (discussed below) has had a parallel deleterious effect on the status of the public-service sector. As demonstrated by the direction of the Green Paper on pluralism and media concentration in the internal market (Commission of the European Communities, 1992b, discussed below), far stricter anti-concentration standards in prevailing national laws would be diluted and levelled through weaker Community-wide anti-trust rules targeted at media ownership structures. A trans-European reduction of such rules to a low, common standard will inevitably strengthen the private commercial structure of media ownership, thereby further corroding the audience and advertising base of an already weakened public service system forced to turn to advertising in the last decade in order to supplement a pattern of diminished public funding.

The guarantee of a stable financing system for the public-service sector in the information age is in essence the central issue determining its fate. The traditional source in Europe has been the licence fee on ownership of television sets, a mechanism that has supported universal provision of general interest programming (Euromedia Research Group, 1992). However, this economic basis of public service has been severely challenged by the EU's audiovisual policy of encouraging dual systems in mutual competition for audience share, in some instances (see Achille and Miège, 1994) favouring predominantly commercial services in a position to overtake, perhaps even absorb, the public sector. Declining audience share makes it difficult in turn to justify public funding, resulting in the depreciation of political legitimacy and yet further inability to create and distribute high-quality general interest programmes.

Germany's Federal Constitutional Court responded to this threat by reaffirming support in 1994 for the licence fee as well as for programme standards—that is to say, for the programming obligations—of the country's two public broadcasting networks: ARD and ZDF (see discussion of case in Bundschuh, 1994). The ruling recognizes citizens' rights for public broadcasting for which the public-service sector must be guaranteed sufficient funding to fulfil its programme brief. But as with the case of public undertakings in telecommunications, it is entirely probable that the European Commission and the European Court of Justice may view public broadcasting as falling within the jurisdiction of the television directive, and therefore defined as an economic good. Doubtless, the directive may be equally useful to public broadcasters in exploiting transnational audience share and in pre-empting protectionist-state policies that benefit national broadcasters, whether commercial or non-commercial. At the same time, however, the directive's 'economic good' formulation situates the licence-fee funding structure in the precarious position of being cast as a competition-distorting, therefore invalid, method of financing under the terms of the Treaty of Rome.

As a result, the long-term prospects of national constitutional rulings in favour of the public system may be handicapped by the implicit threat of isolating broadcasting systems in member states from participation in Community information-society policy. For this reason, having accepted the *de facto* diminution of the public broadcasting networks, communication ministers of member states met collectively to address the problems of public-service media. The outcome of this effort has been a number of pleas to retain, at the very least, a single general-interest programme service for the digital environment where commercial programme content will most likely dominate (see resolution on the future of public-service broadcasting in Council of Europe, 1994).

In short, the future of public broadcasting in Europe, but more especially of public-service programme distribution in the multimedia environment, is inherently linked to the fate of a public-service model of public space and content regulation in the information society. From the Treaty of Rome to the Treaty of Maastricht, the logic of European construction has been founded exclusively on liberal conceptions organized and defined by three characteristics of transnational policy and law:

(1) a supranational collection of growing norms defining the domain of competence at the European level;
(2) an intrinsically juridical or legal nature of union, with the notion of Europe as, above all, a Europe of law producing socio-legal norms derived from directives and rulings applied by Community institutions and upheld by the jurisprudence of the Court of Justice;
(3) economic liberalism as a foundation of Community construction composed of principles of free exchange and free circulation of peoples, goods, services, and capital within a market regulated by particular forms of competition.

These socio-legal characteristics of unification have progressively eroded the power of national laws to address the requirements of a public-service approach to information policy. As argued by Cohen-Tanugi (1992), the impact of Europe on France, for instance, cannot be reduced to a quantitative loss of sovereignty by the path of transfer of legal competencies, but has set in motion a process of progressive erosion of the public-service political model by the dismantling and delegitimization of two of its pillars: the law as expression of the general will, now subordinated to Community law; and the state as the institutional form of public-service principles. Thus the transfer of sovereignty in regulating public broadcasting systems signifies less a displacement of the site of production of public service norms from Paris or Rome towards Brussels, than a transformation of the status of political society: namely, the displacement of political society by a juridical society based on the legal construction of a particular competitive order. This phenomenon can be seen in the struggle to define some limits on media ownership and consolidation in the Community.

AUDIOVISUAL CONCENTRATION: TAMING THE EFFECTS OF LIBERALIZATION

A tolerance for concentration in the principles of Community constitutional law is not valid. Even so, Chapter 4 attempted to demonstrate the manner in which competition policy or anti-trust rules derived from Articles 85 and 86 of the Treaty of Rome (Commission of the European Communities, 1993c) can be employed to undermine the public-service communication entities and without any corresponding deterrence to emerging structural dominance within the private sector. This characteristic of the information society is also discussed at more length in the next chapter. It could be said that the application of competition policy has been targeted as the principal mechanism in accomplishing a set of political aims of information liberalization that will lead to a reconstruction of the role of the state and the creation of a particular competitive order (see Chapter 7). A similar pattern is also evident in the area of audiovisual production and network distribution such as broadcasting, pointing to its own set of social outcomes. The difference in the audiovisual sector is that the opposition to liberalization from cultural and public-service arguments has also appealed to competition rules in managing the form of harmonization which transnational consolidation of the audiovisual market has brought about, through those provisions of the television directive that impose upon states mandatory reception of transnational content distribution.

Thus the institutionalization of Community audiovisual policy cannot be fully understood purely from an examination of the struggle over its implementation either in the domain of high European politics involving the terms of union, or in the sphere of multilateral trade. Important aspects of policy and practice have also emanated from the rule-making authority of the competition directorate, DGIV, in the Commission.

Collins (1994) points to two cases in particular where DGIV has given an indication of the appropriate conditions of broadcasters' rights to programmes: first, the overturning of the German public broadcasting network ARD's deal with MGM/United Artists (see Commission Decision of 15 September 1989 in *Official Journal of the European Communities*, no. 284: 36–44, 3 October 1989 (cited in Collins, 1994); secondly, the ruling in favour of a UK satellite television channel, Screensport, for its right to air sports events even where European public broadcasters had already acquired the sports screening rights (see Commission Decision of 19 February 1991 in *Official Journal of the European Communities*, no. 63: 32–44, 9 March 1991, cited in Collins, 1994). The two judgments appear to be hostile to established public-service broadcasters and favour new commercial entrants to European broadcasting markets, according to Collins (ibid.) who argues they were widely perceived to disadvantage *dirigiste*, that is, interventionist structures and institutions and to favour liberal or non-interventionist structures. As argued, however, the *dirigiste* analysis may be wrongly formulated since the real question for the Commission or for any nation state confronted with liberalization is not whether to intervene but in what form. The confusion over this question arises from a misapprehension of liberalization's competitive order, analysis of which is provided in the next chapter. It may be argued, instead, that the implications of Commission competition rule-making in these two cases points to a strategic and selective interpretation of competition policy to achieve through state action certain proprietary scales of organization and market governance, as against alternative scales and structures of governance which may have been equally valid under the same antitrust constitutional provisions of the Treaty.

In a call for Community action, Roberto Barzanti, former president of the European Parliament Committee on Youth, Culture, Education, Media, and Sport, also assumes that the solution to the failed European audiovisual market pivots on the very act of intervention—termed 'support'—but without addressing what intervention would mean in Community policy or the form it should take with respect to cultural or political ends: 'Unless there is solid support from the outset, the audiovisual industry of all European countries will be thrown into the Single Market like a Christian to the lions in the arena' (Barzanti, 1990: 1).

Barzanti identifies the predator to be the US audiovisual industries whose large-scale organization is the form which must inevitably benefit from a transnationalized information market. This leads him to propose (ibid.) a variety of mechanisms, including the quota but also support for European audiovisual consolidation, which lead right back to the anticompetitive structures that proponents of liberalization first considered the cause of European decline.

In response to concerns in the European Parliament and to rising public opinion opposed to the kind of European unity brought about by the television without frontiers directive (Commission of the European Communities, 1989), as well as to assess the loss of diversity alleged by European industry, the Commission at the end of 1992 published a Green Paper on pluralism and media concentration in the internal market: an assessment of the need for community action (Commission of the European Communities, 1992b). Its purpose was to assess the issue of concentration in television, radio, and the press, to evaluate the need for action, and to suggest possible forms of action. The Commission conducted a wide consultation process, the initial responses to which show no consensus as to whether there is cause for Community action or what form such action should take (see results of the initial consultation process in Commission of the European Communities, 1994*l*, 1993*m*, 1993*n*, 1992*c*). Attempts to propose initiatives for harmonizing media ownership rules within the Community were later defeated by national governments reluctant to subordinate national standards to Community-wide standards (see *Europe*, 1997*a*, 1997*b*) since member states would lose the power to introduce stricter rules on cross-border investments when attempting to counteract the transnational bias in Community information policy (ibid.).

For this reason, concerns raised in the European Parliament (recorded in *Official Journal of the European Communities*, nos. C68, 19 March 1990: 137–8; and C284, 2 November 1992: 44–6) argued for higher levels of Community regulation of media ownership, endorsing the need to constrain content monopolies in the interest of promoting pluralism, diversity of opinion, the place of non-profit broadcasting organizations, and a legal framework for media mergers and takeovers. The degree of merger activity, cross-border consolidation, and concern for media concentration in general prompted the European Parliament to call for action (ibid.), although its proposals also failed to secure the support of the Council and of the European cultural industries (see *Europe*, 1997*a*).

The decline of public-service broadcasting, of course, is linked directly to the liberalization environment created by the television directive, and parallels similar tendencies shown in the telecommunications sector (discussed in Chapter 4). In addition, since liberalization not only undermines the public-service sector but also generates the conditions of proprietary enlargement in the private sector, there has been a dramatic growth in consolidation processes through mergers and acquisitions. Between 1989 and 1990, in the period immediately following passage of the directive, eighty-one mergers and acquisitions within the Community were announced by the media industry, with thirty-seven of these transactions affecting television networks. These figures increased to fifty-seven media industry mergers and acquisitions affecting television networks in 1990 (see data on concentration trends, in Commission of the European Communities, 1992*c*). The international trends of staggering increases in mergers and acquisitions have overtaken these levels (Nesvold, 1996) and show no sign of levelling off under the policies of the information society. There is even growing evidence (ibid.) that the European audiovisual industry could become completely assimilated to the international structure and may even cease to exist as an independent 'European' cultural industry.

Prior to the media concentration Green Paper, the Commission's view on media concentration was contained in its 1990 communication to the Parliament on audiovisual policy (see Commission of the European Communities, 1990h). While the treatment of this issue was brief, it did acknowledge that Community competition law might not be sufficient to address the issues of media concentration (ibid. 21). Yet this debate does not adequately reveal the profound dilemma and structural constraints arising from inherent liberal aims of unification of markets embodied in the Treaty which confronts the Commission in any consideration of an appropriate response to the monopolization of content by a shrinking range of structures of capital ownership. While the concerns of the European Parliament articulate the democratic concept of participatory and information rights for citizens and the public-service concept of minimum standards of universal access to quality information that cannot be adequately served by commercial expression alone, the Commission has been faced with trying to address the democratic deficit through the intrinsically liberal provisions of its own legal mandate in the Treaty.

The Commission and the European Court of Justice may acknowledge that protection of information pluralism is of fundamental importance to the maintenance of democracy in the Community (see Chapter 8), but ultimately the EU is still faced with identifying which basis of intervention should apply in the Community in the context of yet further consolidation of the internal market. In policy terms, the issue of what is the desirable form of regulation to ensure information pluralism has been converted into a concern for whether constraint or antitrust regulation on proprietary expansion—regulation that is automatically implicated in the democratization of public space—will obstruct the expansion of the internal market. This tension pervades the whole of the media concentration Green Paper (Commission of the European Communities, 1992b) and illustrates the tension between the liberalization and public-interest models in addressing the structures of the information market. The problem of information pluralism has thereby been converted into a concern for what happens to the information economy and the demands of cross-border investments when it is necessary to address democratization of information through anti-concentration mechanisms. The answer may not be difficult to imagine. It is useful, therefore, to examine the Green Paper's approach to this tension as a way of understanding how the European approach to the structure of content in the information society is being shaped by the debate over the media concentration Green Paper. The Green Paper provides clues to the preferences for certain regulatory mechanisms in the information society.

First, the Green Paper holds that protection against the erosion of pluralism in the content industry is primarily a matter for member states, although it is necessary for the Community to ensure that its own activities do not adversely affect pluralism (ibid. 59, 103, 113). The Commission thus restricts itself from the outset in its ability to safe-guard pluralism even where it claims the authority to regulate the content and structure of public space through telecommunications, intellectual-property rights, and audiovisual policies. It suggests that where the loss of pluralism is an effect of such Community policies, the responsibilities devolve to the member-state level.

Secondly, the Commission proposes, instead, that stricter antitrust rules in member states regulating the size and nature of proprietary holdings in contents industries should be lowered or subordinated to Community competition rules, otherwise higher levels of ownership regulation may in fact interfere in the operation of the internal market (ibid. 8, 98, 116). The Green Paper serves, therefore, as the appropriate context in which to assess the level of national antitrust laws for communications and to develop a framework for harmonization. Since the logic of harmonization has been essentially a consolidation logic, the Green Paper concludes that standardization of antitrust rules will only work by a general lowering of national rules to a uniform least-restrictive standard. This conforms with the Community's approach to telecommunications liberalization, intellectual property, and audio-visual policy, which together establish a ceiling on the powers of national laws to regulate information other than utilizing the power of the state in ratifying immense economies of scale. Thus the general tendency towards creation of disproportionate power and control over public space by easing antitrust restrictions on cross-national, cross-media, and cross-sector ownership consolidation is reflected in the Green Paper's proposal to harmonize competition law, where in fact, at the encouragement of the European Parliament, it had set out to do just the opposite.

Thirdly, the Green Paper suggests that general competition law and merger control regulation may not necessarily be appropriate for the information industry for, while mergers might affect pluralism, they would not come under competition-law scrutiny unless they also affected competition (ibid. 115). In this argument, the Commission pro-vides evidence of its view of the internal market as an environment that should benefit proprietary expansion in general, but in particular for the cultural industry which is not served well by placing limits on media ownership. The conclusion also represents an implicit recognition of the century-old international, pre-liberalization era assumption among national governments that communications industries are capital inten-sive and constitute 'natural monopolies'. The Commission's argument does not, however, explain the rationality of the political uses of competition in breaking down existing natural monopolies only to substitute them with others, which is one of the essential features of the competitive order of liberalization (see Chapter 7).

Having established that preserving pluralism in the information sector is not a Community objective (ibid. 59–61), the Green Paper placates Parliamentary concern in judging that, since the realization of the internal market actually creates opportunities for media companies, liberalizing ownership restrictions in the single market may actually promote pluralism (ibid. 59). Similarly, the Green Paper argues that promotion of European audiovisual consolidation justified on grounds of cultural policy or industrial policy would also contribute to pluralism (ibid. 60). This is an approach which is often advocated to rationalize consolidation processes and accurately reflects the supply-side reasoning of the competitive order of the information society. As observed at several stages of this study, the supply-side logic of liberalization assumes that the democratic functions of the public realm will be automatically addressed if the power of the state is employed in setting market-compensation levels free and in benefiting large-scale proprietors of content. It is simply unnecessary for the state or any public institution to take action to secure political rights, participatory opportunities, or deliberative conditions to allow the formation of collective will. Democratic processes simply arise as side-effects or natural by-products of the chemistry of capital enlargement and vertical integration.

Yet these side-effects may not necessarily follow, since deregulation of transnational content industries has actually resulted in concentration of ownership within the broadcasting and newspaper industries. Under information-society hyper-deregulation, it will be possible for audiovisual and broadcasting industries to be assimilated into a far denser capital structure through merger with telecommunications, cable, software, and satellite conglomerates. This is the proposal of the infrastructure liberalization in the EU (Commission of the European Communities, 1995a, 1994b) and telecommunications laws in the USA (US Congress, 1995). The second underlying assumption that freedom of ownership consolidation benefits pluralism by multiplying the number of operators and providers, the so-called 'perfect competition' theory, is taken up in the next chapter, both for its fallacious reasoning as well as for the new reality that increased competition does not accurately constitute the political aims of liberalization. The foremost goal of the information society to encourage proprietary enlargement in the information economy is in fact undermined by a market of numerous competitors (see discussion, Chapter 7). Hence the Parliament's reliance on a competitive market to foster pluralism is misguided in terms of the solution preferred by the media concentration Green Paper, which is to suspend application of competition in order to provide incentives for high compensation levels in the communications sector from which process pluralism would derive as a natural by-product (see discussion in Chapter 4 of the incentives strategy increasingly employed in information policies).

The Green Paper's conciliatory discourse, arguing that pluralism and competition are not contrary but identical objectives (Commission of the European Communities, 1992*b*: 82–3), obscures the issue that relying on competition law to achieve a plurality of information, knowledge, and creative forms in the public realm may result in forms of collaboration or mergers that constrain information pluralism while still being in compliance with competition rules. It is to this conceptual equation of pluralism with competition, therefore, that makes it possible for the Green Paper to conclude that the expansion of the internal market in information services under liberalization is more likely to have a positive effect on pluralism than would a restriction of liberalization through application of anti-concentration rules: 'The operation of the Community is not in itself a threat to pluralism; quite the reverse, it may have a positive effect on two factors which determine the level of pluralism: the number of broadcasters and newspapers and the diversity of their controllers [capital ownership]' (ibid. 98). Thus, having reviewed the justifications for intervention to protect pluralism and freedom of expression in the Community's common information space, the Green Paper's final position is that intervention may indeed be necessary, but for the exigencies of the internal market: 'Any need for action on the part of the Community, then, has more to do with ensuring that the single market functions properly than with maintaining pluralism as such' (ibid. 99). In the context of considering the role of government, the Green Paper concludes that the only possible valid policy at the Community level must be a liberalization policy which should be strengthened even further. Thus the irony of the European Parliament's concern with the effects of information liberalization in the Community is that this concern seems to have provided the opportunity to propose additional intensification of those very processes. Action the Green Paper suggests takes the form of standardization of national antitrust laws by reducing them all to a common level, and by enforcing the prohibition at all levels of Community and national rules, against intervening in cross-border concentration.

In conclusion, the study of audiovisual regulation in the European Union has show that liberalization of information requires a great deal more orchestration than is apparent from information-society discourse and policy rationalizations. What does this form of orchestration suggest about the sense in which civil society and political liberty are realized in the information society? First, the release of the public realm to private expansionary interests signifies the governance of civil society by concentrated, large-scale proprietary power over information which restricts entry to public space by other private as well as all non-market entities. It would suggest, therefore, establishment of an unrepresentative and feudal basis for civil society. Secondly, the opportunity for independent social forces, the full range of political and economic interests, to be represented in the public domain and to influence, check, and limit political and social centres of power through deliberative conditions of collective will-formation would be virtually unrealizable under this mode of development of the information society. The definition of society by its political organization as in Montesquieu's and Hegel's conceptions of networks of interlocking associations emerging from the structure of the public realm, which an information revolution could undoubtedly enhance given the appropriate policy environment, is made dim by the vision of liberalization. The self-regulating forces of proprietary relations are given a central place in the information society and define a dimension of life that functions outside the political constitution, rendering the practice of democracy an anachronism.

Finally, this 'feudalization of the public sphere' (Habermas, 1989) makes it possible for all social relations to be integrated into the market of proprietary governance, effacing that crucial distinction and balance between society, the state, and the market which has been historically essential to counter-absolutist struggles since the democratic revolutions of the eighteenth century. One might say that the reform of absolutism or oligarchy in its many modes and forms, some new, others familiar, has been and continues to remain at the heart of the democratic problem (see the analysis of this problem offered by Tocqueville, 1990). In so far as liberalization of the content of information, including conditions of production, exploitation rights, and capital ownership structure, offers indications of a new form of absolutism which deprives individuals of their political rights, it is every bit, if not more, of a challenge to human development as any absolutist peril that preceded the information age.

The next chapter extends the analysis of the emerging competitive order of the information society to define its underlying and larger place in the construction of a new realist basis of transnational and international relations.

7

Realist Internationalism and the Competitive Order of the Information Society

WHILE THE theory and practice of international realism has been around for some time, global liberalization has transformed the basis of interstate relations into a set of powerful forces for compelling nations worldwide into a single design of the social order. The realist-competitive order of information liberalization may emerge as an important force of change by advancing the contemporary political aims of liberal internationalism. These aims, as argued, favour the reconstitution of the world system on the basis of large-scale proprietary interests. The manner in which liberal realism mobilizes the information society as a new form of international relations is addressed here in an analysis of the nature of liberal internationalism and its realist manifestation in the competitive order of the information society. The notion of a competitive order is then related to the realist assumptions and premises of contemporary liberal internationalism, especially in the rapid assimilation of EU competition policy to a deepening international system.

MISCALCULATING COMPETITION

This section attempts to characterize the form of competition which underlies the political arrangements for information liberalization. The argument for releasing competitive processes comprises the principal justification for information-society initiatives in the transformation of public space. The analysis tries to show how claims for competition in the multimedia broadband environment have been miscalculated in information-infrastructure policies. This is because both the concept, and criticism of, perfect competition misapprehend the political aims of liberalization, with their conclusions serving as poor guides in explaining public policy for the multimedia broadband network.

The conception of competition employed by liberalization policies for the information society, either in public discourse or multilateral trade negotiations, emerges from an implicit general theory of the way society should be organized in the information age. The political pressures of liberalization forcing governments to submit national information systems to commercial forces leads to the impression, generally held, that the concept of 'perfect competition' provides the appropriate model for judging the effectiveness of competition in the information sector. It is assumed that to the extent that real competition differs from the model, liberalization of communications is designed to ensure that undesirable, even harmful, effects to economy and society will be far less likely than under any alternative mode of organizing the broadband environment. Thus the premise of perfect competition is thought to inform the reasoning, aims, and objectives of the information society.

On the other side of the debate, it has been suggested (Murdock, 1994; Mansell, 1993; Melody, 1990; Mosco, 1990) that perfect competition is an inadequate explanation of the historical workings of the communications market and logically should be eliminated as a naive basis of public policy. Yet it is seldom considered that perfect competition may not be the basis of information liberalization, and serious examination of the information-society design emerging on both sides of the Atlantic shows very little justification for maintaining that the information society will develop under widespread competitive conditions.

The required conditions of the competitive process which are advanced in the argument of perfect competition are equally assumed in the account of 'imperfect' or 'monopolistic' markets which, to be 'imperfect', assume the possibility of the 'perfect'. According to the generally accepted view of competition in the information market within economic theory (Hayek, 1994; Train, 1991; Vickers and Yarrow, 1988; Smith, 1986; Fowler and Brenner, 1982) and political economy (Gilpin, 1987; Wallerstein, 1989, 1979; Schiller, 1985, 1976), perfect competition presupposes:

(1) a standardized information service or commodity offered and demanded by a large number of relatively small information-service providers, none of which expects to exercise by its action a perceptible influence on price;

(2) free entry into the information market through standardization, interconnection, and interoperability and absence of other restraints on the movement of tariffs and allocation of resources;

(3) complete knowledge of relevant market factors, or 'perfect information' conditions, for all infrastructure operators, and producers, packagers, providers, and distributors of information services who are either entrants or participants in the market.

These are the conditions systematically claimed in the discourse of the information society (see Commission of the European Communities, 1997, 1996*a*, 1996*c*, 1995*a*, 1995*b*, 1994*a*, 1994*b*, 1994*c*; US Congress, 1995, 1994*a*, 1994*b*; U.S. Government, 1995*a*, 1995*b*).

It is apparent from these claims, that the assumption of 'perfect competition' is inherently tied to an assumption of 'perfect information', meaning free, complete, instantaneous, and universally available information as the defining feature of the perfect market. Yet, as Boyle (1996) observes, the assumptions of wealth creation in the information society are also simultaneously based on the commoditization of information by which it is necessary to create incentives for investment through new forms of proprietary-based information exploitation and the restriction on its availability through monopolies, tariffs, and horizontal and vertical consolidation of capital. These ambiguities of claims, assumptions, and arguments raise for a competitive information environment the question: what institutional arrangements are necessary in order that private entities who have perfect knowledge specially suited to innovation, production, and distribution of particular information services are most likely to be attracted to the market to provide those services? Liberalization policies assume that the market naturally can and does, or does not naturally but ought to, function without domination, abuse, or distortion to attract the producer or provider with specialized knowledge and resources.

This concern with the defects of competition conceals a confusion regarding the supply-side political goals of competition in the information society, and leads on occasion to incongruous conclusions about the power of market or competitive restructuring of the information industries to bring about 'diversity' of choice in ideas and information services. It focuses the question on the natural processes of the market rather than on the political order particular forms of competition reflect and sustain. As the analysis here attempts to show, the liberalization model of economy and society embodied in the information society would be no different if competition were assumed to be 'free' in the traditional sense or if it were assumed to be 'unfree' or simply nonexistent. Thus opposition to some liberalization policies for the information market may swing, so to speak, at a 'straw man' in negative appraisal of the defects of competition. That is to say, in efforts to identify or transform the deficiencies of liberalization, most concerns for the consequences of deregulation appear to be inaccurately formulated. Information-society policies show clearly there is not only no likelihood that different structures in information networks and services would be produced if policy provisions ensured an undistorted market open equally to all participants, either producers, distributors, or consumers, but also no likelihood that all those services, information content, and network options at lowest cost would necessarily be produced or constructed if the number of providers dramatically increased. A solution to the economic problem of the information society is in this respect not to be found in the enforcement of competition policy, commonly known as anti-trust law or media-concentration rules, to make competitive processes more just, equitable, or perfect. Instead, the solution lies in understanding the patterns of proprietary consolidation prevailing in, and necessary to, the emergence and development of an advanced information society.

Conclusions concerning policy to which preoccupation with a 'perfect' or 'open' competition model leads are misleading for two reasons. First, if emerging information policies are judged on the basis of open competition, they would have to provide for rules governing 'orderly competition' that allow a fair return on capital investment but not an excessive return. Such has been the idealism of the antitrust, anti-monopoly movement through most of this century, as it has struggled to apply the principles of open competition in selective areas of the communications industries, achieving in the end no more than a symbolic purpose. Horwitz (1989) as well as Garnham (1990), for example, have documented the failure of antitrust regulation in the USA to address endemic information-sector monopolies in telecommunications, broadcasting, and audiovisual production and distribution. The inability of the state to guarantee the conditions of open competition in the information market—whether telecommunications, broadcast, cable, audiovisual production and distribution, software, or digital satellite services—has led to an inevitable outcome: namely, enthusiasm for perfect competition in the political claims of public policy and the support of national and global monopolies in practice evidenced in staggering levels of capital consolidation, mergers, and alliances (see *Wall Street Journal*, 1995; *Washington Post*, 1997). Information liberalization and the sweeping deregulation which it promotes have created unprecedented rates of merger activity and corporate consolidation in the information industries (see *Chicago Tribune*, 1996; Nesvold, 1996).

However, this is only one of many dimensions of the information society whose neglect has made the picture of open competition quite remote from the actual role of competitive processes in sustaining the political basis of the information market. The confusion on all sides in the debate over whether and how to create more open competition conceals from us the important fact that competition is the more important to the political aims of information liberalization and the broadband multimedia age the more 'imperfect' are the objective conditions in which information industries have to operate. Indeed, far from competition being beneficial only when it is 'perfect' or 'open', this chapter is inclined to argue that the uses of competition for liberalization's social objectives is nowhere greater than in sectors such as information where the requirements of capital investment and the nature of information infrastructure and services make it imperative there never should be a perfect market of innumerable participants operating in an unrestricted environment. For information-liberalization policies, the inevitable actual imperfections of competition are as little an argument against competition as the difficulties of achieving greater democratization are an argument against granting voting privileges, or as the imperfections of civil society constitute an argument against civil society.

Legislative and statutory proposals for the information society in the European Union and the USA advocate a global case for removing obstacles to competition; but this does not mean there is political commitment to create a more uniform environment for participation by numerous providers, producers, and distributors than existed prior to liberalization policies. It also does not mean that such policies are in contradiction with themselves by professing competition while achieving consolidation. On the contrary, judged by the conceptual system, policy justifications, political objectives, and most of all by the prevailing assumptions of the public space of the information age, the claims of more competition while encouraging industry concentration and dominance through state activism is entirely consistent with the fundamental terms and central assumptions of information liberalization (see discussion of the market-choice model of public space, Chapter 2).

The second of many points made ambiguous by the competitive order of liberalization is an assumption derived from the assertion, but not the reality, that the fundamental principle of supply-side liberalization policies is the absence of state activity (see this assumption in Branscomb, 1994; Bauer and Steinfield, 1994; Casey and Wu, 1994; Ungerer and Costello, 1988; Bolter, 1984). The claims of liberalization are taken at face value to mean that its framework of privatization and deregulation are opposed to state intervention since a liberalized market would quite evidently consider state action responsible for the decline of competition. Advocates of liberalization contend that the free market should be permitted to regulate itself and that the primary, if not exclusive, evil is state intervention which distorts these self-regulatory mechanisms (see discussion in Nesvold, 1996; Adams and Brock, 1995). Most government mechanisms are viewed as counterproductive and liberalization asks that faith be placed in the operation of natural economic laws to protect the consuming public (Nesvold, 1996; Adams and Brock, 1995).

Such an understanding of the aims of liberalization has left public-interest proponents on the defensive and at a loss for effective counter-arguments justifying the interventionist state (for illustrations of this difficulty, see Boyle, 1996; Nesvold, 1996; Schiller, 1996; Murdock, 1994; Mattelart, 1994; Galtung and Vincent, 1992; Horwitz, 1989). One of the mistaken theses this chapter must consider, therefore, is the assumption on all sides of the debate, that the core philosophical premise of liberalization holds competition to be more effective and more beneficent the lower the level of government activity. Accordingly, the misapprehension regarding the meaning of the state and the competitive order which information-society policies in the EU and the USA are bringing about arises from a disregard for the form of political society liberalization presupposes: one in which the discourse of competition institutionalizes a governance of the public realm and of civil society by information oligopolies.

COMPETITION AS CONCENTRATION

The Green Paper on telecommunications services (Commission of the European Communities, 1987) and the terminal equipment and services directives (Commission of the European Communities, 1988*a* and 1990*a*, respectively) have been key policy instruments for forcing open all sectors of the public realm to restructuring within the European Union. Exposition of the socio-legal bases of these instruments has shown (see Chapter 4) that this restructuring is directed at and constitutionally grounded in, an anti-monopoly political argument. Information liberalization, therefore, can be regarded as a political movement with economic premises for discrediting and abolishing certain forms of constraint—such as public-service obligations—on proprietary rights in the public sphere—a sphere conceptualized solely for the purposes of contractual and proprietary relations. These initiatives are widely regarded as a renewed opportunity to displace public-sector communications monopolies (Noam, 1995*a*, 1995*b*; Bauer and Steinfield, 1994; Scherer, 1991; Kohnstamm, 1990; Ungerer and Costello, 1988) and other regulatory restrictions imposed by the state on private contractual rights in the information economy. But since the type of restrictions targeted by the instruments are those expressly permitted under national policies through statutes and other public acts, information-society initiatives in the EU do not anticipate all the restrictions on private proprietary rights—that is, on commercial freedom—which may potentially prevail in the public sphere of the information age. Instead, they target those particular categories of restrictions on proprietary interests deriving from activities of the state in guaranteeing certain non-commercial conditions of public space in the common interest.

For these reasons, both private-communications undertakings and the Commission have attempted to reach wider than the Article 90 constitutional provision in the Treaty (Commission of the European Community, 1993c) which provides for application of the Treaty to the public sector (for more discussion of this provision, see Chapter 4). Rather, utilizing the provisions of Articles 85 and 86 of the Treaty (ibid.), this competitive approach transforms the political question of the terms of democratic participation in public space into the narrower question of the terms of commercial participation in the market. This is precisely the path adopted in US antitrust regulation (for a discussion of the 1890 US Sherman Antitrust Act, see Hawk and Laudati, 1996; Weaver, 1980) through efforts to establish rules for market players in particular economic sectors, as liberalism's answer to the problem of public-interest responsibility of the state in the democratization of civil society. Hayek defends this approach to the regulation of society against alternative views regarding the first and essential responsibility of the political order:

The liberal argument is in favour of making the best possible use of the forces of competition as a means of co-ordinating human efforts, not an argument for leaving things just as they are. It is based on the conviction that, where effective competition can be created, it is a better way of guiding individual [private] efforts than any other. It does not deny, but even emphasizes, that, in order that competition should work beneficially, a carefully thought-out legal framework is required and that neither the existing nor the past legal rules are free from grave defects. Nor does it deny that, where it is impossible to create the conditions necessary to make competition effective, we must resort to other methods of guiding economic activity. Economic liberalism is opposed, however, to competition's being supplanted by inferior methods of co-ordinating individual efforts. And it regards competition as superior not only because it is in most circumstances the most efficient method known but even more because it is the only method by which our activities can be adjusted to each other without coercive or arbitrary intervention of authority. Indeed, one of the main arguments in favour of competition is that it dispenses with the need for 'conscious social control' and that it gives the individuals a chance to decide whether the prospects of a particular occupation are sufficient to compensate for the disadvantages and risks connected with it. (Hayek, 1994: 41–2)

Yet the argument of this chapter is that the ambiguities, perhaps paradox, of competition policy—that is, of state intervention in markets to ensure successful working of independent or natural competitive processes in the circulation of proprietary forms and the commodities they generate—is that the theory of competition policy is enmeshed in the fundamentally ambiguous relation between pre-political, natural proprietary rights and their free circulation without government, and the difficulties presented in enjoying those rights without the activism of the civil state on behalf of proprietary interests. Yet this would contradict the political arguments of contemporary liberalization which employ claims of liberating competitive processes and enhancing competition in the market economy through elimination of the role of the state, that is, through deregulation (see Commission of the European Communities, 1994*a*; US Congress, 1996*a*; US Government, 1995*a*, 1993).

As seen in the case of the EU, the application of information policies under liberalization is caught between an anti-state, open-competition discourse, and an activist-state, proprietary-bias discourse, which logically cancel each other out. In other words, since they cannot both be present at the same time, the question then is, which end of the antithesis will prevail in the emerging framework of the information society? Should information liberalization seek the absolute autonomy of the market from government rules (often called 'distortion'), or should it seek a redefinition of the role of the state towards the market economy? Should information liberalization be designed to enforce conditions of greater competition among providers and operators, or should it be designed to guarantee freedom from public regulation altogether? As argued here, this is the paradox of the competitive order of the information society which arises from the incapacity of liberalization policies to determine the vanishing point of negative freedom beyond which the state subsists minimally, as against the vanishing point of the invisible hand of the market beyond which the logic of competition gives rise to distortions requiring the state to act. Since the problem for information liberalization is the state (Adams and Brock, 1995), the latter must be evicted from all market relations, but not abolished altogether. What role, therefore, must the state play in the information society?

Smith's defence of the natural law of the market in *The Wealth of Nations* (1986) points to some form of competition policy to ensure fair rules of the competition game, even though the admission of such policy severely undermines the theory of the invisible hand and of the autonomous, inherently efficient resource allocation by an unconstrained self-regulatory mechanism. Smith argues that the market has interests which are 'never exactly the same with that of the public' (ibid. 359). This admission is reflected in the history of antitrust or competition policy and law adopted by liberal democratic states following the lessons of the Industrial Revolution, and legally inscribed in the constitutional basis of the European Union in Articles 85 and 86 of the Treaty of Rome (Commission of the European Communities, 1993*c*).

The EU's approach to the information society, therefore, chooses to employ not just the limited government thesis of liberalization embodied within Article 90 (Commission of European Communities, 1993c), in order to dissolve progressively public-service entities and regulatory models as appendages of the state. The approach has also sought simultaneous application of an activist-government thesis in applying antitrust or competition policy to restructure the information sector in favour of a particular set of proprietary interests. Hence, rigorous application of Articles 85 and 86—legally equivalent to the US Sherman antitrust statute (Hawk and Laudati, 1006)—against information industries is of some significance, with EU or public-sector intervention in numerous cases to enforce a set of market rules allowing particular forms of competition, as opposed to other forms.

The concept of a competitive information market in the EU has been shaped, on the one hand, by a requirement for eliminating the state through privatization and deregulation of telecommunications infrastructure. On the other hand, information-society initiatives have granted enormous power to the state (albeit at a European level) to apply the interventionist mechanisms of the Treaty granting the Community legal power to determine the structure of markets in particular economic sectors. EC competition rules in the telecommunications sector (Commission of the European Communities, 1991a) have emerged from the 1987 Green Paper on telecommunications liberalization (Commission of the European Communities, 1987) which calls for the elimination of public-service monopolies. But this is accompanied by renewed power for the Commission and the European Court to intervene in structuring the information market through Articles 85 and 86 of the Treaty. As the Commission itself has indicated of its intentions (Commission of the European Communities, 1994a, 1994b, 1991a), the net result of information liberalization is the construction of a more powerful state which may now act more definitively on competition grounds to advance transnational proprietary expansion over the information sector.

The notion of competition in the public realm is thus problematic both as an assumption about the benefit of spontaneous market processes as well as for the contradictory value it ascribes to the civil state as simultaneously minimal and strong social agent in relation to the market. Yet there is even further complexity to the question of competition which liberalization politically advocates for the kind of public space it favours in the multimedia age. This concerns the global and multilateral advocacy for competitive processes in information services to generate more 'freedom of choice' for consumers without, in fact, any corresponding industry or government provisions within information policies to bring this about through the enforcement of competition rules. Judging from these developments, it is argued that the competitive order of the information society suggests the use of competition policy in the creation of concentration.

As observed already (see Chapter 4), the international origins of information liberalization can be traced to the Commission's 1987 Green Paper on telecommunications-services liberalization (Commission of the European Communities, 1987), and also to the 1982 breakup of the AT&T monopoly into regional telephone companies (US Government, 1982; US Congress, 1994c). Together, these developments are commonly thought to forecast the competitive environment of the information society (see Ungerer and Costello, 1988; Noam, 1989; Bolter, 1984). In view of subsequent initiatives, the meaning of the Green Paper and the AT&T divestiture must be reassessed as representing the last historical attempts at implementing competition or antitrust law and the beginning of a transition to an entirely different approach to market forces in the information sector. Throughout most of this century, competition policy has imposed a responsibility on liberal states to intervene in civil society in order to create the democratic conditions for economic participation and to ensure that markets work in practice as they should in theory. The dream of perfect competition comprises, in an important sense, economic liberalism's approach to the democratic problem, advocating a form of social organization which guarantees to private parties the conditions of rivalry over the circulation and accumulation of proprietary assets (see defence of this view in Nozick, 1974; Hayek, 1982; Rawls, 1993, 1971).

Building on Smith's (1986) ambivalence regarding the role of the minimal state in achieving competitive equilibrium for the market, modern liberal states have undertaken to address by constitutional instrument (Articles 85 and 86 of the Treaty of Rome), statute (US Sherman Anti-trust Act), or public policy the problem of 'imperfect' or 'monopolistic' markets. This is the normative ground on which the democratic legitimacy of public-service communications monopolies in Europe have been called into question by the USA in multilateral trade negotiations, and by European information policies (Caby and Steinfield, 1994; Mansell, 1993). It is the moral ground on which Judge Harold Greene used US antitrust laws to break up the publicly sanctioned private-communications monopoly of AT&T (US Government, 1982; US Congress, 1994c; Horwitz, 1989), reiterated in subsequent US legislation to abolish private regional telephone monopolies in local voice telephony (US Congress, 1996a, 1995a, 1994a). It may be argued, then, that the tendency of public policy in liberal states over the course of the twentieth century claims an intolerance towards the imperfections of competition as a distinctive method of addressing the responsibility of governments towards the general problem of democratization.

Since the rejuvenation of the liberalization movement in the 1980s, liberal states, by targeting areas in which competition is deliberately suppressed on grounds of common interest other than economic rights, have been able to invalidate alternative categories of democratic rights for citizens including not just welfare benefits for the chronically dispossessed (widely discussed as the 'end of the welfare state'), but also political rights related to information, cultural self-determination, moral rights of creative paternity (creative authors' rights in copyright law), and political rights, that is, rights to receive information and to participate in the public realm. This trend has displaced the focus of competition policy directed at the shortcomings of actual competition among private entities whose rivalry very often results in further consolidation of capital ownership, since larger entities are logically motivated to eliminate or absorb smaller players in the interest of efficiency (see Adams and Brock, 1995).

Under the Reagan and Thatcher political regimes and their post-Cold War legacy in the USA and the European Union, this form of competition policy has thus trained the apparatus of the state to target instruments of intervention where competition is deliberately suppressed, as in the case of public-service monopolies, rather than where it is largely absent owing to the inherent imperfections of its workings in the natural market (the rationale for these policies draws from the theories of Schumpeter, 1947; as well as the theories of the Chicago School of economics described in Adams and Brock, 1995; see policy justifications in Fowler and Brenner, 1982). The approach can be briefly summarized as follows: the real evil is the regular consequence of a suppression of competition regardless of sector, and is on a different, more serious plane from conditions which may be caused by the largely benign imperfections of natural, competitive rivalry among proprietary interests. The form in which this approach is applied to policies of the information society works under an unacknowledged assumption that a monopoly based on the superior efficiency of accumulation processes under private proprietorship—that is, private monopoly—does less harm comparatively to civil society than do public-service entities governed by certain non-commercial criteria, whether universal access, substantive diversity in content and information services, or affordable rates for minimum information services for all.

The workings of this competitive order indicate that enforcement of market competition and competitive conditions among information industries mandated by policy may in fact constitute an obstacle in the development of the broadband network and multimedia services. The information society is thought to be better served by a so-called 'tear up the rule books' argument (*Congressional Quarterly*, 1994a; Commission of the European Communities, 1994a) for sweeping withdrawal of regulatory restrictions. The parameters of this reversal in the historical development of competition law have been largely sketched out by the Delors White Paper on growth and competitiveness, the Bangemann Report on the information society, and the infrastructure Green Paper (Commission of the European Communities, 1993a, 1994a, and 1995a, 1994b, respectively), as well as by the national–global information-infrastructure agenda in the USA (US Government, 1995a, 1993), the US Congress communications legislation (US Congress, 1996a, 1995, 1994a), and global telecommunications agreements (World Trade Organization, 1997). These initiatives in the socio-legal design of the intelligent network, that claim the benefits of competition for society, can serve as the basis for assessing a few of the central issues at stake for the organization of advanced industrialized democracies in the information age.

It should be noted that the political and economic dilemma of regulation for the digital revolution embodied in the paradox of competition policy which this chapter identifies is not held to be problematic because the competitive order of information policies is logically contradictory. The concept of 'paradox' delineated here is not used to signify logical contradiction. Rather, the concept of paradox is employed to describe the pragmatic relationship between the initial conditions of the application of competition, which is a factor of pre-existing proprietary arrangements, and the consequences of its realization. To say that competition in the information market is paradoxical is to say it risks being defeated on its own terms, because the conditions of its realization are defined and established in such a way that they are undermined in the process of realization. Consequently, it is suggested that this form of paradox is in no way self-defeating; rather, it is self-serving for the political aims of liberalization as such. Accordingly, the competitive order of information liberalization can be illustrated in the following self-serving, paradoxical forms.

1. Even as the significance of competition policy applied to a number of communications industries ranging from broadcast to telecommunications is widely debated in the European Union, the USA, and in multilateral and bilateral trade agreements, it is becoming irrelevant to market players. Recent actions of the US Federal Communications Commission in auctioning spectrum for the wireless communications market (*Congressional Quarterly*, 1994b), the US Telecommunications Act of 1996 (US Congress, 1996a) rolling back monopoly restrictions,

and the Commission's orientation (Commission of the European Communities, 1997, 1996*a*, 1996*c*, 1995*a*, 1994*b*, 1994*d*, 1990*a*) in assimilating the liberalization policy paradigm emerging in the USA to mobile, telecommunications, and broadband-infrastructure development in Europe, indicate competition legislation is being overtaken by state activism and market realities favouring market consolidation.

2. Whereas industry and liberal governments at one time pressed for the extension of competition policy to cover growing areas of information infrastructure and services, the utility of such laws in prising open markets for global players is now over. Once the concept of dismantling public-sector monopolies has gained international validity in information policies and trade negotiations, the political aim of the competition order of liberalization has been achieved. As new liberalization initiatives in the EU and USA indicate, strict principles of competition superimposed to correct the invisible hand of the market are being regarded as counterproductive to technology innovation, infrastructure development, and proprietary growth.

3. Antitrust policy is being displaced by liberalization and the two do not necessarily reinforce each other nor do they constitute related processes; as argued here and in earlier chapters, they may even be logically opposed. Competition rules emphasize the public interest in discouraging unfair distortions, uneven development, and unacceptable domination by a few market entities, thus attempting to force the market to behave as its philosophical ideal says it should. Liberalization, however, favours the aims of global strategy in breaking up public-service monopolies worldwide while simultaneously permitting their legal substitution with private-sector monopolies. Evident in the Commission's infrastructure Green Paper (Commission of the European Communities, 1995*a*, 1994*b*) and in recent US legislation (US Congress, 1996*a*), communications industries are being released both from non-commercial public-interest obligations as well as sector ownership barriers into a state of new oligopolistic freedoms for positioning themselves in the battle over global market share.

4. The other major rationale of competition law, namely, its benefit to consumers in provoking downward pressure on tariffs, is also being effaced in the arguments successfully advanced by the major information-industry players in contemporary policy development (Commission of the European Communities, 1994*e*, 1993*c*; US Chamber of Commerce, 1995; International Chamber of Commerce, 1992). The greater the diversity of players competing over provision of services, the communications industries argue (ibid.), the fewer the chances of high-profitability incentives to finance technological innovation and development. Thus competition rules must be suspended in order to guarantee

compensation for industry above the level the market will allow in the global arena (high-margin incentives), on the assumption that liberalization policies nurturing the global strategy of larger economies of scale will result in the necessary technological investment to stimulate proprietary growth.

These are the reasons why both the USA and EU may invoke competition as a public-interest anchor to rationalize the socio-legal framework of the information society—starting with US Vice-President Gore's vision of rewiring the information society by a diversity of competitors rather than by previous 'natural monopoly' or public-service providers (*Congressional Quarterly*, 1994*a*), and rearticulated as well in the mobile and infrastructure Green Papers of the Commission (Commission of the European Communities, 1994*d*, and 1995*a*, 1994*b*, respectively). But the actual provisions of emerging legislation and policy sanction a new age of monopoly by flexible modes which will permit vertical and horizontal integration of communication sectors within single proprietary structures and a restructuring of economic relationships towards concentration in a range of industries (see discussion of these new freedoms of mergers and acquisitions in Nesvold, 1996).

Among the conclusions one may draw from the information-society regulation trend on both sides of the Atlantic is that governments are being forced to recognize that the anti-monopoly political movement of the last decade was only able, through competition policy, to address the problem of *public* communications monopoly but not the condition of monopoly as such. This is because the realities of the global information market make it virtually impossible for structures of network development and advanced information services to emerge on a national or transnational scale except in the context of immense economies of scale, capital concentration, and the intertwining of industry sectors; in other words, by substituting public with private monopoly which must then be provided a new framework of regulatory legitimacy. This legitimacy necessarily emerges as the competitive order of the information society, according to which the role of the state is redefined from guaranteeing the conditions of democratic participation in economy and society, to guaranteeing freedom from regulation for proprietary acceleration into global oligopolies.

The pressure to maintain Europe's place in terms of global-information market share is leading to the de-emphasizing of market-competition rules in public policy which were geared under national laws to relatively greater competitive equilibrium among proprietary interests (see Hawk and Laudati, 1996), aimed at eliminating barriers to market entry for a diversity of providers, and which opposed an oligopolistic competitive order to a participatory competitive order. The decline in competition standards, resulting from a shift from national to European competition regulation in the information sector, mirrors US communications-policy history (Horwitz, 1989) which has been largely incapable of distinguishing the benefit—or 'public interest'— to civil society of supporting private proprietary accumulation, from that of supporting the social and economic democratization of information space for citizens, users, and providers.

Despite the 'limited government' assumptions of the anti-public service movement, it is argued here that the general thesis of the competitive order of the information society holds that competition can be made more efficient and more functional by certain activities of government than it would be without them. While arguing persuasively for abolishing the role of government in the construction of the information society, these policies simultaneously hold that a functioning market presupposes not merely enforcement of contractual rights but enforcement disposed towards specific forms of market rivalry favouring consolidation. What is meant by a competitive order in the construction of a 'common European information space' (Commission of the European Communities, 1994a) is to make competition work with a propensity for greater proprietary expansion and capital accumulation than is possible under unrealizable (Hayek, 1948) perfect competition as assumed by antitrust law.

Liberalization has challenged, through public policy, the organization of democracies by a fundamentalist root model of minimum state–maximum liberty of proprietary monopoly. Yet as is evident, concrete provisions of liberalization do not actually question whether to allow for state intervention; rather, they act to redefine the nature of legitimate intervention thus canalizing the power of government largely towards virtually unqualified freedoms of large-scale proprietary expansion in the information industries. This process of unabated consolidation (see examples cited in *Village Voice*, 1996; *Business Week*, 1996; and discussion in Nesvold, 1996; Schiller, 1996) and ever-accelerating stream of transactions has been possible only through the competitive order of the information society. This policy system has made it possible to employ the power of the state to sanction monopolistic structures in the information market, and allowed the state to make the political choice of withholding the application of competition law in the prevention of vertical integration, strategic alliances, and consolidation leading to information oligopolies. In this respect, the competitive order of the information society has been successful since the paradox has been self-serving for the information industries and certainly not self-defeating.

To explore further these developments, it is necessary to examine the international dimensions of this competitive order whereby the momentum of information liberalization derives not from a model of open competition, but from the realist mode of utilizing the concept of open competition to accelerate structures of global capital concentration in the information industries.

THE BASIS OF LIBERAL INTERNATIONALISM

In an essay on the spread of liberal internationalism, Stanley Hoffman (1995) calls liberalism 'the only comprehensive and hopeful vision of world affairs' (ibid. 177) which has 'succeeded in removing a vast number of barriers to trade and communications' (ibid. 174). Even while admitting that 'the global economy is literally out of control, not subject to the rules of accountability and principles of legitimacy' (ibid. 175), Hoffman maintains that the transnational economic order 'constitutes a triumph of the liberal vision that first appeared in the eighteenth century' (ibid. 174).

Such an account of the new competitive order may overlook a central question regarding the relation between liberal internationalism and modern communications: namely, the extent to which information liberalization enhances or alienates citizens' rights to participate in the decisions of political association. As seen in this study, current 'information-revolution' or technological-innovation arguments, justifying a radical restructuring of the relation between the state and society, are generally employed to emphasize how liberalism would be strengthened by the universal propagation of communication technologies which, by virtue of their technological components, transfer the power of decision-making and oversight to individuals worldwide. The argument that participatory democracy is no longer an issue because it will be implemented by technological means is put forward by liberalization policies (see Commission of the European Communities, 1995*a*, 1995*b*, 1994*a*, 1994*b*; US Congress, 1995, 1993; US Government, 1995*a*, 1995*b*, 1993) and their conceptual justifications (see, for instance, Noam, 1995*a*, 1989; Pool, 1990), though unproved by the social order of liberal internationalism.

As demonstrated in this analysis, these proposals fail to address the profound contradiction between liberal internationalism and democratization. The technological solution of spreading computing and interactive devices in the assumption they possess the inherent capacity to democratize public space, is an approach that disregards some essential questions. These include, for instance:

- Why does the process of technological innovation seem to favour the growth of commercial penetration as against non-commercial, associational organization?
- Will information liberalization allow societies to transform the existing conditions by which issues of common concern in the public arena are to be formulated?
- For all societies affected by the forces of information liberalization, that is, by assimilation to global information regimes, will there be actual enlargement and advancement in how individuals learn of the arguments for and against the various proposals for the development of their societies?

An engagement with these questions is more likely to establish whether liberal internationalism and its mechanism of information liberalization point to a substantive improvement in the prospects for democracy and global development than do policies which merely reference dramatic advancements in technological innovation. This section takes up some of these questions by examining the basis of liberal internationalism and its realist thesis.

The realist approach to international relations is the notion that among societies and states power is the predominant currency and self-interest the predominant motivation (Walker, 1993). While this is also an ancient, neoclassical idea of world affairs (see Machiavelli, 1961; and discussion of Thucydides in Bruell, 1974), in the late twentieth century it has fully merged with liberal internationalism (Forde, 1995) because of essential consistency with liberalism's competitive order favouring private self-interest and the preservation of existing conditions of social power as the basis for the organization of society. This view presupposes the negation of any competing moral outlook regarding the nature of international relations. For instance, contemporary international realism treats liberalization as justified in shedding normative concerns regarding the ethical basis of interstate relations because of liberalization's increasing reliance on its competitive order and on the scientific grounds of technological innovation. A cornerstone of contemporary liberal internationalist theory and practice is the principle that truly scientific processes at work in the logic of competition and technological innovation are inherently value-free with respect to political constitutions and power, proprietary conditions, culture, religion, or social development, and hence applicable to all human societies as a scientific and value-neutral path to a global model of interstate relations. An important defence of this view argues that the only alternative to liberal internationalism in the post-Cold War period is the existence and persistence of anarchy (Grieco, 1988). Only if states respond to the (inevitable) conditions of international anarchy by the terms of this latest form of international realism—which emphasizes private proprietary relations on a world scale as the basis of interstate relations—can nations hope to establish behavioural regularities that are rational, thereby peaceful, scientific, and mutually beneficial to all societies.

Thus universal imperialism via liberal internationalism is justified on the rational grounds of proprietary self-interest held to be a progressive force which deserves liberation on its own account through a foreign policy constituted in realist bilateralism and multilateralism in trade and economic arrangements. What gives modern liberal internationalism its scientific character is its grounding in necessity—the defence of a theory of nature organized around the processes of competitive self-interest. Natural compulsions for private self-interest, mainly with respect to issues of property and accumulation arising from the state of nature, induce both individuals and nations to act in the ways described by realist liberalism. Information liberalization grants profound legitimacy to the arguments and reality of liberal internationalism because it is a verification of this natural necessity of market processes and of its consequences. If the liberalization of trade and information services, or more generally, the exercise of power based only on private-information monopolies, constitutes a genuine law of international behaviour in the sense argued by liberal realists (Donnelly, 1992), no state can be blamed for acting in accordance with liberalization. To the extent that the imperialist behaviour of expanding, large-scale proprietary interests under contemporary information liberalization is referred to nature, hence scientific necessity, it is removed from the realm of ethical discourse, for it is its own exoneration.

The goal of the science of liberal internationalism is to guarantee the survival of existing proprietary structures and the liberal state labouring on its behalf, which can be accomplished only by the pursuit of economic power and the practice of universal pre-emptive imperialism in global communications markets. This realist environment continually challenges the historical achievements of democratic community, and the two irreconcilable poles of morality and necessity suggest an almost tragic perspective for the 'global information infrastructure' and the information age. This issue of the historical achievements of democracy and its irreconcilable conflict with the realist basis of information liberalization oriented to a set of private proprietary ends that are not necessarily democratic is explored in the discussion of the international model of democracy that is being constituted in global information policies and arrangements.

Schumpeter (1947) defends liberalism's model of democracy which he describes as 'the democratic method of institutional arrangements for arriving at political decisions in which individuals acquire the power to decide via a competitive struggle for the people's vote' (ibid. 232–302). Democracy is defined by Schumpeter, not as a kind of society or a set of moral ends or even as a principle of legitimacy, but rather as a method of competitive struggle. The liberal model, therefore, claims the advantages of realism in its emphasis on the descriptive, pragmatic, and sole model appropriate to modern international relations. This realist model of democracy prides itself on providing an operational and empirically descriptive account of the needs and behaviour of nations considered to be democratic. It also tends quite openly to reduce the normative meaning of the term to a set of minimum procedures for bargaining and competition derived from the pre-eminent realism of the market rather than from any model of citizenship or participation.

Competitiveness in acquiring power is, of course, the core of this model of interstate relations. The competitive element is deemed to be the source of creativity, productivity, responsibility, and responsiveness, but is first and foremost the only legitimate behaviour in international relations. Indeed, participation theorists argue that the realist model has denuded the concept of democracy of so many of its elements that it has lost any connection with its original meaning (Cohen and Arato, 1992). Thus the price of the realist model of democracy and international relations is the loss of what has always been taken to be the core of the concept of democracy, namely, the citizenship principle (Arendt, 1958; Habermas, 1989) that carries definite normative assumptions of justice, participation, access, and common interest. For these reasons, among others, liberal internationalism, along with the competitive order of information liberalization to which it gives rise, loses all criteria for distinguishing between information structures comprised of formalistic ritual, systematic distortion, choreographed consent, manipulated public opinion, on the one hand (see Ellul, 1990), and systems of participatory communication structures, on the other.

The realist attack on the fundamental responsibility of the state is predicated on the idea that there is an unlimited growth potential for commercial goods and services that would be unleashed, but only on the condition that the state is pushed back to its proper minimal terrain of guaranteeing property rights and law and order (for moral justifications of this view, see Locke, 1960; Hobbes, 1991; Gray, 1989). Privatization and deregulation, the principal strategies of liberalization, would allegedly restore competition to its natural state and end the inflation of political demands. However, the political presuppositions of this global policy would then conflict with the principles of democracy. Necessarily repressive policies regarding the right to participate in the public sphere for the non-commercial sector, and efforts to abolish information rights

ranging from universal service to content diversity, are scarcely conducive to citizenship and to the creation of consensus.

The global export of the liberal realist model through trade and communication policy (information liberalization), a model essentially of
'society against the state', is often based on an approach in which civil
society is either reduced to market or proprietary interests or to some
notion of an essential, inherited, natural non-political culture. Thus the
policies of deregulation and privatization enforced by contemporary
liberal internationalism on a number of societies are based on the
defence of re-creation of a traditionalist and authoritarian social order.
Social integration is undermined by the expansion of an increasingly
illiberal corporate economy, fostering new forms of dependency and
unaccountable structures of governance on existing or emerging civil
societies in the post-Cold War period.

The 'limited government' claims of liberal internationalism suggest
that information liberalization brings about the generalization of
competition in interstate relations. Yet the basis of information-
liberalization policies points to its realist defence of the conditions of
proprietary consolidation, that is to say, of monopoly. The direction of
global communication policy under liberal internationalism is
developing towards the absolute freedom of proprietary accumulation
and concentration, a global oligarchic logic for which the dissolution of
all alternative models of social development—including democracy—in
the modern world would now seem inevitable.

CONCLUSION

This chapter has called into question the fundamental political claims of
the information society, that perfect or fair competition in the information market can be achieved by market processes. Schumpeter (1947),
among the few influential liberal economists to acknowledge openly the
logical reality of proprietary rivalry in the market, has suggested that
the real liberal obligation towards promoting Smith's (1986) theory of
laissez faire is to fashion a moral and economic defence of monopoly. In
Capitalism, Socialism, and Democracy (1947: 87–106), Schumpeter
argues that the process of 'creative destruction' (ibid. 87) makes
monopolies, as opposed to a plurality of competitors or voices, far more
suitable to the dynamic development of capitalism. Monopolies, he
suggests, are not the enemies of progress; on the contrary, they help
progress along in ways that are impossible for smaller, more numerous
proprietary players. The future of capitalism, in his analysis, rests on the
absolute freedom of proprietary and contractual structures for accumu-

lation, concentration, and consolidation, without investment barriers to cross-sector merger and growth. Without this freedom, that is, the state's support of an obvious paradox, the free market is doomed. The suggestions are that it is more proper for the liberal state to work on behalf of large-scale proprietary interests than on behalf of enforcing a competitive market as such:

> Thus it is not sufficient to argue that because perfect competition is impossible under modern industrial conditions—or because it always has been impossible—the large-scale establishment or unit of control is a necessary evil . . . . What we have got to accept is that it [monopoly] has come to be the most powerful engine of progress and in particular of the long-run expansion of total output not only in spite of, but to a considerable extent through, this strategy which looks so restrictive when viewed in the individual case and from the individual point of time. In this respect, perfect competition is not only impossible but inferior, and has not title to being set up as a model of ideal efficiency. It is hence a mistake to base the theory of government regulation of industry on the principle that big business should be made to work as the respective industry would work in perfect competition. (Schumpeter, 1947: 106)

This, in fact, is the unwritten and unacknowledged, but more accurate assumption of liberalism's approach to a competitive order for the information society evolving in the European Union, in the USA, and now in many other parts of the world. Schumpeter's admission of the reality and superiority of monopoly logic in the free market explains part of the underlying thesis of the organization of public space in late modernity.

In the information-society policy framework still emerging in international relations, communications industries have successfully convinced nation states that universal-service and public-interest criteria are in general becoming less relevant as a policy concern since technological innovations allow the market to address these aims without the necessity of non-commercial, public-interest obligations (see Noam, 1995a, 1994). If fixed into the information-society regulatory design, this strategic proprietary tilt could mean the end of a public-interest rationale in public policy, resulting in significant reconstruction of the role and responsibility of the democratic state through the next century and a reassessment of the place and value of the individual in free societies.

It was suggested that the realist basis of contemporary interstate relations has cast information liberalization as a strategic mechanism central to the global political aims of liberal internationalism. The analysis of the realist forms of information liberalization also suggests a basis for asking in what form a coherent conception of enlarged participation is accounted for in the multilateral design of a global information system. The next and final chapter takes up this question of participatory rights or information rights in the European Union and asks whether the preceding directions of the information society may be transformed to more progressive ends. The analysis examines the possibility of whether diverse public-interest and constitutional traditions for communication rights in different states may serve as the basis on which to develop a set of shared, common principles for the information age.

8

Beyond the Promise of Technology:
Communication Rights in the
Information Society

Introduction

The competitive order of the information society has elevated techno-logical-determinist and proprietary-enlargement policies to a pre-dominant place in the constitution of the public sphere. The question regarding technology drives the modern understanding of information and is gradually substituting for the meaning of freedom of expression and information rights. For example, Noam (1995*a*) suggests the solution to information needs in the information society would come from technologies which multiply the 'me-channel' logic of the innova-tion process:

In that [information society] world, channels will disappear. This leads to the emergence of an individualized 'me-channel' (*canal moi, Kanal Ich*) based on viewer's expressed interest, his past viewing habits . . . This is why the future will not be one of 50, 500 or 5000 channels. It will be a future of one channel, a personalized channel for each individual. The simultaneous mass medium experience will be replaced by individualized experience. This is not narrow-casting. It is custom-casting. (Noam, 1995*a*: 53)

Public-space technology of this kind would extend and deepen privati-zation of the public sphere, multiplying the apolitical dysfunctions of liberalization, and moving human development away from political community. The negative liberty and oligarchic proprietary structures of this competitive order are augmented by ever-newer technological devices for regularizing the defeat of public freedoms and accelerating the confinement of citizens to private interests.

Information policies examined in this study take for granted the con-ception of the citizen whose essence is property, and of the political whose basis is the market. The Internet as a model of the information age is a foretaste of this trend. Interactive communications and techno-logical usage would become more frequent, and perhaps would provide more numerous opportunities for expressions of taste, lifestyle, opinion, and commercial solicitation. But communicative acts on the Internet would still be isolated, privatized acts, unrelated to social processes and social structures or to political participation. Indeed, to have more communication-technological devices and terminal equipment in the home would reinforce communication forms whereby citizens register their vote for candidates, consumer preferences, and information products and services in pursuit of their private interests, thus doing little to restore the right of public freedom in decision-making through deliberative, informative, non-commercial structures for reaching common consensus on the direction of the political order. Individuals would still be alienated in their communication practices in the privacy of the digital network, a vision of freedom which current discourse hails:

[T]he electronic hearth around which entire societies congregated nightly will be no more. But this communal experience of constant information sharing has been only an ephemeral episode in the history of mankind. It clashes with a more individualistic media of the information-rich future. For broadcasters, the challenge is to move from the lumbering age of the audience to the age of the individualized me-channel. (Noam, 1995*a*: 54)

There is little in the liberalization of European media to suggest that the information society will promote democracy by designing a regulatory framework that favours the creation of technological capacities and communication structures for collective deliberation and the maintenance of political life. Registering and communicating individual preference (based on what criteria?) at a multimedia computer linked to a digital network is unlikely, given trends in the design of hardware and software and the availability of forms of content, to develop an understanding of relationships of common interest and political association. Political participation and relations are much more complex matters than can be addressed by discovering the outcome of the aggregation of subjective calculations of preference reflected in discrete market choices. Just as voting under liberal political organization has come to occupy its peculiar place as the sole and sufficient political act, so the liberation of global information industries by the policies and technical advancements of the information revolution suggests little more than the extension of the private activities of private parties as they act to protect their rights of proprietary enlargement or consumer freedoms. The effect of this can only be to deepen the power of the competitive order and the absolutism of the information society as the citizen becomes more firmly secured under the authority of large-scale proprietary governance, facilitated by information structures that are promoted by actions of the state.

In arguing for re-examination of what is by no means a new problem plaguing the historical evolution of political freedom, it may be relevant to ask, at this stage, whether a constitutional defence of participatory political rights is inherently irrelevant given the explosion of technical networks and devices for facilitating human communication, or whether rights of expression and information are merely derailed by the modern communication revolution. In an effort to answer these questions, and departing from the emerging technological-determinist substitution for the problem of information rights, the enquiry of this book will conclude with an examination of the ostensibly political aspects of the information society in two related areas of information and participation rights. First, this chapter will evaluate the place of free-expression rights in the socio-legal and competitive order of the information society. Secondly, in questioning the absolutism suggested by the political reality of information liberalization, the study will reflect on the challenge in Europe of articulating a socio-legal basis for information rights that develops from a deliberative paradigm and which may serve as an adequate defence for the maintenance and expansion of these rights under constitutional reform and political integration in the European Union.

The conceptual legacy of communication rights was taken up at length under the 'principle of publicity' as the central political promise of modernity (Chapter 1), its status and structure was determined by the political mode of public space (Chapter 2), and its significance was seen to be central to standards of validity and legitimacy in the participatory organization of a free society (Chapter 3). It was argued that the political order is embedded in and constituted by the socio-legal foundation of public space, defined within a theory of socio-political practices and public freedoms whereby individuals can gain knowledge and information, and can educate, enlarge, and use their capacities to transform their social contexts. The release from the confines of private subjectivity to support judgements on grounds of public reason is possible only under the conditions of a public realm whose institutional and socio-legal basis is conducive to the exercise of political rights of action, and integral to the formation of collective political judgement.

Measured by this standard, in what sense can it be said that the communication rights of the information society provide avenues for democratic transformation? In order to address the question, this chapter will discuss the issue of free expression, rather than contractual, proprietary, or nationalist criteria, as a basis for regulating the multimedia information society. While the argument of this chapter concludes that rights of expression and information have not had any significant effect on matters of information policy in the European Union, it is none the less important to consider the problems of political integration as a struggle between fundamental human-rights and fundamental economic-rights doctrine, and the implications of this struggle on the construction of the information society. The role of fundamental rights of expression and information are considered first in their transnational context as shaped by US doctrine. This is followed by an analysis of how this model helps to reveal significant elements of convergence and departure that pose a set of significant challenges to the construction of a communication-rights framework in the European Union. Unless such a framework is substantively incorporated into European information policies, it is argued, European democracy under political integration, and in the terms and conditions of participation in the information society, will become entirely dependent upon, and shaped by, the socio-legal power of the economic objectives of the Community.

FREEDOM OF EXPRESSION AND THE INFORMATION SOCIETY: THE INVISIBLE HAND

This study has attempted to demonstrate the acute dependence of the public sphere upon its constitutional guarantees emanating from the information rights of participation in public freedoms. If the EU has won the struggle over which level of public authority has the power to regulate the information society, then each element of its myriad actions that affect information will, in actual practice and perhaps already, dramatically reconstitute the public sphere of European societies. Could it be rational then to constitute a public sphere on such a scale and with such sweeping regulatory power without accounting for the socio-legal basis of fundamental information rights? In looking for models relevant to the aims of union, it is useful to start by reflecting on the dominant transnational model that emerges first and foremost from the US constitutional context.

The right of expression in the USA is a negative right, with a twofold guarantee bestowed by the First Amendment[1] to the US Constitution: it applies to the transmission of information content as well as to its reception (Smolla, 1992; Middleton and Chamberlin, 1994). The negative guarantee of both transmitters' and receivers' rights comprises a restraint or political barrier to state action and has the same function, according to Simon (1991), in the area of political intervention as antitrust laws have in the field of economic intervention, that is, to pro-

---

[1] The First Amendment to the Constitution of the United States reads: 'Congress shall make no law respecting an establishment of religion, or prohibiting the free exercise thereof; or abridging the freedom of speech, or of the press; or the right of the people to assemble, and to petition the Government for a redress of grievances'.

vide the implicit regulatory norm to the courts. As interpreted in jurisprudence and in the policies of the state, the function of the constitutional constraint on government is to stimulate the 'marketplace of ideas' by submitting ideas to the test of acceptability in the market (Smolla, 1992; Simon, 1991). At the outset, therefore, the right of communication, or political right, in the USA is handicapped in three ways. First, it is a negative right and consequently does not allow the state to account in policy and law for conditions governing participation and communication practice except by defaulting to governance by the market, thereby reinforcing the inequalities of existing conditions. The restraint on the state would thus logically benefit those private social interests with the power to exercise the right.

Secondly, and this is obviously an aspect of the first point, releasing the conditions of political practice to the market, that is, to the 'natural' or private sphere, allows communication practice, information content, and access to public space to be determined by proprietary criteria alone. This eliminates from consideration other necessary standards of determination to maintain the liberties of a civil society, for example, criteria of public interest in the regulation of expression, content ownership, and cultural production, representing a broad range of social and economic interests, or criteria of conditions conducive to deliberative as against subjectivist, and non-commercial as against commercial, expression.

Thirdly, the default to the market, meaning the governance of public space by proprietary factors alone, sets the stage for the final absorption of public freedoms to the contractual and precedent-based, private-law framework. As discussed in Chapter 5, this political basis of policy is narrowly drawn to recognize the economic rights of media owners in contractual market relations regulating asset transfers, capital consolidation, and extractive agreements, and is narrowly drawn to account only for prevailing proprietary holdings. Obviously, then, contractually centred policies exclude from judicial and state competence the scrutiny of citizens' rights to determine whether the public sphere serves such needs as sufficiency of information content and adequacy of access.

The inherent tendencies of the First Amendment are further compounded by the historical context of its institutionalization. Since its conceptual and political logic privileges prevailing conditions in the marketplace, the proprietary structures in communication benefit from the prohibition on government to guarantee structures of public space in the common interest. The effects of this political form of information rights can be illustrated with respect to treatment of the rights of viewers and listeners in broadcasting.

The Communications Act of 1934,[2] like its predecessor, the Radio Act of 1927,[3] is based upon a public-trustee concept. In these statutes, Congress decreed a system of short-term broadcast licences to be awarded to private entities who volunteer to serve the public interest—to be a fiduciary for all those kept off the air by the government (Simon, 1991; Horwitz, 1989; Middleton and Chamberlin, 1994). Thus licensees must demonstrate to the regulatory agency, the Federal Communications Commission (FCC), that they have met the public-interest standard—always ambiguously defined—to warrant renewal for another term. Despite this requirement, rationalized on grounds of technical scarcity of the spectrum, government policy has directed attention to the freedom of establishment and freedom to maintain existing establishment of media organizations. In other words, the ownership freedoms of media proprietors have taken precedence over other communication freedoms such as adequacy or sufficiency of content for education, public-opinion formation, or representation of diverse social interests in entertainment and information programming (Porter, 1993b; Simon, 1991).

There has certainly been periodic, though isolated, opposition to the validity of this logic from arguments supporting the political rights of democracy over the contractual freedoms favoured by liberalism. Both the 1927 Radio Act and the 1934 Communications Act, for instance, assert a specific public interest in broadcasting whereby broadcasters are to provide equal opportunity in airtime to candidates for political office, meaning they are obliged to present balanced content or programming. This general obligation was later turned into the FCC's Fairness Doctrine[4] requiring broadcasters to air issues of controversy and to be balanced in that coverage. The constitutionality of the Fairness Doctrine and its related provisions in section 315 of the Communications Act were unanimously upheld in the 1969 US Supreme Court decision, *Red Lion Broadcasting* v. *the FCC* (1969). The Court ruled that 'the First Amendment confers no right on licensees to prevent others from broadcasting on "their" frequencies', because 'it is the right of the viewers and listeners, not the right of the broadcasters, which is paramount' (ibid. 390–1). Under this differentiation of communication rights, the rights of listeners 'to receive suitable access to social, political, esthetic, moral and other ideas and experiences' outweigh the First Amendment claims of broadcasters when the two classes of communication rights conflict.

[2] Communications Act of 1934, Public Law 416, 73rd Congress, 19 June 1934, reprinted in Kahn (1984).

[3] Radio Act of 1927, Public Law 632, 69th Congress, 23 February 1927, reprinted in Kahn (1984).

[4] Federal Communications Commission, 1974, 48 F.C.C.2d 1, 30 R.R.2d 1261, reprinted in Carter *et al.* (1993).

According to Horwitz (1989), public-interest groups and labour unions understood these provisions and rulings to imply that non-commercial voices have an implicit constitutional right of access to the airwaves.

The Court thus seemed to conform with the views of some constitutional scholars, such as Jerome Barron (1967), who argue that the development of communications media has reduced the 'marketplace of ideas' to a romantic fantasy. According to Barron, increased concentration in media ownership has resulted in a marketplace failure, requiring that state-created right of access to mass media be not just allowed, but mandatory.

Such a possibility of affirmative communication rights for US democracy was earlier stated (Schmidt, 1976) by the US Supreme Court in *Marsh* v. *Alabama* (1946). Under this formulation, 'the more an owner, for his advantage, opens up his property for use by the public in general, the more do his rights become circumscribed by the statutory and constitutional rights of those who use it' (ibid.). As an attempt to define a public-service concept of democracy, this ruling could serve as a basis to argue that private systems of public communication must be deemed to be imbued with a public character and thus be regulated by the state. Perhaps Barron (1967) should be credited, in the US critical tradition of the First Amendment, with articulation of what may be termed a 'new right', that is to say, the right of access to the modern media that form the principal content producers, distributors, and rights holders in public space:

A right of access to the pages of a monopoly newspaper might be predicated on Justice Douglas's open-ended 'public function' [i.e. public service] theory. . . . Such a theory would demand a rather rabid conception of 'state action,' but if parks in private hands cannot escape the stigma of abiding 'public character,' it would seem that a newspaper, which is the common journal of printed communication in a community, could not escape the constitutional restrictions which quasi-public status invites. If monopoly newspapers are indeed quasi-public, their refusal of space to particular viewpoints is . . . in violation of . . . the first amendment. (Barron, 1967: 1,669)

According to advocates of this 'new First Amendment right', the access-to-the-media approach is not consistent with the First Amendment in assigning regulatory power to the state to take affirmative steps in creating an ideological balance in public debate. These steps consist of enforcing against owners of communications industries rights of access for groups and individuals who hold minority views, but who cannot afford to own a press medium, be it a newspaper, a broadcast station, or a computer server. Barron's position does not consider, however, that communication-content providers have a public-service obligation to inform and educate their audiences on public issues by standards sufficient to the public-opinion function of a democracy. Rather, the normative question of the structure of public space is constrained in Barron's analysis, to the issue of 'minority opinion'. To that extent, Barron's public service concept of communication rights remains tied to the utilitarian liberal understanding of the autonomic functions of market competition (see discussion of this theory derived from Mill and Milton in Chapter 1).

For this reason, Barron advocates a more balanced juridical adoption of the free-market theory in the realm of ideas, namely, state activism on behalf of proliferating the expression of private opinion, which he terms 'unorthodox ideas' (Barron, 1967: 1,649), though he remains silent regarding the need for state action in obliging the content industry to serve deliberative relations and consensus formation in diversity of expression, ideas, information, and cultural forms. The assumption in this theory of private rights of expression is that unorthodox private opinions will 'make effective the guarantee against repression' (ibid.). The context of freedom is thus firmly grounded in the notion of opinion as inherently private and of its existence in a competitive environment from which the truth shall emerge. Consistent with utilitarian liberalism, Barron attempts no distinction between the exercise of private as against public reason, thus preventing his argument from addressing the structural conditions of public space, whereby widespread representations of social reality and opportunities for confrontation among significant social groups and points of view can actually lead to the construction of common goals and the general interest—not just the expression of attitudes and personal preference of either a majority or a minority.

Still, Barron is to be credited for calling attention to the 'romanticism' of First Amendment jurisprudence that is 'constitutionally insensitive to the problem of getting ideas before a forum' (Barron, 1967: 1,652). He seems to skirt the issue of the inherent bias of private law towards pre-existing stakeholders in the public domain, pointing instead to the fallacies of constitutional interpretation 'which looks only to protecting the communications which are presently being made without inquiry as to whether freedom of speech and press, in defence of which so much judicial rhetoric is expended, is a realistically available right' (ibid.).

The focus on improving the competitive marketplace of ideas and on flaws in judicial interpretation of the theory makes Barron's argument vulnerable to liberal criticism in defence of negative communication rights. This defence (Emord, 1991) rightly observes that Barron's approach 'lacks any developed Constitutional law foundation' (ibid.

292), thereby confirming the argument in this chapter regarding the fundamental handicaps of the US First Amendment. It is indeed difficult, if not impossible, to base an affirmative communication-rights theory— whether liberal, republican, or communitarian—on a constitutional provision directed purely at tying the hands of the civil state and barricading it from the problems and processes of the public realm. There are two underlying assumptions in such an absolute constraint. First, the only threat to freedom lies in the absolutist threat of state authority and not in any other sphere of human life, not even the proprietary relations of civil society itself; and secondly, the barricading of the state from the degenerative problems and dysfunctions that may arise in the public realm is defensible by implicit faith that the marketplace of ideas will address any possible dysfunctions of public space to preclude distortion, domination, or inequality. Structurally, conceptually, and legally it is somewhat implausible, therefore, to attempt to build any rational affirmative or public-service socio-legal basis from the First Amendment.

Yet public-service arguments which appeal for legitimacy to the First Amendment, as both court rulings and the FCC regulations show, continued sporadically up until the 1970s in a quest for some method to construct a legal foundation for affirmative rights. This judicial and policy orientation was abruptly reversed beginning with the *Miami Herald Publishing Co.* v. *Tornillo* (1974) case in which Barron had the opportunity to present his public-service concept of the First Amendment 'access rights' before the Supreme Court. The case involved a Florida right-of-reply statute which provided a political candidate attacked by a newspaper with space to respond. The Court unanimously ruled the statute unconstitutional under the First Amendment, arguing that requiring a newspaper to print replies interfered with the editorial discretion of the publisher, and had a 'chilling effect' on the publisher's First Amendment rights. Writing for the Court, Chief Justice Burger stated:

Faced with the penalties that would accrue to any newspaper that published news or commentary arguably within the reach of the right-of-access statute, editors might well conclude that the safe course is to avoid controversy. Therefore, under the operation of the Florida statute, political and electoral coverage would be blunted or reduced. (Ibid. 257)

The Court thus squarely backed the information rights of the media industries regardless of the scarcity argument, finding the industry's 'treatment of public issues and public officials—whether fair or unfair— [to] constitute the exercise of editorial control and judgment' (ibid. 258). The information rights of citizens to have real knowledge of their social, cultural, and political environment, and to enjoy broadening possibilities for participation in common decision-making, is effaced by the higher information rights of the proprietors of the public sphere to unconditional governance over information content.

Under the revival of liberal fundamentalism during the 1980s, marking also the emergence of liberal internationalism, the policies of the state sought to abrogate these instances of political-rights assertion through regulatory appropriation of the FCC (Porter, 1993*b*; Simon, 1991; Horwitz, 1989). The aim of such proposals was to dismantle completely any vestige of regulatory controls over broadcasting, particularly rules which require broadcasters to operate as 'public trustees'. The FCC's chairman asserted that a marketplace approach to broadcasting regulation 'emphasizes broadcaster discretion as a way to maximize listener welfare' (Fowler and Brenner, 1982: 240), following which in 1987 the FCC eliminated the Fairness Doctrine.[5]

Thus the political form of liberalism reasserted itself and came full circle. Although the US Supreme Court had emphasized the information rights of viewers and listeners to be informed and to have access to knowledge for facilitating participation in society and economy, it had also been powerless to prevent the combined effects of liberalism's institutions of contract, private law, and property which reinforced the opposite and unsubstantiated claim that advancing the rights of proprietary expansion in the marketplace maximizes the public interest. The fact that the cause of democracy cannot be furthered by such means is echoed by the constitutional courts of both Germany and Italy, which have gone further in protecting the rights of listeners and viewers (see Porter, 1993*b*). Further, far from providing evidence of the reality of an 'invisible hand' or 'perfect competition' in the unregulated marketplace, as defended by Fowler and Brenner (1982), the history of communication rights in the USA shows this assertion to be somewhat illusory. As argued earlier regarding the competitive order of liberalization (Chapter 7), its political aims are not achieved through the dilution of government. Using the thesis of Toinet *et al.* (1989) on liberalism in the USA, liberal internationalism does not except the state from its political order. There is, therefore, no absence of the state in the application of policies of the 'invisible hand', nor such a thing as minimum state interventionism.

Indeed, as preceding chapters in this study have endeavoured to show, on the one hand, liberal interventionism in the information society seems to take specific forms in accordance with distinctive political aims, a reality which undermines assertions of autonomous

---

[5] Federal Communications Commission, Fairness Alternatives Report, 1987, 2 F.C.C.Rcd. 5272, 63 R.R.2d 488, reprinted in Carter *et al.* (1993).

market processes whose natural forces serve the public interest through tendencies towards equilibrium, efficiency, and inherent fairness. On the other hand, such regulatory attempts to assist the workings of the invisible hand through critique of its failures and compensation through competition policy, industrial policy, or cultural policy do little to alter conditions since none of these is directed at the political problem of how to organize public space around extending public freedoms, but is directed instead at advancing what may be described as a new basis of governance of society and economy by means of information oligarchy.

Under information-society initiatives in the USA (see US Congress, 1996*a*; 1995; US Government, 1995*b*), the telecommunications industry is likely to gain the same communication rights of the First Amendment granted to broadcasters, which would allow them freedom from non-commercial obligations in the provision of video services. While the US cable industry initially opposed this move fearing competition from telecommunications, the fear of competition is now irrelevant given regulatory signals favouring consolidation across industry sectors through alliances and partnerships (see summary of conflicting industry positions over proposed legislation in US Congress, 1994*a*). Thus the move away from the common-carrier model of regulating telecommunications and cable, whereby a non-discriminatory access obligation is imposed in order to further the political intent of the First Amendment for multiplying the diversity of information sources, is also being set aside by information liberalization (for a discussion of the common-carrier rule obligation, see Geller, 1994; also, Horwitz, 1989). If information-society policies succeed in permitting communications industries, such as cable and telecommunications, to join the category of audiovisual producers, broadcasters, and the print press through reclassification from common-carrier status to programme-content provider status, liberalization's political use of the First Amendment to deny the application of principles of political rights of communication to the structure of public space brings about a definitive end to the promise of modernity which, as argued in Chapter 1, is a promise of progress in political and social participation intended to enable individuals to judge politically and play an active role in the creation and maintenance of their freedom by means of a self-managed democratic system (see discussion of 'principle of publicity' in Chapter 1).

The development of free-expression rights under information liberalization in the European Union is similar in some ways, but is less determined and suggests the emergence of opposite tensions in others. This study has already shown the extension of proprietary dominion over the public realm in the areas of telecommunications liberalization, copyright, audiovisual policy and media ownership rules, and competition policy. Together, they indicate the transformation of information rights from the problem of the participatory and information needs of individuals, into the infrastructure and content-ownership expansion needs of private entities. Protestations of 'human enrichment' (Commission of the European Communities, 1995*b*: 1) notwithstanding, it is held that in terms of actual policy provisions, the regulatory boundaries for the multimedia age preclude development of the network for public-service applications at the same time that it gives full licence to development for commercial applications. In this analysis it remains to be seen whether the emerging grounds for a socio-legal or constitutional guarantee of communication rights in the European Union offer the basis for a counter-trend.

Quest for Fundamental Rights in the European Union

Ball (1996) observes that it is not usual to think of treaties as constitutions capable of providing individuals with enforceable rights based on the obligations of signatory nations. Yet as argued in some detail earlier (see Chapters 4 and 5), the European Court of Justice has interpreted the Treaty of Rome (Commission of the European Communities, 1993*c*) as a constitution in its practice of inferring principles, obligations, and rights. But it also takes the Treaty further than the constitutions of liberal states, Bell (1996) argues, because of an inherent structure of positive powers, competencies, and obligations imposed on Community institutions in contrast with the negative obligations imposed upon nation states by standard liberal constitutions as modelled in the USA. Although these European 'rights', so to speak, are in fact fundamental economic rights granted to entities, the Court has both inferred and appealed to a concept of fundamental human rights which has at once granted them legal validity in Community law and extracted the basis of certain implicit norms (see discussion in Chapter 5). The recognition of common traditions of human rights in the constitutions of member states has opened up the possibility for the Court to develop the socio-legal grounds of requiring Community intervention or regulation in areas where these rights may be affected (see discussion of European public-interest law in Chapter 5).

But in terms of constitutional coherence in the economic mandate of European law, it would seem incongruous, at first glance, to associate the principle of liberty of expression with that of free flow of services. The first liberty has evolved in the domain of the rights of man, the second in that of free trade. The linking of the two in the European Union has occurred from the absorption of information-sector regulation by Community trade law. In so far as information industries are now authorized at the Community level 'to receive and impart information and ideas . . . regardless of frontiers' (ECHR, European Convention for Human Rights, 1950: Article 10, par. 1), European law constitutes a support for liberty of expression. And to the extent that the EU legal regime assures the free circulation of information services and distribution structures, the principle of free trade has come to constitute an essential component of the liberty of expression.

The Commission's Green Paper on television without frontiers (Commission of the European Communities, 1984) which preceded the television directive (discussed in Chapter 6), offers one of the first instances of attempts to construct information policy from a relation between the free-press rights of the media, which are an admission of their political, non-commercial function, and the free-trade rights of media industries, which acknowledge their commercial privileges. The Green Paper assessed the relation between principles of free expression and free trade while attempting to develop a rationale for some link. It concluded that the rights of man form an integral part of the Community's central mission to create a single market, and that far from this being a coincidental correspondence, the relations between Article 59 on free movement of services in the Treaty (Commission of the European Communities, 1993c) and Article 10 of the ECHR constitute a source for the enriched development of both human rights protection and the normative grounding of European trade law. Defending the Community's authority in the area of information and cultural industries, the Green Paper maintains that liberty of expression and the market can mutually enrich each other, thus rendering more effective the principle of communication rights.

It is evident, then, that the EU has strategically identified human rights and fundamental rights of free expression as a desirable legal foundation for trade in information services. At the same time, however, the Community has been actively involved in the applicaton of information liberalization and a competitive order whose logic places actual control of expression within a consolidating proprietary sector. In recent years, Community institutions, including the Commission, the European Parliament, and the European Court, have moved separately to assimilate human rights into the EU's regulatory mechanisms by incorporating the ECHR, a number of international human rights treaties and conventions, common constitutional principles drawn from member states, and the accumulation of human-rights case law (see Commission of the European Communities, 1993j; European Parliament, 1989a, 1989b).

In seeking guarantees of freedom of expression at the European level, unquestionably the only explicit legal basis for information rights could be said to derive from an appeal to Article 10 of the ECHR. In some ways, this has been upheld in several cases in which the European Court emphasized 'the pre-eminent role of the press in a State governed by the rule of law' (*Castells* v. *Spain*, 1992: par. 43). The role of public communications, according to the Court, is to be both 'purveyor of information and "public watchdog"' (*Ligens* v. *Austria*, 1986: para. 42). Indeed, the Court has gone further to emphasize

[that it is] . . . incumbent on the press to impart information and ideas on matters of public interest . . . Not only does the press have the task of imparting such information and ideas: the public also has a right to receive them. Were it otherwise, the press would be unable to play its vital role of 'public watchdog'. (*The Observer and Guardian* v. *the UK*, 1991: par. 59(*b*))

Clearly, isolated rulings such as these do not represent a trend and there is no persuasive evidence to support the conclusion that information rights are constitutionally and legally guaranteed under European law. But if precedent is an important—even if not a determining—factor, then these few instances of Court judgments in favour of the positive information rights of citizens to be informed offer some historical potential for the future development of the political rights of civil society. For example, in an analysis of one decision of the European Court of Human Rights, Duffy (1994) observes that few expected the second major court in Europe, the European Court of Human Rights, to allow parties to utilize Article 10 of the ECHR to redress grievances of monopoly, yet 'this is exactly what happened successfully in *Informationsverein Lentia*' (1994, European Human Rights Report, 17: 93, case cited in Duffy, 1994: 90). In this particular case, Duffy notes that the Court of Human Rights condemned the *de facto* monopoly enjoyed by the Austrian Broadcasting Company as contrary to Article 10:

The court has frequently stressed the fundamental role of freedom of expression in a democratic society, in particular where, through the press, it serves to impart information and ideas of general interest, which the public is entitled to receive. Such an undertaking cannot be successfully accomplished unless it is grounded in the principle of pluralism, of which the state is the ultimate guarantor. This observation is especially valid in relation to audio-visual media, whose programmes are often broadcast very widely. (European Court of Human Rights opinion quoted in Duffy, 1994: 90)

Differences both in formulation and interpretation that exist between Article 10 and the First Amendment are substantive in many respects. The most significant distinction, it was argued in Chapter 5, is that the construction of Article 10 of the ECHR would allow a positive-communication right to be directly inferred and, to that extent, Article 10 offers more extensive protection than the First Amendment guarantee. It states:

Everyone has the right to freedom of expression. This right shall include freedom to hold opinions and to receive and impart information and ideas without interference by public authority and regardless of frontiers. This Article shall not prevent States from requiring the licensing of broadcasting, television or cinema enterprises. (ECHR, European Convention for Human Rights, 1950: Article 10, par. 1)

By granting not only the right of conscience and speech, but also the right to 'receive . . . information', Article 10 would, if correctly applied, allow a positive claim which citizens could exercise on lawgivers to guarantee their information rights against the competing claim of freedom from obligation asserted by information-content providers. Thus, in theory at least, European law could be said to:

- confer a more extensive right on individuals, namely, listeners, viewers, and users;
- carry the legal potential for furnishing the state with a positive legal foundation to regulate the information sector with the aim of advancing a non-commercial common good, and not merely proprietary and contractual goods;
- and place a constitutional obligation on content producers, providers, and distributors by holding these entities to standards of adequacy, sufficiency, and plurality of information forms in their exploitation and governance of the public realm.

As argued in Chapter 3, in order for a free society to maintain the conditions of public freedom and of political rights so that the common good and processes of collective will-formation may be identified and arise by democratic means, it is essential for the body politic to consider how the right of individuals to receive information and to participate in the public arena, which is non-reducible to the market, may be prescribed by law. In codification, even if not in legal and policy practice, the Community has succeeded in establishing that human rights, in particular rights of communication, are now fused into the existing constitutional framework of union. The EU has also succeeded in nominally legalizing a higher level of protection for freedom of information than provided by the First Amendment. Yet two issues central to the actualization of the right remain undetermined.

First, the very fact of the legal guarantee of liberty of expression existing in conjunction with the guarantee of market freedoms says very little, if anything. As is evident in the case of the USA, discussed above, the institutionalization of communication rights within liberalization's competitive order effectively effaces the political, though not the private/subjective rights of individual citizens, and transfers the protection to proprietors of the public realm. Thus the question that ought to be asked, it seems, is not if the right is codified but what its political relation with other rights is. No legal code of free expression can answer the question of how the state in a specific historical context, confronting a particular social order, should act politically. The code gives some guidance on the responsibility of the state to help members of a political association to realize their citizenship in a certain way, as well as how the character of the democratic state and the relationship of citizens to it is best interpreted; and it also clarifies the legal grounds on which a democratic conception of social and political life differs from a non-democratic conception.

But the question of what actions ought to be taken that might be successful in furthering a democratic transformation of social life and in creating relations of public freedom between citizens, that is, deliberative relations, can be answered only by the extent to which state action or public policy can secure the conditions of public space for information, knowledge, deliberation, and judgement among a broad representation of citizens and social interests. It is members of political society who have to arrive at common decisions, not just private opinions, and no free-expression code can provide the political knowledge and experience that is derived from the conditions and experience of actual political participation. This requires public space to be reserved for non-commercial, associative development even while it could not be forbidden for proprietary expansion and commercial development.

One of the issues for the European Union to resolve, therefore, is whether the principle of free trade is constitutionally higher or lower in relation to the principle of liberty of expression. If higher than the communication right, the latter's status is merely formal and negative as in the USA, notwithstanding its more extensive positive formulation in Article 10 of the ECHR. Only in the case where proprietary freedoms of the market are subordinated to the higher principle of political rights to speech and reception of information can the state undertake to defend the democratic development of the public sphere. Fusing the two classes of rights into an undifferentiated group, as the television without frontiers directive (Commission of the European Communities, 1989) attempts to do, works to the disadvantage of the communication rights of individuals, since their political claim to this liberty can be absorbed by the information industries through the market claim of freedom from content regulation under the same set of rights.

This study of the policies of the information society has demonstrated that liberalization's theory of property overwhelms all other rights of man in public policy and law if permitted to merge with these rights without adequate distinction. The transformation of human rights emerging from this process is in a form whereby proprietary and contractual freedoms achieve greater authority from the assimilation of the communication right, thus assigning their interests a higher constitutional status for prescribing the responsibility of the state. The Community, therefore, would need to establish which of the two rights is a first principle before the positive communication right of Article 10 could be realized and embodied in the institutional organization of the EU.

The second issue determining actualization of the communication right in the Community relates to the restructuring of the role of the state under information liberalization. Regardless of the strongest constitutional framework or judicial opinion, if the scope of state action has been reordered to function as a central mechanism in proprietary growth and consolidation, as this study has revealed in analysis of the competitive order of the information society, the possibility for the state to act upon alternative grounds and by other means is already seriously restricted. The policy architecture of the information society, as shown in this study, imposes a fundamental limitation, not on the power of the state to act, but on the form of its intervention. Thus we have seen that Community policy has been forced to expel from enabling provisions alternative grounds of regulation, such as the public interest of universality in the development of advanced information services, the incorporation of moral rights of authors and public-access rights of citizens within information policies for intellectual property protection, and the creation of public-service obligations on cultural industries with respect to provision of non-commercial, broadly representative programme production and distribution.

The Treaty's (Commission of the European Communities, 1993*c*) free-market freedoms and their corresponding rights, on the one hand, and fundamental human rights of information and expression on the other, must be placed by the Court in a normative hierarchy of regulative principles within the Community's constitutional order. For it to have any potential for individual and political development in the information society apart from a symbolic or ideological meaning, the positive information right, when it is in conflict with the attainment of Community objectives of supply-side proprietary expansion in the information economy, must be permitted to limit those objectives in the interest of supporting non-commercial expression in the constitution of civil society. In the absence of a willingness on the part of the Council and the Parliament to adopt positive information rights for EU citizens as the first regulative principle of the information society, it must be left to the Commission and the Court to develop such a normative hierarchy as part of the increasingly complex design of the information society and constitutional framework of the Community. Positive information rights should remain an independent standard, autonomous of Community economic and trade objectives, from which to judge the appropriateness of information policy and the actions taken by the Community.

In the absence of these required adjustments for adequate realization of the information society, the public space in the EU will default to oligarchic information control, by which only one form of expression, commercial expression, will dominate over all other forms. This reality already characterizes the public sphere of countries such as the USA where socio-legal adjustments can never be made, either because of the restricted negative information right or because of information policies which have historically treated the public sphere under a theory of property regulated by contract and private law, thereby preferring the rights of the information industries over the rights of citizens to be informed. The separation of a political sphere composed of procedural voting rights and representative legislative conditions—where public freedoms can at best be only hypothetical—from the sphere of communication structures and practices allows the public realm to be declassified as a political space of universalism, freedom, and equality, thus making it far easier for communication structures to default to regulation by private interests of particularism, atomism, subjectivity, inequality, natural law, and property dominion. No level of constitutional protection for political rights of speech, thought, and knowledge can have significant effect or meaning, other than as formal code, unless the conception and structure of the civil state can account for the political organization of its role on those terms. A constitution emphasizing positive political and information rights and common interest, but institutionalized on grounds of private proprietary interests and of contract, will have just as much effect as would a liberal constitution based from the outset on negative information rights. This is most vividly illustrated in the example of the USA, and in a particular liberalization logic of the EU where neither the tradition of public-interest constitutional law nor that of positive communication rights seems to influence the actual provisions of policy, owing to the transformation of the state by the competitive order of information liberalization and its underlying theory of property.

This study has shown that at least three alternative legal and normative foundations of regulation are currently available to the Community:

* first, there exists the constitutional orientation of public-interest law (Chapter 5);

- secondly, the adoption of human rights, especially rights of information and expression, within the legal framework of the union has been accomplished at all institutional levels (see above); and
- thirdly, a theory of public service prevails in several member states, though often in conjunction with nationalist conceptions of state and society (Chapter 6).

Given these already existing elements, it is certainly possible to reformulate information policies as the rights of viewers and listeners to receive information and ideas. That is to say, if information policies were to be regarded as the objective condition of the communications rights of citizens, the constitutional liberty of expression would most likely be assured. But if such policies are regarded as mechanisms of a particular competitive order or proprietary enlargement process, the communication right would be imprisoned in the formal principle of the constitution but not embodied in the constitution of society. Even more serious, this study shows that the precipitous decline of communications rights of listeners, viewers, and users of modern information networks and services in the policies of public space points to the possibility of the systematic destabilization of political rights of speech, action, and participation (the 'principle of publicity') in the information age of the next century, and hence the inevitable passing of liberty from the promise of modernity.

ABSOLUTISM AND THE RIGHT TO HAVE RIGHTS

This conclusion may seem to support the economic determinist thesis that the rights of man merely serve to disguise relations established in bourgeois society (Marx, 1978c: 40–6). As the institution of human rights has grown beyond political rights to support a dynamic of other rights such as social, economic, and cultural rights (for a discussion of expansion of these rights in the Community, see Newman, 1996; Ball, 1996, Meehan, 1993), it is paradoxical that in the information age the cause of freedom has shrunk in political terms even as it expands in private, technological, economic terms. But does the rise of new rights extending private practices and claims in the information society signify the illusory reality of rights as such, or does it signal a perversion of the principle of rights as political, i.e., participatory communication rights? This question is explored next.

The information society as emerging in the EU and the USA indicates that neither political action, freedom of expression and participation, nor civil society as associative relations are judged as normative standards in information policies, so long as the latter might constrain or obstruct the processes of proprietary growth or damage the competitive order within which the role of the state is circumscribed. It is important then to inquire into the relations of exploitation and absolutism that are concealed behind the formal principles of freedom and equality, as in liberalization's claims of information technology bringing about a new age of freedom and enlightenment for all. Yet this does not imply that the development of freedom should fall into the trap of liberalism itself by confirming that the political rights of man are nothing but a disguised form of bourgeois self-interest (Marx, 1978c: 43). A democratic system cannot be viewed simply as a system whose function is to guarantee the rights of private parties in the market, as argued for both under Lockean liberalism and economic determinism. Further, as Hegel (1952a) and Montesquieu (1989) maintain against arguments like those presented in Locke (1960) and Marx (1978c), civil society is not merely a sphere of proprietary relations, but it is also the sphere of associative and non-commercial corporatist organization among citizens—if that is, and only if, the state's policies and laws can defend public space from total governance by proprietary forces. This is the 'spirit of the law' as Montesquieu (1989) defined it, and the institutional form of freedom as Hegel (1952a) defined it, whereby democracy is not simply a form of government but a political form of the non-commercial foundations of civil society.

This examination of the policy design of public space in the multimedia age has demonstrated that the liberal regime of freedom is being transformed into a mode of absolutism by information liberalization in a manner that is not completely identical with conventional despotism. Tocqueville foresaw not only the possibility of the degeneration of liberalism into despotism, but also the possibility of a system of oppression of a new kind which he cannot name. He writes:

I think, then, that the species of oppression by which democratic nations are menaced is unlike anything that ever before existed in the world; our contemporaries will find no prototype of it in their memories. I seek in vain for an expression that will accurately convey the whole of the idea I have formed of it; the old words despotism and tyranny are inappropriate: the thing itself is new, and since I cannot name, I must attempt to define it. (Tocqueville, 1990: ii, ch. 6: 318, emphasis in the original)

As he sought to 'trace the novel features under which despotism may appear in the world' (ibid.), Tocqueville identified the institution of privatism—including property, self-interest, personal necessity—as a basis for constructing an all-powerful state and the subjugation of citizens. He thus alerts us to the complex and ambiguous historical condition of freedoms perhaps being lost behind a façade of freedom. He describes this power as covering the entire surface of society with a network of regulation that strictly defines the legitimate mode of freedom as a private mode. Such regulation does not destroy freedom but prevents its existence, 'it does not tyrannize, but it compresses, enervates, extinguishes, and stupefies' (Tocqueville, 1990: ii, ch. 6: 319). It confines individuals to their private necessities and delegitimizes the value of their public freedom, but it also liberates contractual and proprietary freedoms to occupy the evacuated political terrain.

Thus Tocqueville's approach to the problem of absolutism, as Lefort (1988, 1981) argues, maintains it would be palpably absurd to apply the epithet 'democracy' where there is little evidence of political freedom. This is not because Tocqueville regards liberty to have only an ideological basis, but because he maintains that freedom is not reducible to the outward forms of freedom. Rather than echo Marx's (1978*c*: 40–6) thesis that the concept and practice of freedom are both inherently ideological, Tocqueville's position seems to stress Hegel's argument that the test of freedom is not in the formal principle of a free society but in its institutional form. Democracy, therefore, is completely contradictory to, and incompatible with, oppression of political rights of action, instead of being just another degree of oppression, as an economic-determinist critique holds (Marx, 1978*c*: 42–3).

The ambiguities of liberal democracy are greatly compounded by furthering one of the tendencies that coexist within it, namely, the tendency to reinforce the power of the state to extend private proprietary control. The state is reconstructed for the benefit of private rights of economic consolidation and the aim certainly is not to ensure the well-being, knowledge, and participation of citizens. Information liberalization as a 'novel form of absolutism', following Tocqueville's (1990) analysis, does not simply mark the destruction of political freedom brought about paradoxically by the extensions of communication; it destroys the power of the state to act in democracy's interest. Thus it is possible to differentiate liberalism from democracy in the policies and laws of the state, in the state's application of human rights as individual/private rights as opposed to political rights, and in the state's reduction of the social order to two terms—the state and the private market—instead of to three terms, the state, the private market, and the non-commercial sector of civil society. But the most important test of democratic legitimacy, as argued in Chapter 3, is whether the common interest is embodied in law, the elaboration of which implies the participation of citizens—in other words, the test of consent that is unrealizable without participatory public space.

When Marx (1978*c*: 42, 44) sees in the freedom of action and freedom of opinion granted to everyone no more than the establishment of a new ideological function of power, he is drawing from the observation of civil society as a society shattered into a diversity of private interests in much the way Tocqueville feared. But the political rights of citizens are not a veil, as Tocqueville simultaneously recognized. Far from having the function of masking the dissolution of associative bonds, political rights testify to the possibility of a multiplication of networks of relations—not merely proprietary relations—which bring liberty and political society into existence and allow the political organization of society to emanate from society as a whole (Aristotle, 1981, Hegel, 1952*a*). The French Declaration of the Rights of Man (1789) holds freedom of opinion not just as an aspect of private property modelled on the ownership of material goods, but as a relational and first principle of liberty (Lefort, 1988, 1981). This approach contrasts profoundly with Locke's judgement of the hierarchy of rights, wherein the first principle is possession of property. Because Marx did not take into account that the constituent element of public freedom is public space, whose appropriation by private interest through the mechanisms of state action (policy and law) is the cause of why civil society grows weaker while proprietary power grows stronger, he was unable to conceptualize the right to resist oppression, or, as Arendt (1973, 1963) and Lefort (1988) argue, 'the right to have rights', that is to say, positive information and political rights.

This is the defining feature of absolutism that eluded the critique of modernity in Weber and Marx. As Arendt (1973) quite rightly observes, totalitarianism is indeed characterized by its disdain of positive information rights, even though it could be organized beneath a recognition of negative rights and the rule of law. Only the loss of the positive right of public freedom can take away the possibility of fighting against tyranny, which for Arendt (ibid. 297) describes the condition of slavery however manifested. Private rights, social rights, and cultural rights can all exist without in fact the existence of freedom, that is, the existence of conditions of public space for judging and being judged. The division between legitimate and illegitimate social orders, therefore, is not the prevalence of human rights *per se*, as liberalism professes, but the presence of public freedoms, thus participatory public space, which means a social order founded upon communication structures allowing for the possibility to deliberate what is legitimate and what is illegitimate. Arendt (1973) maintains that whenever these freedoms are undermined, the entire democratic edifice is threatened with collapse. Under these conditions, which are evident in the regulation of the information society by particular constructions of information policy, even economic, social, and cultural rights may cease to be guaranteed (Lefort, 1988).

Thus the only potential for democratic transformation comes from the 'right to have rights', from the existence, that is, of public space guaranteed by policy and law in the common interest for broadly representative development of questioning and judgement. The debasement of political freedom would stem, not so much directly from the inequalities of the market, as from the debasement of public space itself. Thus the question of communicaiton rights and the democratic, non-commercial development of public space in the information age is far more than an economic, competitive, cultural, or social problem. It is, as Arendt suggests (1958), a fundamental political question, the question that lies at the heart of the democratic project.

This is why the existence of a positive right to receive and be informed in the communication right of the ECHR could, if applied, become the basis for an extraordinary advancement in the democratization of the public realm. Yet it remains only a formal right so long as the provisions of public policy are not constituted by its terms, or so long as the Community as a network of law-making institutions is reconstituted by the competitive order of information liberalization to function as guarantor of economic consolidation. In the USA, where the positive right does not exist, even as a formal principle, the development of public space in modernity confronts no limitations in the processes of dismantling most barriers to proprietary extension through rationales of competition and individual interest. Treating policies and laws of public space as a fundamental political question rather than as an economic, competitive, technological, or cultural question, remains the only approach to the information society that is likely to bring about a potential for the actualization of diversity of expression and ideas. Given the prevalence of negative political rights, the privatization of law, and the absence of Montesquieu's theory of public service or universalism of general welfare embodied in the law, this potential is no longer a historical possibility for the development of the information society in the USA. It continues to be, however, for the European Union, provided the US model of information liberalization has not already reconstituted the three essential institutions of positive rights, public law, and public service into a façade for the absolutism of liberalism's theory of property.

There may be an assumption in Community initiatives (Commission of the European Communities, 1996g, 1989) that some minimal grounds to regulate exist—for example, with respect to cultural content, the interests of minors, and with advertising—and these policies may sanction certain mechanisms to these ends. However, as with communication legislation (see US Congress, 1996a) provided to the FCC, in which the US Congress does not clarify the positive communication right or the political grounds of the public interest to sustain principles and standards of public participation through the decades and to withstand judicial scrutiny, regulatory mechanisms alone, devoid of a positive-communication-rights framework, cannot be expected to survive either constitutional challenges on negative free-expression grounds from the information industry; or, for that matter, on free-trade grounds for circulation of information goods and services required in transnational and multilateral trading arrangements. In the absence of legislative clarification on positive information rights as political rights available under Article 10 of the ECHR, the creation of stronger mechanisms for supporting cultural production in time quotas and financial investment—as was proposed for a revised directive in the EU (Commission of the European Communities, 1996*f*, 1994*g*, 1994*k*; *European Report*, 1995*b*)—will ultimately suffer indeterminacy by reverting to private and contractual-law processes in the courts. Under these circumstances, trade negotiations would ultimately determine if such regulation is constitutionally and internationally permissible.

The outcome may well follow US precedent with EU jurisprudence developing on the basis of private law and the negative free-speech rights of industry alone. Without a political-liberties foundation to justify content regulation on grounds of positive-information rights of citizens, viewers, and users, the participatory potential of the intelligent network and its services can scarcely be realized. Past communications-regulation practice and current information-society trends in the USA offer invaluable lessons in this regard. Favouring the listener or viewer as opposed to the speaker in judicial interpretations of free expression is not the dominant reading of the First Amendment in the USA. The political vacuum in communications law evading clarification of the democratic basis of regulation permits the notion of public interest to stand for freedom from regulatory constraint on consolidation. But such a policy basis, as argued earlier, neglects the possibility that other sources of domination may arise within civil society. Competition law as an economic conception of democracy attempted to address this reality, yet, as explained in Chapter 7, that too now seems to be fading from policy relevance as antitrust is absorbed into the competitive order of liberalization. The most advanced communications network and infrastructure design, and the most rigorous regulatory mechanisms will not stand up in the absence of some form of positive rights clarification. Only an articulation of the political-rights basis of public-interest regulation can in the long run withstand judicial review, multilateral trade negotiations, and international law. Otherwise, it risks dismissal as nationalist protectionism, obstructions to corporate free speech, or barriers to global free trade.

CONCLUSION

This study began by defining the promise of modernity and its unrealized hope of participation in public freedoms. Deficiencies in contemporary modes of public space were then addressed as a way to explore the political basis of constraints on policy and law that disallow liberal democracies from addressing the democratic conditions of the public realm. Thereafter, a participatory approach to the conceptualization of public freedoms drawn from Hegel, Kant, Aristotle, Arendt, and Habermas was taken up, before undertaking a detailed analysis of the socio-legal construction of the information society in the European Union, assessed by the standards of this participatory framework. These policies included the regulatory design of telecommunications liberalization, construction of the socio-legal basis of content ownership or intellectual property rights, content policies regarding audiovisual production and distribution, and the constitutional basis of liberty of expression. In light of the findings, the study concludes with a reflection on two major liberal counter-arguments that could be made against the historical relevance of the political/participatory promise of modernity advanced in this book.

The first counter-argument against the relevance of positive political or communication rights is present in liberal internationalism's universal claim, through policy and political practice, of the irrefutable naturalness of the social order as a proprietary order. It was observed in Chapters 3 and 6, however, that Hegel de-natures this powerful assumption and argues forcefully against basing political society on proprietary relations. Conceiving the state as a contract or a mechanism of proprietary interests allows 'the intrusion of the contractual relation, and relationships concerning private property generally, into the relation between the individual and the state [which] has been productive of the greatest confusion in both constitutional law and public life' (Hegel, 1952*a*: part 1, 'Contract', S75: 59).

Political rights cannot be considered and maintained as unqualified private property, Hegel argues, because they 'transfer the characteristics of private property into a sphere of a quite different and higher nature' (ibid.). Hegel emphasizes that the fundamental mistake of the liberal theory of property is that it confuses the regulation of civil society and the protection of private property with the role of the state itself. Liberalism thus reduces the state to property and contract, as we see most vividly in the case of the state's policies towards the public realm in the information age: '[I]f the state is confused with civil society, and if its specific end is laid down as the security and protection of property and personal freedom, then the interest of the individuals as such becomes the ultimate end of their association, and it follows that membership of the state [in political society] is something optional' (Hegel, 1952a: part 3, 'The State', S258: 156).

But since proprietary interest is a foundation only for private enlargement, it cannot be a foundation for associative enlargement or of political society at all, not even of the most atomic community or discrete alignment of individuals. Thus it is neither obvious nor 'natural' that the first principle of a modern constitutional order and its policies and laws are organized around the right of property, a principle that can only fragment rather than give rise to political community. Hegel argues that a policy regime promoting this fragmentation from a foundation of rights of property points to its inevitable logic of social conditions culminating in the 'irrational, barbarous and frightful' (ibid. S306: 198), that is, in the breakdown of all 'circles of association in civil society' (ibid.), and thus the breakdown of the social order. These conditions are already evident in predominantly liberal states where the plural basis of community has eroded in direct proportion, ironically, to the explosion and advancement of communication technologies and networks maintained on the basis of proprietary control. Hegel's de-naturalization of the proprietary foundations of policy and law, and his argument for political liberty grounded in universal interest as the institutional form of society, renders participatory public space not only relevant to late modernity, but in fact central to universal human development in the information society.

The second issue on the question of relevance derives from liberalism's argument that participatory relations are voluntary relations and, since they arise spontaneously in civil society, require no alteration of the liberal social order. The private sphere, that is, the market, is cast as a model of the truly voluntary sphere which can account for the need for political practice as for educational, cultural, or any other social practice. John Rawls (1993, 1971), the most-noted defender of modern liberalism, argues that the requirement of association in political society is provided for in the voluntarist conception of liberal life. Yet as Pateman (1985) points out, not all institutions and organizations in the private sphere or the market are of this kind; economic organizations or proprietary entities 'provide a sharp contrast to such "voluntary associations"' (ibid. 130). And since governance of the private sphere is unconstrained and facilitated by state intervention, the question of 'associating' is only realizable on the basis of proprietary and contractual relations. Basic features of the liberal institution of right of property show that references to 'voluntary schemes' are therefore misleading and can only be utilized in the private sphere of the market as ideological instruments for referencing, but not addressing, the conditions of cooperative practices among equals.

Rawls's liberal defence of the freedom of association, according to Pateman (1985), proceeds as if the rules governing proprietary participation were just like the rules constituting political participation. But the rules of economic enlargement in the market do not rest on the public freedoms of citizens, nor are they made by elected representatives of citizens. Consequently, liberalism's 'democratic conception' of social life, as has been suggested all along in Locke's theory of freedom as property, stops at the gate of the market. It does not seem to contradict, of course, the notion that the governance of civil society by the market leaves very little non-proprietary, non-commercial space—the 'life-world' as Habermas (1990, 1987) calls it—in social life, since promotion of the realities of proprietary interest is central to the political aims of liberalization. Thus the democratic conception Rawls (1993, 1971) defends could only apply to the social residue which remains after subtracting the effects of the market.

Locke's theory of property and Rawls's apologia for liberalism's justice are designed to justify the idea that participation in the market—the competition argument—whether of ideas, information, cultural forms, goods, or services, is comprehensive with respect to the categories of participation. Accepting this formulation would also lead one to accept the division of members of liberal democracies into two broad classes: those who own property in the form of intellectual property, material property, or capital, and those whose property is mainly in their persons, labour, and creative/technical skills. Accordingly, it would further lead to acceptance that the former have the right to make and enforce the rules that govern the market, and thus that their citizenship is worth more because of their power to influence the actual direction of political community. The question, it seems, is whether citizenship has a meaning that exceeds market power. For Rawls, it does in so far as universal suffrage is non-market participation. Even the most casual examination of liberalism's concept of democracy can discern the hollowness of the assertion that the procedural right of voting compensates for the absence of opportunities for participation for citizens who are less advantaged in the proprietary process, and that they can mend their disadvantage by voluntary schemes in the space which market does not govern, or at the polling booth.

Hence liberalism's counter-argument of the adequacy of voluntary association in the private sphere and of universal suffrage as an answer to the requirements of political liberty lends only stronger support for the rational grounds of a participatory theory of public space and its advocacy of policies to organize the information society according to the 'principle of publicity', and political rights of participation to enlarge individuals' capacities for thought, judgement, knowledge, and action—that is, by the right which makes possible all other rights, including but not merely, property.

The information society as liberalism's political form in late modernity, and its private-law form of regulation, serves to justify social relationships and political institutions that already exist in civil society. The concession to a public-space foundation for a participatory political order of the future cannot be made, for this would undermine the very foundation of liberalism by giving citizens the power to judge for themselves the legitimacy or illegitimacy of the political order, and thus give rise to a self-managing democracy based on information rights, not merely property.

In closing, this study has addressed the significance of the argument for a participatory concept of public space through investigation of the policies of the information society. The analysis has shown that a concept of limited government and *laissez-faire* competition as a necessary precondition for the spread of the information revolution and the transformation to a new form of society, the information society, is invalid on the basis of the socio-legal empirical evidence, and by the standards of the participatory framework employed. The evidence has revealed the empirical problem to reside in the preconditions of actual policy provisions that will make it possible for citizens to claim the liberty promised in modernity's hope of political emancipation through communication, that is, in the knowledge revolution identified by Kant (1991a) to be inseparable from the democratic project. The actualization of the system of information rights depends upon the new importance of substantive law or constitutional law that has arisen in the social and political circumstances of the information society, whereby constitutionally based information policies are required to sustain the structures of civil society for the production of a diversity of non-commercial expression. In the absence of such rethinking and action, constitutional law will decline into procedural trivialization and the legitimacy of the information society will be constructed on the guarantee of only a single form of expression—commercial expression—while other forms are historically effaced or confined to the primitive sphere of private technical relations and subjective preferences, even in the midst of technological profusion.

Finally, the underlying argument of this political study of information policy has been to demonstrate Hegel's (1952a) conceptualization of the central role that law plays in the social order and the operative political philosophy on which it is founded. The significance of the political investigation of law, it is maintained, is that it not only manifests the achievement of a certain form of rationality that excludes other forms, but also shows how the law is a representation of the way in which forms of rationality can be demonstrated to exist in the public realm. In this sense, Weber (1946) too argued the study of law to be the key to the basis of social legitimacy through legal domination, and more recently, Habermas (1992) has made the claim that law cannot be dissociated from the implicit image of society with which it is associated. The contribution of this study is directed, therefore, at the development of a theoretically and empirically grounded argument of the relation between communication rights and the production of legitimate law, and between forms of information policy and the construction of political rights in the information age.

The constitutional reform process in the EU may become one of the most significant turning-points in the reform and historical development of democracy. Universality of thought and law embodied in constitutional models of public service are easily destroyed by unquestioned hegemonic logic, whether authoritarian collectivism or oligarchic liberalism. If the opportunity for serious examination of the constitution of the public realm is marginalized in the agenda of political integration, the possibility for conceiving participatory structures may indeed be lost to the information age as political society disappears under the alienation of reason and the evolution of nationalist and proprietary absolutism.

Appendix
Selected Articles from the Treaty of Rome

Article 30
Quantitative restrictions on imports and all measures having equivalent effect shall, without prejudice to the following provisions, be prohibited between Member States.

Article 36
The provisions of Articles 30 and 34 shall not preclude prohibitions or restrictions on imports, exports or goods in transit justified on grounds of public morality, public policy or public security; the protection of health and life of humans, animals or plants; the protection of national treasures possessing artistic, historic or archaeological value; or the protection of industrial and commercial property. Such prohibitions or restrictions shall not, however, constitute a means of arbitrary discrimination or a disguised restriction on trade between Member States.

Article 85 of the Treaty of Rome:
85(1) The following shall be prohibited as incompatible with the common market: all agreements between undertakings, decisions of associations of undertakings and concerted practices which may affect trade between Member States and which have as their object or effect the prevention, restriction or distortion of competition within the common market, and in particular those which:
(a) directly or indirectly fix purchase or selling prices or any other trading conditions;
(b) limit or control production, markets, technical developments, or investment;
(c) share markets or sources of supply;
(d) apply dissimilar conditions to equivalent transactions with other trading parties, thereby placing them at a competitive disadvantage;
(e) make the conclusion of contracts subject to the acceptance by the other parties of supplementary obligations which, by their nature or according to commercial usage, have no connection with the subject matter of such contracts.
85(2) Any agreements or decisions prohibited pursuant to this article shall be automatically void.
85(3) The provisions of paragraph 1 may, however, be declared inapplicable in the case of . . .[any agreement] . . . which contributes to improving the production or distribution of goods or to promoting technical or economic progress, while allowing consumers a fair share of the resulting benefit, and which does not:
(a) impose on the undertakings concerned restrictions which are not indispensable to the attainment of those objectives;

(b) afford such undertakings the possibility of eliminating competition in respect of a substantial part of the products in question.

Article 86

Any abuse by one or more undertakings of a dominant position within the common market or in a substantial part of it shall be prohibited as incompatible with the common market in so far as it may affect trade between Member States. Such abuse may, in particular, consist in:

(a) directly or indirectly imposing unfair purchase or selling prices or other unfair trading conditions;

(b) limiting production, markets or technical development to the prejudice of consumers;

(c) applying dissimilar conditions to equivalent transactions with other trading parties, thereby placing them at a competitive disadvantage;

(d) making the conclusion of contracts subject to acceptance by the other parties of supplementary obligations which, by their nature or according to commercial usage, have no connection with the subject of such contracts.

Article 90

1. In the case of public undertakings and undertakings to which Member States grant special or exclusive rights, Member States shall neither enact nor maintain in force any measure contrary to the rules contained in this Treaty, in particular to those rules provided for in Article 6 and Articles 85 to 94.

2. Undertakings entrusted with the operation of services of general economic interest or having the character of a revenue-producing monopoly shall be subject to the rules contained in this Treaty, in particular to the rules on competition, in so far as the application of such rules does not obstruct the performance, in law or in fact, of the particular tasks assigned to them. The development of trade must not be affected to such an extent as would be contrary to the interests of the Community.

3. The Commission shall ensure the application of the provisions of this Article and shall, where necessary, address appropriate directives or decisions to Member States.

Article 222

This Treaty shall in no way prejudice the rules in Member States governing the system of property ownership.

References

Achille, Y., and Miège, B. (1994), 'The Limits to the Adaptation Strategies of European Public Service Television', *Media, Culture & Society*, 16(1): 31–46.

Adams, W., and Brock, J. W. (1995), 'Antitrust Ideology, and the Arabesques of Economic Theory', *Univeristy of Colorado Law Review*, 66(2): 257–98.

Anderson, B. (1983), *Imagined Communities*, London: Verso.

Antonelli, C. (1985), 'The Diffusion of an Organisational Innovation: International Data, Telecommunications and Multinational Industrial Firms', *International Journal of Industrial Organisation*, 3:109–18.

Arendt, H. (1975), *Crises of the Republic*, New York: Harcourt Brace Jovanovich.

——(1973), *The Origins of Totalitarianism*, New York: Harcourt Brace Jovanovich.

——(1963), *On Revolution*, London: Penguin.

——(1958), *The Human Condition*, Chicago: University of Chicago Press.

Aristotle (1981), *The Politics*, trans. T. A. Sinclair, rev. trans. T. J. Saunders, London: Penguin.

——(1962), *Nicomachean Ethics*, trans. M. Ostwald, New York: Macmillan.

Arnull, A. (1989), *The General Principles of EEC Law and the Individual*, Leicester: Leicester University Press/Pinter Press.

Ball, C. A. (1996), 'The making of a transnational capitalist society', *Harvard International Law Journal*, 37(2): 307–88.

Barber, B. (1984), *Strong Democracy*, Berkeley: University of California Press.

Barnett, S., and Curry, A. (1994), *The Battle for the BBC: A British Broadcasting Conspiracy?* London: Aurum Press.

Barro, R. J. (1994), 'Party politics of growth', *Financial Times*, 1 November: 18.

Barron, J. A. (1967), 'Access to the Press—A New First Amendment Right', *Harvard Law Review*, 80(8): 1641–78.

Barzanti, R. (1990), 'Audiovisual Opportunities in the Single Market', MEDIA 92, Newsletter of the MEDIA 92 Programme, 09/1990, p. 1. Brussels: Commission of the European Communities, DGX.

Bauby, P., and Boual, J. (1994), *Pour une citoyenneté Européenne: Quels services publics?* Paris: Les Editions de l'Atelier.

Bauer, J. M., and Steinfield, C. (1994), 'Telecommunications Initiatives of the European Communities', in Steinfield *et al.* (1994), 51–70.

Bauman, Z. (1991), 'Living without an Alternative', *The Political Quarterly*, 62(1): 35–44.

Baynes, K. (1992), *The Normative Grounds of Social Criticism*, Albany, NY: State University of New York Press.

Bell, D. (1973), *The Coming of Post-industrial Society*, New York: Basic Books.

Benhabib, S. (1992), *Situating the Self: Gender, Community and Post-modernism in contemporary Ethics*, New York: Routledge.

——(1989), 'Liberal Dialogue versus a Critical Theory of Discursive Legitimation', in N. Rosenblum (ed.), *Liberalism and the Moral Life*, Cambridge, Mass.: Harvard University Press.

——(1988), 'Judgment and the Moral Foundations of Politics in Arendt's Thought', *Political Theory*, 16(1): 29–51.

Berelson, B. (1959), 'The State of Communications Research', *Public Opinion Quarterly*, 23(1): 1–6.

Berne Convention for the Protection of Library and Artistic Works, 9 September 1886, revised, Paris, 24 July 1971, 25 U.S.T. 1341.

Blakeney, M. (1996), 'The Impacts of the TRIPs Agreement in the Asia Pacific Region', *European Intellectual Property Review*, 18(10): 544–54.

Bobbio, N. (1989*a*), *Democracy and Dictatorship*, trans. P. Kennealy, Minneapolis: University of Minnesota Press.

——(1989*b*), 'The Great Dichotomy: Public/Private', in Bobbio (1989*a*), 1–21.

Bolter, W. G. (ed.) (1984), *Telecommunications Policy for the 1980s: The Transition to Competition*, Englewood Cliffs, NJ: Prentice-Hall.

Bork, R. H. (1978), *The Antitrust Paradox*, New York: Basic Books.

Bowman, G. (1992), 'Ethnicity, Identity, Fission: European Community and the Collapse of Federation', paper presented at the Institute of Philosophy and Sociology (Culture Theory Unit) conference 'East European Cultures after Communism: Tradition, Modernity, Post-Modernity', Radziowijce, Poland.

Boyle, J. (1996), *Shamans, Software, Spleens*, Cambridge, Mass.: Harvard University Press.

Braman, Sandra (1990), 'Trade and Information Policy', *Media, Culture and Society*, 12: 361–85.

Branscomb A. (1994), *Who Owns Information?* New York: Basic Books.

British Broadcasting Act of 1990.

Brown, L. N., and Kennedy, T. (1994), *The Court of Justice of the European Communities*, London: Sweet and Maxwell.

Brown, R. S. (1978), *Copyright*, Mineola, NY: Foundation Press.

Bruell, C. (1974), 'Thucydides' view of Athenian imperialism', *American Political Science Review*, 68: 11–17.

Buchanan, J. (1975), *The Limits of Liberty: Between Anarchy and Leviathan*, Chicago: University of Chicago Press.

——and Tullock, G. (1962), *The Calculus of Consent*, Ann Arbor: University of Michigan Press.

Bundschuh, A. (1994), 'New Support for German Public Broadcasters', *The Bulletin of the European Institute for the Media*, 11(1): 1–2.

Business Week (1996), 'Land of the Giants', 11 September: 34.

Caby, L., and Steinfield, C. (1994), 'Trends in the Liberalization of European Telecommunications: Community Harmonization and National Divergence', in Steinfield *et al.* (1994), 36–48.

Canovan, M. (1985), 'Politics as Culture: Hannah Arendt and the Public Realm', *History of Political Thought*, 6(3): 617–42.

——(1983), 'Arendt, Rousseau and Human Plurality in Politics', *The Journal of Politics*, 45: 286–302.

Carey, J. W. (1988), *Communication as Culture*, Boston: Unwin Hyman.

Carter, T. B., Franklin, M. A., and Wright, J. B. (eds.) (1993), *The First Amendment and the Fifth Estate*, 3rd edn., Westbury, NY: The Foundation Press.

Casey, T. J., and Wu, S. (1994), 'Telecommunicatons Privatizations: An Overview', *Hastings International and Comparative Law Review*, 17(4): 781–92.

Castells v. *Spain*, European Court of Justice judgment of 23 April 1992, Series A, no. 236.

Center for Strategic and International Studies (1994), The European Union–United States information infrastructure dialogue: Background Papers, Washington, DC: CSIS.

Chalvon-Demersay, S., and Pasquier, D. (1993), 'In the Name of the Audience', *Reseaux: French Journal of Communication*, 1(1): 27–38.

Chicago Tribune (1996), 'Mergers reach $866 billion', 2 January: 1.

Ciborra, C. U. (1992), 'Innovation, Networks and Organizational Learning', in C. Antonelli (ed.), *The Economics of Information Networks*, 91–102, Amsterdam: Elsevier Science Publishers.

Clark, R. T. (1955), *Herder: His life and Thought*, Berkeley: University of California Press.

Cohen, J. (1989), 'Morality or *Sittlichkeit:* Toward a Post-Hegelian Solution', *Cardozo Law Review*, 10(5–6): 1389–414.

——and Arato, A. (1992), *Civil Society and Political Theory*, Cambridge, Mass.: MIT Press.

Cohen-Tanugi, L. (1992), *L'Europe en danger,* Paris: Fayard.

Collins, R. (1994), 'Unity in Diversity? The European Single Market in Broadcasting and the Audiovisual, 1982–92', *Journal of Common Market Studies*, 32(1): 89–102.

Commission of the European Communities (1997), Common Position of 9 December 1996 on a common framework for general authorizations and individual licences in the field of telecommunications services, *Official Journal of the European Communities*, no. C 41/48, 10.2.97.

——(1996a), Proposal for a European Parliament and Council Directive on the application of open network provision (ONP) to voice telephony and on universal service for telecommunications in a competitive environment replacing European Parliament and Council Directive 95/62/EC, *Official Journal of the European Communities*, No. c 371/22, 9.12.96.

——(1996b), Press conference of Mr Bangemann, Brussels, 27 November 1996, BIO/96/576.

——(1996c), Communication from the Commission on the application of the competition rules to access agreements in the telecommunications sector (COM(96) 649 final), 10 December 1996.

——(1996d), Communication from the Commission on a follow-up to the Green Paper on copyright and related rights in the information society (COM(96) 568 final), 20 November 1996.

Commission of the European Communities (1996*e*), Council Directive of 11 March 1996 on the legal protection of databases (96/9/EC; OJL77/20).

——(1996*f*), Opinion of the Commission regarding the proposal for a European Parliament and Council Directive amending Council Directive 89/552/EEC on the pursuit of television broadcasting activities (COM(96) 626 final), 4 December1996.

——(1996*g*), Green Paper on the protection of minors and human dignity in audiovisual and information services (COM(96) 483 final), 16 October 1996.

——(1995*a*), Green Paper on the liberalization of telecommunications infrastructure and cable television networks, part 2: a common approach to the provision of infrastructure for telecommunications in the European Union (COM(94) 682 final), 25 January 1995.

——(1995*b*), Chair, Mr Jacques Santer's conclusions, G7 Ministerial conference on the information society, Brussels, 25–6 February, Office of the President of the European Commission, Brussels.

——(1995*c*), Green Paper on copyright and related rights in the information society (COM(95) 382 final), 19 July 1995.

——(1995*d*), Directive 95/46/EC of the European Parliament and of the Council of 23 November 1995 on the protection of individuals with regard to the processing of personal data and on the free movement of such data, OJL 281/31, 23.11.1995.

——(1994*a*), 'Europe and the global information society', Bangemann Task Force Report to the European Council, *Cordis*, Supplement 2, 15 July: 4–31, Brussels: European Commission, DGXIII/D-2.

——(1994*b*), Green Paper on the liberalization of telecommunications infrastructure and cable television networks, part 1, 25 October. Brussels: European Commission, DGXIII.

——(1994*c*), Status report on European Community telecommunications policy (DGXIII/A/1, January), Brussels: Commission of the European Communities.

——(1994*d*), Green Paper on a common approach in the field of mobile and personal communications in the European Union (COM(94) 145).

——(1994*e*), Information and communication highways: background documents of the Davignon working party, Brussels meeting, 23 March, Brussels: European Commission, DGXIII.

——(1994*f*), Information technologies: market outlook, background documents of the de Benedetti working party. Munich meeting, 19 March. Brussels: European Commission, DGXIII.

——(1994*g*), Green Paper on strategy options to strengthen the European programme industry in the context of the audiovisual policy of the European Union, 7 April 1994. Luxembourg: Office for Official Publications of the European Communities.

——(1994*h*), *Report by the Think-Tank on the Audiovisual Policy in the European Union*, March, Luxembourg: Office for Official Publications of the European Communities.

——(1994*i*), MEDIA guide for the audiovisual industry, 10th edn., June, Brussels: DGX, Commission of the European Communities.

——(1994*j*), Opinion on the proposal for a Council decision amending Council decision 90/68/EEC concerning the implementation of an action programme to promote the development of the European audiovisual industry, MEDIA, 1991–1995, 94/C 148/02 (OJL no. C 148/3, 30.5.94).

——(1994*k*), Communication from the Commission to the Council and the European Parliament on the application of Articles 4 and 5 of directive 89/552/EEC, television without frontiers (COM(94) 57 final).

——(1994*l*), Transparency of media control: study for the European Commission, DGXV by The European Institute for the Media, November. Brussels: Commission of the European Communities, DGXV.

——(1993*a*), White Paper on growth, competitiveness, and employment: the challenges and ways forward into the 21st century (the Delors White Paper) (COM(93) 700 final).

——(1993*b*), 'Treaty on European Union (signed in Maastricht on 7 February, 1992)', in *European Union: Selected Instruments taken from the Treaties, Book I, Vol. I*, 11–89, Luxembourg: Office for Official Publications of the European Communities.

——(1993*c*), 'Treaty Establishing the European Community (signed in Rome on 25 March 1957)', in *European Union: Selected Instruments taken from the Treaties, Book I, Vol. I*, 91–669, Luxembourg: Office for Official Publications of the European Communities.

——(1993*d*), 'European Liberalisation and Interconnection', speech by C. Berben of DGXIII to CommEd Conference, London, 15 December (CB/dhu – 312p005 AlA), Brussels: Commission of the European Communities.

——(1993*e*), Communication to the Council and European Parliament on the consultation on the review of the situation in the telecommunications sector (COM(93) 159 final).

——(1993*f*), Council resolution of 22 July 1993 on the review of the situation in the telecommunications sector and the need for further development in that market (93/C213/01, OJ C213/1, 6.8.93).

——(1993*g*), Communication from the Commission to the Council, the European Parliament, and the Economic and Social Committee on developing universal service for telecommunications in a competitive environment (COM(93) 543 final, 15 November 1993).

——(1993*h*), Public comments on the 1992 telecommunications review, March, Brussels: European Commission, DGXIII.

——(1993i), Public comments on the 1992 telecommunications review, March (XIII/93/66-EN), Brussels: European Commission, DGXIII.

——(1993*j*), *The European Community and Human Rights*, October 1992. Luxembourg: Office for Official Publications of the European Communities.

——(1993*k*), Council Directive of 29 October 1993 on harmonizing the term of protection of copyright and certain related rights (93/98/EEC; OJL290/9, 24.11.93).

——(1993*l*), Council Directive of 27 September 1993 on the coordination of certain rules concerning copyright and rights related to copyright applicable to satellite broadcasting and cable retransmission (93/83/EEC; OJL 248/15, 6.10.93).

Commission of the European Communities (1993*m*), Audience measure in the EC: internal report prepared for DGXV by the GAH Group, September. Brussels: Commisson of the European Communities, DGXV.

—— (1993*n*), Pluralism and media concentration in the internal market: initial reactions to the Green Paper, information memo, 12 May (IP(93) 351), Brussels: Commission of the European Communities, DGXV.

—— (1992*a*), Council Directive of 19 November 1992 on rental right and lending right and on certain rights related to copyright in the field of intellectual property (92/100/EEC; OJL 346/61, 27.11.92).

—— (1992*b*), Green Paper on pluralism and media concentration in the internal market: an assessment of the need for Community action (COM(92) 480 final).

—— (1992*c*), Study on pluralism and concentration in media: economic evaluation for DGIII by Booz, Allen, and Hamilton, February, Brussels: Commission of the European Communites, DGIII.

—— (1991*a*), Guidelines on the application of the EEC competition rules in the telecommunications sector (91/C 233/02, OJC 233/2).

—— (1991*b*), 'Telecommunications: Issues and Options 1992 to 2010', a study conducted by Arthur D. Little for DGXIII, October.

—— (1991*c*), Communication of the Commission of 26 July 1991 concerning guidelines on the application of the EEC competition rules in the telecommunications sector (OJ C233, 6.9.91).

—— (1991*d*), Council Directive of 14 May 1991 on the legal protection of computer programs (91/250/EEC; OJL 122/43, 17.5.91).

—— (1991*e*), MEDIA guide for the audiovisual industry, 2nd edn., Brussels: DGX, Commission of the European Communities.

—— (1990*a*), Commission Directive on competition in the markets for telecommunications services (90/338/EEC).

—— (1990*b*), Green Paper on a common approach in the field of satellite communications in the European Community (COM(90) 490).

—— (1990*c*), Council Directive of 28 June 1990 on the establishment of the internal market for telecommunications services through the implementation of open network provision (90/387/EEC; OJL 192/10, 24.7.90).

—— (1990*d*), Commission communication on Community accession to the European Convention for the Protection of Human Rights and Fundamental Freedoms and of its protocols, 19 November 1990, SEC(90) 2087 final.

—— (1990*e*), *The European Community Policy in the Audio-visual Field*, Luxembourg: Office for Official Publications of the European Communities.

—— (1990*f*), Commission communication to the Council: action programme to promote the development of the European audiovisual industry, MEDIA, 1991–5, 4 May (COM(90) 132 final).

—— (1990*g*), Council decision concerning the implementation of an action programme to promote the development of the European audiovisual industry (MEDIA), 1991–1995, 31 December (OJL 380/37, 31.12.90).

—— (1990*h*), Communication from the Commission to the Council and Parliament on audiovisual policy, 21 February (COM(90) 78 final).

—— (1989), Council Directive of 3 October 1989 on the coordination of certain provisions laid down by law, regulation, or administrative action in member states concerning the pursuit of television broadcasting activities (89/552/EEC; OJL 298/23, 17.10.89).

—— (1988*a*), Commission Directive on competition in the markets in telecommunications terminal equipment (88/301/EEC, OJL 131/73, 27.5.88).

—— (1988*b*), Communication from the Commission, 'Towards a Competitive Community-Wide Telecommunications Market in 1992' (COM(88) 48 final).

—— (1988*c*), Council resolution on the development of the Common Market for telecommunications services and equipment up to 1992 (OJ C277, 4.10.88).

—— (1988*d*), *The Audio-visual Media in the Single European Market*, Luxembourg: Office for Official Publications of the European Communities.

—— (1987), Green Paper on the development of the common market for telecommunications services and equipment (COM(87) 290).

—— (1985), White Paper on completing the internal market (COM(85) 310 final).

—— (1984), Television without frontiers Green Paper on the establishment of the common market for broadcasting especially by satellite and cable (COM(84) 300 final).

Congressional Quarterly (1994*a*), The information arena: special report, 14 May, supplement to vol. 52(19), Washington, DC: Congressional Quarterly, Inc.

—— (1994*b*), 'New Telecommunications Age hits a Snag in the Senate', 2 July, 52(26): 1776–80.

Constant, B. (1988), *Political Writings*, ed. and trans. B. Fontana, Cambridge: Cambridge University Press. Original works published in 1814–15.

—— (1980), *De la liberté des modernes,* ed. M. Gauchet, Paris: Le Livre de Poche. Original work published in 1820.

Contamine, C., and Dusseldorp, M. van (eds.) (1995), *Towards the Digital Revolution*, Düsseldorf: European Institute for the Media.

Corbeau v. *Régie des Postes,* ECJ judgment of 19 May 1993, C-320/91.

Corbet, J. (1994), 'The Law of the EEC and Intellectual Property', *Journal of Law and Commerce*, 13, spring: 327–69.

Council of Europe (1994), 4th European Ministerial Conference on Mass Media Policy: political declaration, resolutions and statement, Strasbourg: Council of Europe.

—— (1993), The Council of Europe and Media Freedom. Contribution of the Council of Europe to the CSCE conference on free media, Warsaw, November.

—— (1989), European Convention on Transfrontier Television, 5 May.

Curran, J. (1991), 'Rethinking the Media as a Public Sphere', in Dahlgren and Sparks (1991), 27–57.

Dahlgren, P., and Sparks, C. (eds.) (1991), *Communication and citizenship*, London: Routledge.

Dahrendorf, R. (1994), 'The Changing Quality of Citizenship', in B. van Steenbergen (ed.), *The Condition of Citizenship*, 10–19, London: Sage.

——(1988), *The Modern Social Contract: An Essay on the Politics of Liberty*, London: Weidenfeld and Nicolson.

Darnton, J., and Wuersch, D. (1992), 'The European Commission's Progress toward a New Approach for Competition in Telecommunications', *The International Lawyer*, 26(1): 111–24.

David, R., and Spinosi, C. J. (1973), *Les grands systèmes de droit contemporains*, Padua, Italy: CEDAM.

de Jasay, A. (1990), *Market Socialism*, Occasional Paper 84, London: Institute of Economic Affairs.

Delcourt, B. (1991), 'EC Decisions and Directives on Information Technology and Telecommunications', *Telecommunications Policy*, 14: 15–21.

Dewey, J. (1963), *Freedom and Culture*, New York: Capricorn. Original work published in 1939.

——(1927), *The Public and its Problems*, New York: Henry Holt.

Dixon, A. N., and Self, L. C. (1994), 'Copyright Protection for the Information Superhighway', *European Intellectual Property Review*, 16(11): 465–72.

Dietz, A. (1978), *Le droit d'auteur dans la Communauté Européenne*, Brussels: Commission of the European Communities.

Donaldson, J. D. (1996), ' "Television without Frontiers": The Continuing Tension between Liberal Free Trade and European Cultural Integrity', *Fordham International Law Journal*, 20(1): 90–180.

Donnelly, J. (1992), 'Twentieth-Century Realism', in T. Nardin and D. R. Mapel (eds.), *Traditions of International Ethics*, 85–111, Cambridge: Cambridge University Press.

Drake, W. J., and Nicolaïdis, K. (1992), 'Ideas, Interests, and Institutionalization: "Trade in Services" and the Uruguay Round', *International Organization*, 46(1): 37–100.

Duch, R. M. (1991), *Privatizing the Economy: Telecommunications Policy in Comparative Perspective*, Ann Arbor: University of Michigan Press.

Duffy, P. (1994), 'European Briefing', *Solicitor's Journal*, 139(4): 90–1.

Dworkin, R. (1993), 'Authorship of Films and the European Commission Proposals for Harmonising the Term of Copyright', *European Intellectual Property Review*, 15(5): 152–5.

——(1978), *Taking Rights Seriously*. Cambridge, Mass.: Harvard University Press.

Dyson, K. (1980), *The State Tradition in Western Europe*, Oxford: Martin Robertson.

Ehrlich, M. A. (1994), 'Fair Use or Foul Play: The EC Directive on the Legal Protection of Computer Programs and its Impact on Reverse Engineering', *Pace Law Review*, 13(3): 1003–42.

Eisenstein, E. L. (1983), *The Printing Revolution in Early Modern Europe*, Cambridge: Cambridge University Press.

Elkin-Koren, N. (1996), 'Cyberlaw and Social Change: A Democratic Approach to Copyright Law in Cyberspace', *Cardozo Arts & Entertainment Law Journal*, 14(2): 215–95.

Elling, M. (1990), 'The Emerging European Community: A framework for Institutional and Legal Analysis', *Hastings International and Comparative Law Review*, 13(3): 511–30.

Ellul, J. (1990), *The Technological Bluff*, Grand Rapids, Mich.: William B. Eerdmans.

Emord, J. W. (1991), *Freedom, Technology, and the First Amendment*, San Francisco: Pacific Research Institute for Public Policy.

Esser, J., and Noppe, R. (1996), 'Private Muddling through as a Political Programme? The Role of the European Commission in the Telecommunications Sector in the 1980s', *West European Politics*, 19(3): 547–62.

Etzioni, A. (1993), *The Spirit of Community: Rights, Responsibilities, and the Communitarian Agenda*, New York: Crown.

Euromedia Research Group (1992), *The Media in Western Europe: The Euromedia Handbook*, London: Sage.

Europe (1997a), 'Newspaper Publishers oppose the Concentration Directive', 12 March 1997, no. 6932.

——(1997b), 'Commission Discusses Draft Directive on Ownership of Media in the Single Market', 3/4 March 1997, no. 6926.

——(1996), 'Film Industry urges Council to Set up Guarantee Fund', 13 December 1996, no. 6873.

——(1995), 'EU/Television: Motion Picture Association (US) considers New Draft of Broadcast Directive too Protectionist', 25 March, no. 6448: 15.

European Convention for Human Rights (1950), in *European Convention on Human Rights: Collected Texts* (1987), Dordrecht, The Netherlands Martinus Nijhoff.

European Parliament (1994), Constitution of the European Union. Committee on Institutional Affairs, 9 February 1994, EP A3-0064/94.

——(1989a), Human rights and the European Community: nationality and citizenship, report for the European Parliament, October 1989.

——(1989b), Human rights and the European Community: Conference Acts, Strasbourg, November.

——(1989c), Report on the European Community's Film and Television Industry (the De Vries Report), 9 January, PE 119.192/final.

——(1985), Jacques Delors's address to the opening of the European Parliament, 12 March, Commission programme for 1985, Debates of the European Parliament.

European Report (1996a), 'EU and US at odds over Author's Moral Rights', no. 2157, 14 September 1996.

——(1996b), 'European Parliament rejects Television Quotas', no. 2175, 16 November 1996.

European Report (1995*a*), 'Commission Unveils MEDIA II and Calls for Financial Muscle', no. 2015: 4–5, 11 February 1995.

—— (1995*b*), 'TV without Frontiers', no. 2015: 12–13, 11 February 1995.

—— (1995*c*), 'Culture/Audiovisual Services', no. 2016: 14–15, 15 February 1995.

Feketekuty, G. (1988), *International Trade in Services*, Cambridge, Mass.: Ballinger.

Ferguson, H. (1992), *Religious Transformation in Western Society*, London: Routledge.

Financial Times (1995*a*), 'Both Living in Interesting Times: There is More at Stake in the Talks between China and the US than Copyright Issues', 3 February: 15.

—— (1995*b*), 'Streets Resound to Superhighway Buzzwords', 5 February 1995: 1.

—— (1994), 'Uncle Sam's Super-Highway', 13 January 1994: 13.

Forde, S. (1995), 'International Realism and the Science of Politics: Thucydides, Machiavelli, and Neorealism', *International Studies Quarterly*, 39(2): 141–60.

Foucault, M. (1972), *The Archaeology of Knowledge*, trans. A. M. S. Smith, New York: Pantheon Books. Original work published in 1969.

Fowler, M. S., and Brenner, D. L. (1982), 'A Marketplace Approach to Broadcast Regulation', *Texas Law Review*, 60: 207–57.

France v. *Commission*, ECJ judgment of 19 March 1991, C-202/88, ECR 1223, the terminal equipment case.

Francis, E. K. (1965), *Ethnos und Demos Sociologischebeiträge zur Volkstheorie*, Berlin: Buncker und Humblot.

Fraser, N. (1992) 'Rethinking the Public Sphere', in C. Calhoun (ed.), *Habermas and the Public Sphere*, 109–42, Cambridge, Mass.: MIT Press.

French Declaration of the Rights of Man (1789).

Frohnmayer, J. (1994), *Out of Tune: Listening to the First Amendment*, Nashville, Tenn.: The Freedom Forum First Amendment Center, Vanderbilt University.

Fromm, E. (1992), *Marx's Concept of Man*, New York: Continuum. Original work published in 1961.

Fukuyama, F. (1989), 'The end of history', *The National Interest*, summer: 3–18.

Furet, F. (1981), *Interpreting the French Revolution*, trans. E. Foster, Cambridge: Cambridge University Press.

Gadamer, H. (1975), *Truth and Method*, New York: Seabury.

Galtung, J., and Vincent, R. C. (1992), *Global Glasnost*, Cresskill, NJ: Hampton Press.

Gana, R. L. (1996), 'Prospects for Developing Countries under the TRIPs Agreement', *Vanderbilt Journal of Transnational Law*, 29(4): 735–75.

Garnham, N. (1997), 'Universal Service', in W. H. Melody (ed.), *Telecom Reform: Principles, Policies and Regulatory Practices*, 207–12. Lyngby, Denmark: Technical University of Denmark.

—— (1990), *Capitalism and Communication*, London: Sage.

Garrett, L. L. (1994), 'Commerce versus Culture: The battle between the United States and the European Union over Audiovisual Trade Policies', *North Carolina Journal of International Law and Commercial Regulation*, 19(3): 553–77.

GATT (1993), see Trade-Related Aspects of Intellectual Property Rights (TRIPs), Annex 1C in the General Agreement on Trade and Tariffs in the Uruguay Round of Multilateral Trade Negotiations, MTN/FA, 15 December 1993, UR-93-0246. Reprinted in 'Results of the Uruguay Round of Multi-lateral Trade Negotiations—The legal texts 2–3', ed. GATT Secretariat, 1994.

Geertz, C. (1973), 'After the Revolution: The Fate of Nationalism in the New States', *The Interpretation of Culture*, 234–54, New York: Basic Books.

Geller, H. (1994), '1995–2005: Regulatory Reform for Principal Electronic Media', position paper, Washington, DC: Annenberg Washington Program.

Gellner, E. (1983), *Nations and Nationalism*, Oxford: Basil Blackwell.

Gerbner, G., Mowlana, H., and Nordenstreng, K. (eds.) (1993), *The Global Media Debate*, Norwood, N.J.: Ablex.

Giddens, A. (1985), *The Nation-State and Violence: A Contemporary Critique of Historical Materialism*, ii, Cambridge: Polity Press.

Gilpin, R. (1987), *The Political Economy of International Relations*, Princeton: Princeton University Press.

Golding, P., and Murdock, G. (1979), 'Ideology and the Mass Media: The Question of Determination', in M. Barrett, P. Corrigan, A. Kuhn, and J. Wolff (eds.), *Ideology and Cultural Production*, 198–238, London: Croom-Helm.

Goldmann, L. (1971), *Immanuel Kant*, London: New Left Books.

Gramsci, A. (1971), *Selections from the Prison Notebooks*, ed. and trans. A. Hoare and G. Nowell-Smith, London: Lawrence and Wishart.

Gray, J. (1993), *Post-liberalism*, London: Routledge.

—— (1989), *Limited Government: A Positive Agenda*, London: Institute for Economic Affairs.

Grieco, J. M. (1988), 'Anarchy and the Limits of Cooperation: A Realist Critique of the Newest Liberal Institutionalism', *International Organization*, 42: 485–507.

Habermas, J. (1994), 'Citizenship and National Identity' in B. van Steenbergen (ed.), *The Condition of Citizenship*, 20–35, London: Sage.

—— (1992), *Faktizität und Geltung*, Frankfurt: Suhrkamp. Reviewed in M. Deflen, 'Habermas, Modernity and Law: A Bibliography', *Philosophy & Social Criticism*, 20(4), 1994: 151–66.

—— (1990), *Moral Consciousness and Communicative Action*, trans. C. Lenhardt and S. W. Nicholsen, Cambridge, Mass.: MIT Press.

—— (1989), *The Structural Transformation of the Public Sphere*, trans. Thomas Burger, Cambridge, Mass.: MIT Press.

—— (1987), *The Theory of Communicative Action, vol. 2*, trans. T. McCarthy, Boston: Beacon Press.

Habermas, J. (1984), *The Theory of Communicative Action, vol. 1*, trans. T. McCarthy, Boston: Beacon Press.

—— (1982), 'A Reply to my Critics', in J. Thompson and D. Held (eds.), *Habermas: Critical Debates*, 219–83, Cambridge, Mass.: MIT Press.

—— (1979), *Communication and the Evolution of Society*, trans. T. McCarthy, Boston: Beacon Press.

—— (1973), *Legitimation Crisis*, trans. T. McCarthy, Boston: Beacon Press.

Hall, S. (1986), 'Cultural Studies: Two Paradigms', *Media, Culture & Society*, 2(1): 57–72.

Hamelink, C. J. (1983), *Cultural Autonomy in Global Communications*, New York: Longman.

Hamilton, A., Jay, J., and Madison, J. (1961), *The Federalist*, ed. J. E. Cooke, Middletown, Conn.: Wesleyan University Press. Original work published in 1787.

Hamilton, M. A. (1996), 'The TRIPs Agreement: Imperialistic, Outdated, and Overprotective', *Vanderbilt Journal of Transnational Law*, 29(3): 613–34.

Harris, L. E. (1995), 'Moral Rights on the Information Superhighway', *InterMedia*, 23(1): 18–20.

Hart, H. L. A. (1954), 'Definition and Theory in Jurisprudence', *Law Quarterly Review*, 70, January: 37–60.

Hartley, T. C. (1988), *The Foundations of European Community Law*, Oxford: Clarendon Press.

Hawk, B. E., and Laudati, L. L. (1996), 'Antitrust Federalism in the United States and Decentralization of Competition Law Enforcement in the European Union: A comparison', *Fordham International Law Journal*, 20(1): 18–49.

Hawley, E. W. (1966), *The New Deal and the Problem of Monopoly*, Princeton: Princeton University Press.

Hayden, R. (1991), 'Constitutional Nationalism in Yugoslavia', paper presented at the 90th Annual Meeting of the American Anthropological Association, Chicago.

Hayek, F. A. von (1994), *The Road to Serfdom*, Chicago: The University of Chicago Press. Original work published in 1944.

—— (1982), *Law, Legislation and Liberty, Vol. 2: The Mirage of Social Justice*, London: Routledge.

—— (1948), *Individualism and Economic Order*, London: Routledge.

Hegel, G.W.F. (1953), *Reason in History*, trans. R. Hartman, New York: Macmillan. Original work published in 1837.

—— (1952a), *The Philosophy of Right*, trans. T. M. Knox, Oxford: Oxford University Press. Original work published in 1821.

—— (1952b), 'World history', in Hegel (1952a), 216–23.

—— (1952c), 'International law', in Hegel (1952a), 212–16.

Heidegger, M. (1985), *Being and Time*, Oxford: Oxford University Press.

—— (1977), *The Question concerning Technology and Other Essays*, trans. W. Lovitt, New York: Harper and Row.

Held, D. (1991), 'Democracy and Globalization', *Alternatives*, 16: 201–8.
—— (1989), 'Sovereignty, National Politics and the Global System', in *Political Theory and the Modern State*, 214–42. Cambridge: Cambridge University Press.

Hills, J. (1993), 'Telecommunications in a Transitional Market: Central Europe and the Case of the Slovak Republic', unpublished paper presented at the International Association of Mass Communication Research conference in Dublin, Ireland, June.

—— (1990), 'The Telecommunications Rich and Poor', *Third World Quarterly*, 12(2): 71–90.

—— (1986), *Deregulating Telecoms: Competition and Control in the United States, Japan and Britain*, Westport, Conn.: Quorum Books.

Hobbes, T. (1991) *Leviathan*, ed. R. Tuck, Cambridge: Cambridge University Press. Original work published in 1651.

Hobsbawm, E. J. (1990), *Nations and Nationalism since 1780*, Cambridge: Cambridge University Press.

Hoffman, S. (1995), 'The Crisis of Liberal Internationalism', *Foreign Policy*, 98, spring: 159–77.

Hoffmann-Riem, W. (1992), 'Trends in the Development of Broadcasting Law in Western Europe', *European Journal of Communication*, 79(2): 147–71.

Hohfeld, W. N. (1978), *Fundamental Legal Conceptions as Applied in Judicial Reasoning*, Westport, Conn.: Greenwood Press. Original work published in 1919.

Horkheimer, M., and Adorno, T. W. (1972), *Dialectic of Enlightenment*, trans. J. Cumming, New York: Seabury.

Horwitz, R. B. (1989), *The Irony of Regulatory Reform*, New York: Oxford University Press.

—— (1986), 'Understanding Deregulation', *Theory and Society*, 15(1–2): 139–74.

International Chamber of Commerce (1992), 'Toward Greater Competition in Telecommunications', position paper no. 17, Brussels: International Chamber of Commerce.

International Media Law (1994), 'Cable and Satellite in the Single Market: Part 1, Copyright Issues', 12(3), March: 21–4.

Italy v. *Commission*, ECJ judgment of 20 March 1985, C41/83, 1985, ECR 873.

Jakubowicz, K. (1992), 'Polish Broadcasting Act revisited', *Bulletin of the European Institute for the Media*, 9(4): 12–13.

Jameson, F. (1991), *Postmodernism or, the Cultural Logic of Late Capitalism*, Durham, NC: Duke University Press.

Jaszi, P. A. (1996), 'Goodbye to All That—A Reluctant (and Perhaps Premature) Adieu to a Constitutionally-Grounded Discourse of Public Interest in Copyright Law', *Vanderbilt Journal of Transnational Law*, 29(3): 595–611.

Jay, M. (1985), 'Habermas and Modernism', in R. J. Bernstein (ed.), *Habermas and Modernity*, 125–39, Cambridge, Mass.: MIT Press.

Johansson, P. O. (1991), *An Introduction to Modern Welfare Economics*, New York: Cambridge University Press.

Johnson, O. (1993), 'Whose Voice?: Freedom of Speech and the Media in East Central Europe', paper presented at the Association for Education in Journalism and Mass Communication Annual Conference, August.

Jorna, K., and Martin-Prat, M. (1994), 'New Rules for the Game in the European Copyright Field and their Impact on Existing Situations', *European Intellectual Property Review*, 16(4): 145–53.

Kahn, F. J. (ed.) (1984), *Documents of American Broadcasting*, Englewood Cliffs, NJ: Prentice-Hall.

Kant, I. (1991*a*), 'On the Relationship of Theory to Practice in Political Right', 73–87, and 'On the Agreement between Politics and Morality according to the Transcendental Concept of Public Right', 125–30, in Kant (1991*b*). Original works published 1793–5.

——(1991*b*), *Kant: Political Writings*, ed. H. S. Reiss and trans. H. B. Nisbet, Cambridge: Cambridge University Press. Original works published in 1784–97.

——(1991*c*), 'Idea for a Universal History with a Cosmopolitan Purpose', in Kant (1991*b*), 41–53. Original work published in 1784.

——(1990), *Foundations of the Metaphysics of Morals* and *What is Enlightenment?*, trans. L. W. Beck, New York: Macmillan. Original works published in 1784–5.

Kaplan, L. (1994), 'The European Community's "Television without Frontiers" Directive: Stimulating Europe to Regulate Culture', *Emory International Law Review*, 8(1): 255–346.

Kapteyn, P., and van Themaat, P. V. (1989), *Introduction to the Law of the European Communities*, London: Graham and Trotman.

Katz, E., and Lazarsfeld, P. (1955), *Personal Influence*, New York: Free Press.

Keane, J. (1991), *The Media and Democracy*, London: Polity Press.

——(1988), 'The Modern Democratic Revolution', in T. Mastnak and R. Riha (eds.), *The Subject in Democracy*, 36–48, Ljubljana, Slovenia: Delavska enotnost, for Institut za marksisticne studije ZRC SAZU.

Knutsen, T. (1991), 'Answered Prayers: Fukuyama, Liberalism, and the End-of-History Debate', *Bulletin of Peace Proposals*, 22(1): 77–85.

Kohlmeier, L. M., Jr. (1969), *The Regulators: Watchdog Agencies in the Public Interest*, New York: Harper and Row.

Kohnstamm, M. (1990), 'Conflicts between International and European Network Regulation', *Legal Issues of European Integration*, 2: 45–100.

Koopmans, T. (1991), 'The Birth of European law at the Crossroads of Legal Traditions', *American Journal of Comparative Law*, 39, summer: 493–507.

——(1989), 'Equal Protection: The Social Dimension of Community Law', *Michigan International Law*, 11(1): 1–10.

Krasnow, E. G., Longley, L. D., and Terry, H. A. (1982), *The Politics of Broadcast Regulation*, New York: St Martin's Press.

Kurlantzick, L. (1994), 'Harmonisation of Copyright Protection', *European Intellectual Property Review*, 16(11): 463–5.

Laclau, E. (1988), 'Politics and the Limits of Modernity', in T. Mastnak and R. Riha (eds.), *The Subject in Democracy*, 36–48. Ljubljana, Slovenia: Institut za marksisticne studije ZRC SAZU.

Lange, P. (1993), 'Maastricht and the Social Protocol: Why Did they Do it?' *Politics & Society*, 21(1): 5–36.

Lanvin, B. (ed.) (1990), *Global Trade: The Revolution beyond the Information Revolution*, Montpellier: IDATE.

Lasok, D., and Stone, P. A. (1987), *Conflict of Laws in the European Community*, Abingdon: Professional Books Ltd.

Lazarsfeld, P., Berelson, B., and Gaudet, H. (1948), *The People's Choice*, New York: Columbia University Press.

Lefort, C. (1988), *Democracy and Political Theory*, trans. D. Macey, Minneapolis: University of Minnesota Press.

—— (1986), *The Political Forms of Modern Society*, trans. A. Sheridan, Cambridge: Polity Press.

—— (1981), *L'Invention démocratique: les limites de la domination totalitaire*, Paris: Fayard.

Lepsius, M. R. (1992), 'Beyond the Nation-State', *Telos*, 91, spring: 57–76.

Ligens v. *Austria*, ECJ judgment of 8 July 1986, Series A, no. 103.

Lippmann, W. (1922), *Public Opinion*, New York: Harcourt Brace.

Lipset, S. M. (1994), 'The Social Requisites of Democracy Revisited', *American Sociological Review*, 59(1): 1–22.

Llewellyn, K. N. (1960), *The Common Law Tradition: Deciding Appeals*, Boston: Little Brown.

Locke, J. (1960), *Two Treatises of Government*, introd. by P. Laslett, New York: Cambridge University Press. Original work published in 1690.

Long, C. (1990), 'Competition in the Markets for Telecommunication Services: The European Commission's Services Directive and its Draft Competition Guidelines', *International Business Lawyer*, 18: 511–16.

Lopatkiewicz, S. M. (1995), 'The U.S.: A Laboratory for Change?' unpublished paper presented at the International Institute of Communications' Digital Media Forum, 20–1 March, Washington, DC.

Lukes, S. (1985), 'Justice and Rights', in *Marxism and Morality*, ch. 4, Oxford: Oxford University Press.

Lyotard, J. (1984), *The Postmodern Condition: A Report on Knowledge*, Minneapolis: University of Minnesota Press.

Machiavelli, N. (1961), *The Prince*, trans. G. Ball, Harmondsworth: Penguin. Original work written in 1512–13.

MacIntyre, A. (1984), *After Virtue*, Notre Dame: University of Notre Dame Press.

—— (1966), *A Short History of Ethics*, New York: Macmillan.

McLuhan, M. (1964), *Understanding Media: The Extensions of Man*, New York: New American Library.

Macpherson, C. B. (1973), *Democratic Theory: Essays in Retrieval*, New York: Oxford University Press.

Maggiore, M. (1990), *Audiovisual Production in the Single Market*, Luxembourg: Office for Official Publications of the European Communities.

Mansell, R. (1993), *The New Telecommunications*, London: Sage.

—— and Jenkins, M. (1992), 'Networks and Policy: Interfaces, Theories and Research', *Communications & Strategies*, 1st trimester (5): 31–50.

Marcuse, H. (1972), *Studies in Critical Philosophy*, London: New Left Books.

Marsh v. *Alabama*, 326 U.S. 501 (1946).

Marshall, T. H. (1950), *Citizenship and Social Class*, Cambridge: Cambridge University Press.

Marx, K. (1978*a*) 'The German Ideology' in Tucker (1978), 146–200. Original work published in 1932.

—— (1978*b*), 'Economic and Philosophical Manuscripts', in Tucker (1978), 66–125. Original work written in 1844.

—— (1978*c*), 'On the Jewish Question', in Tucker (1978), 26–52. Original work published in 1843.

—— (1974*d*), *Grundrisse: Foundations of the Critique of Political Economy*, in Tucker (1978).

—— (1970), *Critique of Hegel's Philosophy of Right*, trans. and ed. J. O'Malley, Cambridge: Cambridge University Press. Original work published in 1844.

—— and Engels, F. (1975), *Collected Works*, iii, New York and London: International Publishers.

Mattelart, A. (1994), *Mapping World Communications: War, Progress, Culture*, Minneapolis: University of Minnesota Press.

May, E. (1994), 'Il était une loi . . .', *Audiovisuel*, no. 28, February: 2–6.

Meehan, E. (1993), *Citizenship and the European Community*, London: Sage.

Melody, W. H. (1990), 'Communication Policy in the Global Information Economy', in M. Ferguson (ed.), *Public Communication: The New Imperatives*, 16–39, London: Sage.

—— (1989), 'Efficiency and Social Policy in Telecommunication', *Journal of Economic Issues*, 23(3): 657–88.

Miami Herald Publishing Co. v. *Tornillo*, 418 U.S. 241 (1974).

Middleton, K. R., and Chamberlin, B. F. (1994), *The Law of Public Communication*, New York: Longman.

Mill, J. S. (1974), *On Liberty*, London: Penguin. Original work published in 1859.

Milton, J. (1978), *Areopagitica*, ed. R. Jebb, Philadelphia: R. West.

Moebes, A. (1993), 'Copyright Protection for Audiovisual Works in the European Community', *Hastings Communications and Entertainment Law Journal*, 15(23): 399–415.

Mommsen, W. J. (1989), *The Political and Social Theory of Max Weber*, Chicago: University of Chicago Press.

Montesquieu, C. (1989), *The Spirit of the Laws*, trans. A. M. Cohler, B. C. Miller, and H. S. Stone (eds.), Cambridge: Cambridge University Press. Original work published in 1748.

Morgan, K. (1989), 'Telecom Strategies in Britain and France: The Scope and Limits of Neo-liberalism and *Dirigisme*', in M. Sharp and P. Holmes (eds.), *Strategies for New Technology*, 19–55. London: Philip Allan.

Mosco, V. (1996), *The Political Economy of Communication*, London: Sage.

—— (1990), 'The Mythology of Telecommunications Deregulation', *Journal of Communication*, 40(1): 36–49.

Mosteshar, S. (1994), 'Surprises in Store: Future Mandatory Rental Rights', *International Business Lawyer*, 22(1): 37–42.

Mouffe, C. (ed.) (1992), *Dimensions of Radical Democracy*, London: Verso.

—— (1988), 'Radical Democracy: Modern or Postmodern?', in T. Mastnak and R. Riha (eds.), *The Subject in Democracy*, 9–20, Ljubljana, Slovenia: Institut za marksisticne studije ZRC SAZU.

Mowlana, H. (1994), 'Shapes of the Future: International Communication in the 21st Century', *Journal of International Communication*, 1(1): 14–32.

Mulgan, G., and Paterson, R. (1993), *Hollywood of Europe?* London: British Film Institute.

Murdock, G. (1994), 'The New Mogul Empires: Media Concentration and Control in the Age of Convergence', *Media Development*, 41(4): 3–6.

—— ((1993), 'Communications and the Constitution of Modernity', *Media, Culture & Society*, 15(4): 521–39.

Negrine, R., and Papathanassopoulos, S. (1991), 'The Internationalization of Television', *European Journal of Communication*, 6(1): 9–33.

Nesvold, H. P. (1996), 'Communication Breakdown: Developing an Antitrust Model for Multimedia Mergers and Acquisitions', *Fordham Intellectual Property, Media & Entertainment Law Journal*, 6(2): 781–869.

New York Times (1994), 'Gore Outlines Data Highway Policy', 12 January 1994, section C: 4.

—— (1993), 'With Time Waning, Europeans Reject US. Movie Compromise', 14 December 1993, p. 1.

Newman, M. (1996), *Democracy, Sovereignty and the European Union*, New York: St Martin's Press.

Nicholas, D. (1990), 'Global Business needs Better Telecommunications for Trade Purposes', in R. B. Woodrow (ed.), *Uruguay Round Trade in Services Perspectives*, 93–6, Geneva: Applied Services Economic Centre.

Noam, E. (1995a), 'The Stages of Television: From Multi-channel to the Me-channel', in C. Contamine and M. van Dusseldorp (eds.), *Towards the Digital Revolution*, 49–54, published proceedings of the Sixth European Television and Film Forum, Liège, Belgium, 10–12 November 1994, Düsseldorf, Germany: European Institute for the Media.

—— (1995b), 'From the Network of Networks to the System of Systems', in Meheroo Jussawalla (ed.), *Telecommunications: A Bridge to the 21st Century*, 25–38, Amsterdam: Elsevier Science B.V.

—— (1994), 'Is Telecommunications Liberalization an Expansionary Process?' in Eli Noam and Gerard Pogorel (eds.), *Assymetric Deregulation*, 7–16, Norwood, NJ: Ablex.

—— (1989), 'Network Pluralism and Regulatory Pluralism', in P. R. Newberg (ed.), *New Directions in Telecommunications Policy*, vol. 1, 66–91, Durham, NC: Duke University Press.

Nozick, R. (1974), *Anarchy, State and Utopia*, New York: Basic Books.

Nussbaum, M. (1992), 'Human Functioning and Social Justice', *Political Theory*, 20(2): 202–46.

Oakeshott, M. (1975), *Hobbes on Civil Associations*, Oxford: Basil Blackwell.

Pataki, J. (1992), 'Political Battle in Hungary over Broadcasting Dismissals', *RFE/RL Research Report*, 1(30): 26–30.

Pateman, C. (1985), *The Problem of Political Obligation*, Berkeley: University of California Press. Original work published in 1979.

Patterson, L. R., and Lindberg, S. W. (1991), *The Nature of Copyright*, Athens, Ga.: University of Georgia Press.

Patterson, O. (1991), *Freedom in the Making of Western Culture*, New York: Basic Books.

Pelczynski, Z. A. (1984), 'The Significance of Hegel's Separation of the State and Civil Society', in Z. A. Pelczynski (ed.), *The State and Civil Society*, 1–13. Cambridge: Cambridge University Press.

Pinder, J. (1991), *European Community: The Building of a Union*, Oxford: Oxford University Press.

Pool, I. (1990), *Technologies without Boundaries*, Cambridge, Mass.: Harvard University Press.

Porter, V. (1993a), 'The Consumer and Transfrontier Television', *Consumer Policy Review*, 3(3): 132–8.

——(1993b), 'The Freedom of Expression and Public Service Broadcasting', *Journal of Media Law and Practice*, 14(2): 46–50.

——(1992), 'Euroville Bound? An Analysis of the EC's Attempts to Establish an International Framework for Copyright in Transfrontier Television Broadcasts', *Media Policy Review*, no. 5, September: 11–15.

——(1989), 'The Re-regulation of Television: Pluralism, Constitutionality and the Free Market in the USA, West Germany, France and the UK', *Media, Culture & Society*, 11(1): 5–27.

Postema, G. J. (1989), *Bentham and the Common Law Tradition*, Oxford: Clarendon Press.

Prosser, T. (1992), 'Public Service Broadcasting and Deregulation in the UK', *European Journal of Communication*, 7(2): 173–93.

Rawls, J. (1993), *Political Liberalism*, New York: Columbia University Press.

——(1971), *A Theory of Justice*, Cambridge, Mass.: Belknap Press of Harvard University Press.

Red Lion Broadcasting Company v. *Federal Communications Commission*, 395 U.S. 367 (1969),

Regli, Brian (1996), 'Mapping a Course for Sustainable Infrastructure Development', *Telecommunications Policy*, 20(8): 557–72.

Reichman, J. H. (1996a), 'Compliance with the TRIPs Agreement: Introduction to a Scholarly Debate', *Vanderbilt Journal of Transnational Law*, 29(3): 363–90.

——(1996b), 'The Duration of Copyright and the Limits of Cultural Policy', *Cardozo Arts & Entertainment Law Journal*, 14(3): 625–54.

Reuters (1989), 'U.S. still worried "Fortress Europe" will hurt AmericanTrade', AM Cycle, 11 September, available in LEXIS, Nexis Library, Wires File.

Robertson, A. H., and Merrills, J. G. (1993), *Human Rights in Europe: A Study of the European Convention of Human Rights*, Manchester: Manchester University Press.

Robins, K., and Morley, D. (1992), 'What Kind of Identity for Europe?', *Intermedia*, 20(4–5): 23–4.

Rome Convention for the Protection of Performers, Producers of Phonographs, and Broadcasting Organizations, 26 October 1961, 496 U.N.T.S.

Rorty, R. (1989), *Contingency, Irony and Solidarity*, Cambridge: Cambridge University Press.

——(1983), 'Postmodernist Bourgeois Liberalism', *The Journal of Philosophy*, 80(10): 585–98.

Rosenau, J. N. (1980), *The Study of Global Interdependence*, London: Pinter.

Rousseau, J. J. (1973), *The Social Contract and Discourses*, trans. G. D. H. Cole, London: Everyman's Library. Original works published in 1755.

Rousseau, P. (1995), 'Will Economic Power Replace Political Power?' in C. Contamine and M. van Dusseldorp (eds.), *Towards the Digital Revolution*, 127–30, published proceedings of the 6th European Television and Film Forum, Liège, Belgium, 10–12 November 1994, Düsseldorf, Germany: European Institute for the Media.

Rowland, W. D. (1986), 'American Telecommunication Policy Research: Its Contradictory Origins and Influence', *Media, Culture & Society*, 8(2): 159–82.

——(1982), 'The Process of Reification: Recent Trends in Communications Legislation and Policy-Making', *Journal of Communication*, 32(4): 114–36.

Sakamoto, Y. (1991), 'The Global Context of Democratization', *Alternatives*, 16: 119–28.

Samuelson, P. (1994), 'Comparing U.S. and EC Copyright Protection for Computer Programs: Are they More Different than they Seem?' *The Journal of Law and Commerce*, 13: 279–300.

Sanchez-Tabernero, A. *et al.* (1993), *Media Concentration in Europe: Commercial Enterprise and the Public Interest*, Düsseldorf, Germany: European Institute for the Media.

Sandel, M. (1982), *Liberalism and the Limits of Justice*, New York: Cambridge University Press.

Sayer, D. (1991), *Capitalism and Modernity: An Excursus on Marx and Weber*, New York: Routledge.

Sbragia, A. (ed.) (1992), *Euro-politics: Institutions and Policymaking in the 'New' European Community*, Washington, DC: The Brookings Institution.

Scannell, P. (1992), 'Public Service Broadcasting and Modern Public Life', in P. Scannell, P. Schlesinger, and C. Sparks (eds.), *Culture and Power*, 317–48. London: Sage.

Scherer, J. (1991), 'Telecommunications Laws in Europe', in J. Scherer (ed.), *Telecommunications Laws in Europe*, 1–32. Frankfurt, Germany: Baker & McKenzie.

Schiller, H. I. (1996), *Information Inequality*, New York: Routledge.

——(1985), 'Electronic Information Flows: New Basis for Global Domination?' in P. Drummond and R. Paterson (eds.), *Television in Transition: Papers from the First International Television Studies Conference*, 11, London: British Film Institute.

Schiller, H. I. (1976), *Communication and Cultural Domination*, New York: M. E. Sharpe.

Schlesinger, P. (1991), 'Media, the Political Order and National Identity', *Media, Culture & Society*, 13(3): 297–308.

Schmidt, B. C., Jr. (1976), *Freedom of the Press vs. Public Access*, Palo Alto, Calif.: Aspen Institute Program on Communication & Society.

Schramm, W. (1983), 'The Unique Perspective of Communication: A Retrospective View', *Journal of Communication*, 33(3): 6–17.

Schumpeter, J. (1991), *The Economics and Sociology of Capitalism*, ed. R. Swedberg, Princeton: Princeton University Press.

——(1947), *Capitalism, Socialism, and Democracy*, New York: Harper & Row.

Schwarze, J. (1988), *The Role of the European Court of Justice (ECJ) in the Interpretation of Uniform Law among the Member States of the European Community*, Baden-Baden, Germany: Nomos.

Schwartz, B., and Wade, H. W. R. (1972), *Legal Control of Government Administrative Law in Britain and the United States*, Oxford: Clarendon Press.

Sepstrup, P. (1991), *Transnationalization of Television in Western Europe*, London: John Libbey.

Servaes, J. (1992), 'Europe 1992: The Audiovisual Challenge', *Gazette*, 49(1–2): 75–97.

Shapiro, M. (1992), 'The European Court of Justice', in Sbragia (1992), 123–56.

Shaughnessy, H., and Cobo, C. F. (1990), *The Cultural Obligations of Broadcasting*, Manchester: European Institute for the Media.

Shelden, J. (1994), 'Television without Frontiers: A Case Study of Turner Broadcasting's New Channel in the Community—Does it Violate the Directive?' *Transnational Lawyer*, 7(2): 523–43.

Siebert, F. S. (1965), *Freedom of the Press in England 1476–1776: The Rise and Decline of Government Control*, Urbana, Ill.: University of Illinois Press.

Simon, J. (1991), *L'Esprit des règles: réseaux et réglementation aux États Unis: cable, électricité, télécommunications*, Paris: L'Harmattan.

Siune, K., and Truetzschler, W. (eds.) (1992), *Dynamics of Media Politics: Broadcast and Electronic Media in Western Europe* (for the Euromedia Research Group), London: Sage.

Skinner, Q. (1986), 'The Paradoxes of Political Liberty', in S. McMurrin (ed.), *The Tanner Lectures on Human Values*, vii, 225–50, Cambridge: Cambridge University Press.

Smith, A. (1986), *The Wealth of Nations, Books I–III*, introd. by A. Skinner, London: Penguin. Original work published in 1776.

Smith, A. (1989), 'Public Interest and Telecommunications', in P. Newberg (ed.), *New Directions in Telecommunications Policy*, 334–58. Durham, NC: Duke University Press.

Smith, A. D. (1992), 'Nationalism and the Historians', in A. D. Smith (ed.), *Ethnicity and Nationalism*, 58–80, Leiden, The Netherlands: E. J. Brill.

—— (1979), *Nationalism in the Twentieth Century*, Oxford: Martin Robertson.

Smith, C. N. (1993), 'International Trade in Television Programming and GATT: An Analysis of why the European Community's Local Program Requirement Violates the General Agreement on Tariffs and Trade', *International Tax & Business Law*, 10(2): 97–115.

Smolla, R. A. (1992), *Free Speech in an Open Society*, New York: Vintage Books.

Spain v. *Commission*, ECJ judgment of 17 November 1992, C-271, 281, 289/90, the services directive case.

Steinfield, C., Bauer, J. M., and Caby, L. (eds.) (1994), *Telecommunications in Transition*, Thousand Oaks, Calif.: Sage.

Strauss, L. (1973), *What is Political Philosophy?*, Westport, Conn.: Greenwood Press.

Streeter, T. (1990), 'Beyond Freedom of Speech and the Public Interest: The Relevance of Critical Legal Studies to Communications Policy', *Journal of Communication*, 40(2): 43–63.

Swanson, D. L., and Nimmo, D. (1990), *New Directions in Political Communication Research*, Newbury Park, Calif.: Sage.

Tassin, E. (1992), 'Europe: A Political Community?' in Mouffe (1992), 169–92.

Taylor, C. (1993), 'The Motivation behind a Procedural Ethics', in R. Beiner and W. J. Booth (eds.), *Kant and Political Philosophy: The Contemporary Legacy*, 337–60, New Haven: Yale University Press.

—— (1990), 'Modes of Civil Society', *Public Culture*, 3(1): 95–118.

—— (1989a), *Sources of the Self*, Cambridge, Mass.: Harvard University Press.

—— (1989b), 'Cross-purposes: The Liberal-Communitarian Debate', in N. Rosenblum (ed.), *Liberalism and the Moral Life*, 159–82. Cambridge, Mass.: Harvard University Press.

—— (1985), *Philosophical Papers*, ii, Cambridge: Cambridge University Press.

—— (1979), *Hegel and Modern Society*, Cambridge: Cambridge University Press.

The Observer and Guardian v. *the UK*, ECJ judgment of 26 November 1991, Series A, no. 216.

Tocqueville, A. (1990), *Democracy in America*, 2 vols., ed. P. Bradley, New York: Vintage (copyright 1945 by Alfred Knopf). Original work published 1834–40.

Toinet, M. F., Kempf, H., and Lacorne, D. (1989), *Le Libéralisme à l'américaine: l'état et le marché*, Paris: Economica, coll. Politique Comparée.

Tomlinson, J. (1991), *Cultural Imperialism*, Baltimore: The Johns Hopkins University Press.

Touraine, A. (1992), *Critique de la Modernité*, Paris, Fayard.

Train, K. (1991), *Optimal Regulation: The Economic Theory of Natural Monopoly*, Cambridge, Mass.: MIT Press.

Tucker, R. C. (ed.) (1978), *The Marx–Engels Reader*, New York: W. W. Norton.

Turner, B. (1992), 'Outlines of a Theory of Citizenship', in Mouffe (1992), 33–62.

Unger, R. M. (1983), *The Critical Legal Studies Movement*, Cambridge, Mass.: Harvard University Press.

Ungerer, H., and Costello, N. (1988), *Telecommunications in Europe*, Luxembourg: Office for Official Publications of the European Communities.

US Chamber of Commerce (1995), Report of findings of the national information infrastructure survey, US Chamber of Commerce Telecommunications Infrastructure Task Force. Washington, DC: US Chamber of Commerce.

US Congress (1996a), Telecommunications Act of 1996, Public Law No. 104–104, 110 Stat. 56.

—— (1996b), Summary of testimony of E. H. Smith, president of the International Intellectual Property Alliance before the Subcommittee on Trade of the Committee on Ways and Means, 11 September 1996.

—— (1995), Proposed telecommunications deregulation bill, S. 652. Washington, DC: US Government Printing Office.

—— (1994a), 'The Information Superhighway and the National Information infrastructure (NII)', *CRS Report for Congress*, 22 March, Washington, DC: Congressional Research Service, Library of Congress.

—— (1994b), Proposed telecommunications infrastructure bill, S. 1822. Washington, DC: US Government Printing Office.

—— (1994c), 'Telecommunications Services: Provisions in the Uruguay Round and in NAFTA', *CRS Report for Congress*, 11 August, Washington, DC: Congressional Research Service, Library of Congress.

—— (1994d), 'The Information Superhighway: An Annotated Glossary', *CRS Report for Congress*, 2 June, Washington, DC: Congressional Research Service, Library of Congress.

—— (1994e), 'The American Telephone & Telegraph Company divestiture: Background, provisions, and restructuring', *CRS Report for Congress*, 20 June, Washington, DC: Congressional Research Service, Library of Congress.

—— (1994f), Proposed telecommunications infrastructure bill, HR 3626, Washington, DC: US Government Printing Office.

—— (1993), US Telecommunications Services in European markets', a report of the Office of Technology Assessment, TCT-548, August, Washington, DC: US Government Printing Office.

US Constitution (1787).

US Government (1995a), Global information infrastructure: agenda for cooperation. Information Infrastructure Task Force, February, Washington, DC: US Government Printing Office.

—— (1995b), Notice of proposed rulemaking in the matter of market entry and regulation of foreign-affiliated entities. Federal Communications Commission, IB Docket No. 95-22, FCC 95-53, 17 February 1995, Washington, DC: US Government Printing Office.

—— (1995c), 'Intellectual Property and the National Information Infrastructure', report of the working group on intellectual property rights, or White Paper, 5 September, 1995.

—— (1993), The national information infrastructure: agenda for action. Information Infrastructure Task Force, September, Washington, DC: US Government Printing Office.

—— (1990), Comprehensive study of globalization of mass media firms: comments of the Committee for America's Copyright Community. National Telecommunications and Information Administration, Notice of Inquiry, MM Dkt. No. 900241.

—— (1982), *United States* v. *AT&T*, CA No. 82–0192 (DDC), Modification of Final Judgment, United States District Court of the District of Columbia, 24 August.

Usher, J. (1981), *European Community Law and National Law: The Irreversible Transfer?* London: University Association for Contemporary European Studies/George Allen & Unwin.

Velkley, R. (1989), *Freedom and the End of Reason: On the Moral Foundation of Kant's Critical Philosophy*, Chicago: University of Chicago Press.

Venturelli, S. (1993), 'The Imagined Transnational Public Sphere in the European Community's Broadcast Philosophy: Implications for Democracy', *European Journal of Communication*, 8(4): 491–518.

Vickers, J., and Yarrow, G. (1988), *Privatization: An Economic Analysis*, Cambridge, Mass.: MIT Press.

Village Voice (1996. 'Merge Overkill: When Big Media gets Too Big, What Happens to Open Debate?' 16 January: 30.

Walker, R.B.J. (1993), *Inside/Outside: International Relations as Political Theory*, Cambridge: Cambridge University Press.

Wall Street Journal (1995), 'Mergers, Acquisitions Soar in Information Technology', 26 July 1995: B8.

Wallerstein, I. (1989), *The Modern World-System III*, New York: Cambridge University Press.

—— (1979), *The Capitalist World Economy*, Cambridge: Cambridge University Press.

Walzer, M. (1992), 'The Civil Society Argument', in Mouffe (1992), 89–107.

—— (1990), 'The Communitarian Critique of Liberalism', *Political Theory*, 18(1): 6–23.

—— (1983), *Spheres of Justice*, New York: Basic Books.

Washington Post (1997), 'Big Mergers Get Bigger in the '90s', 27 October 1997: 1.

Weaver, S. (1980), 'Antitrust Division of the Department of Justice', in J. Q. Wilson (ed.), *The Politics of Regulation*, 123–51, New York: Basic Books.

Weber, M. (1977), *Economy and Society: An Outline of Interpretive Sociology*, trans. G. Roth and C. Wittich (eds.), New York: Bedminster.

—— (1947), *The Theory of Social and Economic Organization*, trans. T. Parsons (ed.), New York: The Free Press.

—— (1946), *From Max Weber: Essays in Sociology*, trans. H. H. Gerth and C. W. Mills, New York: Oxford University Press.

Weber, M. (1930), *The Protestant Ethic and the Spirit of Capitalism*, trans. T. Parsons (ed.), London: Allen & Unwin.

Weizsäcker, C. C. von (1984), 'Free entry into Telecommunications', *Information Economics and Policy*, 1: 197–216.

Wellmer, A. (1985), 'Reason, Utopia, and the Dialectic of Enlightenment', in R. J. Bernstein (ed.), *Habermas and Modernity*, 36–66. Cambridge, Mass.: MIT Press.

Wilkins, K. L. (1991), 'Television without Frontiers: An EEC Broadcasting Premiere', *Boston College International and Comparative Law Review*, 14, winter: 195–211.

Wilkinson, C. (1994), 'The Future European Information Society: How can Intellectual Property Rules Foster its Creation?' Paper by Commission of the European Communities, DGXIII adviser, presented to Joint ECIS/ACIS Symposium, Copyright in a Digital Age, Brussels, 21 April.

Williams, A. (1992), 'Harmonisation and Protection of Copyright', *International Media Law*, 10(6): 46–7.

Williams, H. (1983), *Kant's Political Philosophy*, New York: St Martin's Press.

Williams, R. (1961), *The Long Revolution*, London: Chatto & Windus.

Wnuk-Lipinski, E. (1993), 'Left Turn in Poland: A Sociological and Political Analysis', research paper from the Institute of Political Studies, Warsaw: Polish Academy of Sciences.

——(1992), 'Paradoxes of the Polish Transformation', research paper from the Institute of Political Studies, Warsaw: Polish Academy of Sciences.

Wolff, R. P. (1973), *The Autonomy of Reason: A Commentary on Kant's Groundwork of the Metaphysics of Morals*, New York: Harper & Row.

Wolin, S. (1983), 'Hannah Arendt: Democracy and the Political', *Salmagundi*, 60: 3–19.

Woodmansee, M. (1984), 'The Genius and the Copyright: Economic and Legal Conditions of the Emergence of the "Author"', *Eighteenth-Century Studies*, 17: 443–5.

World Congress of International Performing Rights Societies (1994), Opening address by Sabine Leutheusser-Schnarrenberger, German Federal Minister of Justice, Munich, 18–19 September.

World Intellectual Property Organization (1996), WIPO Copyright Treaty adopted by the Diplomatic Conference in Geneva on 20 December 1996, CRNR/DC/94.

World Trade Organization (1997), Fourth Protocol to the General Agreement on Trade in Services ('Global Telecoms Agreement'), S/L/20.

Wuthnow, R. (1989), *Communities of Discourse: Ideology and Social Structure in the Reformation, the Enlightenment, and European Socialism*, Cambridge, Mass.: Harvard University Press.

Xavier, Patrick (1996), 'Monitoring Telecommunications Deregulation through International Benchmarking', *Telecommunications Policy*, 20(8): 585–606.

Index